"God's Treasure-House in Scotland;" a
history of times, mines, and lands in the
Southern Highlands. With ... map, etc.

James Moir Porteous

The BiblioLife Network

This project was made possible in part by the BiblioLife Network (BLN), a project aimed at addressing some of the huge challenges facing book preservationists around the world. The BLN includes libraries, library networks, archives, subject matter experts, online communities and library service providers. We believe every book ever published should be available as a high-quality print reproduction; printed on- demand anywhere in the world. This insures the ongoing accessibility of the content and helps generate sustainable revenue for the libraries and organizations that work to preserve these important materials.

The following book is in the "public domain" and represents an authentic reproduction of the text as printed by the original publisher. While we have attempted to accurately maintain the integrity of the original work, there are sometimes problems with the original book or micro-film from which the books were digitized. This can result in minor errors in reproduction. Possible imperfections include missing and blurred pages, poor pictures, markings and other reproduction issues beyond our control. Because this work is culturally important, we have made it available as part of our commitment to protecting, preserving, and promoting the world's literature.

GUIDE TO FOLD-OUTS, MAPS and OVERSIZED IMAGES

In an online database, page images do not need to conform to the size restrictions found in a printed book. When converting these images back into a printed bound book, the page sizes are standardized in ways that maintain the detail of the original. For large images, such as fold-out maps, the original page image is split into two or more pages.

Guidelines used to determine the split of oversize pages:

- Some images are split vertically; large images require vertical and horizontal splits.
- For horizontal splits, the content is split left to right.
- For vertical splits, the content is split from top to bottom.
- For both vertical and horizontal splits, the image is processed from top left to bottom right.

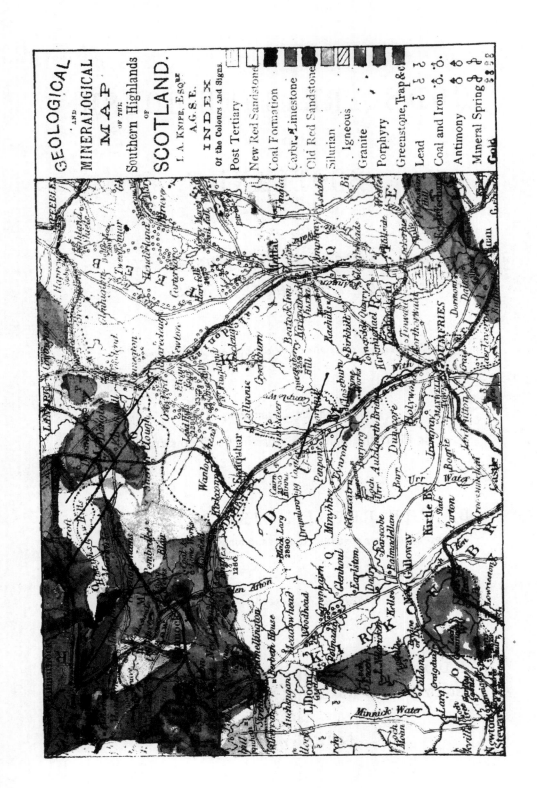

"GOD'S TREASURE-HOUSE

IN

SCOTLAND;"

A HISTORY OF
TIMES, MINES, AND LANDS IN THE
SOUTHERN HIGHLANDS.

With Geological and Mineralogical Map and Illustrations.

Dedicated, by Permission, to
His Grace the Duke of Buccleuch and Queensberry.

BY THE REV. J. MOIR PORTEOUS,
AUTHOR OF "THE GOVERNMENT OF THE KINGDOM OF CHRIST," ETC.

"The Gold of that land is good."

LONDON: SIMPKIN, MARSHALL, & CO.
EDINBURGH & GLASGOW: JOHN MENZIES & CO.
1876.

To His Grace

Walter-Francis Montague-Douglas-Scott,

THE

Fifth Duke of Buccleuch and Seventh of Queensberry,

HIGH STEWARD OF WESTMINSTER, CAPTAIN OF THE QUEEN'S BODYGUARD
IN SCOTLAND, &c., &c.

*UPON WHOSE LANDS AT WANLOCKHEAD
A PLENTIFUL SUPPLY OF THE PRECIOUS MINERALS
HAVE BEEN OBTAINED;*

The Generous Patron of Arts, Literature, and Agriculture;
whose Benevolence as a Landlord is universally esteemed;

AND WHO, WITH

THE DUKE OF ARGYLL, GAVE A NOBLE EXAMPLE TO THE PROPRIETORS
OF SCOTLAND, IN THE
GIFT OF THE PATRONAGE OF HIS NUMEROUS PARISHES TO THE PEOPLE
WITHOUT COMPENSATION,

WHEN IN 1874

THE BILL REPEALING PATRONAGE AND RECOGNISING FREEDOM OF ELECTION
OF MINISTERS OF RELIGION WAS PASSED INTO LAW:

This Work,

DESCRIPTIVE OF THE DISTRICT FORMERLY TERMED

"GOD'S TREASURE-HOUSE IN SCOTLAND,"

IS MOST RESPECTFULLY DEDICATED

BY

James Moir Porteous, Minister at Wanlockhead.

May, 1876.

PREFATORY NOTE.

AN HISTORICAL AND STATISTICAL ACCOUNT OF THE PARISH OF SANQUHAR, DUMFRIESSHIRE,—including WANLOCKHEAD, ITS MINES AND MEN, written at the request. of the Editor of the *Dumfries and Galloway Courier*, appeared in 1875 for twenty weeks in the columns of that journal. Several persons, whose opinions are deserving of weight, having stated that it was read "with very great interest—it is very complete, and will be referred to in future times for the present state of the parish," and it being desired in a more permanent and accessible form, after much research, the history, ancient and modern, has been extended so as to include Crawford, Crawfordjohn, Leadhills, Wanlockhead, and Sanquhar, embracing the geology and mineralogy of the district, with accessible and condensed information as to the gold, silver, and lead workings, details as to properties and people, together with Church History from the Reformation to the present date.

With a few exceptions, the requisite information has been readily furnished, and to all who have thus aided him the author tenders grateful acknowledgments.

No expense or pains have been spared to render the work, that which it is hoped it may be found, a useful handbook of the district and of its rich " treasures."

WANLOCKHEAD, *May* 1876.

CONTENTS.

APPENDIX.

ILLUSTRATIONS

OF

"GOD'S TREASURE-HOUSE IN SCOTLAND."

———+———

"God's Treasure-House in Scotland."

" *O see ye not yon bonnie road,*
That winds about the ferny brae ?
That is the path to fair Elf-land,
Where thou and I this nicht maun gae."

THOMAS THE RHYMER.

IN visiting Scotland by Carlisle from the south, after passing Beattock Station (for Moffat Spa), on the Caledonian Railway, the traveller begins to realise that he is entering upon the "land of the mountain and the flood." Ascending a romantic glen, he at length emerges into the wild moorland of Crawford, and obtaining a sight of the Lowther Mountains on the left, the train descends from the watershed—the source of the Clyde—with accelerated speed, until the lonely station of Elvanfoot, and five miles farther the sweet village of Abington, are reached.

Or again, proceeding from Dumfries by the Glasgow and South-Western line, after passing Thornhill Station, and obtaining a glimpse of the glorious scenery of Nithsdale, where sits as queen the Castle of Drumlanrig—one of the princely residences of the Duke of Buccleuch and Queensberry—a view is then had of the Lowther and Dalveen hills on the right, at the bridge of the Carron, and nine miles farther the visitor is brought nigh to the old "Peel" and burgh of Sanquhar.

9

The central district lying between these positions on these lines of rail, was in old times, because of its valuable minerals, termed "*God's Treasure-House in Scotland;*" and in connection with the entire range of hill-land in the south and west, it has not less fitly been known as "*The Southern Highlands.*"

Multitudes sweep along these lines unconscious of the fact, for there is little to arrest the eye or tell the tale, but there has been located for centuries an industrious and happy population.

The story will not be found destitute of interest to many far outside as well as within the localities of Leadhills, Wanlockhead, Crawford, Crawfordjohn, and Sanquhar, in regard to that "House," its Treasures, its "Old Town," its Gates of Zion.

Part I.

THE HOUSE.

" Long ere the dawn, by devious ways,
O'er hills, through woods, o'er dreary wastes, they sought
The upland muirs, where rivers, there but brooks,
Dispart to different seas."　　　　GRAHAM.

THE ground in the south of Scotland gradually rises out of the flat isthmus in England between Newcastle and Carlisle, terminating in a lofty range of mountains running quite across the island from the Cheviots on the east, to Loch Ryan on the west. Nearly midway between these two, the Dumfriesshire parish of SANQUHAR stretches from that point of the Lowther range called the Five Cairns, or East Lowther, where it parts from the parishes of Crawford and Durisdeer on to the Blacklorg Hill, where it salutes those of New Cumnock and the Galloway Dalry.

The Lanarkshire parish of Crawford, Crawford-Lindsay, or Crawford-Douglas, was also known as Douglas-Moor, and one portion as Friar-Moor.

It extends a distance of eighteen miles from its southern extremity, Queensberry Hill, to the Hill of Heatherstane in the north ; and has a width of ten miles from Annanhead Hill on the east, to the Dod Hill on the west, beyond the village of Leadhills. Throughout that extent upwards of fifty hills afford abundant pasturage, many of them being green to the summit. These hills have a grandeur peculiarly their own. If the bold frowning precipice is not a predominant feature, the majesty of bulk, swell, and rest cannot fail to impress the beholder. In the

11

heavy coaching days, the traveller to Dumfries seldom forgot the delight he experienced in descending the Pass of Dalveen, still visited by those who love the mountain, the mist, and the water-fall—" the lang glen" immortalised by Burns.

On the site of the Lowthers, Lothus, the fabled giant, wearied with his gigantic efforts to put all things to right, lay down to rest ; but his sleep was troubled, and these great swelling hills are the memorial of his tossings to and fro—no inapt illustration of the sorry unrest of very many whose puny efforts at their base or beneath the surface weary and wear out their little day. But rising from fable and earthly cares, they form a grand illustration of the matchless strength and endurance of Him who " hath weighed the mountains in scales and the hills in a balance." As on Waldensian heights, the aid of that Almighty One has been invoked while grateful ones sheltered here have sang—

> " For the strength of the hills we bless Thee,
>   Our God, our fathers' God:
>   Thou hast made Thy children mighty,
>   By the touch of the mountain sod."

Adjoining to Crawford, and divided from it by the Gonar Water, is the third *quoad civilia* parish of Crawfordjohn. The name Crawford is thought to have arisen from a ford of the Clyde near the Castle ; crows having built for centuries on the trees by which it is surrounded. It is " the ford of the craws." " Crawfordjohn" points to the church and village, built by John the stepson of Baldwin. It was afterwards the property of John de Crawford.

These two parishes were early traversed by the Roman military way, or " Watling Street." Camps and stations are still visible. The cart, the mail, and in 1848 the railway followed each other for miles parallel with the river Clyde.

Communication with the Nith valley is had not only along the " Muir" and down the Pass of Dalveen, but by a country road of fifteen miles' length by the Gonar, Leadhills, Wanlockhead, and the Mennock, from Abington. This is joined at Leadhills by five miles of a " parish road" from Elvanfoot. Recently covered conveyances have been added to open " machines" at the hotel, Leadhills, and now the latter are also to be had at Abington to assist the weary traveller.

Dean Stanley, in describing the character of the hills of Palestine, says, " As a general rule, not only is it without the two main elements of beauty—variety of outline and variety of colour—but the features rarely so group together as to form any distinct or impressive combination. The tangled and featureless hills of the Lowlands of Scotland and North Wales are perhaps the nearest likeness accessible to Englishmen of Palestine south of the plain of Esdraelon;" and in a footnote he refers to Dr Richardson, who "compares the approach from Jaffa to the road between Sanquhar and Leadhills," in his 2d vol. p. 223 (Sinai and Palestine, p. 135).

Dr Richardson says, "The features of the scenery (near Jerusalem) brought strongly to my recollection a ride from Sanquhar to Leadhills, where the mountains give a favourable idea of the hills of Judea. There is, however, one remarkable point of difference. In Scotland the traveller passes through an excellent road, among an honest and industrious population, where the conversation of the commonest will often delight and surprise the man of letters. Among the hills of Palestine the road is almost impassable, and he finds himself among a set of infamous and ignorant thieves, who would cut his throat for a farthing, and rob him of his property for the mere pleasure of doing it."

That "Mennock" road, ascending six miles from the bed of the Nith, and winding at the base of lofty hills which, with their sloping sides, convey impressively the idea of *rest*, is particularly grand and striking. The Rev. Mr Rankin said, "The road along Mennock to Wanlockhead, being in a deep sequestered glen, in many places cut out of the rock, the bold acclivity and verdure of the hills on each side, the purling of the limpid stream below, and the music of the birds from the brushwood, render it the admiration of strangers, beautifully romantic and delightful."

The view from the top of Auchenlone forms a truly magnificent panorama, taking in such near heights as Tinto (2236), Culter Fell (2330), and the Pentlands. Then westward, beyond Cairntable in Ayrshire, Benlomond, the Paps of Jura, and Ailsa Craig. Again, following the valley of the Nith southward, Criffel below Dumfries, the Solway Firth, the Isle of Man, and the mountains of Hellvellyn and Skiddaw in Cumberland; whilst eastward the swelling tops of the Cheviots may on a clear day be distinctly surveyed.

Dr Brown, in his "Enterkin," says, "The road is little more than a bridle one. You ascend steadily and gently, to a great height, the high hills lying all around—not sharp and ridgy like the Highland mountains, 'curling their monstrous heads, and hanging them,' like the fierce uplifted waves of a prodigious sea—they are more like round-backed, lazy billows in the after-swell of a storm, as if tumbling about in their sleep. They have all a *sonsy*, good-humoured, *buirdly* look. . . . The east side of the Lowthers is an easy ascent, and, as we saw it, the vast expanse was covered with thick, short, tawny grass and moss, one unbroken surface to the summit of 2377 feet, it was like the short, close-grained fur of a lioness —the hills lying like her cubs, huddling round their mighty mother."

PASTURAGE.

These southern uplands are best adapted to the feeding of sheep. Few black cattle are ever seen upon the hills. The bounty of Providence has supplied these moorlands with a wonderful and unnumbered variety of natural grasses, suited for all conditions ; and which, by infinite wisdom and good-ness, are made to spring up continuously, so that a rich supply of good and tender food can generally be found by the flocks. This will be evident if collections from upwards of a hundred kinds known to the shepherds be examined. Of mosses alone one hundred and fifty-four varieties are found in old pastures. Where these are in excess the feeding is impoverished, being "full of fog." And yet one sprig of moss may be of great value, even to man. Mungo Park laid himself down to perish in the midst of a vast wilderness, when, by the sight of a little moss, he was roused from despair to trust in the living God.*

TEMPERATURE.

The locality is bleak and desolate in the extreme, with a corresponding climate. The inhabitants may frequently exclaim :—

" A pleasant climate this of ours !
Who would now turn out a dog ?
To face the peasoup-coloured show'rs—
Fog !

" To-morrow—true !—a change may see—
This climate changes oft, but vain
Is any change ! What will it be ?—
Rain !

---

* For " Natural Grasses," see Appendix A ; " Sheep and Shepherds," B.
14

> " The next day may be altered too—
>   Variety again prevail;
>   Our ears may both be black and blue—
>   Hail !

> " And after that—well, goodness knows
>   What cheer this climate next may show,
>   May nip our noses, pinch our toes—
>   Snow !"

From meteorological observations taken at the two stations in 1873, the cold was some four degrees more intense at Wanlockhead than at Drumlanrig ; in the wettest month there were nine more wet days, although a less quantity of rain fell, at the former. The two wettest months were January, when 12·52 inches fell, and July 12·95. The height of gauge above sea-level being 1330 feet. The greatest fall in twenty-four hours was in September 2, 1870. The heat is lower, and the dryness of the atmosphere is less, in summer. The wind blew at Wanlockhead thirty-seven days more from the east, sixty-two less from the south, and seventy-nine more from the west; whilst not one calm or variable day was experienced. The mean temperature at Drumlanrig for the year was 45·6°. With prevailing east winds the cold is intense, and with prevalent west winds or from the south come the heaviest and most powerful rainfalls.

Of one of the wild mountain passes leading from the Clyde to the Gonar, a couplet runs—

> "Little kens the auld wife, that sits by the fire,
>   How the wild wind blaws in '*Hurl-burl Swyre.*'"

Still not only the purest air, but a plenteous supply of the purest water is obtained. Very many of the mountain springs never run dry, and it is not hard, but as soft as rain-water, fit for all household purposes. Notwithstanding, many think that "it can scarcely be supposed that any one would voluntarily choose to reside there at so high an elevation."

The curling-stone is frequently thrown in the hill region when the plough is busy in the valleys. With the exception of the winter of 1874, the climate has within twenty or thirty years undergone a remarkable improvement. Formerly cottages had to be dug out in Wanlockhead, now the country road is seldom blocked up for more than a week or fortnight.

To be out upon these hills in a snowstorm is no light matter. Snow drifting, roads blocked up with deep wreaths, and all communication with the outer world cut off. Oftentimes—

"Atween an' Wanlock hills the snaw gade swirlin' by like stoure,
And like a spell its glamor fell athort the mirksome muir.
A' efternune the feathery flecks cam' flichterin' through the air,
Wi' scarce a wauf o' win' tae drift the whiteness here nor there ;
But e'er the blude-reid sun had sunk aneth Glengaber's broo
A norlan' blast begoud tae blaw wad chill't ye thro' an' thro'."

REID.

Even then enjoyment can be had by the lover of nature, and matter for praise gathered up by the Christian. The mountains lie as recumbent creatures, white, radiant, and spotless. The sharp, clear frosty day is felt to be truly invigorating. The sun shines out bright and warm, and as mountains and valleys are covered with a thick sheet of pure white snow, the prospect is grand in the extreme. The tops of the hills shine as if with burnished gold, whilst the fantastic wreaths that seem sculptured out of the clefts and crags sparkle as if studded with millions of diamonds.

But come hither,

"When the summer is in prime,
Wi' the flowers richly bloomin',
An' the wild mountain thyme
A' the moorlands perfumin',"

then the bracing air of the mountains is delightful. Abounding in Galloway, very few adders are found on these hills ; so that rambles there are safe as well as full and free.

Occasionally, too, phenomena of an interesting nature are observable. In July 1872 a very singular waterspout was observed at Wanlockhead. In form it resembled a long serpent, winding, twisting, now descending very near to the mountain-tops, and then writhing up again into the bosom of the cloud of blackness from whence it proceeded. The heat had been intense all the morning, and, as on several previous days, some peals of thunder were heard, followed at some distance of time by forked flashes of lightning. After this the darkness became intense from the presence of a thick cloud immediately above the Stake Moss Hill, and close upon the village. Then a terrific blast of wind came forth with a noise resembling thunder. A portion of the cloud seemed to descend in a lighter form, and out of it this light blue serpentine spout dropped down towards the earth. After exhibiting itself thus for about half an hour the spout gradually merged itself into the cloud. It was afterwards discovered that the water-spout had burst upon the Lowther Mountains. Not only was the Mennock stream swollen thereby, but the road leading to Sanquhar was deluged with water. Had it burst upon any of the cottages of the lead-miners, the consequences might have been serious. As it happened, it was an object of delight and wonder.

In spring-time, again, the mountains seem all on fire—

> "While far the withering heaths with moor-burn blaze !
> The pillared smoke ascends with ashen gleam;
> Aloft in air the arching flashes stream ;
> With rushing, crackling noise the flames aspire,
> And roll one deluge of devouring fire."   LEYDEN.

The top of the East Lowther or Five Cairns is interesting from the fact of the burial of suicides there in old times. The oldest horse that could be got to pull the oldest broken-down cart, with wretched harness—mostly string and ropes—were made to drag the body thither. Refused Christian sepulture, it was here disposed of, where three lairds' lands and parishes met, and therefore out of possessable and disputable land, and the old cart and horse, &c., were left there as unfit for further use on earth. But seldom was the desecrated body allowed to lie. A man was bribed to go at dead of night, whither he was led, and to hurl on his barrow to the doctor's house the bundle which he and his assistant had dragged or tumbled in the sack down from the mountain height. And then if noises were heard in the doctor's dwelling, fears were allayed by observing, "Oh! it's only old Betty at her pranks again." So runs traditionary story.

GEOLOGICAL FORMATION.

The hills and valleys composing the basins of the Nith and Clyde have been felicitously described by Professor Geikie, and also in the "Memoirs of the Geological Survey."

"The continuous band of hilly ground from St Abb's Head to Portpatrick," says the former, "consists fundamentally or hard greywacke and shale, with occasional limestone bands of Lower Silurian age squeezed into endless foldings, as the great piles of a carpet, as by pressure from the north-west and south-east. The scenery of this broad belt of hilly ground is distinct from that of any other part of the kingdom.

It maintains, indeed, a great uniformity and even monotony throughout its whole extent. . . . It divides itself naturally into two not very unequal portions, each of which, while retaining the same family likeness, possesses, nevertheless, certain individual and distinguishing features of its own.

"The valley of the Nith passes completely across the Silurian region, and its course serves as an approximate boundary line between the two districts. . . . The country between Nithsdale and St Abb's Head [has] long-connected chains of hills, nearly destitute of lakes, but with numerous confluent valleys, whose united waters, after a course of many miles, enter the sea as important rivers.

"The north-eastern half of the Silurian belt from Nithsdale to the German Ocean may be regarded as a wide, undulating tableland, cut into coalescing ridges by a set of valleys which are usually narrow and deep. It has no determinate system of hill-ranges, the grouping of its eminences seeming in most cases to be defined by the circumstances which aided or retarded the excavation of the intervening hollows. In the higher parts of the district the smoothness and verdure of the hills are here and there exchanged for bold rocky scarps, bare crags and cliffs, and deep narrow defiles, that remind us now and then of parts of the Highlands. Such is the nature of the romantic Pass of Dalveen, among the Lowther Hills. . . . In no part of Scotland is the relation of valley to watercourse more strikingly shown. The valleys are usually narrow and deep, and the streams either fill up the whole bottom, or wind from side to side in short curves, laving the base of the opposite hillsides alternately. . . .

"The Lyne Water and the Nith actually take their rise beyond the Silurian belt altogether, and flow completely across it. The springs of the Nith well out of the north flank of the uplands, and the infant river descends into the Ayrshire coalfields, as if to wind away towards the Firth of Clyde. Instead of turning in that direction, however, at New Cumnock it bends round to the south-east, and then entering the Silurian tableland, traverses its entire breadth, and merges into the Solway.

"The Clyde valley is most interesting. Drawing its waters from the very centre of the southern uplands, it flows transverse to the strike of the Silurian strata, until, entering upon the rocks of the lowlands at Roberton, it turns to the north-east along a broad valley that skirts the base of Tinto. The Clyde there approaches within seven miles of the Tweed. Between the two streams, of course, lies the watershed of the country, the drainage flowing on the one side into the Atlantic, and on the other into the North Sea. Yet instead of a ridge or hill, the space between the rivers is the broad flat valley of Biggar, so little above the level of the Clyde that it would not cost much labour to send that river across into the Tweed. Indeed, some trouble is necessary to keep the former stream from eating through the loose sandy deposits that line the valley, and finding its way over into Tweeddale. That it once took that course, thus entering the sea at Berwick instead of at Dumbarton, is probable, and if some of the gravel mounds at Thankerton could be reunited it would do so again.

"'It is a singular circumstance,' says Stoddart in his 'Angler's Companion for Scotland,' 'that salmon and their fry have occasionally been taken in the upper parts of the Clyde above its loftiest fall, which, being eighty feet in height, it is utterly impossible for fish of any kind to surmount. The fact is accounted for in this way. After passing Tinto Hill, the bed of the Clyde approaches to a level with that of the Biggar Water, which is close at hand, and discharges itself into the Tweed. On the occasion of a large flood, the two streams become connected, and the Clyde actually pours a portion of its waters into one of the tributaries of the Tweed, which is accessible to, and frequented in winter by, salmon.'

"Before farming operations were carried to the extent to which they have now arrived, large boulders, now mostly removed, were scattered so abundantly over the mossy tract between the river Clyde and 'the Yelping Craig,' about two miles to the east, that one place was known familiarly as 'Hell Stanes Gate' (road), and another 'Hell Stanes Loan.' The traditional story runs that the stones were brought by supernatural agency from 'the Yelping Craigs.' Michael Scott and the devil, it appears, had entered into a compact with a band of witches to dam back the Clyde. It was one of the conditions of the agreement that the name of the Supreme Being should never on any account be mentioned. All went well for a while, some of the stronger spirits having brought their burden of boulders to within a few yards from the river; when one of the younger members of the company, staggering under the weight of a huge block of greenstone, exclaimed, 'O Lord! but I'm tired.' Instantly every boulder tumbled to the ground, nor could witch, warlock, or devil move a single stone one yard farther. And there the blocks lay for many a long century, until the rapacious farmers quarried them away for dykes and road-metal." (See " Scenery of Scotland in connection with Physical Geology.")

These mountain ranges, then, are generally composed of granite or trap rock. "If," says a geologist, "we take the granite rocks of Galloway as the base, we have superincumbent upon them—first, the greywacke of Leadhills and Wanlockhead; second, the red sandstone over which the Clyde is precipitated at Lanark; and third, the coal formation of the Middle and Lower Wards, consisting of bituminous shale, grey limestone, and clay ironstone, thus affording a beautiful illustration of the Transition and Carboniferous epochs."

In these deposits interesting specimens can be obtained. Dr Grierson of Thornhill brought recently before the Society of Inquiry a series of specimens of graptolites from the black shale of the Silurian rocks at Wanlockhead. "These graptolitic markings," he observed, "have a special interest as being the forms of a race of beings supposed to be allied to the hydrozoa, which have existed in the mud of the world's first seas, and been raised by the earth's central powers to form mountains."

"The largest and highest fragments which remain of the original tableland out of which the existing valleys have been carved, form the group of the Wanlockhead, Leadhills, and Lowther Hills, . . . and the high grounds about the sources of the Afton, Euchan, Snar, and Ken waters. In the Lowthers the highest point is 2403 feet above the sea, and a space of about two and a half square miles exceeds an elevation of 2000 feet; while on the south-west side of the Nith the area above 2000 feet amounts to rather more than a square mile, its highest point being the Black Craig of Afton, which has an elevation of 2298 feet. The only cliff of any size in the district is Glenwhorgan Craig, in the valley of the Scar Water, which has a height of upwards of 400 feet. . . On the south side of the Lowther Hills, in such valleys as that of the Enterkin or of Dalveen, and in their tributaries, though the slopes are steep, they are almost always grassy or heathy; and where rock does roughen them, it is for the most part only in detached little crags and hummocks." *

The principal heights of the Lowther range are—Lonsiewood

* For geological groups and minerals, see Appendix C.

Law, 2028; White Law, 1941; Dun Law, 2216; Dungrain Law, 2186; Green Lowther, 2403; Lowther Hill, or "the Five Cairns," 2377; and Auchenlone, 2068. These hills are green to the top, with

> "*Banks of moss, spongy and swelling soft.*"

FISHING-GROUND.

In the valley of the Clyde the river rises from the high ground mentioned, where

> "Annan, Tweed, and Clyde a' rise from ae hillside;
>   Annan ran, Tweed ran, Clyde fell and brak' his neck ower Corralinn."

It has another source in Queensberry Hill; and in this district receives the burns of Pitrenick, Peden, and Glenochar, with the Powtrail and Daer Water. Then Clyde's Burn, or Little Clyde. Below this, Elvan, Midloch, Camps, Glengonar (with Glencaple), and the Duneaton, into which falls the Snar, &c.

The Elvan, or clear stream, which two miles above is termed the Shortcleuch, drains one valley running up to the Lowthers, and the Gonar another running above Leadhills. These "burns" are influenced by mining operations. Still "Clutha" suffers not, for

> "The course of Scotia's pride is wild and free,
>   As rushes she along in noisy glee,
>   Then rushes o'er the linn with deaf'ning roar."

These are open to the angler, and yield good trout-fishing. Salmon are sometimes found above the falls; for, as has been said, in heavy spates the upper waters of the Biggar mingle with those of Clyde, so that these salmon are properly Tweed fish.

The Daer or Darr, rising in Queensberry, joins the Clyde near Elvanfoot, which (with the Powtrail and other burns) is twelve miles long, contains yellow trout and grayling, the average being half a pound. The months of April, May, August, and September are the best. These, with the Duneaton, eighteen miles, are all open, and are favourite streams with anglers, who have good inns at Abington, Crawford, and Elvanfoot, where increased accommodation is much desired.

On the other side of the Lowthers liberty to fish is obtainable from J. G. Clark, Esq., Dabton, Thornhill, Chamberlain to the Duke of Buccleuch. The Crawick, with the Spango and smaller feeders, are good burn streams. Its tributary, the Wanlock, for a reason to be named, contains no fish. Crawick runs twelve miles through green hills and richly-wooded banks, and falls into the Nith not far from Sanquhar. The Mennock or Minnick, rising in the Lowthers, after a run of six miles through solitary and magnificent hill scenery, by the side of a good road to Wanlockhead, falls into the Nith at Mennockfoot village. It receives the Glendyne two miles up, winding up a glen much resorted to by Peden and the Covenanters. Enterkin, rising near the source of the Mennock, flows by that ancient and precipitous pass between the hills memorable for Covenanting rescues, and falls after four and a half miles' run into the Nith at Enterkinfoot village, the visitor finding good accommodation at the Hopetoun Arms in Leadhills, or in the Queensberry Arms at Sanquhar.

The Nith, rising in Ayrshire, for twenty miles, in the property of the Duke of Buccleuch, is an important river, passing here through lovely scenery. The streams which fall into it on the other side are the Kello, running ten miles amidst rocky hills, and the Euchan, which, with the former, rises in Blacklorg Hill (2231 feet), at the extremity of Sanquhar parish. These with their tributaries also yield good trout, and are best fished in May, June, or July. There are grayling in the Nith, and sea-trout is to be had in the end of the season.

THE SHOOTINGS

are generally retained in the hands of the proprietors, although that of Eliock, on the richly-wooded banks of the Nith, was lately rented for £380.

The great advantage of the pursuit of game is the occupation and invigoration of the upper classes during the autumnal months, as a relaxation from the severities of Parliamentary and city, or the strait-laced round of conventional, life. Nowhere can a better field be presented for such bracing enjoyment than in this treasure-house. There have usually been an abundance of grouse, patridges, black game, hares, and in the Nith valley of roedeer, &c. The modern method of lying behind a turf dyke or hut, and shooting game driven thither, is generally regarded as "poor sport," whilst very many birds creep away and die of their wounds. Poachers, who once were frequent visitors and escaped with loads of booty, are now unknown ; and such an occupation is never dreamt of even by the mining population, although they have both time and ample opportunity. The frequent presents of game sent them by his Grace the Duke of Buccleuch have doubtless secured this good result. Far more game is killed in Kirkconnel than in Sanquhar. All is given away but what is required for consumption at Drumlanrig Castle.

Power to the tenant to kill ground game on the Buccleuch estate is given to twenty-six tenants, and to five to kill partridges, while the privilege is given to all who desire it.

The birds of prey, of song, and of the migratory species are those which are abundantly common in the south of Scotland. The bullfinch, goldfinch, and squirrel are found in Eliock woods, &c. Few except the snow-bird and the lark are seen in the hilly parts of the parish. Wild otters, badgers, weasels, wild cats, polecats, and foxes, formerly known, are now almost extinguished.

Abington, as a centre for Crawford and Crawfordjohn, was long the meeting-place of the coursing clubs, and although the "coursing trains" have rather spoiled that exercise, the "Caledonian" still keeps there its annual tryst. Thus in these southern uplands—

> "To him who in the love of nature holds
> Communion, . . . for his gayer hours
> She has a voice of gladness, and a smile
> And eloquence of beauty ; and she glides
> Into his darker musings, with a mild
> And healing sympathy, that steals away
> Their sharpness ere he is aware."
>
> W. C. BRYANT.

CRAWFORD BARONIES.

"This is the state of man ; TO-DAY he puts forth
The tender leaves of hope, TO-MORROW blossoms,
And bears his blushing honours thick upon him.
The THIRD day comes a frost, a killing frost ;
And when he thinks—good easy man—full surely
His greatness is a-ripening—nips his root,
And then he falls." SHAKESPEARE.

BY the Romans, inhabitants of the upper part of Clydesdale during the first century were termed the Damnii. They were an athletic, warlike, indomitable race, fighting in chariots with swords, lances, and bucklers, having made considerable progress in the useful arts. Avoiding pitched battles, they yet cut off stragglers, intercepted supplies, and attacked encampments, so that this district was held by them against the invading foe. "Celts," and other implements and antiquities still preserved, tell of these unwritten periods of our national story.*

The history of the "Treasure" runs thereafter for centuries along with, and concentrates itself around the proprietors of, "Tower Lindsay," a fine old ruin unfortunately almost hid by the cutting of the railway from the eyes of passengers. It occupies one of the most magnificent sites, in the midst of old trees upon a knoll on the north side of the river Clyde, surrounded by an extensive amphitheatre of hills. Within its walls, or those of a more ancient castle, the "Wallace wight" is said to have put fifty of an English garrison to the sword by his own hand.

* One stone celt used for cutting or to strike a foe, when secured by thongs to a wooden shaft, measuring $10\frac{3}{4}$ by 4 inches, and another of greenstone tapering to the end, 16 by 4 inches, are in the possession of Mr Macqueen, Abington.

The greater portion of Crawford parish being possessed by William Lindesay, it obtained the name of Crawford-Lindsay.

David de Lindsay and Walter de Lindsay witnessed charters confirmed by William the Lion from 1200 to 1227; proving that the family had lands in the upper part of Clydesdale before the marriage of David with the heiress of Crawford.

Two brothers, William and Walter de Lindsay, obtained lands in Clydesdale, &c., from David I. Sir Alexander de Lindsay was one of the magnates who agreed to the marriage of Margaret of Scotland with Prince Edward of England in 1290. He swore fealty to Sir William Wallace in 1297, and submitted to Edward the same year, but soon afterwards ranged himself against the English. On the submission of Comyn to Edward, Alexander was excepted from the conditions, and ordered to be banished.

Sir David de Lindsay was Keeper of the Castle of Edinburgh, 1346—

> "Syne wes Edynburchis Castale
> Gyvyn, and the towne all hale,
> To Schyr Daivy the Lyndssay,
> That was trewe, and of stedfast fay.
> Intil his tyme wyth the cuntre
> Na ryot, na na stryfe made he."
>   WYNTOUN.

Robert II. granted the castle and barony of Crawford to Sir James Lindesay. The cousin and heir of Sir James was created Earl in 1398, with a charter and jurisdiction of regality. The fourth Earl having espoused the cause of James II. against the insurgent barons, was created Duke of Montrose; and although not formally forfeited, the barony of Crawford-Lindsay was forcibly taken from him, on the fall of James III., and bestowed on Archibald, Earl of Angus, or "Bell-the-Cat." It is well known how this title was given to Angus. James had lavished his partiality on favourites, especially on Cochrane, a builder. James was king, but Cochrane ruled. This could not be endured by the feudal lords. They assembled in Lauder Church; then Lord Gray told the old story of the mice who resolved to hang a bell on the cat to warn the mice of its approach, and that the good scheme lacked only one bold enough to put it on. Then "I will bell the cat," cried Angus. Just then a knocking was heard, Cochrane admitted. His chain of gold and jewelled hunting horn were torn from his neck by Angus, and Cochrane shortly after hanged by a hair "tether" over Lauder Bridge.

Angus in turn was forfeited; and on the accession of Mary, 1542, the Earl was reinstated. When the Queen came of age, 1567, this restoration was confirmed. James V. frequently visited the Castle for sporting purposes, personally giving evidence of the loose morality of his Court.

In its old extent the barony was valued at £200. In 1359 it contributed 20s. to the Ward of the King's Castle at Lanark. The present Earl of Crawford is considered the head of the Crawford Lindsays. Dr W. Lauder Lindsay of Perth, whose writings are well known, is a descendant of the same family. The title *Crawford-Douglas* arose from the barony having passed into the hands of the Hamilton branch of the Douglas family. In the time of Anne, Duchess of Hamilton, with consent of her husband, she bestowed the barony of Crawford on a younger son, who was created Earl of Selkirk and Lord Daer—a title taken from a neighbouring stream. The barony remained in the possession of the Selkirk family until the latter part of last century, when it was sold to Sir George Colebrooke, Bart. His grandson, Sir Thomas Edward Colebrooke, M.P., is the present proprietor, whose country residence is the pleasant mansion of Abington House.

The barony of CRAWFORDJOHN was possessed in the reign of King Malcolm by John de Crawford, who was succeeded by his son, Sir Reginald de Crawford, Sheriff of Ayr, who obtained the lands of Loudon by marriage with the heiress of James the son of Lambin (whence Lamington). John de Crawford, one of his sons, inherited the barony in 1228. "*For the soul's weal of himself and his wife Ossanna*," he (1232 to 1249) gave to the Cistercians of Newbattle his lands "from the place where the burn of Lauercatsalanue [Lettershaws] falls into the stream of Glengonar, upwards by the said burn to the top of the hill, thence westwards, as the waters descend into Glengonar *above the mine*, to the march between my lands and Nithsdale." That land now forms part of Crawford parish, but prior to 1683 Glengonar stream was its boundary.

Ambassadors of Henry III. co-operated with certain barons in Scotland in counteracting the influence of Walter Comyn, Earl of Monteith, in 1255. Johannes de Crawford and his brother Hugh were among these, and it is probable that John was rewarded by a grant of the barony of Crawfordjohn, as it does not appear to have been so erected till that period; and the township of John of Crawford would clearly distinguish it from the neighbouring barony.

This barony was divided between two daughters on the death of John, one of whom married David de Barclay. In 1359 the Sheriff collected 20s. from one-half of the barony of *Crawfordjohn-Barclay.* Thomas de Moravia, who married the other, was connected by marriage with Robert de Bruce, and in 1357 became hostage in order to the liberation of King David. His daughter Jean, who inherited the half barony in 1361, carried it to her husband, Archibald the Grim, Lord of Galloway and Earl of Douglas. It remained with that family till the ninth Earl was forfeited for rebellion against James II. in 1454.

The lands of "Albintonne and Glengonaryg" in this barony were, under the Great Seal, granted in 1458 to Sir Walter Scott of Kirkurde for his good service in the battle of Arkinholm. The whole of this half of the barony was in 1464 bestowed on James, Lord Hamilton; and in 1512 a confirmation of the grant was made to James, second Lord Hamilton and Earl of Arran. But it is found that Hugh, son of David de Barclay, inherited the former portion, 1397. Marjory, his heiress, married Malcolm Crawford of Greenock, and in 1529 it was exchanged by Laurence Crawford with Sir James Hamilton of Finnart; and Sir James then took possession of the entire barony, he having been declared legitimate. Soon after the barony was exchanged and given up to James V., and it continued to be annexed to the Crown till the next reign.

On the forfeiture of James Hamilton in 1543 being rescinded, the half of the barony became the property of Lord James Hamilton, and the other of Sir James of Finnart; but his grandson having no male heirs, disponed it in 1611 to James, second Marquis of Hamilton. The reunited barony remained in this possession till 1693, when Anne, Duchess of Hamilton, conveyed it to her younger son, the Earl of Selkirk. In 1710 the other principal heritors were Mackmoron of Glespin, Somerville of Birkcleuch, and the Maxwells of Calderwood, who held the lands of Abington. At the close of last century, that and the adjoining barony of Crawford-Douglas, as stated, were bought by *Sir George Colebrooke, Bart.* In both cases, however, the right to the minerals was reserved.*

* See Murray's "Upper Ward of Lanarkshire;" and for Earls of Crawford, present proprietors, rental, and condition of these parishes, see Appendix D, E, and F.

Part II.

ITS TREASURES.

" On Tintock-tap there is a mist,
And in the mist there is a kist,
And in the kist there is a caup,
And in the caup there is a drap;
Take up the caup, drink aff the drap,
And set the caup on Tintock-tap."

THE barrenness of the surface of these southern uplands is largely compensated by the valuable minerals contained in the bowels of the hills. At present lead, with its proportion of silver, is one great source of wealth. In ancient times gold was found in such quantities as to give rise to the designation of "God's Treasure-House;" and still the precious metal can be had by patient search.

The southern gold-field ranges over a very extensive tract. Robert Seton's Memorandum in the time of James V. stated that gold was found at Newtown in Angén (?); Cartburn in Annandale; Solway Sands, near the town of Annand; Glen Naip (or App), betwixt Carrick and Galloway; Galloway, in the barony of Tareagles; in a hill called Coloshere; and in the hill of Skrill (or Skreel of Bengairn, near Kirkcudbright).

Kersop upon Yarrow Water, in Philiphaugh, is mentioned by Colonel Borthwick in addition to many other places. A tract of from forty to sixty miles of the South has been found to be gold-bearing; but this central field, of some ten miles in length, was the Paradise whose four rivulets were compared to the four rivers that flowed in Eden.

"In Clydesdale and Nydsdale, within the kingdom of Scotland [is a place] which may be compared unto it [the Garden of Eden], or called a second garden, though not so pleasant and fruitful, yet richer under ground than above for gold. And there be foure waters or rivers, the heads whereof discend out of mountaines and mosses, or hard rocks and craggs. These rivers are also divided, by God's omnipotent power, into foure heads," which Atkinson goes on particularly to describe as Wanlock, Mennock, Shortcleuch, and Gonar. He also states that "the Lord Marques Hambleton is superiour under his Majesty" upon "Fryar Moore;" "the Earl of Lowdian, *alias* Lord Newbottle," "upon Alwayne" on Shortcleuch. "Lord Sanquer *superiour upon Robbart Moore*, on the Wynlocke; and the Lord of Closebarne is fewer thereof;" and "Lord Dumlanyricke superior upon Mannocke Moore, on Mannocke Water, which descendeth unto the river of Neede or Neeth, and so unto Dumfresse; and then to Carlile, and so unto the sea."

GOLD AND GOLD-FINDERS.

" Of everilk mettelles we have the riche mynes,
Baith gold, silver, and stanes precious."

Sir David Lindsay.

EARLY FINDERS.

AT a period when the aristocracy of Caledonia dwelt in holes dug in the ground covered over with branches, and when the bear, wolf, and wild horse roamed in the primeval forest—ages before written records were known, our ancestors found, formed, and prized ornaments of gold. This fact has been unfolded when the stone "cist" and its skeleton remains have been examined. That which was most prized in life was then buried with the dead. They had no intercourse with foreign lands, or at least none such as would bring the precious metal hither. The conclusion is irresistible that it was native gold they wore.

These weighty gold ornaments buried with the honoured dead prove that the early inhabitants possessed it in considerable quantities. Their keen eyes beheld the little nugget or shining dust swept down by mountain streams; and their collars of twisted or engraven gold tell of the advance made from the teeth, shell, or bone ornaments of savage life. Long before a bronze sword, iron, or the fusion of metals were known, gold was possessed.

"Britain produces gold, silver, and other metals, the booty of victory," was the language employed by Agricola, when Galcacus led them to attack the Caledonians (Tacitus, Vita Agricola). Although the Romans had sufficient land within their power, it is uncertain whether they knew of the existence of gold in this locality. But if the Romans were ignorant of its presence, the Celtic tribes of the sixth and seventh centuries were

31

not. Torques or ornaments of great weight and value were not only found upon the persons of their chiefs, but upon their horses and armour. Bards of the ninth century, recording the savage inroads of the Norsemen, describe them not only as "feeders of wolves," but also as "exactors of rings" from the Scottish "forlorn wearers of rings." And there can be no doubt that the rings they came so far to exact were of native gold.

Of the twenty specimens of gold ornaments preserved in the Antiquarian Museum in Edinburgh, one is a lunette or plate of gold shaped as the crescent of the moon, with incised lines and punctures, which was found on the farm of Southside, near to Coulter. Another is a plain hoop ring weighing 1 oz. 8 dwt., which was found in digging at the parish church of Kilpatrick-Durham, in Galloway.

Two fine specimens of an ornament were found in 1858 on a piece of newly broken-up ground on the farm of Southside, in the parish of Kilbucho, about three miles from Biggar. They were at first thought to be merely pieces of tin, and were taken to the farmhouse and thrown behind the kitchen fire. A relative of the farmer, who had visited America, happened to have his attention attracted by their singular appearance, and on examination found that they were composed of the finest gold. They were taken to Biggar and weighed, and ultimately found their way into the hands of Adam Sim, Esq., who presented one of them to the Antiquarian Society, Edinburgh. The other is still in his possession at Coulter Mains. Each of them weighs 1 oz. 8 dwt. 13 grs. They are both exactly alike, in the form of a crescent or half-moon, measure at the broadest part $1\frac{3}{8}$ in., terminate at each extremity with a button or small disc, and have a slight ornamentation, consisting of faint lines and small depressions. They were got where bronze celts and other remains of a remote antiquity have been found.* Some supposed these to be Druidical remains, representing the shape of the moon when the sacred mistletoe was cut on the sixth day of the moon's age.

IN TWELFTH AND FIFTEENTH CENTURIES.

The earliest official notice of Scottish gold is in the twelfth century (1125), when King David I., that "sore sanct for the

* Biggar and the House of Fleming, p. 12.

Croon," granted a tenth of all the gold found in Fife and Fothrif to the Church of the Holy Trinity in Dunfermline.

In James I.'s Parliament, held in Perth 1424, it was provided that wherever gold and silver mines were discovered within the lands of any lord or baron, if it can be proved that three halfpennies of silver can be produced out of the pound of lead, the mine should, according to the established practice of other realms, belong to the King (Tytler's History, vol. iii. pp. 63, 201).

IN SIXTEENTH CENTURY.

Hector Boethus says, " In Clydesdale are the gold mines and diamonds, rubies and hyacinths, discovered in the time of James IV." (Hist., p. 6.)

James IV. maintained a gay court. Masques, pageants, tournaments, with accompanying revelry, involved a large expenditure. He was, moreover, the patron of new inventions. His straits combined with prevailing credulity led him to establish a quack in the Palace of Stirling. Alchemy possessed the minds of men, and nothing was so renowned as the pursuit of the philosopher's stone. Bishop Lesley gives this account of the experiments in the royal laboratory, and how the stone took wings to itself from the castle walls :—

" This tyme thair wes ane Italian with the King, quha wes maid Abbot of Tungland, and wes of curious ingyne. He causit the King believe that he, be multiplyinge and utheris his inventions, soold mak fine gold of uther mettall; quhilk science he called the Quintassence, quhairupon the King maid grait coste, but all in vaine. This abbot tuik in hand to flie with wingis, and to be in France befoir the saidis ambassadouris; and to that effect he causit mak ane pair of wingis of fedderis, quhilkis beand fessinit upon him he flew off the castell wall of Striveling, bot shortlie he fell to the grund, and brak his thie bane. Bot the wyte thairof he ascryvit to that thair wes some hen fedderis in the wingis, whilk yarnit and covet the mydding and not the skyis."

A far more successful enterprise was prosecuted in the search for gold in the mines of Crawford, which seem to have been well known as its treasure-house. About the year 1502 a nugget of gold weighing 2 lbs. 3 oz., or 12,960 grs., worth (valuing gold at £4 per oz.) upwards of £100, was found.

In 1511, 1512, and 1513 a number of payments are recorded

at Crawford Muir mines to Lebald Northberge, the master miner; Andrew Ireland, the finer; and Gerald Essemer, a Dutchman, the melter. These operations were carried on under Sir James Pettigrew. But the fatal field of Flodden, where James IV. ended his reckless life within the unbroken ring of his nobility in the year 1513, when many wept and sang, if they could, that

"The flowers o' the forest are a' wed away,"

for a time laid an arrest upon the scheme.

During the regencies after the King's death the search for gold was in some measure revived. The treasurer, James, Bishop of Murray, records in 1515: "Item, deliverit to my Lord Postulate of the Yles, for to pas to Crawford Mure, and there to set workmen, and mak ordinances for the gold myne, to gud compt. in ane hundreth crownes of wight (xxxx. Ii.)" That was under the Queen Regent; and it appears from the correspondence of Wharton, the English Lord Warden of the Marches, that in July 1526, under the Regent Albany, when the Earl of Angus had possession of the young King, a lease of the gold mines was granted to certain Germans. By means of a large bribe, the bullion laws of the kingdom were allowed to be contravened, and the precious ore was exported to be refined in Germany.

When Scotland's morn began to dawn; when feudal chains, Popish oppression and corruption, were losing hold of the people; and when a spirit of enterprise in trade and freedom began to be developed, the search for gold began to be prosecuted on a more systematic and extensive plan.

The "Miscellanea Scotica" (Lond. 1710, 8vo) gives preface of translation of a "French Account of the Life of James V.," in which particulars are given, derived from a paper "On the Gold Mines of Scotland" in the Cotton Library (Otho, E. x. 12), of which only a fragment is preserved, it having suffered by fire in the year 1726. It mentions that the gold mines were found in Crawford Muir by the Germans; that above £100,000 worth (English money) was obtained, and that in another place pieces 30 oz. weight were found.

Lesley, Bishop of Ross, in his "Descriptio Regionum et Insularum Scotiæ," describes the gold mines at Crawford Muir as if first discovered in the reign of James IV. He also gives an account of the success of the German artists employed to refine the gold. Their grant, dated 19th July 1526, is preserved in "De Rebus Gestis Scotorum," Romæ, 1578, 4to, p. 452.

The MS. referred to appears to be a report of an inspector of the gold-bearing area. It is preserved in the Cottonian Collection in the British Museum. Without date and imperfect, it yet tells its own tale:—

"I have been enformed in Kinge James the fou[rth's time] Scottishmen did begin to washe golde, and in King Ja[mes] . . . somers there was three hundred psons wch did mainta[in themselves by washing] golde; but for theis last 40 yeres there hath been little . . . foresaid eightie yeres manie Gills, waters, and valleis have [yielded] therein of greater value than an hundred thousand pounds y[early] . . . people workinge for golde, no vains of gold have been knowne to be f[ound]." The MS. then goes on to narrate numerous localities where gold has been found, and gives a lot of the empirical jargon of the period as to the indications where the different metallic ores—including gold, silver, tin, lead, copper, and iron—are to be found; it then proceeds, "Bie report of sundrie workmen, some whereof afirme that at Pontahields, . . . Winlock Water, and in sundrie other places, they have founde golde in bignes of cherristones, and some greater peeces, lyinge between two rocks in a yallowe . . . blewishe mother or leeder" "bie testemonie and voluntarie othes of such as have founde peeces of golde, and have seene founde bie others, one peece of 30 ounces, and some of greater waight which were flat and mixed wth spar, and some wth keele, and some wth brimstone, and the Lorde of Markestone did show . . . three-quarters of an ounce, and some lesser [peeces] . . . those peeces were torne by the force of water . . . of ye waters since that time wherebie I doe [think keele and] brimstone are leaders to ye vaines of golde." The writer of the MS. goes on to remark upon the ignorance of the gold-washers of the district in neglecting the indications which he perceived of metallic ore; and further says that many trials for gold had been made on the side of the hills, and that he having "made two daies triall in ye toppes and sides of ye hills, did likewise finde noe golde." The MS. concludes with the remark "that there hath ben . . . plentie of golde gotten in ye waters of the said cloughes and Gillies 80 fad[oms] above the foresaid waters in ye valleis, wch golde being ponderous . . . must bie common reason descend: so as consequentlie, whereas some peeces of [gold] of above 30 ounces weight have been found in the said Gillies, the same must . . . growe there aboute or bie violent waters be dryven out of higher places wher they did grow wthin ye circumference of those places where the golde is founde."

In this Cottonian MS. it is stated again that "gold hath ben gotten bie washinge bie ye L. of Markes[ton] . . distant from Leadhill Howse in Crawford Moore, 28 myles, and [gold] hath ben gotten in Langham Water, 14 miles, and Megget Water . . . Phinlande, 16 miles distant from Leadhill Howse, and in many other [places] bie testimonie of sundrie reputed honeste; wch golde to have ben gotten . . . so far distant one from another, doth showe there are either manie se[ames] . . . ye golde so founde is generallie dispersed, and doth but ly in ye supfice[al] not in the solid and knit vaines." *

The King had not only sent ambassadors to France, he went in person, and espoused Madeleine, the fair and graceful eldest daughter of Francis I. The marriage and the train of the royal pair were very brilliant. Not less so her reception in Scotland. Stepping on shore at Leith, she kissed her adopted country and gave thanks to God. Tradition tells that when the French ambassadors, hunting with James at Crawford Castle, made light of the country because of its barren appearance, the King wagered that it could produce richer fruit than their own; and that he won the wager when at the banquet he introduced covered dishes filled with beautiful gold coins called " Bonnet pieces." This act of gallantry—which probably the King could ill afford—was repeated by presenting to his lovely French bride at the dessert these specimens of " Scottish fruit." But her joy was short-lived; for only forty days elapsed from her triumphal entrance into the capital, until she lay sleeping the sleep of death.

Another beautiful and majestic Frenchwoman, Mary of Guise, the widow of the Duke of Longueville, soon thereafter became Queen of Scotland. With Mary of Guise came woeful times, as the Reformation struggle fully proved; but the arrival of this Mary of Lorraine brought a fresh impetus to the search for gold. Workmen from that duchy were introduced into the

* See " Historical Notes on the Gold of the South of Scotland," by P. Dudgeon, F.R.S.E. & S.

Crawford mines, and by their superior skill, trained as they had been in the great mining field of France, secured very large results. Mr John Mossman received charge of these miners. Entries of payments in the royal treasurer's books are not only found in 1539 and 1540 for "interpreters to pass with the French mynours till they learn the language," as well as for the subsistence of these "mynours," but account is also taken of the amount of gold received.

A grant was also made of "ane Scottish boy that speaks French, to serve them till they get the Scottish language."

Another record connects the gold found with the Castle of Crawfordjohn, which has long ago disappeared. James V. made it or the neighbouring Castle of Boghouse his headquarters for hunting in 1541. The treasurer recorded, "Item, deliverit to George Carmichael, son of the Captain of Crawford, for 3 ounces of gold, which he delivered to the Queen's grace, the time she was in Crawfordjohn, price £6, 8s. the ounce." At that period there were many castles or strongholds in the neighbourhood.

Snar Castle, the remains of which are traceable, was about that time held by a notorious mosstrooper known as "Jock of Snar." The "Priest's Hole" in its neighbourhood is said to have been the scene of a ducking given to a friar, whom on his return from an expedition he found occupying his place. Whether the priest lost his life tradition saith not.

Again it is recorded that in 1541, gold amounting to "one ounce, two unicore, half-unicore wicht," was delivered to the royal jeweller "to garnus ane cairtuithe" (coral) for my Lord Prince. These accounts also show that the value of the gold was £6, 8s. per ounce. The Chamberlain Rolls show that in 1542 gold was issued from the mine to form the Regalia; 35 ounces being devoted to the Queen's crown, and 3 pounds 10 ounces to that of the King. $19\frac{1}{2}$ ounces were also appropriated to form a belt for the Queen. The cost of making these amounted to £15. Ocular demonstration may thus be had by a visit to the Regalia of Scotland in the Castle of Edinburgh, that a large amount of gold was there obtained.

That search was necessarily arrested by the troubles of his closing years. Assuming the reins of government in 1524, James V. seems to have died of a broken heart after his defeat at Solway Moss, exclaiming, as if prophetically, regarding the Crown, "Ay! ay! It cam' wi' a lass; and it'll gang wi' a lass."

No notice of these workings exists during the minority of Mary, Queen of Scots, whilst the Earl of Arran was Regent. Their revival was coincident with the regency of the Queen Dowager. Then a charge is recorded, "For a copper kettle sent to the English miners at Crawford Mure, £3, 1s.; and also seven stones of lead to fine gold with." The dire events that rapidly succeeded each other until the abdication of Mary in 1567, and the tragedy at Fotheringay in 1587, could not be favourable for the prosecution of this peaceful and profitable enterprise.

During the minority of James VI. capitalists and workmen from England renewed the search for gold. Cornelius de Voss (also called Hardskins), a Dutch artist and lapidary of great merit, "a most cunning picture-maker, and excellent in the trial of minerals," with a partner of the name of Nicholas Hilliard, a goldsmith, who after the accession of King James to the throne of England became "principal drawer of small portraits, and embosser of our medals of gold," along with other London merchants, commenced operations with a capital of £5000 Scots. Commissioned by letter from Queen Elizabeth, and obtaining a licence from the Regent Murray, Cornelius procured much gold at Leadhills. In thirty days they sent eight pounds weight of gold, worth £450 sterling, to the Mint at Edinburgh. Thus encouraged, and to secure the favour of those in power, the company was enlarged by the addition of several Scotch members. The conditions of all the grants given to gold-seekers were, that (1) all gold found was to be sent to the Mint in Edinburgh to be coined; and that (2) one-tenth of the coinage was to be retained to the Crown, and nine-tenths to be delivered to the finders.

The bullion laws prevented the exportation of the precious metals, unless in exchange for payment of imports, or for needful travelling charges. Unless these laws were relaxed, Cornelius could make no remittances to his London associates, and therefore he was prepared to pay well for the favour. It is probable, however, that there would be some grumbling at the largeness of the bribe required. By the arrangement entered into, ten parts were appropriated by the Earl of Morton; ten by Robert Ballantyne, the secretary; ten by Abraham Paterson, a Dutchman in Edinburgh; five by James Reade, an Edinburgh Burgess, leaving only ten parts for Cornelius and his English friends. The Dutchman mentioned is identified with "Abraham Grey or Great beard," who under the Earl of Morton procured gold from Crawford Muir. From that gold "a faire deepe bason, conteynand, by estimation, within the boynes thereof an English gallon of liquor, was made by a Scotch man, in Cannegate Street, att Edinborough," which being filled with the gold coins called unicorns, was presented by the Earl to the French king, with the statement that it was the produce of Scotland, "where that metal does increase and engender within the earth, out of the two elements fire and water." Poor Regent! his theories and activities were soon terminated by the axe of the Scottish Maiden.

Cornelius does not appear to have been well satisfied with the arrangement that had been made, for in 1572—the same year in which John Knox expired—returning to London, his privileges were assigned to another Dutch painter named Arnold Bronckhurst, but under the condition that the proceeds of the mine should be forwarded to Cornelius and his friends. This plan did not succeed. The Regent Morton would not now relax the bullion laws, and Bronckhurst could not obtain the Regent's confirmation of the agreement unless he became a sworn servant of the King of Scotland.

In 1583, the King, considering that the mines have decayed by the "non-putting of men of knowledge and judgment to the inventing and seiken of the samen," grants the "haill golden, silver, copper, tin, and leedin mynes, within this realme of Scotland, to Eustachus Roche, medicinar" (a Fleming), and his partners for the space of twenty-one years. This compact was confirmed by Act of Parliament in 1584, and a number of minute and curious conditions were added. This new start was soon arrested, several of Roche's partners failing to fulfil their engagements, and his foreman proving dishonest; so that by another Act of Parliament in 1592 the engagement terminated. The reasons given in this Act are thus quaintly put: "That the said inconvenience has ensued by reason our said Sovereign Lord and his most noble progenitors was in use commonly to let the said hail mines within their dominions to one or two strangers, for an small duty, who neither had substance to cause labour or work the hundredth part of any one of the said mines, nor yet instructed other lieges in this realme in the knowledge thereof; which is more than notour be the doings of the present tacksman of the mines, who neither works presently, nor has wrocht these many years, nor ever has searched, sought, nor discoverit any new metals since his entry, nor has instructed any of the lieges of the country in that knowledge; and which is most inconvenient of all, *has made no sufficient payment of the duty to our Sovereign Lord's treasury.*" The office of a Master of Metals was thereafter created by this Act, whose duty was to further the King's commodity therein. It also enacts regulations and grants certain mining privileges.

Meanwhile, George Douglas, the younger, of Parkhead, who in 1585 was operating in Leadhills, "was slaine with the fall of the bray after a great weete; and was found three days after that, and had good store of gold about him; and he was before accounted always a poore man, but he was burried better than any of his kindred had bin of long time before." This success he attained and termination he met with in the valley of the Shortcleuch.

An Act of Parliament in 1587 ratified a charter of James VI., which granted to "our well-belovit Counsellare Mark, last Commendator of Newbattle, and now Baron of Newbattle, the barony of Crawfordmure or Friar's Mure, which ly in that part of the kingdom *which is most exposed to robbery, theft, and forays.*" "A description," writes Murray, "which is fully borne out by the remains which still exist, as every farmhouse appears to have been built in the form of a fortified tower or peel, the lower story forming a vault, in which the few cattle they possessed were enclosed, and the upper ones occupied by the family, who in many cases must have ascended by a ladder. From several points in the parish the remains of nearly a dozen of this class of keeps can still be counted." The remains of one of these strongly built forts may be seen at Glendorch.

"KNIGHTS OF THE GOLDEN MINE."

" Alas ! who was the first,
So curious and accurst,
Who digged out of the mine,
Man's mind to undermine ;
Heavie weights of golde ore,
Better concealede before :
And pearle crept into ground
Pale for feare to be found ;
Galing golde, wringing rings,
Precious, but perilous things?

BOETHUS tr. by ACOSTA.

EVIS BULMER obtained a grant to work the gold mines in Scotland, 1578–92. Atkinson says that "Mr Bulmer had workemen and laborers up Mannocke Moore to search out this natural gold in Nidsdale, and gott there some small quantity thereof ; but he builded no house to dwell in there, which was an hinderance, &c. Uppon Winlocke Water, on Robbat Moore, likewise in Nydesdale, he caused search diligently for naturall gold, and gott sometimes a pretty quantity togeather. He brought home a watercourse there to wash and scower the naturall gold from the earth, that had before bin descended from the mountains, ever since Noah's flood : Neither builded he houses there to dwell in, but they all went to the lead-hill unto Thomas Floods, his house to diett ; whereas Mr Bowes had theire built a dwelling-house that might have sufficed him ; yet he repaired it not. But some say that he alsoe found out the suspected vaine of gold which Mr Bowes had discovered ; a good parte or quantity thereof he brought unto the Queene of England, but had not the same in abundance, which I hardly beleeve.

"Upon Shortclough Water, or Crayford Moore, he brought

41

home another goodly watercourse, and intended there sondry·
dammes to contayne water for the buddles, and for scowrers,
&c., for the washing of gold, . . . and purposed to have built
there another dwelling-house and storehouse."

"The cause why they removed from Short-clough brayes to
Long-clough head was for that the workemen had bin shodding,
hunting, and chasing after a piece or ij of great gold, which
they found there within two foote of the mosses. It was
weighed to be vj ounce weight, as they report that found the
one peece, the other was five ounce and better, which was
supposed to descend from the bedd of gold; but no bedd as
yett thereof was found thereat, for it was cleene gold of itselfe.
No king, prince, superiour or any other governour, ever saw
naturall gold more perfitter then it was, neither ever shall see,
and especially of God's owne handy worke." These things
"are to be discovered within the bowells of the earth amongst
rocks and craggs, called God's treasur-house."

At "Fryer Moore, in Glangonner Water, he gott there
reasonable good store;" upon "Short Clough Water, on Cray-
forde Moore, he often found good store thereof; and he gott as
much gold there as would maintaine iij times so manie men as
he did keepe royally."

It appears that in 1576 Bulmer was engaged as a person
skilled in mining by Thomas Foulis, an Edinburgh goldsmith,
in working a most profitable lead mine. The narrative of the
successful working of these lead mines by his successors to the
present time must be afterwards detailed. Meanwhile the
history of Bevis Bulmer, who is styled an "ingenious gentleman," is not without interest. Descended from the great
Yorkshire family of that name, and connected early with
mining operations in the north of England, he was induced
by Foulis to come to the Crawford mines. Foulis confined
himself to the search for lead. The speculative disposition of
Bulmer was more attracted by the richer metal. Obtaining
letters of recommendation from Queen Elizabeth, the Scotch
Government granted him a patent "to adventure and search
for gold and silver mines" in the Leadhills.

At first Bulmer seems to have had great success. He had
a staff of 300 men. Whether tribute was paid for the privilege
is not recorded. The search, although prosecuted only in the
summer months, was, for three years' washings, successful to
the extent of £100,000 sterling. The gold was deposited in a
house in Wanlockhead, but Sir Bevis had another upon the

Gonar. And it is said that over the doorway of that house were inscribed the words—

> "In Wanlock, Elvan, and Glengonar
> I won my riches and my honour."

There he kept a large stock of sheep and cattle on the lands he had purchased. The house was removed last century, but one of the heights above it still bears the name of Bulmer's Hill. Extending from its north base, a small field and a few trees mark the spot where Bulmer resided. Bulmer Moss lies south of Wellgrain Law (1813 feet), east of Waterhead toll.

Mounds of rubbish on the Elvan or Shortcleuch are still called "the gowd scars," and a row of houses in Wanlockhead, termed "The Gowd-Scar Row," are monuments of these enterprising works of the sixteenth century. They ceased as unprofitable when the workman's day's wage rose to fourpence ! The quality of the gold is said to have varied from £76,000 to £136,000 per ton. Bulmer had a stamping-mill erected at the head of the Longcleuch Burn, a tributary of the Shortcleuch, for he had found there "the little string or vein powdered with small gold."

The thirst for gold was not quenched by these successes. Not satisfied, Bulmer returned to England to embark in other adventures. There he presented Queen Elizabeth with a porringer made of Scotch gold, along with the statement in rhyme :—

> "My mind and hart shall still invent
> To seek out treasures yet unknown."

In return for this attention Bulmer was constituted the "Farmer of Duty on sea-borne coals." This proving a failure, in 1587 he began to work lead mines at Mendip in Somerset; but shortly after entered on a new silver-lead speculation in Devonshire, by which each partner cleared £1000 a year. That wrought out, he began by an engine to supply the west of London with water, when he presented Sir Richard Martin, Master of the Mint, with a silver cup made out of the last silver cake taken in Devon, "weighing 131 oz., being 11 oz. 17 pennyweights fyne in goodness by the assay." This gift is recorded "26th October 1594." Mr Bulmer's picture was engraved upon it along with some doggerel lines.

Engaging thereafter in Irish mining, the produce was refined at his Devonshire works; but all this was not enough. On the accession of James to the English throne (1603) the King held a long discussion with Bulmer on mining and mines, and opened to him "a plot" to make them productive. It was that twenty-four gentlemen should each advance £300, and in return to receive the honour of knighthood, each to be termed "a Knight of the Golden Mynes, or a Golden Knyht."

Mr Bulmer replied to the King, who asked whether the gold mines in Scotland would be easily discovered and profitable, that "all mynes are uncertaine within the earth; for God hath hidden his manifold blessings within the corners of the earth, amongst crevesses and holes, even in secrett places; and it is not to be doubted but that your Majesties golden mines may be discovered, if it might please your Grace to inure them."

King James proposed to Bulmer: "Lastly, to erect a church or chappell for all the workemen, where they might make theire prayers to God, for theire soules health. And then the workes of theire hands will be blessed, and come to a good end, to God's glory, the Kings profitt, and a benefitt to the commonweale, as in other countries and nations."

"Only one knight was made, and he was called Sir John Cleypoole; for he had ventured with Mr Bulmer before £500, starling, at the gold mynes in Scotland." Although this scheme was defeated by the opposition of the Earl of Salisbury, Bulmer was knighted, and returning to Leadhills as "Sir Bevis Bulmer," he resumed former operations there. Just then a silver vein having been discovered at Hilderston in Linlithgow, Bulmer removed thither; and finally to Alston Muir in Cumberland, where he died in 1613. There a rude inscription on a building stated that it was erected by Sir Bevis Bulmer,

> "Who won much wealth and mickle honour
> On Shortcleuch Water and Glengonar."

Who would have imagined that, notwithstanding all his energy, success, and honour, he would have died *in poverty!* But this is declared to have been the end of that, as it has been of many another, speculator. Atkinson states that "he had always many irons in the fire besides these which he presently himself looked on, and oftentimes intricate matters in hand to decyde, and too many prodigall wasters hanging on every shoulder of him. And he wasted much himselfe and gave liberally to many for to be honoured, praised, and magnified, else he might have been a rich subject, for the least of these frugalities [?] were able to robb an abbot. By such sinistor

44

means he was impoverished, and following other idle, veniall vices to his dying day, that were not allowable of God nor man ; and so once down, aye downe ; and at last he died in my debt £340 starling, to my great hindrance : God forgive us all our sinnes."

Sir Bevis Bulmer is thus a notable beacon of warning to all who thirst insatiably—for gold.

GEORGE BOWES was another gold-seeker of eminence, who, as stated, held a commission from Queen Elizabeth ; for Scotland was at that time considered an "El Dorado" by her southern neighbours. It is recorded that he was empowered "to dig and delve as he would ;" and that at Winlocke Head he discovered "a small vaine of gold, which had much small gold upon it." He swore his men to secrecy, and after working the vein for some time he caused the shaft to be closed up, and took oath of his men to keep it concealed. The locality of this vein, looked for and alluded to by several parties as never refound, is not unknown to the miners at Wanlockhead. Pieces of gold of 30 oz. weight were found in this neighbourhood in the reign of James V., "mixed with the spar, some with keel, and some with brimstone."

Bowes also worked at "Long-clough brayes or head up the great hill, where he discovered a small string thereof. This vaine had the sapperstone [?] plentiful in it, which sometimes held naturall gold, a little, not much." There Mr Bowes erected a stamping-mill, and by this means "used to gett small mealy gold." He returned to England with a purse of gold valued at seven-score pounds. The Queen of England was so encouraged by his success that he was commanded to return in spring to resume the search. But the spring returned not for George Bowes. Visiting mines in Cumberland, he turned aside to look, fell down a shaft, and was killed.

STEPHEN ATKINSON, a native of London, who served as apprentice to Francis Liver, a refiner of gold and silver, and was taught mining skill "by Mr B. Bulmer, an ingenious gent," was admitted a "Finer" in the Tower of London, 1586, and spent his "golden tyme" in England and Wales. He was brought to Leadhills by Sir Bevis.

A letter dated 29th April 1616, was given by the King at Newmarket, which in modern spelling runs : "Right trusty and well-beloved cousin and councillor, and right trusty and well-beloved councillors, we greet you well. Whereas the bearer hereof, Stephen Atkinson, being desirous, at his own charges, to seek minerals in Crawford Moor, hath made humble suit unto us, that he might be permitted to do so. And forasmuch as the working in the said moor can be prejudicial to none, but on the contrary, if any vein be found, it may prove beneficial to us, we have thought good by these presents to require you (if you see no reason to the contrary), that you give order that he may be permitted to work and seek in such places of the said moor with such number of people as he shall think fitting, freely and quietly without any stop or molestation. And this specially recommending to you, we bid you farewell."

On the 11th June 1616, Atkinson obtained by Act of the Scottish Privy Council power to continue the search for gold. It says, "Whereas Steven Atkinsoun, Englishman, has vndertane and promiest to the Kingis most sacred Majestie, that vpon his awne propper chairges and expensses he sall make ane new searche, tryall, and discouerie of the mynes, seames, and minerallis in Crawfurde Mure, with Saxeere, the Calumere, and the Salyneere stanes, and of all mettall of gold and silver, etc. . . . grantis full power and commission by these presentes to the said Stevin, and his seruandis and suche utheris as he sall adjoyne vnto him, alsweel countrymen as strangeris, during his lyfetyme to searche, seik, worke, dig, try, discouer and find oute all suche seames and mynes of gold and silver. . . . Provyding alwayes, like as it is heirby expreslie ordanit, commandit, and declairit, that the said Stevin sall bring into his Majesties Conezie-house at Edinburgh, the whole gold and silver that sall be discouerit to be coined, one-tenth part to be his Majesty's due, and nine-tenths of the coined money to be delivered to the said Stevin."

In 1619 Atkinson composed his treatise, entitled "Discouerie and Historie of the Gold Mynes in Scotland," in hope of exciting the interest of King James. This "dainty dish" was admirably flavoured to suit the royal taste. It is not only full of allusions to Kings David and Solomon, and the comparisons mentioned of the four streams to those of the garden of Eden; it relates a professed prophecy, delivered by two shipwrecked philosophers in the reign of Joshua, said to be King of Scotland, 160 B.C. It was to the effect that there would be a great light and discovery of gold mines when a king was born "having a privy signe marke or token upon his body, the like unto none shall have, who shall reigne, rule, and governe in peace, and be supreme head of the Kirke, and a prince of mae kingdoms than is Scotland." James must have felt highly flattered, especially when, in addition to his boasted supremacy, he thought of the lion mark imprinted on his side.

Besides the alleged prophecy, the King is encouraged to search for the precious metals by five resemblances to King David, all religious "deeds" but one, viz., "the opening of the secrets of the earth"—this treasure-house in Scotland to make his Majesty the richest monarch in the world. This was to be accomplished by the royal "plott" of the "Knights of the Golden Mynes."

Atkinson prayed for a patent on the grounds that the search for minerals (1) tends to the glory of God in discovering secret blessings, (2) and to the ennobling his Majesty's crown and dignity; (3) to the advancement of the entire kingdom, if successful, and (4) to the satisfaction of the adventurer "better than the hart of man doth deserve. For thereby God remunerates, the asker to have, the seeker to find, the hunter to follow, till that great blessing of God be laid open, (viz.) God's treasure-house; even that bedd, or vaine, of gold and silver myne, *valued at ten thousand times* the charge of the adventurers and labor: My desire, for this cause, humbly prayeth, that a patent might be granted, of a suite both lawfull, honest, and reasonable, such a one as hath not bin used in the kingdom of Scotland." After enumerating the richness of the mines of other lands, Atkinson thus concludes: "My opinion is that as good rich mynes as any before spoken of be within the kingdom of Scotland, but some other men cannott be perswaded hereunto; neither that God hath placed any such treasure within the bowells of the earth, *especially in Scotland.* But God who knoweth the secretts of all harts, hath shewed the like examples to moyners, and pioners, which seeke for the secrets of the earth out of meneralls and menerall stones, amongst rocks and craggs. And even then it will be finished, when it shall please the Almighty God to stirr up men's harts thereunto, and till then it cannot be. Neither is it to be done by wishers and wonlders, but only by the King's Majesties. The plott had already been devised; it would cost him nothing but only a stroke with his sword upon the shoulder of man; for which the one-halfe of the profitt doth fall unto his Majesty, the other halfe to lay open the gold and silver moynes in Scotland." He then prayed that the prophecies may be fulfilled, and that the "same gold and silver mynes will become to be an everlasting happiness to all successive ages, which God grant for his Majesties sake. Amen. Amen."

This notable device failed, as the King had already expended £3000, and had not obtained 2 oz. of gold from these mines in return (see Laing's Hist. of Scotland, iii. p. 56).

Atkinson met with as little favour from London merchants. "I offered," he said, "to put in security that it should be restored againe to Mr Morray, so that he would be pleased to let it be but seene unto merchants of London that had promised me to adventure; for want whereof (as I thinke) they fell quite from me, excusing the cause thereof, and alledging, that it is more fit for princes than for subjects. And, therefore, said some of them to me, If thou wilt adventure in any other nation of a hotter climate, we will take better advise thereof, and we will both respect yourselfe and your knowledge, for we love to adventure, where our forefathers have don before us; and to tell you the naken truth of it, we have no mind at all in Scotland to adventure."

DR JOHN HYNDLIE received a grant in 1621, notwithstanding the rejection of Atkinson's pleas. This was given in a long missive, dated "at Roystoun, the twelff day of October, the zeir of God I^m vj^c tuentie ane zeiris," and giving as a reason that "whereas his Majesties mines of gold within the bounds of Crawford Moor, Friar Moor, Crawfordjohn, Robertmoor, Glenim, Auchensoul, Auchingreuch, and Castlegilmour, have during diverse years bygone been neglected, and no care nor order taken for working them," &c. But he also failed to make them productive; and since that period systematic operations for gold as an article of commerce have been abandoned.

IS THE GOLDEN TREASURE GONE?

" Prudent men . . . compared those Scotts gold mynes unto God's treasur-house, placed by God himselfe within the centur of the earth. . . . But others . . . will not be perswaded that any goodnes can be produced out of Scotts ground, and are doubtfull whether the sonne and moone and starrs shine there or not."—Atkinson's Discoverie, p. 9.

WHILE few dispute that large quantities of gold were found in the sixteenth century, the language of incredulity which Atkinson encountered is as common still. " It is fabled," says a writer in 1867, " that gold exists upon some parts of the Ochil range of hills; but since Bulmer's day there has been no gold found in Scotland. No eye has ever seen it, although very many have sought for it. Indeed, our golden age is ended;" and he calls for thanksgiving because " we have nothing to attract the vagrant blackguardism of the world to our shores." The one fact that a boy picked up a nugget bigger than a bean, and worth £9, at Helmsdale, a few years ago, answers that assertion.

Three questions arise out of such declarations: (1) Was this " House " robbed of the whole of its nuggets and grains? (2) Would it be possible to work the " gold mynes " afresh with advantage? (3) and without involving such an assemblage?

1. *Has the House been emptied?*

This question has been conclusively solved. Eyes that could not be deceived have seen it; and further, it can be found whenever a persevering and proper search is made for it; while occasionally nuggets are found when they are not sought for.

GOLD-DUST.

" For three centuries gold has been collected in small quantities from the alluvia of the streams in the Leadhills and Wanlockhead district" (Mem. Geol. Survey, s. 15). In all the burns flowing down on both sides of the Lowther watershed it has been obtainable, in Glenclach and Wanlock—near the village, on " Robbart Moor," and even in the soil dug out in making graves at Meadowfoot. About 1850 two miners got as much at Longcleuch as sold in Glasgow for £42.

The gold is generally found in minute particles at the bottom of a rush from the hills, or in the bed of the burns by careful and tedious washing. As much as will form a ring or small chain is occasionally obtained. Individuals in the villages possess specimens both in the natural and wrought conditions.

In the year 1863 the Leadhills miners in turn made a search for gold at their leisure hours with considerable success. The principal gold-bearing ground was found to be that which Bulmer and others had proved to be most productive at the head of the Longcleuch Burn. The average quantity obtained per day was about 12 grains. Some obtained small nuggets as large as a bean. In a few months many thousand grains were collected. There, and in other places wrought, the débris is above 15 feet deep, the whole of which produces more or less gold—on an average 5 grains per cubit yard of earth. But between this and the rock, a mixture of clay, gravel, and oxide of iron, varying from 1 to 10 inches thick, is very rich in gold, producing 10 grains per cubit foot. I have been informed by men who wrought on the Longcleuch that the gold-bearing way appeared to be a watercourse; that about a foot square was particularly rich; and that it was only abandoned because the shaft fell in, and the men had no materials wherewith to remedy the matter or prosecute the search. Others were successful in reworking débris thrown out by their companions. Amount collected, 1940 grains.

The gold collected was presented to the Countess of Hopetoun, who had it made into ornaments, which she displayed to the miners in their cottages. Thrice since then, on the marriage of three gentlemen connected with the mining company, a miner collected 80 grains each time for wedding rings.

In the British Museum 28 grains, labelled " From Wanlockhead stream washings," are held to be genuine.

NUGGETS.

Tradition says that "a lump of gold as large as a horse's head lies buried in the ' Limpen,' " a burn on " Robbart Moor." Whether such a " welcome stranger " be ever found there, it is unquestionable that small nuggets varying from 60 to 90 grs. have been found without search, and some of much larger dimensions.   (1.) One got at Lochnell foot brought above £2. (2.) Several years ago a little girl playing with companions upon the steep face of the Dod Hill exclaimed, " Æh ! what a bonnie stane ! I'll tak' it hame to my faether."   The " bonnie stane" was found to be a nugget of gold.   It passed through the hands of the late Dr Watson of Wanlockhead, and afterwards of the late Dr Martin of Leadhills, whose sons have placed it " on loan" in the Edinburgh Museum of Science and Art. It weighs 640 grs. troy, or 1 oz. 6 dwt. and 16 grs. (3.) On the Leadhills side small nuggets the size of a fourpenny-piece have frequently been found.   One man secured two, weighing respectively 30 and 60 grs., for which he received at the rate of 10d. per grain.   (4.) Another found a piece as large as from the point of the little finger to the first joint.   (5.) A crooked piece brought £10.   (6.) A miner obtained a nugget which equalled the weight of seven guineas, which he very handsomely presented to the Earl of Hopetoun. (7.) The largest piece found in 1863 weighed 72 grs.   (8.) In 1874 a nugget weighing 209 grs. was found, and purchased by the Countess of Hopetoun.

These facts prove that the House was not robbed of all its treasures in former days.   And

" The gold of that land is good."

A memorandum left by Robert Seton anent the metals "in Scotland, especially gold," who had returned from Mexico about the reign of King James V., gives a list of forty-four places in Scotland where gold was found, in which " Long-Cleuch" is mentioned.

In an " Account of the Metalls and Mineralls found in Scotland, given to Sir Robert Sibbald by Col. Borthwick, who had the direction of some of the mines," it is said that " gold is found in severall places in Scotland; the most famous place is Crawford-moor, where it was found by King James the Fourth and King James the Fifth, and is yet found by passing the earth through searches, and the same brought down with speats of raine. I have seen it as big as a cherry. *It is exceeding fine gold.* The ore as it was tryed at the Kings Mint, London, *afforded eleven parts of gold, and the refuse was silver."*

Gerald Malynes, writing in 1622, says that the Crawford gold was *twenty-two carats fine* (Lex. Mercatoria, p. 183).

There is still found a considerable difference in the colour of the gold. In Glenkip and in Glendorch it is *white as silver;* on Duneaton, *much darker;* in Glengonar, *pale;* in Shortcleuch, *red;* Mennock, *rough;* Glenclach, like *small pin-heads;* while on Wanlock it is like *small scales.*

RECENT ANALYSIS.

Mr Dudgeon of Cargen placed some clean grain gold, washed from a burn at Wanlockhead, for analysis in the hands of a chemical expert, Professor A. H. Church, of the Royal Agricultural College, Cirencester. That gentleman published a report, from which the curious fact appears that native gold, so called, contains only about 86½ per cent. of the pure metal, the remainder being all silver, with the exception of rather more than one-third per cent. of iron. The analysis is thus given in Mr Dudgeon's " Historical Notes :"—

Gold	86·60 per cent.
Silver	12·39 ,,
Iron	00·35 ,,
Other substances, and loss	00·66 ,,

Professor Church also gives an analysis of a specimen of Sutherlandshire gold. " It was found to contain no iron, but the gold was even less than that of the Wanlockhead specimen—that is, rather less than 79¼ per cent., the remaining 20¾ parts being exclusively silver. The specific gravity of the two specimens was respectively 16·50 and 16·62, that of absolutely pure gold being 19·3. By way of comparison, we may mention the composition of some Ashantee native gold, also lately examined by Professor Church—gold rather over 90 parts, and almost 10 parts of silver, with a trace of iron, and a very minute trace of copper, the specific gravity being 17·55. So long as the natural auriferous alloy contains a maximum of gold, and practically no other metal than silver, the usage is to employ the term " native gold," which is certainly quite allowable, although to the uninitiated it does seem to be a scientific term that is rather unscientific."

QUARTZITES.

That quartzites, gold *in situ* or in vein quartz, have been found within this " Treasure-House " seems an undoubted fact. Whether these were *natives* of the district, is a question that has not yet been satisfactorily solved.

(1.) Pennant mentions specimens weighing 30 oz. or 2½ lbs. (Wales, vol. i. p. 90 ; and Boyle, vol. v. p. 30.) (2.) A valuable stone with gold is reported to have been found near Wanlockhead, weighing 10 lbs., containing 150 grs. of gold. (3.) In 1803 Professor Trail of Edinburgh is said to have found auriferous quartz—*in situ*—at Wanlockhead. (4.) A nugget of 8 or 10 grs.. was found in a quartz vein about the year 1855, when a shaft was being cut for lead. This vein of quartz is half an inch thick, and is a " ledger wall " slanting downwards from that shaft opposite the old smithy in the Meadowhead lead vein in Leadhills. Another quartz vein, containing " indications " (oxide of iron), is 2 feet wide at Reingray-foot on the Shortcleuch. This is above the site where the old shepherd's house stood. In that one vein at Meadowhead are to be found gold, silver, lead, copper, antimony, and sulphate of iron. (5.) Another piece was found on Bulmer's Hill by C. Griffin, solicitor, Leamington. (6.) Another, on an old dyke at the head of Leadhills, as large as a child's head, some sixty years ago. It was said to have found its way into the British Museum.

T. Davies, Esq., of the British Museum, writes me : " The specimen in massive quartz-rock in our collection I suspect to be Australian. We had only the dealer's assurance that it was purchased out of an old collection made in the Wanlockhead district. The specimen is about 5 in. × 2 × 2, and contains but little gold in one or two places. It consists of massive quartz without any other rock whatever, and may have been part of a vein, judging from the appearance of one of its sides. The only other specimens (in addition to the 28 grs. of Wanlockhead gold already mentioned) of gold from Scotland we have, are a nugget from Turrich, Glencoish, Perthshire, 1010 grs. ; a small grain (8 grs.) from Tweeddale ; and a nugget and some grains from Helmsdale, Sutherland, (1 oz. 188 grs. avoirdupois). The specimens of gold from

Wanlockhead were purchased of Mr Wright, a London dealer in minerals, in 1864."

(7.) The gold is generally got *in position* high up the hill, and seldom lower than 4 feet below the surface. In Long-cleuch, &c., iron-sand abounds. When got in connection with quartz, the gold is often spread in a very thin leaf on the top of the ironstone or oxide of iron. Specimens of this kind, requiring the use of the glass to be seen, found on the Broad Law, are in my possession. (8.) The Duchess of Buccleuch, Sir T. E. Colebrooke, and others, are also in possession of interesting specimens; but it is only very rarely that gold has been found in this district in the matrix—*i.e.*, in vein quartz. Mr Dudgeon writes of an interesting specimen.

It was found at Wanlockhead in 1872 by Andrew Gemmell, miner, and is of considerable size, weighing about 10 lbs. Gemmell unfortunately broke it into a number of pieces, and sold them to various individuals in the district. With the assistance of Mr Clark of Speddoch, Mr Dudgeon obtained the loan of all the pieces from their respective owners, and having joined them together, he has had an exquisite copy of the restored mass executed in chromo and gold, which forms the frontispiece of the "Notes," which is at once a handsome and most interesting illustration of them. This discovery was first made public by Dr Grierson exhibiting a specimen at the "Society of Inquiry" in 1873. The specimen portion contained gold equal to the third or fourth of a sovereign, along with iron-ochre diffused over one of the surfaces of the quartz.

Dr Lauder Lindsay says that it is probable that all interested may have an opportunity of inspecting the Gemmell quartzite, as there is a prospect of having it repieced and placed in the Museum of Science and Art in Edinburgh.

There is no doubt whatever as to this find, or as to its being genuine auriferous quartz; but there exists considerable dubiety amongst the best-informed men as to the *nativity* of this quartzite. As, first—

1. No one in Wanlockhead who is acquainted with the prevailing quartz, which is simply *a thin rider* underneath and above the veins of lead, or going in and out through these veins, asserts that it is a native of the district; and no vein of quartz similar to this specimen has ever been met in with by the miners. A. Gemmell can only appeal to the fact that he found it here, which no one ever disputed. Others will only go the length of saying, "*It may be a native.*"

2. No other instance, but one, of a quartzite—that is, of *a piece of quartz* WITH A VEIN OF GOLD RUNNING THROUGH IT —has been known to the miners of Wanlockhead, although frequent instances are known of *gold with quartz or spar attached* both here and in Leadhills district. The other is that of a smaller piece, said to be found on the public road, near to a horse-watering basin, towards the foot of Mennock. This evidently must have been dropped or brought there in some way, as there is no quartz at that neighbourhood.

3. Immediately on looking at the portion sent to Dr Grierson's Museum, a Wanlockhead man, who had wrought in the Ingleston and Ballarat gold-fields, exclaimed, " Surely that has come from the Maxwell Reef. If not, it is exactly similar." He and others who have wrought at gold-finding, here, in Australia, and in California, do not entertain the idea that it is a native of Wanlockhead.

4. How then, it is asked, can this find be accounted for ? One reply is, that it may have been dropped in the removal of quartzites and minerals that same year, and over that same ground—" The Landlord's Brae." These belonged to a retired miner, whose sons had been successful in Australian gold-fields. They had exhibited a very large quartzite at the London International Exhibition, which was afterwards broken and thereafter removed from one cottage to another. The only difficulty as to this supposition is, that if so, the loss ought to have been ascertained and proclaimed, whereas nothing of the kind was named.

Be this as it may, the prevailing impression in Wanlockhead is that the specimen, somehow or other, came from afar. And, as Dr Lindsay suggests, this " missing link " can only be supplied by a persevering search for gold in the rocks or *in situ* in the locality.

2. *Would the search prove advantageous ?*

This second question has received conflicting replies. The late Mr Nevin, manager at Leadhills, seemed to think that the gold-bearing drift or alluvial had been wellnigh exhausted. Sir Roderick Murchison states that "as no rich auriferous sand or gravel is known in any part of the British Isles, we may rest satisfied that in our own country . . . the quantity of gold originally imparted to the Silurian or other rocks was *very small*, and has for all *profitable objects* been exhausted" (Siluria, 3d edit. p. 479). The discovery and successful working of the gold-field in Sutherland until the permission was withdrawn, and other considerations, seem to show that this opinion was formed from incorrect data. Gold is still found in the drift from the hills. A person I could name, in three hours obtained a few grains after others who had wrought all day had left the spot. Another person collected as much as made a ring for himself in the burns that flow into the Mennock. Mr T. A. Readwin of Glogau gold mine in Wales, writes in the "Mining Journal" (October 1875), "I found gold easily enough, four years ago, when near Lead-hills." "The glittering sand," says Dr John Brown, "is still occasionally to be found, and every now and then a miner, smit with the sacred hunger, takes to the deluding, feckless work, and seldom settles to anything again."

In one summer a Wanlockhead miner made £20 by gold-finding over and above his remuneration as a lead miner.

It must be confessed that *the search will " not pay " for mere amateur labour*, nor apart from the employment of capital and of the most skilful and scientific appliances. In 1564 a licence was granted to John Stewart of Yarlair to search for gold, &c., between the Tay and the Orkney Isles. In 1740 Sir John Erskine, with four partners, formed a company to resume the search, but were unsuccessful (Jacob's Hist. of Metals, vol. vi. p. 292). In the reign of George III. another attempt was made under the manager of the Wanlock-head lead mines, but the price of labour was too high (William's Hist. of Min. King., vol. ii. p. 365).

The Earl of Hopetoun resumed the search for gold prior to 1790, but in a short time it was discontinued as being less profitable than common labour. And though gold-dust was "found on the tops of the rocks, the search was regarded rather as an amusement than a serious occupation."

On the other hand, there can be little doubt that the "mines" at Longcleuch and Robbart Moor, if permitted to be opened and wrought, might be made productive. They could easily be found. It is said that in making a watercourse on Robbart Moor, the shaft of the gold mine fell in. It was not reopened, and is now built up by the wall of the new lead-crushing and washing mill.

Another question remains—

Can no yield be obtained from the rocks of the district?

It appears to me that Dr Lindsay has laid the country under obligations by his continuous suggestive and practical replies ; and possibly a new impetus will be given to the inquiry when his new work on " The Gold-Fields and Gold-Diggings of Scotland" appears.

The positions he maintains in support of an affirmative answer are such as these :—

1. A parallelism between the auriferous states of Otago and Scotland, Leadhills district being a second edition of Tuapeka.

2. Gold-drift is usually superjacent to, or in proximity of, gold rocks *in situ.*

3. Auriferous quartzites containing a much larger percentage of gold than the ½ oz. per ton of those in Bute will be found if properly looked for.

4. Even where no gold is discoverable by the eye or the lens, experience proves it may be found in remunerative quantity; and that this is the most permanent gold industry.

This fact is sustained not only by his own experience in New Zealand, but by the evidence of the Rev. W. B. Clarke of Sydney in his "Researches in the Southern Gold-Fields of New South Wales," in which are some striking facts, as " that a heap of detritus, from which all gold has been apparently taken out, will yet supply gold after it has been exposed to atmospheric action." Again, from quartz, where its presence could not be detected, "I have been able, even by a rude process, to obtain between 2 and 3 grains of pure gold, and a portion of a grain of pure silver." Evidence to the same effect is produced from others.

PROPORTION OF GOLD IN QUARTZ.

A gold-bearing vein of quartz 4 or 5 inches thick is to be found on the Broad Law. About the year 1858, at the expense of the manager at Leadhills, an analysis was made at Glasgow of three kinds of quartz ; and one was found to contain a twenty-eighth part of a grain in 1 lb. of quartz—that is, equal to 80 grs., or 3 dwts. 8 grs. troy. The quartz was taken from the Longcleuch. This was a somewhat different result from the improbable one proclaimed by Calvert in his " Gold Rocks, 1853," that the quartz of Leadhills would produce from 3 oz. 10 dwts. to 4 oz. per ton. It would be of importance, however, could another, and perhaps more thorough assay be taken for gold in the quartz of the district. But taking that assay as correct, if what Musprat states in his "Chemistry" regarding Australian quartz would equally apply to Scotch— viz., that 1 dwt. of gold would pay out of a ton of crushed quartz—then assuredly 3 dwts. 8 grs. would prove a higher award.

Were it so that the quartz could not give a sufficient yield, still it would be worth consideration, whether this could not be wrought along with some one or other of the nine gold-bearing districts of Scotland. In addition to this (1) Lowther House, the precious treasure is found in (2) Tweedsmuir, Peeblesshire; (3) the Lammermuir Hills; (4) the Galloway, (5) Breadalbane, (6) Braemar, (7) Clova, Forfarshire, (8) Argyle, and (9) Central (Ross-shire and Inverness) Highlands.

The gold on the Ballywater, near St Mary's Loch, and another Tweed burn was found to give a considerable yield. A miner who sought for it there, assures me that if permitted, and able, he could gather 1 oz. per week, which, if reckoned at 2d. per grain, would be worth £4. A person whom he instructed in the art found a piece which weighed 70 grains in 1862. Quartz-bearing ground which abounds there and on Ettrickside are from ¼ to 3 and 4 feet thick.

The question may therefore be pressed, Were the presence of so much of the most precious metal proved to be located on some distant shore, whether some earnest and persevering efforts would not be put forth to obtain it? What the single-handed and poor miner cannot attempt, afford to experiment upon, or accomplish solely by his washing-dish — a well-organised, wealthy, and skilful company, with the aid of machinery and scientific experience, might secure. These finds without search, the results of that of 1863, &c., together invite to a more thorough search than has yet been attempted since the death of Bulmer.

Mr Atkinson adduces some principal points which he had learned during thirty years' intercourse with Mr Bulmer, as that (1) "whosoever is a menerall man must be of force a hasserd adventurer;" (2) adventuring a little and happening to win, he must not be overjoyed; (3) venturing and losing, he must not be discouraged; (4) and finding a rich vein of metal, "he must not esteeme thereof, for it is like a man stonge with a nettle; sayth he. And if he do seeke in hope to find, albeit thereby noe profitt nor princippal doth come, yet must he thinke himselfe a rich man, and beleeve that he hath, or shall have that he hath not; and if he cannot embrace the lessons he cannot be a right menerall-man; sayth he."

What may be accomplished by such an investigation or "prospecting" as is necessary may be gathered from details given by Dr Lindsay of practical operations in 1874 in the Island of Bute : " The gold was found by an *exploring party*, started about three or four years ago, consisting of (1) Mr William Cochrane, watchmaker, native of Rothesay, now in Wisconsin, America ; (2) Mr Leckie, retired jeweller, from Australia, and now back to Australia; and (3) Mr Cameron. We started, fully prepared with wash-basins (instead of cradles), with mercury, with geologists' hammers and other tools, and examined all the burns on the north and north-east part of the island, and also all the shore-glens and hillsides, wherever we came across any quartz strata, and there are a number in Bute,—some of them being about 4 feet in thickness, going through from one side of a hill to the other. We washed the [sand or gravel of the] burns in a number of spots, and we were rewarded in our labours by finding in Chapleton Burn, which runs down from Baron Hill, a small piece of gold of beautiful colour, 14 grains in weight. Mr Leckie so happened to be absent that day ; and it was after washing in the basin several hundredweights of sand and gravel from the bottom of the burn, and forcing the quicksilver through chamois leather, that we came on the piece [of gold]. We took it home, and evaporated the mercury off the gold. We also took home every night a large piece of quartz, broke it in two, kept a specimen, and put a ticket on it to show where it was got. We pounded [the other half] to powder, ran it through with mercury and water, kept the mercury, evaporated it, and in *many cases* got a residue of gold; then evaporated to dryness the quartz, washed it with *aqua regia*, precipitated all other metals except gold and platinum by treating a diluted solution with carbonate of soda, then filtering it, and treating it with proto-sulphate of iron. In one case we got as much, after making a rough calculation and a large allowance for mistakes, at the rate of ½ oz. [of gold] to the ton-weight of quartz crushed.

" We examined the place where this last piece of *quartz* was got. There is a great deal of quartz about the shore. We got no indications of gold there ; but in a burn which runs down from the plantation over strata of quartz and mica, right above where the gold was got, we got indications of it. . . .

" With the *advice of some old diggers*, the first three of us started, fully prepared with tools and material of the newest kind, in a small way. . . . Sometimes we could discern the gold in very small specks without the use of a glass. . . . We washed some part of every burn, . . . and *in almost every case* we got a small residue of gold after the evaporation of the mercury. On one occasion I came across a small piece, 14 grains in weight (in Chapelton Burn). . . . We evaporated the crushed quartz to dryness, and then boiled it in *aqua regia* for some time over the fire ; then washed out the quartz with water to dilute the acid. Sometimes we had a residue of chloride of *silver*."—*Recent Gold Discoveries, by Dr Lindsay, Perth.*

These experiments agree with the interesting description given by Fownes (Watt's) in his " Manual of Chemistry :" " Gold, in small quantities, is a very widely-diffused metal ; traces of it are constantly found in the iron pyrites of the more ancient rocks. It is always met with in the metallic state, sometimes beautifully crystallised in the cubic form, associated with quartz, iron oxide, and other substances, in regular mineral veins. Its atomic weight is 197 ; its symbol, Au. (*aurum.*) The sands of various rivers have long furnished gold derived from this source, and separable by a simple process of washing ; *such* is the gold-dust of commerce.

" When a vein-stone is wrought for gold it is stamped to powder, and shaken in a suitable apparatus with water and mercury ; an amalgam is thus formed, which is afterwards separated from the mixture and decomposed by distillation. Formerly the chief supply of gold was obtained from the mines of Brazil, Hungary, and the Ural Mountains ; but California and Australia now yield by far the largest quantity. The new gold-fields of British Columbia and of Colorado are also very productive.

" *Native* gold is almost always alloyed with *silver*. The purest specimens have been obtained from Schabrowski, near Katharinenburg in the Ural. A specimen analysed by Gustav Rose was found to contain 98·96 per cent. of gold. The Californian gold averages from 87·5 to 88·5 per cent., and the Australian from 96 to 96·6 per cent. In some specimens of native gold, as in that from Linarowski, in the Altai Mountains, the percentage of gold is as low as 60 per cent., the remainder being silver.

" Pure gold is obtained from its alloys by solution in nitro-muriatic acid (*aqua regis*), and precipitation with a ferrous salt, which reduces the gold, and is itself converted into a ferric salt thus :—

$$6 \text{ sulphate iron } + 2 \text{ chloride gold } =$$
$$= 2 \text{ persulphate iron } + \text{ chloride iron } + 2 \text{ gold.}$$

The gold falls as a brown powder, which acquires the metallic lustre by friction.

" Gold is a soft metal, having a beautiful yellow colour. It surpasses all other metals in malleability, the thinnest gold-leaf not exceeding, it is said, $\frac{1}{200,000}$ of an inch in thickness, while the gilding on the silver wire used in the manufacture of *gold-lace* is still thinner. It may also be drawn into very fine wire. Gold has a density of 19·5 ; it melts at a temperature a little above the fusing-point of silver (bright red heat). Neither air nor water affects it in the least at any temperature ; the ordinary acids fail to attack it singly. A mixture of nitric and hydrochloric acids dissolves gold, however, with ease, the active agent being the liberated chlorine " (pp. 416, 417).

Where are the Quartz Veins ?

A gold-quartz vein in Britain, except in North Wales, has not as yet been found, though eagerly sought for. Whence, then, the gold ? Glacier action and glacier drift, along with the elevation of the country from the sea, are the theories usually adduced. These, with some change in the Equatorial Current or Gulf Stream, would account for the carrying and deposition in certain localities. The golden nugget interrogated is supposed to say, " Believes that he came out of glacial drift a long time ago." Where did he come from before he got into the drift ? The king of stones and men, the Yellow Dwarf, who reigns wherever his kind are scarce, seems to wink his eye, and say, " You wish to know where nuggets grow ? ' Speech is silver, silence is gold.' " He keeps his own counsel like a true Scot. Sir Roderick Murchison, than whom perhaps there is not a more competent authority, states " that, looking to the world at large, the auriferous vein stones *in the Lower Silurian rocks* contain the greatest quantity of gold " (see " Gold-Dig. in Sutherland "). This statement, and another of his conclusions, that " granites and diorites have been the chief gold-pro-ducers," are of vast consequence when taken along with the geological formation of the Southern Highlands. They seem to indicate that a well-considered and systematic search in these fields would not go unrewarded.

THE BRITISH GOLD-FIELD,

in addition to (1) places in Scotland that have been named, embraces (2) in Ireland—Londonderry, Antrim, Wicklow, Wexford, and Kildare—the largest nugget in Europe, 22 oz., being found in Wicklow ; (3) in England—Cornwall, Devon, Somerset, Gloucester, Worcester, Salop, Bedford, Derby, Chester, Lancashire, Westmoreland, Cumberland, Northumberland, Durham, and York ; (4) in Wales—Carnarvon, Flint, Cardigan, Caermarthen, Pembroke, and Merioneth.   In 1843, Mr Arthur Dean obtained rich gold in Cwmhesian, and maintained that " a complete system of auriferous veins existed through the whole of the Snowdonian, or Lower Silurian, formations of North Wales."   Five hundred tons of minerals yielded more than $\frac{1}{2}$ oz. of gold to the ton.   When " poor copper ore " at Glogau was tested, $14\frac{1}{2}$ oz. of gold were obtained from 100 lbs. weight.   Thereafter the Crown got a small harvest in licences, and speculation and loss followed, till the Vigra and Clogau mines were sold by order of the Court of Chancery, and bought by Messrs Readwin & Williams.   Dormant gold mines wrought for a time were suspended, with the exception of Clogau, " not so much on account of the paucity of gold as of the difficulty of extracting it by the means at command at the time."

CROWN RIGHTS.

Formerly, either from avarice or the exigencies of State, the Crown laid claim to all metals ; subsequently this was abandoned as to the baser metals, gold and silver being retained for the purpose of coinage, and to support the dignity of the Crown.   The justices and barons in the " great case of mines " (1568) unanimously agreed " that by the law all mines of gold and silver within the realm, whether in the lands of the Queen or her subjects, belong to the Queen by prerogative, with liberty to dig and carry it away."   The law was, however, uncertain in the case of these precious being mixed with the baser metals.   This led to distrust, and greatly destroyed the enterprise, till a declaratory Act was passed in the reign of William and Mary.

The law has been illustrated by the practice of the Office of Woods and Forests, since the gold discoveries in Wales in 1854, and has been thus detailed by Mr T. A. Readwin : " 1. Where the gold is found in combination with other metals, the *whole* of which, with the necessary easements for working, *are* vested in the Crown ; the Crown deals with the case *in the same manner as an ordinary licence to search for minerals*—£30 per annum minimum rent, and one-twelfth royalty on the gold.   2. Where the gold is found in combination with the minerals specified in the Acts of William and

Mary, and which are *not* vested in the Crown, the Crown *proposes to accept a royalty in lieu of the right of pre-emption.* 3. Where the gold is found in a virgin state, or secreted in rocks, and not in combination with the ores and minerals specified in those Acts, on lands where the minerals are *not* vested in the Crown, the Crown requires the parties interested *to take a licence on payment of a nominal annual rent, and a royalty upon the gold raised."*

The " Otago Times " of November 24, 1875, states that the Southern Escort had brought in 2252 oz. 17 dwts. of gold from four districts, and that 6579 oz. 6 dwts. had been brought from ten districts by the Northern Escort ; that the shares of re-constituted companies were taken up in *one day ;* that the Bendigo washings were expected to yield 700 oz. ; and that £8500 had been " netted " by the shareholders. Whether similar success shall ever be attained in the Southern Gold-Fields of Scotland remains to be seen. These things are at all events self-evident : (1) This Treasure-House formerly rewarded systematic search ; (2) the field has been proved to be unexhausted ; (3) skill and science of a higher order than previously known could now be introduced ; and therefore (4) a company possessing these, capital, permission, limitation, and encouragement of proprietors, along with assistance from Government, are indispensable, so as to avoid the " assemblage of the blackguardism of the world," which all would deprecate, and to secure a thorough trial with hope of reward for the toil. There appears to be no good reason why proper regulation might not be secured in this as in any other legitimate enterprise ; and thus as satisfactory a solution be given to the last as to the former questions.

From all this it appears that, comparatively small, poor, and barren as Scotland is, especially in her Northern and Southern Highlands, God has therein filled her house with the richest treasure—precious gold. To know that *He* has put it there for man's use is warrant sufficient to take it from His hand gratefully—a duty and a privilege.

And yet, that is merely the gold that perisheth. His statutes are greater treasures far—

" *They more than gold, yea, much fine gold, to be desired are,*"

for they tell of Him who redeems, not with corruptible things as silver or gold, but with His own precious blood ; and that,

" *Yea ! He shall live, and given to Him shall be of Sheba's gold.*"

THE LEADHILLS.

LEAD AND SILVER.

" Entrusted safely each to his pursuit,
Earnest alike, let both from hill to hill
Range ; if it please them, speed from clime to clime ;
The mind is full—no pain is in their sport."

WORDSWORTH.

ANCIENT WORKINGS AT LEADHILLS.

"THE search for gold brought about the discovery of lead in the sixteenth century." This is the common mode of reasoning. No such thing. Lead mines were wrought in the Leadhills in the thirteenth century. The mineral wealth of this "Treasure-House" is referred to in a grant of lands in Crawford Muir to the monks of Newbattle by Sir David Lindsay, in 1239, in which a mine on Glengonar Water is named. That mine had been sunk for lead, as appears from a suit raised before the Lord Auditors in Parliament. This was at the instance of Patrick, Abbot of Newbattle, against James, Lord Hamilton, for the spoliation of 1000 stones of lead ore, which he had carried off from the Abbey lands in Friar or Crawford Muir. Lord Hamilton was ordered to restore that quantity of lead ore. In the Chamberlain Rolls of 1264 the sum of 42s. is entered in the accounts of the Sheriff of Lanarkshire for the conveyance of lead from Crawford to Rutherglen. And in 1467 a charter of resignation of the lands conveyed by his ancestors was granted by David, Earl of Crawford. This included "the mines and leadpit." Thereafter, as stated, the gold mines were also wrought and let on lease.

On the 23d January 1562—shortly after the Reformation had been accomplished—a royal grant was made to " Johne Achisone and John Aslowane, burges of Edinburgh," " to work and wyn in the lead mynes of Glengonar and Wenlock," and to transport the ore to Flanders, that the silver may be there extracted; paying to the Queen "fortie-five unce of uter fyne silver for every thousand stane wicht of lead." Another grant was made on the 26th August 1565, for five years, "to John, Earl of Atholl, to cause wyn fourthy thousand tron wicht of lead in the nether leid hoill of Glengonar and Wenlock." *

The failure of Roche, who leased the workings of the "haill mynes within this realme of Scotland from 1583, and the creation of the office of a Master of Metals in 1592, have been detailed.

In 1581 George Douglas of Parkhead in Douglas Water, along with his sons James and George, were forfeited. Three years after, their estate was annexed to the Crown. Taking refuge in the north of England, George, the younger son, took advantage of his position, and acquired considerable skill in the working of the lead mines there; and in 1585, when his attainder was reversed, he returned and applied his knowledge to good account in his native district, till his death as related, exception having been made by giving him a share of the universal lease of Roche.

An exception was farther granted in favour of Thomas Foulis, a goldsmith in Edinburgh. In 1578 Gavin Smith, mining engineer, mentioned in a letter to Lord Burleigh that Thomas Foulis had in 1576 visited the north of England to procure the assistance of a person skilled in mining operations. That Foulis had begun to treat with Smith, but finally engaged Bevis Bulmer, who was then working for Foulis a profitable lead mine in Scotland. Foulis was deeply impressed that a Spanish proverb generally proved correct. It was to the effect that "he who works a gold mine becomes poor, while he who possesses a copper one acquires a fortune." Accordingly Foulis confined his exertions to the search for lead. Bulmer, as has been seen, earnestly and successfully looked out for the gold. The fact of the death of Bulmer in debt, with the prosperity attendant upon Foulis and his heirs on to the present day, is no inapt illustration of that proverb.

Foulis was the most enterprising adventurer of those times. His rights and privileges are mentioned in the Act of 1592, and his success was such that he purchased the lands where the mines lay. A grant was made to him in 1593 by James VI., which narrates that the gold, lead, &c., mines in Craw-

---

* See pp. 122, 123 for obligations, contracts, and leases given to these and other parties.

ford Muir and Glengonar were given to him for twenty-one years in consideration of the great sums due to him "and his dearest spouse;" and in 1594 Parliament confirmed these rights, declaring that they included the mines lately possessed by Douglas of Parkhead. These were, however, hazardous times in which to carry on valuable mineral operations. He required in addition to obtain a proclamation in 1597 to suppress the disorders of "broken men of the Borders," who robbed his servants when conveying his lead of "horses, armour, clothing, and their haill carriage." Certain burgesses of Lanark and Glasgow were also accused by him in October of the same year of having possessed themselves by force of a quantity of his lead on its way to Leith, who were ordered to restore what they had taken, or to pay value for the same.

Foulis died about the year 1611. He was succeeded (1612) in the lands of Glendorch, in the parish of Crawfordjohn, by his brother David; and in the lands of Leadhills, with the mines therein, by Robert Foulis, advocate in Edinburgh—probably another brother. This advocate was succeeded by his two daughters, Anne and Elizabeth, in 1633. Elizabeth dying in 1637, Anne became sole heiress. Meanwhile, David, the possessor of Glendorch, usurped the inheritance of Anne, who was then in her minority. To obtain redress, the Court of Session must be appealed to. The advocate who successfully conducted her case was Mr James Hope. This contested case led to another equally successful, for this talented advocate gained the heart and hand of his client; and this second led to his third success, of such skill in mineralogy that mining was brought by him to a perfection up till that period unknown in Scotland.

In 1661—a year memorable because of the ejectment of two thousand ministers in England and four hundred in Scotland, in order to the enforced establishment of Prelacy—a grant of these mines under the Great Seal was ratified by Act of Parliament in favour of Sir James Hope of Hopetoun and Dame Anne Foulis, his spouse. In this Act the privileges and intromissions of the grantees and miners are thus referred to. First, the King takes the miners employed under his special protection, and exempts them from all taxes, both in peace and war; but this is not to extend "to such proportion of excise for ale and beir brewed in the house of the grantees as shall be payed by other heritors for the ale and beir brewed in their houses."

Second, heavy penalties are imposed on any person who attempts to seduce the workmen from their employment, or who fraudulently removes any materials, lead or lead ore. No person is to be permitted to intromit with the workmen without a certificate from Sir James; and the officers of customs are required to take "special notice of the shipping of such mettals or ore, and to record the quantities thereof, with the names of the pretended owners thereof, and vessels in which the same are shipped. And in default of such wryting or testificate, to make seasure thairof in name and for the use of the grantees." Lastly, the grantees are empowered to make and mend roads, in order to the conveyance of the metal to seaports.

From that period to the present the mines have remained in the possession of, and have been worked with varied success for, the Hopetoun family. So great is the value of the lead which has been raised from beneath one of the mountains at Leadhills, that a competent authority has declared that "*it would suffice to pave its surface completely with gold guineas set on edge.*" Subsequent purchases and operations have largely increased the original value of the estate possessed by Thomas Foulis.

Robert, Earl of Lothian, was served heir to his father in the barony of Crawford or Friar's Mure in 1609. But the feuars of Thomas Foulis being mentioned in the Act of Parliament which confirmed the grant of minerals as belonging of old to the Abbey of Newbattle, he must then have been in actual possession. The daughters of Robert Foulis, Anne and Elizabeth, were served heirs to him in 1633. In 1637 Anne became sole heiress by the death of her sister. Shortly afterwards she married Sir James Hope.

As stated, in 1661 a charter of Charles I., in favour of her and her husband in liferent, and their son Thomas Hope, was confirmed, in fee. This conveyed to them the lands and barony of Waterhead and Leadhills, *alias* Glengonar; and in 1683 the entire barony, formerly in possession of the monks, became vested in the Hopetoun family. In that year Charles Hope of Hopetoun, *who had been created a peer*, was served heir to his father in the lands of Crawford Mure, Friar Mure, or Douglas Mure, which were all united in the barony of Hopetoun.*

* See Appendix G.

LEASES AND LITIGATIONS.

Two distinct companies obtained the mining-field on lease in 1747. The Scots Mining Company held the north-western portion. Its shareholders were chiefly gentlemen in London, whose descendants originated the Sun Fire Office. Although embracing but a fourth of the whole, the capital subscribed amounted to £10,000, in £100 shares. Mr Marchbank & Company held the south-western portion. In addition to these, the Hopetoun family reserved and worked a portion east of Glengonar Burn. Mr Marchbank & Company having resigned for want of success, the Scots Company obtained the south-western portion in 1772, and carried on the works with vigour. At that same time Mr Popham, a Master in Chancery, and others obtained that part reserved by the Hopetoun family, and they termed themselves the Leadhills Mining Company. Having but poor success, they ceased operations in 1805. Then the Scots Company obtained the north-eastern portion ; and the south-eastern, after a rest of three years, was leased by Mr Horner, from Darlington, and others, who carried on the works with vigour till 1817, when Mr Horner died. The family of that gentleman being large, and the property divided, want of capital and mining knowledge led to the abandonment of the mines by his sons in 1828.

The Leadhills Mining Company purchased the lease from Mr Thomas Horner. They were, however, unable to commence work, as they could not obtain water for their engines and wheels, the use of a watercourse having been interdicted them by the Scots Company. This resulted in a lawsuit between the Leadhills Mining Company and the Earl of Hopetoun on the one hand, and the Scots Mining Company on the other. This lawsuit, which lasted upwards of twenty years, and cost some £25,000, led to no satisfactory result. At length—after the mines had been thoroughly inspected, reports and suggestions presented by Captain Vivian and others *—a compromise was entered into in 1861, by which the Scots Mining Company relinquished their lease, and the Leadhills Mining Company obtained possession of the entire mining-field.

Prior to this the Leadhills Mining Company had only been

* See Appendix H, Report by Messrs Hedley and Scaife.

able to carry on limited operations in the year 1846; consequently the village was almost depopulated, and the miners with their families, with grievous lamentations, were compelled to leave their native village and seek employment at Newton-Stewart, Carsphairn, Dalmellington, and other places where mining operations were carried on. Instead of some 1400, the inhabitants were reduced to 896 in the year 1861. Numbers of the cottages were then unroofed and ruinous. The place had become a doleful and desolated dwelling.

LEADHILLS MINING COMPANY.

The following interesting account of the EXTENT and PROGRESS of the works since 1861 was written by J. Nevin, Esq., the late manager, and father of the present, in 1864:—

"The whole of these lead mines were let in 1861 to a company of Scotch gentlemen, of which the principal partner is William Muir, Esq., Leith, who, under the name of the Leadhills Mining Company, are now prosecuting them with a vigour hitherto unknown in lead mining in Scotland. The mining-field extends over about 10 square miles, but the principal workings are in and around the village of Leadhills, where, within an extent of 4 square miles, there are upwards of forty veins, the majority of which run in a north-easterly and south-westerly direction; but these again are intersected by others whose bearings differ. All the veins in this district are more or less productive of lead ore, and in many of them, according to old records, 6 feet wide of solid galena was often met with; whilst in more than one vein, ore has been found in a solid mass, varying from 10 to 14 feet in width. These large knots or bunches of ore did not extend, however, to a length of more than a few fathoms, nor continued to any great depth, and were therefore soon wrought out.

"The rocks in the district are of the inferior stratified series, below the transition or greywacke group, and consist principally of gneiss, mica, and clayslate, through the close texture of which it is difficult to penetrate. The veins vary very much in thickness, being frequently as many feet as in other places they are inches wide; and have generally a considerable underlie, sometimes at an angle of thirty degrees. The walls are principally composed of iron pyrites, and their contents, as is the case with other mineral veins, differ much. In some places galena alone is found. In others, galena, mixed with sulphate of baryta and quartz; whilst in other places, again, the sole contents are either sulphate of baryta or mineral soil. Perhaps in no other mining district is there such a variety of lead ores as is found here. Besides galena, no less than seven pieces occur in phosphates, carbonates, sulphates, and their compounds. Copper ore is also found ; but the quality being poor, and the quantity obtained small, it will not pay working. A vein of antimony is also known to exist, but is not considered rich enough to pay the cost of exploration.

"These mines are to a certain extent drained by two adit levels, the higher of which extends over the greater part of the mining-field, and is about fifty fathoms or 300 feet below the surface at its extremity. The lower adit level is not yet driven much farther than the village, which is about the centre of the principal workings, but is now being continued as part of the underground railway, hereafter described; and when it reaches the extent of the mines already opened out, will be about eighty fathoms from the surface. The former lessees, it appears, have not availed themselves of the facilities these adit levels afford of bringing the work to bank by an underground railway, but have carried on their operations by means of shafts, of which there are great numbers. The cost of sinking these shafts would amount to no inconsiderable item in the expenditure, as the total depth of the same is fully equal to the distances between them. This being the case, the courses of the principal veins are clearly delineated on the surface by the lines of shafts, which, with the refuse heaped up about them, produce a very unpicturesque effect, and add much to the barren appearance of the district. From these adit levels to the surface nearly all the veins have been wrought out, and have yielded a considerable quantity of lead ore ; but, through neglect, these old workings, as well as the adit levels, were nearly all closed, so that when the present lessees commenced operations in 1861 more than three-fourths of the mines were inaccessible and abandoned. Since then great exertions have been made to reopen the whole, and more particularly the adit levels, so as to drain off the water—which levels are being extended throughout the whole of the mining-field. Although these mines have been wrought for upwards of three hundred years, yet it is only in two of the principal veins that operations have been carried to any great depth below the lower adit level. In prosecuting these workings, steam and hydraulic power were employed to draw the water and work. These workings are again being resumed, and it is intended to carry them to a still lower depth, when more powerful machinery will be required than has hitherto been employed for pumping purposes, as they were formerly abandoned for the want of sufficient power to draw the water.

"At present the lessees of these mines are forming an underground railway, so as to bring the whole of the work excavated to a central depot and washing-place at the surface. This railway is at the lowest point accessible—namely, at the lower adit level ; will be carried throughout the whole of the works, and will be at least 5 miles in length when completed. It is being laid with malleable-iron rails, 40 lbs. per yard, on which it is intended that a locomotive of twelve-horse power should run, with waggons attached ;

thus bringing out the whole of the work produced at a much cheaper rate than by any other means that could be adopted. The excavation for this underground railway is 7 feet in height, by 4½ feet in width, and being principally driven in hard rock —the cost of which will probably average £10 per fathom—the expense of completing the same will be about £45,000. It would have taken at least twenty years to finish, but shafts are being sunk on the line of this railway, from which it is intended to drive both right and left, so as to get it completed with as little delay as possible. When this level or underground railway is carried out to the extent proposed, the facilities for working these mines to advantage will be equal, if not superior, to any other mine in Great Britain.

"In order to have sufficient power for driving their hydraulic and other engines, the present lessees have constructed a series of reservoirs. One of them covers upwards of 13 acres of land, and contains about 60,000,000 gallons of water—the embankment being 40 feet in height. The different water-races from these reservoirs to the works are upwards of 8 miles in length, and are being laid with clay pipes, spigot and faucet joints, some of which are 20 inches in diameter, costing about £650 per mile.

"For working these mines water-power alone is now employed, and at present there are four hydraulic engines for pumping, one hydraulic engine, and four water-wheels for drawing work, one water-wheel for crushing and dressing the ores, and one ditto for driving the blasts at smelting-works—the united horse-power of which is upwards of 550. One of these hydraulic engines, recently erected, is the largest in Scotland, having a 2-feet cylinder and 10-feet stroke, with a pressure of water of 216 feet; and when double-acting is equal to 139 horses. Other two of these powerful engines will shortly be erected, when the available horse-power will be greatly increased.

"The present washing-floors and mode of conducting the washing operations are, like the previous working of the mine, capable of great improvements, the machinery being old and antiquated. Preparations are therefore being made to construct a new washing-floor at the terminus of the underground railway, when all the recent improvements in crushing and dressing lead ores will be introduced and covered over, so that operations may be carried on, independent of the weather, at all times of the year. From this washing-floor a railway will be laid to the smelting-works, which are on the Glengonar Water, 2 miles below the village of Leadhills.

"These smelting-works consist of two roasting-furnaces, one reverberatory furnace, four ore-hearths, and one slag-hearth, and are capable of smelting 50 tons of lead per week. The blast for the hearths is given by a water-wheel working two air-cylinders in connection with an air cistern or reservoir, from which the air is conducted in pipes to the hearths. In consequence of the ores not containing much silver—namely, only about 5 oz. per ton—

72

desilverisation, or the extraction of the silver from the lead, has not been practised at these works; but as 4 oz. per ton will pay the cost, and a great improvement in the quality of the lead is made thereby, buildings are being erected to carry out the process. At present there is only a short chimney-flue from these works, in which not more than 2 per cent. of the fumes from the hearths are collected, and as fully 10 per cent. of the lead ore smelted escapes in fumes, the loss is considerable. In order to remedy this, new flues are being commenced with, the dimensions of which are 5 feet in width by 6 feet in height, and will be carried to the distance of 1000 yards, where apparatus for condensing the remaining fume will be erected."

Tennant wrote, in 1772, that "the veins vary in their depth. Some have been found filled with ore within two fathoms of the surface; others sink to the depth of ninety fathoms. The ore yields in general about seventy pounds of lead from a hundred and twelve of ore; but affords very little silver. The varieties are the common plated ore, called *Potter's*, the small or steel grained ore, and the curious white ores, lamellated and fibrous, so much searched after for the cabinets of the curious. The last yields from fifty-eight to sixty-eight pounds from the hundred; but the working of this species is much more pernicious to the health of the workmen than the common. The lead is sent to Leith in small carts that carry about 7 cwt."

The produce of the mines has been known to vary from 10,000 to 18,000 bars of from 112 to 120 lbs. each. The sale also has been various. After the commencement of the French Revolution, the demand failed, so that £40,000 worth remained at Biggar, half-way, and an equal quantity at Leith, for a time. Soon after the demand raised the price to double that amount.

The Earl of Hopetoun received a sixth bar for rent from the two mining companies.

In 1700 the crop amounted to nearly 18,000 bars.
In 1786   „   „   only to 10,080 „

The description given years ago of the smelting-works applies as appropriately now: "Descending from the successive platforms where the bruised ore is washed till it is almost pure dust of lead, we put our heads into the noisy vault, where the great water-wheel was revolving and letting fall a drip which filled the place with the sound of mighty splashings. The blast of the furnaces roared under our feet, and all around about us every light substance, such as coal dust and shreds

73

of peat, was blown about like chaff. At the furnace were men enduring the blaze of the red heat on this sultry day. They work for five or six hours; but only for five days in the week. They were piling up the glowing coals upon the bruised and washed ore in the receptacle in the furnace; and from under the front of the fire we saw the molten lead running down its little channel into its own reservoir, leaving behind the less heavy dross, which was afterwards to be cast out in a heap in the yard. The mould for the pig stood close by, at a convenient height from the floor. We waited till there was lead enough in the reservoir to make a pig. One man ladled out the molten metal into the mould, while another skimmed off the ashes and skum with two pieces of wood. It was curious to see this substance, which looked exactly like quicksilver, treated like soup; and the process of cooling begin from the edges, and the film spreading slowly towards the centre, till all was solid; then, the pigs set on end against the wall, looking light and movable from their lustre, when just out of the mould, and to remember that one might as well try to lift up the opposite mountain as to move one of them unaided."

Lead was also obtained some thirty years ago on the small estate of Snar, which runs north-east in a valley on the north side of the hill which divides it from the Wanlock and Gonar glens. At one time the two sides of the Snar stream were owned by the Hamilton and Colebrooke families. The late Mr Thompson, who resided at Little Crawick, having sold the Hamilton portion which he possessed, Sir Edward Colebrooke was induced also to part with his share. This transfer took place about the year 1845, and Snar is still in the possession of John A. Johnstone, Esq. of Archbank, near Moffat. It is entirely pastoral, feeding some fifty or sixty score of sheep, who are cared for by two shepherds at Snar and Snarshead respectively. The mines, which were wrought by the late James Hunter, Abington, and others, were abandoned forty years ago, not for want of lead, but of *machinery to remove the water.* The proprietor appears to be unwilling to have his stock injured by lead operations. As, however, the mineral as well as pastoral privileges were purchased, and it being possible to work the Snar veins from Leadhills without breaking the soil in Snar valley, it is extremely probable that these treasures may by-and-by be explored; all difficulties solved; proprietor and community benefited.

In the zenith of the lead trade in Leadhills in 1810, about 1400 tons annually were produced, which, according to the current price, valued above £45,000. Price and quantity decreased to 700 or 800 tons annually. Workmen were also reduced till only eight men were employed by the Scots Mining Company, whose manager was Mr Borron. The rent of the Earl of Hopetoun at that time was every sixth bar produced.

From the year 1861 to the present time an annual crop of from 800 to 1600 tons of lead has been obtained, realising from £17, 12s. 6d. to £24 per ton—its present value being £22. More lead is now being obtained than for many years before. One knot of ore in Raik vein, from 3 to 24 inches broad, and 60 fathoms long, has yielded in three months about 530 tons of solid lead, which has been raised at £4 per ton, including drivings and sinkings. Last year the crop yielded 1150 to 1200 tons, or from 23,000 to 24,000 bars of 1 cwt. each; this year probably 1500 tons, or 30,000 bars. The lordship is one-ninth to the Earl of Hopetoun, with fixed rent of £52, 10s., the company having all minerals—gold, silver, and lead—at its command. If the Susannah vein should be worked by steam, the lordship for it would be only one-twelfth; but that seems to be nearly exhausted. The veins principally wrought at present are termed Raik, Brow, and Brown's. The greatest depth from the surface is 115 fathoms.

This successful enterprise has not been accomplished apart from an immense expenditure of skill, perseverance, and capital. Since 1864, four water-wheels for drawing and pumping, from 18 to 30 feet diameter; two hydraulic engines for do. do., of 8 and 19 inch cylinders; and one turbine, 6 inches diameter, for driving fan and sawmill and turning-lathe, have been erected.

Then about the year 1868 some two and a half miles of underground railway were opened, which, with cross-cutting, cost £7213. Again, in 1873, the embankment on the reservoir was raised 5 feet, so as now to contain 80,000,000 gallons of water, at a cost of £120; and some 9 or 10 miles of clay pipes are laid, costing £2280. Further still, new washing-floors for sorting the ore, under cover, were erected in that same year, with two water-wheels for crushing and driving; jigging-machines, and slime-washing apparatus, were erected. Only eleven hands are there employed, and dressed ore can thus be produced at the small cost of 5s. per ton, exclusive of slime ores. Besides, improvements were effected at the smelt-mills in 1864 and since; and in 1868 the workshops were re-modelled, whereby they are large, healthy, commodious, and profitable.

Hitherto the company, having large expenditure, have reaped little; but they have in contemplation (1) the extension of the railway to the smelt-mills, to be wrought either by a steam or an air-compressing locomotive—the latter being most suitable to the locality. (2) The erection of chambers to catch the lead fumes. It is understood that one-tenth of the lead passes away with the smoke. At the works of Mr Beaumont in Northumberland 7 or 8 per cent. are retained, whereas only some $2\frac{1}{2}$ are secured at the Leadhills works. Having abundance of hill-ground, and the recent successful experiment at Wanlockhead before them, the Leadhills Company will doubtless realise that, for their own interest, the fumes which now poison the surrounding heath ought by all means to be detained. (3) The "desilverisation," or, if by the new and cheaper process, "dezincification" of the lead, is also in view. It is considered that only 4 or 5 oz. of silver to the ton exists in this lead, that the yield and the cost would be, at this rate, 20s. per ton; but then the lead itself sells at a higher figure, while the oxidised lead is also of greater value. So that, in time, it may be anticipated that works will be found at Leadhills second to none in the kingdom. At present there are 276 hands employed—viz., 162 miners, 26 underground labourers, 10 mechanics, 5 enginemen, 14 carters, 33 washers, 26 smelters, and 4 agents. In addition to surrounding aid, 20 horses—10 belonging to the company—are constantly at work. These extensive mines have been admirably conducted by John French Nevin, Esq., since 1867.

"LEAD,

whose atomic weight is 207; symbol, Pb. (*Plumbum*), is an abundant and useful metal, altogether obtained from the native sulphide, or *galena*, no other lead ore being found in large quantity. The reduction is effected in a reverbatory furnace, into which the crushed lead ore is introduced and roasted for some time at a dull red heat, by which much of the sulphide becomes changed by oxidation to sulphate. The contents of the furnace are then thoroughly mixed, and the temperature raised, when the sulphate and sulphide react upon each other, producing sulphurous oxide and metallic lead.

" Lead is a soft bluish metal, possessing very little elasticity; its specific gravity is 11·45. It may be easily rolled out into plates, or drawn out into coarse wires, but has very little tenacity. It melts at 315·5°, or a little above, and boils and volatilises at a white heat. By slow cooling it may be obtained in octohedral crystals. In moist air this metal becomes coated with a film of grey matter, thought to be suboxide, and when exposed to the atmosphere in the melted state it rapidly absorbs oxygen. Dilute acids, with the exception of nitric acid, act but slowly upon lead."—*Fownes' Manual of Chemistry, Watt's edition*, 1872, pp. 449, 450.

ANALYTICAL TESTS FOR GOLD, SILVER, AND LEAD.

RE-AGENT.	GOLD (Au.)	SILVER (Ag.)	LEAD (Pb.)
Ferrous sulphate ($FeSO_4$).	Brown precipitate, fusible by the blowpipe to a bead of metallic gold.		
Stannous chloride ($SnCl_2$).	Brownish purple precipitate, called " Purple of Cassius."		
Hydro-chloric acid (HCl).		White curdy precipitate, insoluble in nitric acid, soluble in ammonia, darkens in daylight.	White precipitate, soluble in excess of water, readily soluble in hot water, not changed in colour by ammonia.
Iodide of potassium (Ki).		Yellow precipitate, insoluble in nitric acid or ammonia.	Yellow precipitate, soluble in boiling water.
Potassium bichromate ($K_2Cr_2O_7$).		Crimson precipitate, soluble in nitric acid or ammonia.	Yellow precipitate, soluble in caustic soda.
Dilute sulphuric acid ($H_2SO_4 + H_2O$).			White precipitate, soluble in caustic soda.
Caustic soda ($NaHO$).		Brown precipitate, insoluble in excess, soluble in ammonia.	White precipitate, soluble in excess.

Example.—If to a solution of a substance supposed to contain gold a few drops of a solution of ferrous sulphate be added, and a brown precipitate be produced, fusible by the blow-pipe to a bead of metallic gold, you may be sure that gold is present.—*R. Midgley.*

WORKS ON THE WANLOCK.

" So silent is the place, and cold,
So far from human ken,
It hath a look that makes me old,
And spectres time again."

AYTOUN.

FORMER OPERATIONS.

KNOWN from the thirteenth century, workmen were employed in mining for lead on the Wanlock by James IV. in 1512.

In 1529 Ninian Crichton obtained the royal licence to work in the mines within the barony of Sanquhar for three years, the minerals of the country being retained in the hands of the King. It would seem to have been a hundred and forty-eight years after the expiry of that lease before the working was thoroughly set about. The subsequent history of these works, which include a circle of about two and a half miles, and join at the boundary with those of Leadhills, was graphically told by the Rev. Thomas Montgomery in 1835 :—

" The lead mines at Wanlockhead were opened by Sir James Stampfield about the year 1680, and were wrought by him with some success, but not to any great extent, till the Revolution in 1691. He was succeeded by Matthew Wilson, who procured a lease for nineteen years, and wrought the vein called Margaret's in the Dodhill. He carried his workings quite through that hill, from Whitecleuch to Wanlock stream, and was very successful in his discoveries. He was again succeeded in 1710 by a company for smelting lead ore with pit coal. They had a lease for thirty-one years, and wrought to a considerable extent in the veins of Old Glencrieff and Belton-grain, but were not very successful in their operations. At length, after much discouragement, they had the good fortune to find out the veins of New Glencrieff, where in a very short time they raised a great quantity of lead ore. In 1721

78

a numerous company was formed of persons residing in different parts of the kingdom, under the name of the Friendly Mining Society. They entered into partnership with the smelting company. . . . The two companies thus united carried on their operations in all the four principal veins then known, to a considerable extent, till 1727. They then separated from each other, and prosecuted their works in different grounds. The smelting company entered on the east side of the Wanlock stream, and vigorously continued their operations till 1734, when, having suffered great loss, though they had raised much lead, they resigned their lease. An individual partner in the company, however, Mr Wightman, retained liberty to work in the southern part of their boundary. He confined his operations to the south end of Margaret's vein. But they were very unprofitable, and terminated with his death in 1747. The mining liberty which had been possessed by him was unoccupied till 1755, when it was entered on by Messrs Ronald Crawford, Meason, & Co. . . . They continued their operations in Margaret's vein forty-three years. For carrying off the water they erected three steam-engines. The first was in 1778, and supposed to be the second erected by Mr Watt in Scotland. The Friendly Mining Society, or Quaker Company, having resigned their lease in 1734, were succeeded by Alexander and William Telfer. . . . They succeeded in raising great quantities of ore, which sold at a high price. At the expiration of their lease in 1755, Messrs Ronald Crawford, Meason, & Co. were also their successors, who now possessed the whole of the mining liberties at Wanlockhead. This enterprising and eminently successful company continued the works which had been left by Messrs Telfer till 1775. About this period they discovered good ore in Belton-grain vein above water-level, and continued working there till 1800. Then finding the ore above water-level to be mostly wrought out, they were under the necessity of erecting one steam-engine, a second in 1812, and a third in 1817. The works were profitable till the free-trade system was introduced, and foreign lead was allowed to be imported to Britain, without being subject to the payment of duty. From that period the company must have suffered great loss. The veins also presented great poverty. . . . During the period which elapsed from 1823 to 1827, the company sank forty fathoms under level, and erected two steam-engines underground, but the quantity of ore found did not answer their expectations. . . . The five engines last mentioned possessed collectively 268-horse power. Previous to the erection of these and of those on Margaret's vein, the water was raised from the mines by hand-pumps and water-wheels. The steam-engines have now all been removed, and a water-pressure engine has been erected, which is succeeding remarkably well. It carries away all the water which was formerly removed by the two steam-engines underground; it works with little attention, requiring merely that the water be kept regularly upon it, and thus greatly lessens the expense which was formerly incurred. The company at their commencement in

1755 had a lease only of nineteen years ; but an Act of Parliament was obtained afterwards authorising the extension of it till 1812, which was subsequently extended thirty years farther. The lessees in 1835 were the Marquis of Bute, three shares, and Mr M'Leod, one—in all, four shares. The company during fifty years have expended at Wanlockhead the sum of £500,000. By the terms of their lease, they delivered *a sixth part* of the lead raised to the proprietor as rent or lordship. But by a new agreement . . . they delivered a much less quantity. During fifty years, 47,420 tons of lead were raised. The success of the company was various. In the year 1809 were raised nearly 1037 tons of lead, sold at £32 per ton. In 1811 its price was £24 per ton. In 1829 and 1830 respectively were raised 596 and 461 tons, when its price was only £13 per ton. The number of persons employed in the works in 1835 were 4 overseers and clerks, 154 miners, 12 washers; 8 smelters, 10 smiths, carpenters, and engineers, 20 boys who assist in washing—amounting in all to 208. The work was, and still is, let by bargains, generally for three months—that is, the workmen receive a certain stipulated sum for the quantity of ore per ton which they raise, or for the fathom of dead work which they perform in that time. They relieved each other by courses every six hours (now every eight), and in twenty-four hours the same course does not go to work more than once. Each miner, on an average, was supposed to earn about £20 during the year. Agreeably to the contract of lease, some spare pickmen are always at work for making new discoveries of lead.

" The veins or mineral depositories hitherto wrought are five in number—viz., Old Glencrieff, New Glencrieff, Belton-grain, Margaret's, including Charles or Bay, Straitstep, and Cove, including Lochnell. They lie distant from each about 120 fathoms. Belton-grain, which lies nearest the east, is about 300 fathoms from the Cove. They have been wrought to the depth of 60, 75, 93, and 136 fathoms from the surface. The tops of the veins lie generally to the west, and they slope or *hade* eastward at an angle from sixty-eight or forty-five degrees from the horizon. According to the language of the miners, they *hade* one fathom in three, or sometimes in two ; by which is meant that they make one fathom in horizontal length to three or two in height. They do not generally run straight forward, but in a winding direction. From this cause none of the drifts are straight lines, but vary in working southward, from five to fifteen degrees east to south of fifteen degrees west of south. on all the workings the medium point is found to be almost south and north, so that the veins cannot be said to vary much in their course. The rocks which they traverse lie in beds at the same angle with themselves. These are the indurated argillaceous mountain rock, or what miners call the grey and blue whinstone. The veins are from a few inches to four feet in width. The bearing and the barren parts are very various in their length. The former are found from 1 or 2 to 70 or 80 fathoms, as in Belton-grain.

The latter are sometimes more and sometimes less extensive, and when they do occur are called 'checks' by the miners. The length and depth of the bearing parts always maintain a proportion to each other. The length, however, is generally something more considerable than the depth. Few of the veins have been found to contain much ore beyond the depth of 100 or 120 fathoms. They generally contract in their extremities, and diminish in their course toward the bottom. *Clay beds* are found occasionally to interrupt them. The course of Belton-grain vein may be traced on the surface by the ground being somewhat slackened or hollowed. A similar hollow is perceivable on the surface of the ground over some of the other veins.

"The structure of the veins is very various. The ore frequently lies in a regular form, but sometimes it is irregular, and mixed with what are called *vein-stones*, as *lamellar heavy spar, calcspar, rockcork*, &c. The ores are *lead glance, blende, manganese ochre, copper pyrites, green lead ore, white lead ore, lead vitriol*, and *brown hematite*, all in small quantities except the lead ore. The *contents of a bearing vein* are often found as follows : On the under or lying side is lead glance or galena, then a layer of ochre of manganese several inches thick, above it a layer of quartz interspersed with iron pyrites, then another layer of manganese mixed with quartz, pieces of lead glance and carbonate of lime, followed by greywacke, which constitutes the walls of the mine. Besides lead glance or common galena, the following minerals are also found—viz., sulphate, phosphate, carbonate, and arseniate of lead. The vanadiate of lead has been found in the refuse of the old workings, where it was for a time taken for arseniate of lead. These different specimens are now and then found occupying the same drusy cavity, and when seen before being injured or removed from their relative position exhibit a fine lustre and beautiful crystallisation. The druses, or *laeugh* holes, as they are termed by the miners, are also frequently studded with quartz, carbonate of zinc, &c. Sulphuret of zinc or zinc-blende is found in considerable quantities in some of the veins, particularly in Margaret's. Specimens of iron also occur, as ochry-red iron ore, but iron is always reckoned by the miners as unfavourable to their prospects in procuring lead. The *lead glance* at Wanlockhead was found by analysis to contain a small quantity of *arsenic, antimony*, and *silver*. The last mentioned was from *eight to ten ounces in the ton* of lead."

The veins of lead are sometimes bounded by a girdle of white quartz, popularly called "riders." The surrounding rocks are generally greywacke or greywacke slate, frequently yellowish at the surface and black at the centre, sometimes so hard as to strike fire with steel, but easily exfoliating with the weather, or falling to powder from exposure. A kind of exfoliating rock, popularly called "Stemin," is used for plugs to cork in the powder put in prepared holes in the

F

rocks prior to blasting, as no fire can be struck from it. Accidents, notwithstanding, occur when the "needle" or "pricker," which prepares the way for the fuse, is struck on one side. Then it "ratts" on the bottom or side, and so fires the powder. In this way many men have lost life, or have been seriously maimed.

The lead is of a light blue colour, with some lustre, which soon tarnishes. It is not malleable or ductile, and is one of the heaviest metals next to gold and platina. When a wide piece or belly is found, and where the veins meet, it has been known to measure 14 feet; the reflection upon it of the lights carried is very dazzling. Werner supposed the veins filled by aqueous matter descending from above in a state of solution; Hutton that the contents of the veins were injected from beneath in a state of igneous fusion, and the dispute of old ran high between the Neptunists and Vulcanists. From the lie of the veins, although interwoven, nearly north and south, their origin appears to be connected with magnetic influence. But here, as in everything, man must acknowledge his ignorance of the ways of Him who is wonderful in counsel and excellent in working.

The specific gravity of lead, cast, is 11·35; while that of gold, pure and cast, is 19·26; and of silver, pure and cast, is 10·47. Copper, cast, is 8·79; and zinc, cast, is 7·20. This specific gravity is the relative gravity of this body to another, assumed as a standard of comparison; which is generally pure water at 60° F., as being least subject to variation, and 1000 oz. avoirdupois being assumed as its specific gravity.

From a list of 168 men employed in working 31 "bargains" or contracts in Wanlockhead in the year 1783, in the possession of Mr John Laidlaw at Crawick, it appears that the companies ranged from two to eight men, and that the prices for driving were from £1, 10s. to £8, 15s. per fathom, and £1 per ton; raising ore, from £2, 5s. to £3, 10s. per ton; sinking, £4 to £5 per ton, or £6, 10s. per fathom; repairing old level, 12s. per fathom; washing ore, from 7s. 6d. to £5, 5s. per ton; smelting, 5s. 6d. to £1, 17s. 6d. per ton.

RECENT OPERATIONS.

Any one looking at the Geological Survey map of the district, where the Government officers have the veins laid down from a plan made out by the present manager, may observe that the veins do not run in parallel lines, but form a network, with the lines running in a northerly and southerly direction.

At the termination of the lease above mentioned in 1842, the Duke of Buccleuch took the mines into his own hands, and wrought them by a manager (James Stewart, Esq.) successfully till his decease in 1871, when he was succeeded by his son, Thomas Barker Stewart, Esq.

About the year 1830, when the late Mr James Stewart became connected with the management of the works, the mines were very poor, and more than half the workmen had to find employment out of their native village. By the substitution of hydraulic-pressure engines for steam-power and manual labour for pumping, the lower workings were made more accessible at a much cheaper rate, and by skilful and energetic prosecution of all underground and other works, with the introduction of improved machinery, both underground and on the surface, all the miners who desired it then found employment at home, and the mines became remunerative. Since that time bread has been provided for a considerable portion of the community, large sums of money circulated, and a satisfactory profit returned to the proprietor.

From the year 1835 mining operations have been conducted in Cove Vein and Lochnell Mine, which is in a portion of Cove Vein, in the north end of Belton-grain, north and south ends of New Glencrieff, Straitsteps, and Bay or Charles Veins —all of which have been more or less prolific, the workings in New Glencrieff and Lochnell particularly so. For its durability, for the extent and depth of its workings, and for its productiveness, New Glencrieff might challenge any other lead vein in Scotland. The low level has been driven along lead-bearing ground for nearly a mile. The lowest workings are 130 fathoms, or 780 feet, below the surface at the engine-shaft mouth. The vein has been operated on first and last between fifty and sixty years. The débris that has been raised during the last twenty years is estimated to weigh many thousands of tons, and the lead obtained in that period fully 12,500 tons, representing at the present price of lead a capital of £287,500.

The mines presently in operation are those in New Glencrieff, in Bay, and in Straitsteps veins. A trial is also being made on East and West Stayvoyage veins, which run across the county march from Leadhills grounds, near the turnpike road. A shaft has been sunk, and a steam-engine erected for pumping and winding. In connection with the mines four powerful hydraulic engines and a water-wheel of 28 feet diameter are used underground for pumping. The water for turning the hydraulic machinery is obtained by carrying all the streams that form the higher tributaries of Mennock and Wanlock Waters to the positions where power is required, by many miles of glazed clay pipes laid with cement. There are also used one steam-engine, two water-balance machines, and two horse-gins for winding materials out of the mines. At High Glencrieff the largest working siphon in Scotland has been long in operation. Mr T. B. Stewart obtained a medal from the Royal Scottish Society of Arts in 1858 for a model and description of this siphon.

PREPARATION.

There are several processes through which the lead ore is put after it has been drawn out of the mines. (1) By means of waggons on rails, it is taken to the coups or departments into which the produce of each partnership is deposited. It *was* then (2) separated into three kinds—(*a*) round, (*b*) small, (*c*) good and bad; and then that which is mixed with rock or quartz was (3) broken by the crushing-machine, wrought by a water-wheel 28 feet in diameter. It was next (4) washed by several processes — (*a*) "trucked," (*b*) "sieved," and (*c*) "buddled," these operations being so conducted as to preserve all the lead ore possible. This year a new method began.

The ore-dressing machinery and washing-floors that have been in use for about thirty years were the best of their kind at the time they were erected, but are now considered out of date. These have been removed, and new machinery erected instead. This is now in operation, and is the most complete and perfect arrangement in the kingdom. It consists of a powerful Blake's stone-breaker and revolving-table; sets of Green's patent and improved crushers, classifiers, and jaggers; besides Zenner's and Green's improved machines for dressing the small ores and sludges. The machinery works in three spacious and handsome sheds constructed of ashlar and brick work, the walls being supported by Norman buttresses. It is moved by two large water-wheels and a steam-engine of 12-horse power. It is self-acting, and dispenses with a great amount of manual labour formerly required. A man and two or three boys are sufficient to supply and attend to it. The raw material is supplied at one end of the machinery, while the pure ore is delivered at the other separated from all impurities, with the different sizes by themselves.

From the dressing-floors the ore is next (5) carted to the mills and weighed; it was then (6) roasted in furnaces, although this has been much discontinued; and finally, (7) it is smelted into bars.

DESILVERISATION.

From the smelting-house the bars are now (8) taken to the neighbouring refinery, where they are put through a series of pots—sixty to eighty bars being refined at a time. After they are melted, the temperature of the lead in the pot is gradually lowered. The lead, as it cools, like other metals, consolidates in a crystalline form, and it is found that the portion of lead that crystallises first contains only about half the proportion of silver in the original lead, and what remains in the fluid state has taken up an extra quantity of silver in proportion to that given up by the other. The crystallising process is thus carried through the series of pots until one portion of the lead operated upon is considered poor enough of silver to be sent to the market, and another made rich enough to be sent (9) to the refining-furnace, in the bottom of which there is a large cupel made of bone and pearl ashes to resist the intense heat. The very argentiferous lead being now melted in a small side pot, and poured into this furnace, a cross blast of air, along with flame, is passed along its surface, which oxidises the lead, and at the same time sweeps off the oxide as it forms, until pure silver alone remains in the cupel. This is a most beautiful and interesting process, which, by permission of the manager, strangers have the opportunity of witnessing. The oxidised lead or litharge, as it sweeps and drops off, is like a sea with rocks of burnished gold, on which, as the plate of silver "sets," scenes such as Aladdin's lamp alone could conjure up are brought into view. Vast plains are beheld on which armies in battle array confront each other. At times thrones are erected, on which sit kings and queens in crown and royal robes, sceptre in hand, giving judgment e'er the contest begins. Again, burning mountains pour forth fire and smoke, while their sides roll over with burning lava. Or, once more, cities of palaces, with gates of pearl and walls of jasper, and whose streets are paved with pure gold, are filled with multitudes that no man can number.

The plate is now removed and cut before it is quite cold, so as to be packed and sent to the silversmiths. The average quantity obtained per annum is 5750 oz., which, at 5s. per ounce, would bring £1437, 10s. The litharge dropped from the cupel is powdered and put into barrels, and becomes an important mercantile commodity for colour-making and other purposes. It sells higher and weighs heavier than it would without the oxidisation. About 316 barrels of 3 cwts. each are sent from the works annually. The average number of bars of lead of about fifteen to the ton obtained per annum is 13,256 during the last five years.

The proportion of silver to the ton of lead averages 7 per cent. It is said that the process will pay if there be 3 oz. of silver to the ton of lead, and that lead containing little or no silver is worth £1 more, it being more easily wrought. The lead ores of Devonshire and Cornwall are considered the richest in silver, averaging 35 to 40 oz. per ton. Those of the Isle of Man come next, and average about 20 oz. The Irish ores average about 10 oz., while the Scotch ores only average about 7 or 8 oz. The quantities vary very much, some ores yielding as high as 120 oz. of silver, while others contain so little that it is not worth separating.

In olden times, when the smelting-works stood near the site of the smiths' shops, and also at the foot of the village, silver-refining furnaces were kept in operation; but seeing that no supplementary process of desilverising lead either by steam, zinc, or by crystallisation, known as Pattinson's process, was then discovered, the undertaking could not be successful, except with very argentiferous lead. At present, as stated, the lead, after being smelted from the ore, is submitted to the process of crystallisation, but a new process of desilverising by steam has been lately introduced at some works, and the manager expects to have it established at Wanlockhead mills as soon as other improvements in hand are completed.

Wanlockhead is the only work in Scotland where desilverisation of lead is carried out. The present smelting-mills and silver-furnace were erected in 1845, for which, and other purposes in connection with the works, about 920 tons of coal are annually required. The present new smelting-hearths and smoke-condenser were completed and set to work in the end of 1873. The new hearths present a very unique and handsome appearance, having the Douglas crest shown *in relievo* on an iron plate above each fire. They are of the most improved construction, and produce lead faster, of a better quality, and economise fuel better than the older hearths. The necessary blast is supplied by a new machine called a Root's blower.

On the occasion of the marriage of Lady Margaret E. D. Scott to Donald Cameron, Esq. of Lochiel, in 1875, her lady-ship was presented by the workpeople with *entrée* dishes made of silver from Wanlockhead.

SILVER.

"Silver, whose atomic weight is 108, and symbol, Ag. (*Argentum*), is found in the metallic state as sulphide, in union with sulphide of antimony and sulphide of arsenic; also as chloride, iodide, and bromide. Among the principal silver mines may be mentioned those of the Hartz Mountains in Germany, of Konsberg in Norway, and more particularly of the Andes in both North and South America.

"The greater part of the silver of commerce is extracted from ores so poor as to render any process of 'smelting' or fusion inapplicable, even where fuel could be obtained, and this is often difficult to be procured. Recourse, therefore, is had to another method—that of '*amalgamation*'—founded on the easy solubility of silver and many other metals in metallic mercury.

"The amalgamation process adopted in Germany—which differs somewhat from that in use in America—is as follows: The ore is crushed to powder, mixed with a quantity of common salt, and roasted at a low red heat in a suitable furnace, by which treatment any sulphide of silver it may contain is converted into chloride. The mixture of earthy matter, oxides of iron and copper, soluble salts, silver chloride, and metallic silver is sifted and put into large barrels made to revolve on axes, with a quantity of water and scraps of iron, and the whole is agitated together for some time, during which the iron reduces the silver chloride to the state of metal. A certain proportion of mercury is then introduced, and the agitation repeated; the mercury dissolves out the silver, together with gold, if there be any, also metallic copper and other substances, forming a fluid amalgam easily separable from the thin mud of earthy matter by subsidence and washing. This amalgam is strained through a strong linen cloth, and the solid portion exposed to heat in a kind of retort, by which the remaining mercury is distilled off, and the silver left behind in an impure state.

"Considerable loss often occurs in the amalgamation process from the combination of a portion of the mercury with sulphur, oxygen, &c., whereby it is brought into a pulverulent condition, known as 'flouring,' and is the more liable to be washed away, together with the silver it has taken up. This inconvenience may be prevented, as suggested by Mr Crookes, by amalgamating the mercury with 1 or 2 per cent. of sodium, which by its superior affinity for sulphur and oxygen prevents the mercury from becoming floured.

" A considerable quantity of silver is obtained from argentiferous galena. In fact, almost every specimen of native lead sulphide is found to contain traces of this metal. When the proportion rises to a certain amount, it becomes worth extracting. The ore is reduced in the usual manner, the whole of the silver remaining with the lead; the latter is then remelted in a large vessel, and allowed to cool slowly until solidification commences. The portion which first crystallises is nearly pure lead, the alloy with silver being *more fusible than lead itself*: by particular management this is drained away, and is found to contain nearly the whole of the silver (Pattinson's process). This rich mass is next exposed to a red heat on the shallow hearth of a furnace, while a stream of air is allowed to impinge upon its surface; oxidation takes place with great rapidity, the fused oxide or litharge being constantly swept from the metal by the blast. When the greater part of the lead has been thus removed, the residue is transferred to a *cupel* or shallow dish made of bone-ashes, and again heated: the last portion of the lead is now oxidised, and the oxide sinks in a melted state into the porous vessel, while the silver, almost chemically pure, and exhibiting a brilliant surface, remains behind.

" Pure silver may be easily obtained. The metal is dissolved in nitric acid; if it contains copper, the solution will have a blue tint; gold will remain undissolved as a black powder. The solution is mixed with hydrochloric acid or common salt, and the white, insoluble, curdy precipitate of silver chloride is washed and dried. This is then mixed with about twice its weight of anhydrous sodium carbonate, and the mixture, placed in an earthen crucible, is gradually raised to a temperature approaching whiteness, during which the sodium carbonate and the silver chloride react upon each other; carbon dioxide and oxygen escape, while metallic silver and silver chloride result: the former melts into a button at the bottom of the crucible, and is easily detached. The following is perhaps the most simple method for the reduction of silver chloride. The silver-salt is covered with water, to which a few drops of sulphuric acid are added; a plate of zinc is then introduced. The silver chloride soon begins to decompose, and is, after a short time, entirely converted into metallic silver; the silver thus obtained is grey and spongy; it is ultimately purified by washing with slightly acidulated water.

" Pure silver has a most perfect white colour and a high degree of lustre: it is exceedingly malleable and ductile, and is probably the best conductor both of heat and electricity known. Its specific gravity is 10·5. In hardness it lies between gold and copper. It melts at a bright red heat. Silver is unalterable by air and moisture: it refuses to oxidise at any temperature, but possesses the extraordinary faculty of absorbing many times its volume of oxygen when strongly heated in an atmosphere of that gas, or in common air. The oxygen is again disengaged at the moment of solidification, and gives rise to the peculiar arborescent appearance often remarked on the surface of masses or buttons of pure silver. The addition of 2 per cent. of copper is sufficient to prevent the absorption of oxygen. Silver oxidises when heated with fusible siliceous matter, as glass, which it stains yellow or orange, from the formation of a silicate. It is little attacked by hydrochloric acid ; boiling oil of vitriol converts it into sulphate, with evolution of sulphurous oxide ; nitric acid, even dilute and in the cold, dissolves it readily. The tarnishing of surfaces of silver exposed to the air is due to hydrogen sulphide, the metal having a strong attraction for sulphur."—*Fownes' Manual of Chemistry, Watt's edition*, 1872, pp. 351–353.

SAVING LEAD FROM SMOKE.

Lead becomes rather volatile when subjected to a high temperature, and therefore a smoke-condenser is thereafter ready, prepared (10) to precipitate the fumes of lead carried off in the smoke from the furnaces and smelting-hearths. The new apparatus erected for that purpose consists of a series of spacious brick and woodwork chambers. The smoke is first conveyed to the condensing-chambers, where it is submitted to the action of water in the form of spray ; it is next admitted to the refrigerating-chambers and flues, where, in long passages which wind round the hillside, it is exposed to fully 100,000 superficial feet of cooling surfaces. The erection, which, it is understood, cost about £3000 sterling, was first cleaned out after working seven months, and produced about 58 tons of lead, worth, at market value, £1300 sterling. The product taken from the apparatus is estimated to exceed 100 tons of lead, worth £2300 sterling. This new arrangement thus not only pays for the expense of cleaning out and smelting the product, but will return the full capital expended in construction in less than a year and a half. No silver, however, is obtained from this produce.

MINING MEN.

" Go, if thou lov'st the spot to tread
Where man hath nobly striven,
And life, like incense, hath been shed,
An offering to heaven."   F. HEMANS.

 LADY, when asked to show her jewels, begged for time; and when a band of rosy-cheeked boys and girls came home from school, the mother led them into the presence of her friend with the exclamation, " Now, these are *my* jewels!"   In like manner some might be disposed to present those who have wrought, or still do labour within the bowels of these mountains, and to exclaim, " These, rather than minerals, are the treasures of the Southern Highlands."

They are located in two villages within the valleys of the Gonar and the Wanlock, separated by a high ridge of hill, and a mile and a quarter apart.

LEADHILLS

—a title now applied to the *quoad sacra* parish—or, as termed by the villagers, " Leedhill," is appropriately named, although for a time after the works came into the Hopetoun family it had been styled " Hopetoun." It lies at the head of the valley through which the Gonar stream flows down to the Clyde. Leadhills and Wanlockhead are the highest inhabited places in the south of Scotland. Leadhills lies on the sides of the valley, some of the houses in rather a low position. The area widens out and undulates above, and by the successful cultivation of the miners some 300 acres of land have been reclaimed, which afford potatoes and crops of hay. Corn does not ripen in this upland district. This green surrounding of

90

the village forms a pleasing contrast to this otherwise bleak, barren, heathy district. Highest cottages, 1412 feet above the sea.

Possibly only a few rude huts were erected at first near Bulmer's Field, at the "gowd scars" on the Shortcleuch, here, and upon the Wanlock, when, as migratory birds, the search for mineral treasure was prosecuted merely during summer. When these efforts became more systematic and successful, more permanent residents and buildings would be found. These would increase with the energetic prosecution of the works after Thomas Foulis assumed the helm, and then so rapidly did the population multiply that 1400 were located here in the middle of the eighteenth century. The litigations referred to reduced the population more than a third, and the village was one of the poorest that could be found.

Dr John Brown in 1865 said :—

"It is a dreary, unexpected little town, which has lain great part in ruins for many years, owing to the suspension or spiritless working of the mines, during a long, baffling House of Lords lawsuit. Things are better now under the new company, and we may soon see it as tidy and purpose-like as the Duke's neighbouring Wanlockhead. The people are thoughtful and solid, great readers and church-goers. They have a capital library. Like all natives of such forlorn, out-of-the-world places, they cannot understand how any one can be happy anywhere else ; and when one of them leaves the wild, unlovely place, they accompany him with wondering pity to the outskirts of their paradise, and never cease to implore and expect his return for good."

By the happy change in 1861, the steady progress manifested in the conduct of the works, and the generous treatment experienced by the miners under the management of the Messrs Nevin, father and son, together with the privileges enjoyed from the Hopetoun family, their numbers have risen to 1113, as given by the census of 1871.

The impressions of strangers have been frequently given, and it is somewhat amusing to note their observations upon this place and people. Thus Pennant in his "Tour in Scotland," vol. ii., 1772, says :—

"The place consists of mean houses, inhabited by about 1500 souls, supported by the mines, for five hundred are employed in the rich *sous terrains* of this tract. Nothing can equal the barren and gloomy appearance of the country round ; neither tree nor shrub, nor verdure, nor picturesque rock, appear to amuse the eye; the spectator must plunge into the bowels of these mountains for entertainment, or please himself with the idea of the good that is done by the well-bestowed treasures drawn from these inexhaustible mines, that are still rich, baffling the efforts of two centuries."

The miners and smelters were subject here to the lead-distemper, or *mill-reek*, as it is called, which brings on palsies, and sometimes madness, terminating in death in about ten days; but by an improved blast, smelting is now a healthy occupation.

Another account, ascribed to Miss Martineau in 1852, says:—

"The village, we were told, was 'just behind there;' and there it was — the strangest of British villages. The customary diet was that which we saw the two quarrymen enjoying at the road-side—oatcake and milk. Meat is an almost unknown luxury, even in the form of bacon. We had not before, nor have we now, a high opinion of the wholesomeness of oatmeal diet; but it is certainly the fact, that the people of Leadhills, living on a poor soil, at a height of 1280 feet above the level of the sea, have a remarkably healthy appearance, notwithstanding the presence of the fumes of the smelting, and the absence of a meat diet. The men work as in Cornwall, on tribute, sharing the success of their enterprises with the proprietors. They change the name of a mine quaintly enough, according to their approbation or displeasure towards it. We saw one which had till lately been called the 'Labour-in-vain Vein.' After a lucky turn which disclosed new riches (more lead with a little gold), it was called 'California'—a title, by the way, which shows that some tidings from the world without reach this secluded spot. . . The miners must be very like children in their impressibleness, and in the precarious character of the innocence which has been maintained in the absence of temptation. One other kind of intercourse is provided by the annual arrival of Lord Hopetoun, or his sporting friends, in August. We saw an elegant moorhen moving tamely on in the heather, not far from the smelting-houses; and this game so abounds on the hills that the sportsmen come home to dinner at 'the Ha'' with their thirty or forty brace each. Looking round on the very small cabbage-patches of the miners, remembering their oatmeal diet, without even a smell of bacon to their bread, pondering also the average of nine shillings a week, which leaves so many with only six, we inquired whether poaching could, in such a wild scene, be kept within bounds. The answer was, that the poacher would forfeit everything if detected. It is wonderful, and must be the result of strong compulsion of circumstance, that hungering men can see wild creatures fluttering in the herbage on the far-spreading moors, away from every human eye but their own, and can abstain from taking what can hardly appear like property. . . . At the very top of the settlement, when we have passed all the cottages, and 'the Ha',' and the potato-patches, and the heaps of lead ore, we come to a place which takes all strangers by surprise: a charming house, embowered in trees, with honeysuckle hanging about its walls, flowers in its parterres, and a respectable kitchen-garden, where the boast is that currants can be induced to ripen, and that apples have been known to form, and grow to a certain size, though not to ripen. This is the agent's house. The plantation is really wonderful at such an elevation above the sea; and it is a refreshing sight to the stranger arriving from below. There may be seen, growing in a perfect thicket, beech, ash, mountain ash, elm, plane, and larch, shading grass plats and enclosed walks, so fresh and green that on a hot day one might fancy himself in a meadow garden, near some ample river. In this abode there is a carriage, and a servant in livery—a great sight, no doubt, to the people, who can hardly have seen any other, except when sportsmen come to 'the Ha',' with all their locomotion and pleasure. In connection with this abode is the office of the company, where the books are preserved as far back as 1736."

It is to be regretted that the spirit of jealousy fostered by the law plea referred to, led to the burning of all books and papers when the present company came into possession. The late manager had not even a plan of the mines to guide him in his operations. His anxiety and enterprise can better be imagined than described, which, humanly speaking, must have shortened his days. The same energetic character has been inherited by his son, who possesses a magnificent collection of mineral specimens. And the view given is accurate. The manager's house is said to be on the same level with Tinto, and that the soil in which these trees grew was brought from the low country, every cart removing lead bringing back a load of mould; and further, that a Jacobite hid himself for many years in this retired mansion. It has evidently been built at different times, room being added to room, and is not the more comfortable on that account. In addition to a homestead and counting-room, a bowling-green with a garden, and an acre of ground, are surrounded and interlined with trees—all the more valuable that they are so rare in the locality.

As this place was far distant from the cultivated parts of the country, oatmeal and barley were purchased by the overseers of the mining companies, and reserved in stores, out of which all the individuals employed received weekly a certain quantity for their families, which formed part of their pay. Years ago that system took end, the miners obtaining a settlement at the end of every quarter, together with a monthly allowance of £2, 10s. per man. In addition to good shops, a co-operative store has supplied them with provisions. It numbers sixteen members, with upwards of £300 capital. In the year 1875 its sales amounted to £3032, 18s. 8d., which, after paying all expenses, left a profit to the shareholders of £350. It has been remarked that the common people employed in the mines bear little resemblance to their brethren in other quarters. They are of a sober and intelligent character, work in the mines only six hours (now eight) out of the twenty-four, and have therefore much leisure, and employ a considerable portion of it in reading.

The library was originally established by an overseer named Mr Stirling, who was a famous mathematician. Prior to its existence the miners were in no degree superior to ordinary colliers; but a taste for literature speedily produced its ordinary concomitants—decency, industry, and sobriety of manners, pride of spirit, and a desire to give a good education to their children. Similar effects have also been produced by a library at the neighbouring mines of Wanlockhead. This benefit has also been ascribed to Allan Ramsay the poet.

THE FAMILY OF RAMSAY.

Captain John Ramsay, son of Ramsay of Cockpen, and cousin to Lord Dalhousie, was manager of the mines at Leadhills before 1650—his son Robert, who married Alice Bower, succeeded to the same post. He was the father of Allan Ramsay the poet, who was born at Leadhills in 1686, and remained there until 1701, when in his fifteenth year he was apprenticed to a wigmaker in Edinburgh, his father having previously died, and his mother having been married again to a neighbouring proprietor of the name of Crichton. Allan in 1712 married Christian Ross, the daughter of a W.S. in Edinburgh. His poems, which were at first written in detached sheets or pamphlets, soon became so popular that previous to 1718 he renounced his business and devoted himself to literary pursuits. In 1721 he published his poems in a quarto volume, acquiring by the publication 400 guineas. In 1724 he published the first volume of his collection of songs, entitled "The Tea-Table Miscellany." A second and third volume were published within three or four years after. In 1721 he had published a pastoral under the title of "Pattie and Roger," followed by a sequel entitled "Jennie and Meggie." These were so much approved of that he was induced to rearrange them in the dramatic form in which the "Gentle Shepherd" now appears. His fame extending beyond Scotland, an edition of his poetical works was published at London in 1731, and another in Dublin in 1733.

Ramsay established the first circulating library in Scotland, and he also at his own expense built the first regular theatre. His society was sought by many of the Scottish nobility and gentry.

Sir J. Clerk, Sir W. Bennett, Sir A. Dick, Lord Elibank, and other distinguished men were his intimate friends. Towards the close of his life he built an octagon house, which still stands in Ramsay Gardens, Edinburgh, and is now the property of his descendant, Mr Murray of Henderlands. He died in 1758, and was buried in the classical graveyard of Greyfriars.

His son Allan, who frequently visited Leadhills, rose to considerable eminence as a painter. Having been introduced to George III. by Lord Bute, his accomplished manners and familiarity with the German and French languages so pleased the Queen that he obtained an appointment in the Royal household, and was appointed painter to their Majesties, succeeding Sir Joshua Reynolds. He married a daughter of Sir A. Lindsay of Evelick, and niece of the celebrated Earl of Mansfield.

Amongst his paintings, which were mostly portraits, may be mentioned that of his sister Janet at Newhall; the Duke of Argyll in the Assembly Rooms, Glasgow; George III. and his Queen, the Earl of Bute, Horace Walpole, in the possession of the Rev. T. W. M'Cririck of Stockton. A. Ramsay was one of the most refined men of his day. His taste was shown in a large and handsome collection of articles of virtu, some of which became the property of Mr M'Cririck—a gift from his cousin, General Ramsay, the son of Allan.

Allan died in 1784, leaving a son, John, who distinguished himself in the Peninsular War, and two daughters, Amelia and Janet, who were married respectively to Sir A. Campbell of Inverness and Captain Malcolm. In 1861 Lord Murray of Henderlands erected in Princes Street Gardens, Edinburgh, a beautiful marble statue of his ancestor, Allan Ramsay the poet. The statue was executed by Steell. On the pedestal are medallions of Lord Murray, General Ramsay, Lady Campbell, Mrs Malcolm, and Allan Ramsay the younger.

Ramsay once and again described himself, and said,

> "Then for the fabric of my mind,
> 'Tis mair to mirth than grief inclined:
> I rather choose to laugh at folly,
> Than show dislike by melancholy;
> Weil judging a sour, heavy face
> Is not the truest mark of grace."

Ramsay, Burns, and others having written in the Scottish dialect, have rendered it permanently interesting; and it is found a spoken language, almost as Ramsay wrote it, in Leadhills and Wanlockhead to this day. On one occasion he thus alluded to the manner in which he was handsomely patronised by one of the southern lairds, probably with the "gowd" of his native district:—

> "The chief required my snishing-mill,
> And well it was bestowed;

> The patron by the rarest skill,
>   Turned all the snuff to gowd.

> " Gowd stamped with royal Anna's face,
>   Piece after piece came forth ;
> The pictures smiled, given with such grace,
>   By one of so much worth."

Of Allan Ramsay it may be said in his own words—

> " While on burn banks the yellow gowan grows, .
>   Or wandering lambs rin bleating after ewes,
>   His fame shall last."

DR MARTIN.

Another eminent native was the late Dr Martin. He was born in Leadhills on the 3d of January 1790. His father, Robert Martin, was lead agent and bailiff to the Earl of Hopetoun. "Three of his sons became professional men. James, the eldest son, received his education in the village school and at Sanquhar. Thence he proceeded to Edinburgh to study medicine. At the beginning or close of a session he would walk the distance from Leadhills to Edinburgh in a single day. His practical professional apprenticeship was spent under an eminent surgeon in Dumfries. In 1811 he qualified as L.R.C.S.E., and, smitten by the enthusiasm of the age, he at once joined the medical service in the army. At that time our country was involved in all the excitement and stress of the Peninsular War. In the spring of 1812 Dr Martin joined the medical staff of the forces in Spain, acting under the immediate command of Lord Wellington, and he accompanied them during the whole of the subsequent course of that brilliant and immortal campaign. Immediately after his arrival he was present at the storming of Badajos, and gave active professional assistance under the fatal fire of that terrible night of the 7th of April. No man who witnessed it could ever forget such a sight, and to his latest days he would occasionally describe it to his more intimate friends in the most graphic terms. He entered the city next morning, and saw it sacked, but his own share of the booty, as he would humorously relate, consisted only of a handful of simple labels from a hatter's shop. After the capture of Badajos he accompanied the Allied army during those extraordinary military manœuvres in the direction of Tormes which have hardly a parallel in history, and whose result decided the tactic superiority of Wellington over Napoleon's greatest generals, and guaranteed the certain recovery in time of the whole Peninsula. Then followed the battle of Salamanca, the enthusiastic entry into Madrid, the flight of the ignoble 'King of the Cooks,' and the disconcertment of the whole strategy of the skilful Soult. He mastered Spanish thoroughly, and came into constant contact on the general march, or upon incidental expeditions, or while bivouacking in the country villages, with the most varied forms of the priestly, civilian, and peasant life of that interesting land of old faith, renown, and chivalry. He also passed through the campaigns of 1813 and '14, which were a series of the most brilliant movements and victories, embracing the advance through Spain, the difficult operations in Biscay, the decisive battle of Vittoria, the driving of the French fugitives in a storm of war over the Pyrenees, and the last conflict with Soult on the plains of France. On the abdication of Napoleon, the forces of Wellington, covered with glory, returned to England, and it must have been with a proud heart that the brave surgeon reached his own home among the hills in the summer of '14.

"Dr Martin had escaped danger, and was able for active service. He accordingly got attached to another regiment bound for the West Indies, and thus missed being present at the last act in the great drama, of which he had seen so much, as it terminated so tragically on the field of Waterloo. He heard of the final victory just as the vessel in which he had embarked was weighing anchor in the Channel. In the West Indies he found work enough of a different kind, amid the gay and dashing life of the young officers and the planters' families of the isle of Dominique. A terrific outbreak of yellow fever broke out after he had been settled some years, decimating the garrison, and cutting off many of his most intimate friends. When exhausted by excessive work he himself caught the infection, and made a narrow escape with his life. He was sent home invalided, but recovering, he returned again to his post. His health, however, had been so weakened that he was once more compelled to retreat before the fatal climate, and even to withdraw from the service in which he would otherwise have undoubtedly risen to high rank. Retiring on half-pay, he resumed his medical studies for a short time in Edinburgh, and graduated M.D. of the University in 1826. He then went to France, and was about to settle in the practice of his profession in the fair town of Avranches in Normandy, whither some of his old friends and companions in arms had retired.

"A sudden family affliction induced him to settle down, still in his prime and vigour, among the quiet hills which he loved so well, and there he was to spend the long evening of his life-day. He took up the village practice and carried it on with unremitting attention for many years. His remarkable skill, both as a physician and a surgeon, proved a blessing to the whole neighbourhood, directed as it was by a heart so tender and a sense of duty so unfailing. Some years ago the inhabitants of the district appropriately expressed their sense of his merits and services by a very handsome present of silver-plate. He had succeeded his father in representing the Hope-toun family in the village affairs, and deservedly enjoyed their confidence and friendship; and for some years past (said the 'Dumfries Courier') occupied a sort of patriarchal position in the village." Dr Martin died at Edinburgh, 9th February 1875, and was buried at Leadhills. He has left behind him three sons and two daughters, all of whom except one have gone to Australia.

A stone, supported by four pillars, erected to the memory of Dr Martin, bears the following inscription: "James Martin, born at Leadhills 3d January 1790, died at Edinburgh 10th February 1875. Having served as a surgeon to the forces under Wellington in the Peninsular War, and afterwards in the West India Islands, he returned with honour from active service to his native village, where he spent his later years, physician and friend of its inhabitants. Faithful in his profession, careful in the discharge of duty, affectionate in every family relation, distinguished in a constant public life, beloved in private by many attached friends, and honoured by all who knew his career, his wisdom, and his exemplary character."

The graveyard stands on a knoll near the lower part of the village. It is well enclosed by wall and trees. The small stone which marks the first interment has been recently defaced. Its inscription stated that "Here lyes Euphan Wright, aged 60 years, who departed this life, April 25th, 1741, and the first that was buried here."

The tombstone of the patriarchal John Taylor is most sought after by visitors. It reads thus: "Sacred to the memory of Robert Taylor, who was during many years an overseer to the Scotch Mining Company at Leadhills, and died May 6th, 1791, in the 67th year of his age. *He is buried by the side of his father, John Taylor, who died in this place at the remarkable age of 137 years."*

A MAN OF SIXSCORE YEARS AND TEN.

The tombstone bears that it was erected to the memory of John Taylor, miner, aged 137.

This John Taylor, the son of a miner in Aldstone, Cumberland, seems to have been born in the year 1637, and as he died in 1770, he must have been 133 years of age when he died. This is ascertained by a celebrated eclipse of the sun which took place in the year 1652, and the age at which young men were allowed to work underground. Losing his father when four years of age, he washed ore when a boy for twopence a day. For three or four years he had been a kibble-boy in the mine, and was at the bottom of a pit called Winlock shaft on that "mirk Monday." One Thomas Millbank called down to him to tell the men below to come up and behold the wonder, for a curious cloud darkened the sun, and the birds were falling to the earth. This event John Taylor frequently described.

"My late father," says Mr John Thomson of Grovehill, in writing to me on the 18th October 1875, "entered upon the lands on both sides of the Elvan about the year 1780 (ten years after the old man's death), and the universal impression in the district then was that he had entered upon his 133d year when he died—137 is simply a myth. He lived at Gold Scars, about two miles below Leadhills. You will notice vestiges of a house there still. The place is endeared to me by a thousand associations. When a child I remember of being carried on the back of the shepherds, seventy years ago, to the sheep-handlings there ; and when an elder boy, I have gathered many many scores of particles of gold at the same place. A family of the name of Moffat lived in the cottage then. Their descendants are still in Leadhills. The old man Taylor removed to Leadhills a year or two before he died, to be near his descendants. It appears at first glance rather incongruous that a miner should have married into a large landholder's family ; but such was the fact. He became acquainted with his future wife when employed by Scott of Harden to make trials for lead ore in the vale of Ettrick. His son was, I think, an overseer in Leadhills, and his grandson John was an overseer at Wanlockhead. His brother, James Taylor, has the sole merit of the discovery of the utilisation of steam to sailing vessels. Mr Miller of Dalswinton simply stood in the capacity of a landlord going to erect a house. He furnished the materials and paid for the workmanship, but had nothing to do with the merit of the plan.

"The last of the males of Polmood died out, and old John Taylor's descendants were most unquestionably the righteous heirs of the estate; but John and James, with astounding stupidity, did not assert their rights in time. Robert Taylor, the son of John, spent £1200 on it about 1800–10, but unfortunately too late. The late Lord Jeffrey told my sister that the whole of the Scotch bar were clearly of opinion that her husband had a just title, but it could not be established because one little link of evidence was lost. I have heard a thousand anecdotes of the old man, we being the nearest neighbours but one to the Gold Scars, and they were the common topic of conversation; but, alas! after a lapse of seventy years I cannot recall them."

When twenty-six, John Taylor went to the lead mines at Blackhills, county Durham. After nine years he was sent to report on mines in Islay. Returning to the north of England, he made trial, as stated, for lead in Ettrick. The death of Scott of Harden, and the accession of a minor, terminated that engagement. He was next employed at the Mint in Edinburgh, where Scottish coin was converted into British. Re-engaged at Islay, he married his only wife, by whom he had nine children. In 1730 he was at the mines in Strontian, Argyleshire. There attacked by scurvy, he removed to Glasgow, and for a time wrought as a day-labourer. Then at Hilderstone, near Bathgate, he wrought at the York Buildings Company's silver mine. Finally, he removed to Leadhills in 1733, working regularly as a miner till 1752, having spent upwards of a century in unceasing labour.

In 1758, when his wife died, he had a recurrence of the scurvy, but otherwise enjoyed good health. His teeth were firm and good till 1764, when he gave up the chewing of tobacco from motives of economy, and then lost the best of them in a few months.

When 116 years of age he went over the hills to fish, " but the snows came upon him and blocked up his way on every side. He gave himself up for lost. But he stuck his fishing-rod upright in the snow, and made another struggle for his

life, to a place where he was found. When he had recovered
he went back, plucked his rod out of the snow, and returned
to begin his new lease of seventeen years of life." ·"Dickens'
fishing story," adds my friend Mr Thomson, "looks queer.
Still I believe it can be reconciled as a fact, for in my own
recollection the summers were much hotter and the winters
more intense than at present. A snowstorm the end of September in these high regions would be nothing uncommon."

Latterly the seasons had a visible effect upon his frame. He
weakened in the course of latter winter and strengthened again
during the summer. In cold weather he found it necessary to
keep his bed, and take a glass of brandy once or twice a day
to warm his stomach. In October 1766, when 128 years old,
he walked from his own house to the village of Leadhills, two
miles of hilly road, and having entertained his children and
grandchildren together, returned the same day on foot. He
was a thin spare man, about 5 feet 8 inches high, black haired,
ruddy faced, and long visaged, had always a good appetite;
and when obliged to go to work—as miners are at all hours—
found no difficulty of making a hearty meal at midnight as at
midday. His breakfast was usually oatmeal porridge, dinner
meat and broth, and his chief drink malt liquor. At no period
of his life was he addicted to indulgence in intoxicating liquors,
and if his daily labour produced as much as supplied the wants
of his family and kept him out of debt, no man in the world
enjoyed life with a happier relish. "At length," says Chambers' account of him, "having been sometime craddled in a
second childhood, with hardly any remains of either bodily or
mental faculties, this veteran of 133 years expired in the
month of May 1770."

How strange must have been the meditations of this man,
ere his faculties gave way, regarding the conflicts and changes
of Church and State during his length of days! Born the
year before the second Reformation, he must have known of
the stirring struggles of the Covenanters, and of the grinding
despotism which not only ground them down, but which led
to the Revolution of 1688. The arrival of William of Orange,
and then the Union with England, which met with such
determined opposition north of the Tweed, were, however, all
over before his marriage in Islay; and he came to Leadhills
when the deposition of Ebenezer Erskine must have made
somewhat of a stir, although in those days little of it may
have been felt in the Southern Highlands.

A tall granite stone, surmounted by a Greek cross, is erected over the remains of Mr Grierson of Ogscastle and his parents. This is the only variation from the usual "head" or "throuch" stones. The graveyard is in a most disagreeable condition, the old system of raised graves being practised, and there being no walks, it is a most distressing operation to convey a corpse over them to its last resting-place. But the modern system of placing the earth dug out in wooden boxes at the grave mouth—ready to lift and let the mould fall in—has been adopted, and a visit by the miners to our modern cemeteries would be sufficient to convince them of the importance of having the mould laid and kept level, and of securing broad walks, so as to make this place of graves, instead of being a repulsive, an accessible and interesting spot.

PROVISION FOR THE POOR.

The Lady's Fund

consists of an endowment by a Countess of Hopetoun, which yields from £10 to £15 per annum, and is administered by Mr Gill, the agent of the Earl of Hopetoun. Last year thirty "old miners or miners' widows" received 10s. each in the month of August.

The poor used to receive a sum of £2, 10s., distributed on Quarter-day, in addition to 10s. for exigencies, the seventeen paupers in Leadhills being supported by the Earl of Hopetoun and collections at the chapel.

For the last three years there have been thirty-six registered poor, to whom, with six vagrants, £308, 18s. has been paid by the Parochial Board.

The Grierson Bequest for the Poor and Deserving Persons in Leadhills.

In the year 1873, James Grierson, Esq. of Ogscastle, son of William Grierson, miner in Leadhills, died. James having saved a little, went to America to push his fortune, but at first was so unfortunate as to be reduced to his last three-pence. Receiving some money he had left behind him, he began to trade with mules, and then by a strange turn of the wheel of fortune he continually prospered, till he scarce knew the amount. Having made his fortune in Buenos Ayres, and having no family, he bequeathed one-half of his estate for the benefit of the poor and of students attending the Edinburgh University. His trust-disposition and settlement of 22d March 1872, after disposing of two-fourths to his wife and relatives, says, "I direct my trustees to lay out and invest in such way and manner, and on such security heritable or personal, as they may deem proper, another fourth of said residue, and apply the annual proceeds thereof for the benefit of such poor and deserving persons residing in and natives of the parish of Leadhills as my trustees shall deem proper, with full power to them, should they consider it advisable, to transfer said fourth of said residue to the minister and kirk-session of the parish of Leadhills, in order that said minister and kirk-session may administer the same for the benefit of said poor and deserving persons , and the receipt of said fourth of said residue by the said minister and kirk-session shall be a sufficient exoneration and discharge to my trustees in regard to said fourth of said residue."

It is understood that this fourth has already realised the sum of £9250, and that eventually upwards of £5000 more may possibly be available for this object. So that, properly administered, this endowment ought to make a comfortable provision for poor and deserving persons in Leadhills second to none in Scotland.

This benefit is divided half yearly in sums of from £1 to £2, some seventy persons being participants. In this cheerless climate, where coals are expensive, being brought from afar, this fund cannot but promote comfort in many homes of the deserving poor.

EDUCATION.

The Leadhills school is managed by the School Board. There are over 200 scholars, with an average attendance of 180. Each miner, married or single, is rated at 1s. 8d. per quarter for school fees. It is well conducted by a male teacher with four pupil-teachers, a female teacher not being yet secured.

The school accommodation was recently extended, and an excellent schoolmaster's house is being erected at the expense of the Earl of Hopetoun.

THE GRIERSON BURSARIES.

Mr Grierson further directed, in regard to the fourth portion of his estate to be invested on security, " for the purpose of founding one or more bursaries in the University of Edinburgh, and which shall be known and called the Grierson Bursaries. The said bursaries to be in connection with the Faculties of Arts, Medicine, Law, and Divinity, as may from time to time be thought advisable. . . . Declaring always that in bestowing said bursaries a preference shall be given to young men natives of the parishes of Crawford and Leadhills."

This portion also realised £8000, and then it is understood that there may be £1250 more available.

The Senatus have apportioned (1) £100 yearly to the Faculty of Arts in four (five?) bursaries of £20 each. These are open to students entering the University for the first time, and in no other classes than the Junior Latin, Greek, or Mathematics, the preference to natives as above. (2) £100 to the Faculty of Law, one bursary of £40 and two of £30, with £40 open to competition. (3) £80 to the Faculty of Medicine. (4) £37, 10s. for competition in the Faculty of Theology, along with (5) two bursaries of £20 and £25 open to competition to students of the first year (see University Calendar).

The trustees appointed by Mr Grierson for the carrying out of these bequests were Mr Robert Grierson, merchant in Leadhills (deceased) ; Mr Archibald Kerr, merchant, Liverpool ; Mr Robert Paterson, Cameron Cottage, Lasswade ; and Mr John Ross, S.S.C., with power to appoint others in place of those deceased or discharged.

HOLDINGS.

The hill land reclaimed by the miners, from which good crops of hay are obtained, now measures nearly 394 imperial acres. And its value when sold is almost as high as the finest land in the Lothians. Upwards of 100 cows are possessed, which, under the care of herd-boys—who are fed by the owners in turn—browse upon the heathy hills in summer. The yield of butter is considered extra fine, and a large supply of milk is carried to Wanlockhead, where cows have become scarce.

There are 253 houses built in rows. Formerly these were low and thatched with heather, having a dismal appearance outside, and being ill-ventilated and unaccommodating within. Since 1861 nearly 220 cottages have been rebuilt or repaired by the miners themselves. In this work they have received

£600 in loans of from £12 to £20 at five per cent., and repayable at from 15s. to 20s. per quarter, from the company. These cottages are now roofed with Welsh slate, are higher in the ceiling, and more commodious generally. Their whitewashed walls, and in some cases tasteful borders, give a cheerful aspect to the place. These cottages are not only held rent-free, but are accounted, with their crofts, the property of the miners, which they are permitted to dispose of when they leave the place, or cease to require them, although all property in the village is held without lease at the pleasure of the Earl of Hopetoun.

That (1) generous assistance, together with (2) permission to sell house or property, and the fact that, (3) in addition to a fair wage, the full benefit of finding a good piece of lead in their workings is given to the miners, have made Leadhills one of the most prosperous of Scottish villages.

The property remains in the right of the Earl of Hopetoun, and changes are subject to the approval of John Gill, Esq., bailiff and lead agent on behalf of the Earl. But the people have unbounded confidence, both in this gentleman and in the Hopetoun family. Some years ago a plentiful supply of water was introduced, the people willingly paying their share of the expense, and they showed their gratitude for the assistance received by collecting gold for the Countess.

A BRANCH OF GOOD TEMPLARS,

instituted in 1872, has increased from 16 to 87 members, with 117 juveniles; the working of which, in addition to a tax of 3d. for males and 1½d. for females per quarter for the Grand Lodge, involves an expenditure of upwards of £17, defrayed by weekly contributions.

MUSIC.

A brass band has existed for some years, and sacred music is cultivated in a class, conducted by the precentor of the Established Church, and a Sol-fa Association by Mr Galbraith.

A VOLUNTEER CORPS

(No. 107), J. F. Nevin, captain, was formed in 1875. It numbers 81 young men, including the 15 members of the band. They are regularly drilled by Sergeant Swain.

LEADHILLS CURLING CLUB

consists of seven rinks. It has friendly contests with Crawford and the Lanarkshire Curling Clubs, &c., gaining generally all the games played for, and carrying off four medals. The possession of curling-stones is looked forward to with great interest by the young men; and boys are beheld on frosty days pulling or carrying these heavy granite toys up the hills, or upon the ice, besom in hand, sweeping lustily, and apparently forgetting that there is such a thing as cold.

A FLOWER, CATTLE, AND POULTRY SHOW,

by Mr Nevin's exertions, has had considerable success, and has stimulated the rearing of stock and of vegetables. Some £18 are expended in prizes.

SAVINGS BANK.

The Post Office was opened for Savings Bank business, March 2d, 1863. Number of depositors' accounts, 108—of which 60 were open and 48 closed to the 31st December 1873.

		£	s.	d.
Amount due to depositors, Jan. 1, 1873,	.	446	12	1
„ of deposits in 1873,	. . .	194	7	0
„ of interest,	. . . . .	10	7	5
		£651	6	6
„ of withdrawals in 1873,	. .	193	5	6
„ due to depositors, Dec. 31, 1873,	.	£458	1	0

Under the attentive care of Mr and Mrs Newbigging, the transactions have since increased; and the more the advantages of opening a personal account are considered, young men will refrain from thoughtless and useless squandering of their money. A considerable deposit is also found in a branch of the Commercial Bank recently opened at Leadhills.

Letters are conveyed by a daily runner from Abington, and thence by another to Wanlockhead, every lawful day, who return with despatches in the afternoon. Telegraphic communication between Sanquhar and Leadhills was opened in 1873, which, with Post-Order Office, might easily be granted to Wanlockhead Post Office.

DANGER FROM EXPLOSIVES.

The workmen being generally steady and thoughtful, accidents from explosives are of rare occurrence. Powder has been mostly employed, and gun-cotton tried has found little favour. Latterly dynamite has been much used, except in places that are badly ventilated, and hitherto without accident. An explosion, however, occurred on the 21st February 1876, by which a young miner and his sister were badly hurt, and the house and furniture wrecked. Indeed it seemed a miracle that they escaped alive. It was the first time he intended to use it, and while putting on his mining garments, he incautiously put the pieces of dynamite to heat upon the "hob" of the fire. His sister was toasting bread upon the girdle, and he tying his shoes with his back to the fire, when the explosion occurred.

This seems to have arisen from a false impression, that unless in addition to a certain amount of heat, *a knock be given* to the cartridge, it will not explode. It cannot be matter of surprise that the inexperienced should entertain that idea, when such an intelligent person as Mr Downie, the manager of the Dynamite Co., held the same opinion to his own destruction. A cargo of dynamite had been found to be damaged by sea-water upon its arrival in Ireland. Instructions were issued from the works in Ayrshire to unship it by a skilful workman, and throw it into the sea. Mr Downie undertook the duty himself. To convince the engineer and others how safe it was, and that without a blow it would fuse away upon the fire without exploding, he began to pitch piece after piece upon the fire, when all at once it went off, and blew him to atoms out of the door into the sea, so that his remains were never beheld. A Mr Prentice, at Stowmarket, is also said to have met with his death in a similar manner. It thus appears that when the glycerine flows by heat, explosion ensues without the blow; this occurs when slowly heated to 420° Fahrenheit.

The miners generally carry it in their pockets to the mines, the natural heat of the person being sufficient to prepare it for the shock given by firing the fuse. The explosion is very powerful, *striking down* while powder strikes up. It will also effect its work if the bore-hole be simply filled with loose sand or water. Thus because of its great power, and adaptation to wet workings, it is much in use, although some say that it is more costly : dynamite costing 2s., while powder is but 5d. per lb.

This is another proof that even cautious men become fool-hardy in continually working with dangerous materials. Most explicit directions—printed in English, Gaelic, and Welsh—are given with every case of dynamite ; and these ought to be not only inculcated, but inspection made as to whether the regulations are observed. They are to the effect that it ought not to be thawed otherwise than by warm water, and at a safe distance from dwelling-houses, &c.—*never near fires or hot-plates, never put into warm water ; but into a water-tight vessel, and that vessel put into warm water.* Safe warm-water warming-pans are to be had, but are seldom used. Iron rammers are also to give place to wooden in the use of the dynamite cartridges, and very careful clear directions are given as to the mode of attaching fuse and percussion-cap, and of firing it with safety.

CENSUS OF CRAWFORD, CRAWFORDJOHN, AND LEADHILLS, 1871.

	Separate Families.	Houses.			Persons.			Children aged 5 to 18 receiving Education.	Rooms with one or more Windows.	Temporarily absent.			Temporarily present.		
		Inhabited.	Uninhabited.	Building.	Male.	Female.	Total.			Male.	Female.	Total.	Male.	Female.	Total.
CRAWFORD* .	412	374	14	6	928	901	1829	289	958	7	12	19	16	6	22
CRAWFORDJOHN†	181	166	10	3	394	459	853	118	567	4	14	18	12	10	22
With Ecclesiastical Subdivision.															
CRAWFORD . .	148	132	9	2	360	364	7 4	119	432	...	...	...	...	...	...
CRAWFORDJOHN	179	164	10	3	390	455	845	118	561	...	...	...	...	...	...
LEADHILLS, *q.s.*‡	266	244	5	4	572	541	1113	170	512	...	...	...	...	...	...
Leadhills Village . . .	249	227	5	4	526	507	1033	164	484	...	...	...	...	...	...
Registration Districts.															
CRAWFORD— Crawford .	149	133	9	2	362	365	727	...	434	...	...	...	...	...	...
Leadhills .	263	241	5	4	566	536	1102	...	404	...	...	...	...	...	...
CRAWFORDJOHN	181	166	10	3	394	459	853	...	567	...	...	...	...	...	...

ROOMS WITH WINDOWS.

	1.	2.	3.	4.	5.	6.	7.	8.	9.	10.	11 to 15.	16 to 20.
CRAWFORD— (1.) Crawford	27	65	21	10	5	3	4	1	1	1	5	1
(2.) Leadhills	112	126	7	7	2	4	2	...	1	...	...	2
CRAWFORDJOHN	70	32	26	18	11	9	4	6	1	...	3	...

* 65,407 acres.　　　　† 26,357 acres.
‡ Population of part of Crawford, 1105 ; and of part of Crawfordjohn, 8 ; total, 1113.

WANLOCKHEAD.

WANLOCKHEAD MINERS.

" *A lanely wee toun,*
Far hid amang hills o' the heather sae broon ;
Wi' its hooses reel-rall, keekin' oot at ilk turn
Like an ill-cuisten crap in the howe o' the burn.
Ane here and ane there, wi' a fitroad atween,
In the daftest construction that ever was seen.
And there the cauld Winter first comes wi' his snaw,
And he likes it sae weel that he's laith to gae 'wa' ;
For there's three months o' bluister tae ilk ane o' sun,
And the dour nippin' cranreuch's* maist aye on the grun'.
Ay, whiles the corn's green on the lallan's, they say,
Or the hinmaist snaw-wreath dwines awa' on the brae."

ROBERT REID.

THE Wanlock or Gray-Glen runs in a south-easterly direction up from the Crawick stream for four miles towards the Lowther Mountains. The designation is very apt in pointing out the dreary aspect of heather, bent, and shingle which alone meet the eye on the hillsides, and the covering of thick grey mist or " white rouk " with which it is so frequently enveloped. The Wanlock stream, though fed by numerous rills, partakes of the same grey or bluish-white colour from its previous service in the preparation of the lead.

Near to the head of the stream, and clustering round the base of the Dod Hill, as two sides of a triangle, lies the village of Wanlockhead, which occupies the north-east corner of the civil parish of Sanquhar. It contains 176 houses, of which only twelve have a second flat. They used to be mostly thatched with heather, but these roofs are now giving place to the slate. Although requiring frequent repair, the thatched cottages, with a "but and a ben," constructed with box beds

---

* Hoarfrost.

and inner doors, were warmer, and probably better adapted to this high and cold locality exposed to penetrating winds. These, formerly rebuilt by the miners, used to be held as their own property so long as their descendants remained in the village. Now cottages are only rebuilt by the proprietor, for which the nominal rent of barely $2\frac{1}{2}$ per cent. on the outlay is charged. Forty new cottages have been erected since 1835.

The Rev. R. M. M'Cheyne, who visited Wanlockhead in 1841, after a recent visit to the Holy Land, stated that this village impressed him as being very similar to Hebron, near to which Abraham dwelt. The late Dr Simpson described it thus: " An ancient place, but still more interesting than ancient. The village is squatted at the head of a lonely glen and in the heart of a batch of mountains that rise to a great height, between the counties of Lanark and Dumfries." On the occasion of the visit of the Prince of Wales to Drumlanrig in 1871, huge bonfires were lighted up on the tops of two of these mountains, the East Lowther and Auchenlone, the workmen giving their labour gratuitously.

It is rather singular that no road has been formed along the gentle ascent of the Wanlock from that which passes at its foot from Sanquhar to Crawfordjohn; especially as one comes down to the smelting-works about a mile and a half below the village, passing the graveyard and village of Meadowfoot; but it is hoped that railway connection may yet be obtained by this easy route. Communication is maintained with Sanquhar, nine miles distant, by the hill-paths of Glendyne or Cogshead, and by road through the Mennock valley, entered by a narrow pass or " hass," reached from the village by a steep ascent. Two cottages are about 1500 feet above sea-level.

At present the works give employment to—Manager, overseers, and clerks, 5 ; miners, 112 ; labourers, 36 ; ore-washers, 11 ; boys, 36 ; blacksmiths, 4 ; joiners, 4 ; woodmen (in mines), 4 ; smelters, 15 ; refiners, 15 ; other hands, 32—total, 274. In addition to their employment as miners, several have little shops, and are butchers, tailors, cloggers, &c. The miners have also reclaimed a considerable amount of hill-land, so as to yield hay for their cows. They enjoy the right to pasture cows and sheep on about 500 acres of heather and coarse grazing-land, round the village, at the nominal rent of £25. The women at one time earned a considerable sum at muslin work, but since its failure those not required for household duties at home are drafted into service.

The village doctor is supported principally by the Duke of Buccleuch, and has an excellent house. Medicines and the doctor's salary, except what is derived from a deduction of 4s. per annum from each workman, are provided by his Grace.

A good school, for male and female teachers, a schoolmaster's house, and nearly the full endowment, are also provided, those having children in attendance being required merely to pay a nominal fee for their education. The school has not been put under the Board, and is not yet subject to official inspection. A miner is a kind of deputy policeman, but the post is a sinecure, as crime and poaching are almost unknown. There is no inn and no bakery in the village.

REMUNERATION AND THE POOR.

For a long period the miners rejoiced in the privilege of supporting their own poor, 1s. out of every £5 earned being put into "the box" for occasional demands. Another plan was termed "The Old Men and Widows' Bargains." When a man was too old to go down into the mines, a substitute or "forehead labourer" took his place at 10d. per day, as one of the company or partnership of eight or sixteen men who bargained to work a certain portion of the mines. This, along with a "venture" above ground after his six hours below, sufficed for his subsistence, whilst the aged miner received his share of the concern, subject to this deduction of 10d. per day. This plan allowed old people to live respectably and comfortably, each deriving an annual benefit of from £12 to £18. On the death of any miner his widow received this benefit for a year and a half. If he was killed in the mines, this benefit was retained by the widow during her lifetime. As it has long been customary to marry very early (and mostly among themselves), it was a hard struggle to bring up a family; but when the aged miner retired with his pension, his children were generally in the way of doing for themselves. And not only did the miners profit by this arrangement; whilst most creditably maintaining a healthy spirit of independence in the support of their own poor, the master of the works shared in the benefit. Lads who had served for some years in washing the lead ore were put into these bargains when advancing to maturity, and served another apprenticeship as miners, so that it used to be

113 H

confessed that, generally, miners as well qualified could scarcely be met with elsewhere. Whether this want may not be felt, and compensation require to be made, remains to be tested. The young men at that time cheerfully accepted their position in the expectation that they themselves would participate eventually in the advantage. Owing to some misunderstanding, in 1870 this very creditable and benevolent practice terminated, and the poor of the village were, much against their wishes, placed upon the Parochial Board. Were it possible to return to that method, most of them would rejoice. And still there is, by a gift of coals to the poor in the winter (which are driven by the manager's permission), a manifestation of the same benevolent intention on the part of the people. The poor's roll, adjusted in May 1872, shows thirteen, and those of 1873 and 1874 give eighteen persons connected with Wanlockhead who are more or less aided by the Board.

A change took place in the system of payments at the close of 1870. Although not, strictly speaking, within the scope of the Truck Commission, it reported that whilst "there was no reason to believe that, apart from the system, the men were otherwise than kindly treated, little doubt can be entertained as to the great evils of an arrangement by which men receive in January 1871 the balance of wages due to them since January 1869, while in the interval goods on credit are supplied to them by their employer and their employer's servants. The lead mines at Wanlockhead ought, in our opinion, to be brought within the Truck Acts." This was unnecessary, as a change immediately took place, the settlement being now quarterly, with £2, 10s. a month in advance for "subsist;" and generally the change is for the better. Some left the place, tempted by the rise in wages in coal and iron districts; but although no corresponding advance was obtained here, able-bodied men were never so comfortable as under the present manager. The average earnings of the miners will be as much by their week of five days as can be obtained by a surface labourer—indeed higher, as the miners have generally full work the year round. An average of 19s. for day-wage men, and 21s. for miners, is supposed to be reached. Notwithstanding, some think the men were as strong, healthy, and comfortable in the old times when such luxuries as tea and toast were unknown, and porridge, potatoes, and peameal bannocks formed the staple fare, while wages were comparatively low.

The miners of Wanlockhead have for centuries maintained a high character, not only for honest industry, but for intelligence and moral worth.

One proof of superior intelligence and energy is furnished in the fact that the first trial of steamboat navigation on Dalswinton Loch, about 1786, was the work of three men drawn from thence. James Taylor, grandson of the very aged man referred to, and graduate of Edinburgh University in 1785, became tutor in the family of Mr Patrick Miller of Dalswinton. Being conversant with the steam-engines of this district, he contended with Mr Miller that steam-engines alone were powerful enough to propel vessels through the water, who at length sent for William Symington, engineer, and John Hutchison, blacksmith, from Wanlockhead, to make the machinery, which was fitted to a small vessel. Mr William Symington was a schoolfellow of James Taylor's, who introduced him as an ingenious young man. In 1787 Mr Miller published a description of a triple vessel propelled with paddle-wheels moved by cranks, originally intended to be worked by men. In 1789 Mr Symington was employed to construct one on the Forth and Clyde Canal, which, destroying the banks, was removed. It has been said that the family of Mr Miller, Lord Brougham, and the poet Burns were present at the first trial on Dalswinton Loch.

John Taylor, who was manager for the company at Wanlockhead, was considered to be the most eminent engineer ever known in the locality. Many of his operations remain an enduring monument of his genius and industry, such as the cutting of a level to bring water through below "the Hass" from the Mennock to the Wanlock valley. On one occasion the mines were very low. At Belton-grain, had the cutting gone on as usual, no lead would have been found, and the enterprise would have been abandoned. Taylor was persuaded that it existed on a lower level, and when the company demurred, offered to make trial at his own expense. Then twenty fathoms lower a rich vein was struck, yielding four times the amount obtained in any vein now wrought. By these and other exact calculations and energetic labours, John Taylor may be said to have laid the foundation of permanent prosperity for the mines of Wanlockhead.

Mrs Taylor, the widow of J. Taylor, on account of his application of the steam-engine to navigation, received £50 and then £100 from Government.

" The people have deeply engraven on their hearts a love for their native place and all her historic associations ; and I have noticed," says one of their descendants, " that all the natives of these lonely villages have a deep-rooted veneration for everything, and even every one who belongs to them— rivalling the clanships of our Celts, without their ferocity."

Wanlockhead has produced some distinguished men for various departments of active service in Church and State— editors, ministers, missionaries, lawyers, &c. Smollett, the author of the continuation of the history of England, while residing with his sister, Mrs Telfer, in what is now the Duke's shooting lodge, wrote his not very admirable " Humphrey Clinker."

SOCIAL HABITS

are to some extent cultivated. Friends assemble to eat the " blythe-meat " at births and christenings. Formerly, but not now, a pound of tea was known to suffice for a large party at the marriage-table, blythe-meat, christening, and during the interval. When any accident occurs, all private differences are laid aside ; sympathy and willing assistance are universal. Coffins for the dead are supplied from the workshop, partners dig the grave and perform other last offices, so that a trifle to the keeper of the mortcloth is the only absolute expense incurred.

A marriage at the village is generally an occasion of rejoicing, and is the chief topic discussed for a length of time. When a member of the band is married, the whole population turn out to witness the procession. Sounds of martial music are heard in the distance, and then more plainly reverberating amongst the hills, until, preceded by the brass band of the village, the bridegroom and his party of friends are conducted to the cottage of the bride's friends. By her side the bridegroom takes his place ; and in reply to the questioning of the village pastor, and in the presence of as many friends as can be crowded into the little kitchen, he vows to be unto her a faithful and loving husband till death should part them. The necessary document being duly signed and attested, congratulations over, refreshments partaken of, there and in the other cottages filled with friends, pence collected and handed to the minister, the bestman then comes forward and offers his arm to the bride to head the procession, which, two and two, goes forward, the bridegroom being brought on at the end by the father, along with the minister. The band in their smart apparel, having formed at the door, precedes, playing their liveliest tunes. The bride, of course, is the centre of attraction, especially to the wives and daughters, who, plaids over head, press forward to get a close inspection; and such notes of admiration are heard as "Eh! but she is braw and bonnie!" Arrived at the new dwelling, which has been plenished with drawers, cupboard, presents, and necessaries, the new wife, who is saluted with a shower of oatcakes, is led to the fireside to "poke the ribs" with the tongs, in proof that she has taken possession; and then, again, at the head of the procession, the company are at length seated at tables laden with good things in a room or rooms—(no proper hall being as yet possessed.) These having been partaken of, the company, crossing their arms and joining hands, sing—

> " Weel may we a' be,
> Ill may we never see ;
> God bless the Queen,
> And this companie."

Three times this is repeated—" to fl'ie the rattens"—with rounds of applause, and then, the ceremonies being concluded in truly orthodox fashion, the minister retires, and the ladies prepare for the evening's enjoyment.

Relaxation is indulged in by fishing, chiefly in the Clyde. One of the choicest relaxations to a miner is *a "night's" fishing*—for although the whole of the following day may be occupied in thrashing the waters, he sets away over the Lowthers to the Daer or Powtrail in the afternoon, spending the night in the delightful exercise. The manly games of running, wrestling, putting the stone, quoiting in summer, and curling during winter, are also cultivated.

THE CURLING

is detailed by Mr James Brown in his "History of the Sanquhar Curling Society:"—

"In 1777 a document, drawn up in quite an official and diplomatic style, records that the subscribers—William Gilchrist, Alexander Miller, &c., of Wanlockhead—had been duly initiated into the secret of the craft by the Sanquhar Society, and enrolled as members, the usual condition being imposed upon them that they should not divulge the secret to any one, or take it upon them to confer the degree of the order. A number of curlers at Wanlockhead having made application to these members for admission, an application was presented to have the restrictions placed upon them removed, and the power conferred upon them of admitting new members, and giving them the 'word.' The application was granted. . . .

"The distance between the two places necessarily led to the formation of a separate society, and since 1831 games between the two societies have been of frequent occurrence. It became a rule between them to play their games at Sanquhar and Wanlockhead alternately, regardless of who was winner or loser—a departure from the ordinary rule of the losers going to the ice belonging to the winners. Games between Sanquhar and New Cumnock began in 1844. The wide extent of the latter, and her great command of men, rendered the possibility of Sanquhar competing with her at her full strength with any prospect of success extremely problematical, and New Cumnock declined to break her numbers. Sanquhar determined, however, to make a gallant attempt, and while her own enrolled strength was at the time only seven rinks of eight men each, she had to muster eighteen rinks of nine men. Every available man who could be got who had ever thrown a stone, however slight his acquaintance with the art, was pressed into the service. So urgent, indeed, was the call that some who had never even played a stone were taken out the previous evening, and by the light of the moon received their first lesson. The want of stones was no less severely felt than the want of men ; and many a weaver's 'pace' (stones which were hung on the beam for the purpose of keeping the web on the stretch, to which use old and disused curling-stones were frequently put) was unstrung, while others were hauled out from among the coals below the bed (a common place for the storing of coals in those days), their soles, it may well be conceived, not being in the best condition. With such raw recruits and weapons the greater part of the Sanquhar players were 'harried' —could not reach the 'tee.' One rink was 'soutered,' and others trembling on the very brink.

"The disaster was most complete, Sanquhar falling by 168 shots, crushed by sheer force of numbers. The help of Wanlockhead was adopted—Wanlockhead being part of the parish of Sanquhar. The aid asked was promptly rendered, and quickly the change was felt. Now the parties were on somewhat equal terms. In 1847 the 168 shots were reduced to 12, and in 1848 converted into a victory for Sanquhar by 2 shots, since which time down to 1867, when circumstances had again deprived her of the help of Wanlockhead, Sanquhar kept her honour bright.

"The 'foreign spiel,' as it was called at Wanlockhead, was an event which caused great excitement in the village, and in which the women even greatly interested themselves. Up betimes in the morning, and well breakfasted, with a 'comforter' from 'Noble's' in the pocket, and well-trimmed besom in hand, they set out, and from the summit of Sanquhar moor (which was the usual scene of action) on a hard, crisp, frosty morning, the mist creeping gradually up the hillside and disappearing above the horizon like a ball of fire, to see them come in sight over the distant hill-top or come pouring down Glendyne and Mennock, reminded one strongly of the scenes so graphically described by our late lamented townsman, Dr Simpson, of those days when our Covenanted forefathers were wont to wend their way over these same hills to the conventicle in some quiet, moorland spot.

"Tall, strapping young men, strong and hardy, they possessed every quality necessary to make good curlers. Their discipline, too, was absolutely perfect. At the time when there were eight men in a rink, this was most apparent. Arranged three and three on each side of the rink, they waited with the greatest attention till the stone was delivered, following it quietly, but eagerly, in its course, till, at the call of the skip, 'soop her up,' down came the besoms like lightning, hands were clasped, the feet kept time to the rapid strokes of the besom, and no exertion was spared until the stone was landed at the desired spot, when a good long breath being drawn, the player was rewarded with a universal shout, 'Weel played, mon!' All who have seen Wanlockhead curlers play will admit that in the matter of sweeping they 'bear the gree.'

"In Kinglake's 'History of the Crimean War,' notice is taken of the different sounds that proceed from the soldiers of different nations when engaged in battle. It is said, too, that in the British army the roar or cry given forth by the regiment belonging to the different nationalities of which it is made up—English, Scotch, and Irish—is as distinct and marked as are the characteristics of the different races. In the same way the sound proceeding from a rink of Wanlockhead curlers was unmistakable, and not for a moment to be confounded with any other.

"Better curlers we need not hope to see, and more trusty allies Sanquhar curlers could not desire to have. One of their old veterans, hearing that a neighbouring parish, which had been experiencing an extraordinary run of success, thrashing everybody round about, and, Alexander-like, beginning to despair of finding an equal on this lower sphere, threatened to challenge *the moon*, exclaimed, 'Tell them to ca' at Wanlockhead on the road up.' We agree in thinking that probably they would have been saved the journey further."

BENEFIT ASSOCIATIONS, ETC.

The principle of association for mutual benefit, long acted upon in this district, is further evidence of the mental and moral worth of this community of mountaineers. (1.) The "Leadhills Reading Society" was instituted November 23d, 1741; that of Wanlockhead in November 1756. The payment of 5s. constitutes a member, and 2s. being the annual subscription, the advantages of a varied supply of books on arts, science, philosophy, biography, history (civil, ecclesiastical, and natural), law and politics, religion, travels, voyages, poetry, plays, &c., are brought within the reach of all. There are 2470 volumes in the library, and 68 readers—fewer by far than formerly. This reading society has been of incalculable benefit. (2.) The miners' first worker's society was founded on February 16th, 1862, with 140 members. Each member on the sick list had his work kept up for twelve months, each member working a shift in his turn; and any member who was unable for his work by an accident in the mines got his work wrought for eighteen months. This society was closed at the end of 1870. The second, or Friendly Society, was founded in January 1871. The number of members at present is 134. Each member pays into the society 14s. per annum, and the sick benefit per week is 8s. for the first three months, 6s. for the next nine months, and 4s. for the next six months, and 2s. per week for any length of continued sickness. (3.) The Heather Bell Lodge of the Independent Order of Odd-fellows, a branch of the Manchester Friendly Society, was opened at Wanlockhead April 19th, 1867. At December 1874 there were 191 subscribing members. The amount of funds at same date was £397, 19s. 4½d. The sick benefit to members is 8s. per week for six months, 4s. per week for the next six months, and 2s. per week for any continued illness. The funeral gifts are—for members, £8, and £4 for a member's wife. Besides an initiation fee, the monthly contribution varies from 1s. to 2s., according to age, there being thirteen monthly contributions per annum. (4.) A few individuals are also members of a similar Forester's Benefit Society, which has also a gala day, marching in procession with green sashes and banners through the two villages. Formal ceremonies are also gone through at the funeral of members. This "Allan Ramsay" Court in Leadhills admits to membership on payment of a fee varying from 5s. to 14s., and 1s. to 1s. 4d. of a monthly sick fund. The benefits are 9s. per week for 26 weeks, 7s. 6d. for the next 26 weeks, and 5s. per week for the remainder of sickness, with £12 for a member's funeral, and £7 for a member's wife.

Upwards of twenty years ago a public-house was conjoined with the toll-house, and scenes of riot were occasionally witnessed. Toll and public-house both have been abolished. Confirmed drunkards are almost unknown, but after the quarter's settlement needless visits are often paid to Lead-hills.

CO-OPERATIVE SOCIETY.

In the beginning of 1871 the former meal store was handed over to the miners by the Duke of Buccleuch, who has since enlarged the building for their accommodation. A Co-operative Society was instituted, and has since been carried on by the miners with marked success. The following general statement of its affairs was rendered to the Registrar in February 1875 : Number of members, 160 (in 1875, 180); amount of share capital in £1 shares, £432, 7s. (now £507); cash received for goods during the year ended, £1823, 15s. 3½d. (in 1875, £3458, 17s. 11½d.); average stock-in-trade, £145, 11s. 0¼d.; entire liabilities, £505, 15s. 3d.; do. assets, £544, 10s. 9½d.; value of fixtures, £20; disposable profit, £62, 4s. 4½d.; reserve fund, £12, 4s. 4½d. Dividend declared to members, 5 per cent. with 1s. 6d. bonus per £ on purchases; 1s. 4d. at the Leadhills Store.*

A Young Men's Association for Mutual Improvement was formed in January 1873, by means of readings, conversations, essays, social meetings, and lectures—courses being delivered in the winter months. The management is conducted by a committee of 12, the two ministers being consulting members. Its finances for a year were—receipts, £11, 6s. 7d.; expended, £3, 15s. for coals for the poor, and £4, 18s. 10d. for soirées and association expenses—leaving a balance of £2, 12s. 9d. There are upwards of 40 members. A similar association was organised in Leadhills. A Sabbath Morning Fellowship Association also meets in Wanlockhead. Cottage prayer-meetings, tract distributing, &c., are also in operation.

BRASS BAND.

A band of instrumental music has been in existence for several years, consisting of 14 members. In 1871 the band were presented with a magnificent set of brass instruments by the Duke of Buccleuch, made by the celebrated Mr Besson, London, costing, it is understood, nearly £90. It consists, with large drum, of 14 pieces—viz., 6 cornets, 1 baritone, 1 euphonium, 2 E-flat saxhorns, 2 E-flat bombardons, 1 tenor trombone, and 1 E-flat clarionette. The band had also the

* See Appendix for other statistics.

assistance of an able master for nearly two years by the kindness of his Grace. On fête-days, as the annual games in June, society or Sabbath-school walks, the marriages of its members, &c., the strains of the band are heard resounding amongst the hills.

It is expected that, in accordance with their petition, a hall for reading-room and other purposes will be erected by his Grace.

The miners at Wanlockhead, some thirty-four years ago, possessed the privileges which have so highly promoted the advancement of Leadhills and the comfort of families. Those who reclaimed land from the hill by patient, toilful industry, or erected cottages by personal labour and expense, were entitled to these properties, not only to be heired by relatives, but, if necessary, to be sold or let. And in reply to a petition, the miners were informed " that whatever privileges they enjoyed under the Marquis of Bute, the same would they possess under his Grace of Buccleuch." Unfortunately that document was lost; and first sanction was required as to the party coming into possession, and eventually, when the key or the land was required, it had to be given up, otherwise employment ceased. Besides, the miners complain that no adequate compensation has been received in several cases. Consequently, little or no land has since then been reclaimed, many have been disheartened or have left, and the village has fallen behind its sister. Still, in all this no blame is thrown upon the proprietor; the general impression being that were there a resident bailiff, such as Mr Gill, to act on behalf of his Grace, these and other grievances, real or supposed, would be rectified.

OBLIGATION ON THE PART OF THE CONTRACTORS FOR WORKING THE LEAD MINES OF GLENGONNER AND WENLOCK-HEAD, IN THE REIGN OF QUEEN MARY.

(Copied from the books of Privy Council.)

"Apud Edinbur^t, xxiij Januarii, Anno lxij°, &c.

" In presence of the Quenis Majestie and Lordis of Secrete Counsale, comperit Johne Achisone, maister comyeor, and Johne Aslowane burges of Edinburgh, and gaif in this thair band vnderwritten, and desirit the samin to be insert in the bukis of Secrete Counsale, with lettres and executorialis of horning or poinding to be gevin therupoun for compelling of thame to fulfill the samin in forme as efferis. Quhilk desire the Quenis Hienes and Lordis forsaidis thocht ressonable and therfore ordanit the samin to be insert in the saidis bukis, with lettres and executorialis to be gevin in maner theron foirsaid. Off the quhilk the tennour followis. We, Johne Achisone and Johne Aslowane burges of Edinburgh, be the tennour heirof, bindis and oblissis ws faithfullie to the Quenis Majestie, and hir Hienes thesaurar, in hir name, Forsamekill as hir Grace hes grantit and gevin licence to ws, oure partinaris and seruandis in our name, to wirk and wyn in the leid mynis of Glengoner and Wenlok, samekil leid vre as we may gudlie : and to transport and carie furth of this realm to Flanderis, or ony vtheris partis beyond sey, twenty thousand stane wecht of the said leid vre, comptand sex scoir to the hundreth trone wecht, comprehenhand therein five thousand stane wecht of the said vre, ellis send be ws to Flanderis, as hir Hienes licence grantit to ws thairupoun beris. Hierfoir we bind and obliss ws faith-fullie to the Quenis Majestie, and hir said thesaurar in hir name, to deliver to hir Graces comyiehous, betuix this and the first day of August nixt to cum, fourtie five vnce of vter fyne siluer for every thousand stane wecht of the saidis tuentie thousand stanis of leid vre, extending in the hale to nyne hundreth vnces of vter fyne siluer, without ony forther delay. And heirto we bind and obliss ws faithfullie be thir presentis, and ar content that this oure obligatioun be actit and registrat in the bukis of Secrete Counsale, with lettres and executorialis of horning and poinding, to be gevin therupon, for compelling of ws to fulfill the samin in form as efferis. Subscribit with our handis, at Edinburgh, the xxiij day of Januar, the zeir of God I^{m}V^{c} lxij zeris."

A CONTRACT BETWIXT HENRY AND MARIE, KING AND QUEEN OF SCOTS, AND JOHN EARL OF ATHOLL, dated at Edinburgh, the 26th August 1565, is preserved in the General Register House, by which "thair Majesties hes gevin and grantit, and be the tennour heirof, gevis and grantis licence to the said Erle, his assignais, factouris, and servandis, ane or ma, to wyn, or cause to wyn, fourtly thousand trone stane wecht, comptand sex scoir stanis for ilk hundreth off leid ure, and mair gif the samin may gudlie be wyn within the nether leid hoill of Glengonare and Wynlock ; now occupiit be Johne Ache-soun and Johne Aslowane, for the space of fyve yeris, nixt efter the dait heirof," &c.—"For the quhilkis causis the said Erle oblesis him and his airis, to pay to thair Majesties, thair thesaurare now present or being for the tyme, or to quhome thair Hienessis sall depute to that effect, for every thowsand stane wecht, trone wecht as saidis, of the said leid ure, fiftie unces of fyne silver, in maner and at the termis following," &c.

This is signed by

MARIE R. HENRY R.
JHONE, ERLL OF ATHOLL.

A LEASE TO OTHER PARTIES is also preserved, in which "it is appoyntit, contractit, and finalie endit betuix the richt hicht and Illustre Princessis Henrie and Marie, King and Queen of Scottis, on that ane part, and James Carmichaell, Maister James Lyndsay, and Andro Stevinsone, burgessis of Edinburgh, on the uther part, as followis, That is to say, thair Majesties hes gevin and grantit licence, and be the tennour heirof, gevis and grantis licence to the saidis burgessis, thair partinaris, assignayis, factouris and servandis, ane or ma, to win, or caus be win, fourtie thousand stane wecht, comptand sex scoir stanis for ilk hunder of leid ure, and mair gif the samin may gudlie be win out of ony ground within this realme ; Saifand the mynd and werk of Glengonar and Wenlok, presentlie occupeit be Johne Achesone and Johne Asloane, and that for the space of ten yeiris, nixt efter the dait heirof, and to transport and cary the samin furth of this realme, to the partis of Flan-ders, or ony uther partis quhair thai pleis during the said space," &c. Paying to their Majesties "for every thousand stane wecht, trone wecht transporting as saidis, of the said leid ure, fourtie fywe uncis fyne silver," &c.

This is subscribed by

MARIE R. HENRY R.   MR JAMES LYNDESAY.
JAMES CARMICHAELL.   ANDRO STEVINSOUN.

SANQUHAR.

Part III.

THE "OLD TOWN" PARISH.

" I am a bending, aged tree,
That long has stood the wind and rain ;
But now has come a cruel blast,
And my last hold of earth is gane.
Nae leaf o' mine shall greet the spring,
Nae simmer sun exalt my bloom ;
But I maun lie before the storm,
And ithers plant them in my room." BURNS.

THE Dumfriesshire Parish of Sanquhar embraces all round seven parishes and three counties, besides that to which it belongs. It measures 15 miles between its two principal heights ; 10 miles from its northern to its southern point ; and 6½ miles in breadth from the points where the river Nith meets with and parts from the parish. Its outline is very irregular, and when regarded from its W.S.E. point of view is not unlike the face and neck of an old Scotch " grannie " stretched aloft to watch the approach of some enemy from the south. The Royal Burgh of Sanquhar lies in the north-west centre of the parish, almost equidistant from the sea-coast, 27 miles north of Dumfries, and 33 miles south-west of Ayr.

The parish is divided into two sections of high lands by a lovely valley, which acts as a natural drain by means of

THE RIVER NITH.

It rises out of the spur of Bendeoch, near Dalmellington, and runs west for 10 miles. If continued, it would have fallen into the Clyde. Its course was changed by upheaval of strata. A Countess of Dumfries, wishing to divert it westward, was prevented. (One of the lochs at the Cumnocks still flows both ways.) Flowing for 20 miles, it runs tortuously north-west to south-east for 7 miles through this parish, thereby receiving six tributaries (three on each side) on its way to the Solway Firth. Though low in summer, the Nith is at times an object of grandeur, and even of terror and destruction. Rocky obstructions prevent many salmon from ascending so far, but trout are to be had in the various streams and burns. The "Yochan" may have received its name from one of the three Pictish kings who bore that title.

The high hills either rise out of each other, and lead to the formation of long winding valleys, as that of the Mennock Pass or Glendyne, or they are conical and frequently elliptical or oval in their form.

OLD DESCRIPTIONS.

In an account of the Presbytery of Penpont by the Rev. Mr Black, minister of Closeburn, given in "A Large Description of Galloway, by Rev. A. Symson of Kirkinner, 1684," Nithsdale is called "Nithia a Nitho arune, which river doth run out of a small fountain near Dalmellington in Kyle." It also states that "Nidesdale is a Sheriffdom, where my Lord D. of Queensberry, his Majesty's High Treasurer, is Heritable Sheriff. But the jurisdiction of the Sheriff is here not considerable, partly for that the interest of the Duke is interwoven in many of the parishes, and there be some whole parishes belonging to his Grace, whereby his whole interest, being a regality, is subject to his Bailie, and partly for that there are several Baronies in this shire, all which are subject to the jurisdiction of their immediate superiors."

Sibbald's description in 1733 was thus given :—"Another branch of Dumfrise is Nidisdale, encompassed with a ridge of hills on all sides, and in the bottom has abundance of corn. It is divided into the *Overward*, containing the parishes in the Presbytery of Penpont; and the *Netherward*, containing those of the Dumfries Presbytery. Here Sanchar is famous for its castle, the residence of the Duke of Queensbury, who has built a noble house at Drumlanerick, and is now adorning it with stately avenues, gardens, and terras walks."

In the "MSS. Collection of the Several Shires, by Sir James Balfour, Lyon King at Arms, with considerable additions by Sir Robert Sibbald," a brief account is given of the "Stewartry of Annandale and *County* of Nidisdale : "—" Close to Annandale on the west lies Nidisdale, abounding in arable and pasture grounds ; so named from the river Nid, by Ptolemy, falsely written Nabius for Nodius or Nidius, of which name there are other rivers in Britain, full of muddy shallows as this Nid is. It springs out of the lake Lough Cure, (?) upon which stood anciently Corda, a town of the Selgovæ. It takes its course by Sanghar, a castle of the Crightons, who were long honoured with the title of Barons of Sanghar, and the authority of hereditary Sheriffs of Nidisdale."

THE DESIGNATION

of this parish for centuries has been "Sanquhar," so denominated, says Symson, "from Sanctus Quarus, who lived here." The derivation of the term has been disputed. The Rev. William Rankin, in the statistical account of 1793, says that "it approaches almost to certainty that the ancient form was *Sanch-Car* (or *Caer*) from the Celtic—the first syllable signifying in that language 'ratifier with the touch,' and the last 'a town.'" From this interpretation he infers that the name has an allusion to the touching of the place with a sacred wand by the president of a popular assembly during the ceremony of consecration. This is ingenious and plausible. The Rev. Thomas Montgomery, in the account published in 1835, says that " *Caer* signifies a fort, and *Sean* old." This last is confirmed by a minister in Ross-shire, who has made Celtic topography his study. He writes me that "both interpreters are at one as to the Cathiri portion (pronounced Căhir). As to Sanch or Sean, I prefer the latter interpretation, the former being by far too recondite. Celtic names are, as a rule, very simple. The great difficulty involved in the decipherment consists in the great antiquity of the Gaelic in which they are couched, no inconsiderable number of the words used in topography having become obsolete. But the law which rules the names is descriptive of two or more of the physical features. In composition Sean, old, takes the form of Seann (pronounced Sang), and Seann-Chathari (Sang-Chahir)—Sanquhar—not, however, necessarily, *old-fort*, but ' *old-town.*'" This title, as he also shows, points to an antiquity far beyond " British times."

In the charters of David II. and Robert I. in the fourteenth century, the name is spelt Senechar and Sanchaer. The "quh" is thus a modern substitute for the "ch." Thus the designation means the " *old-town* " parish of Nithsdale, and "kith and kin" may possibly be claimed for its early inhabitants with a band of allies in the very heart of Asia. A recent traveller to Zanskar, struck by the Scotch pronunciation of the Tibetan mountaineers, ascertained from a Gaelic scholar that the Highlanders of Scotland and the inhabitants of this province belong to the same race. Bonnets, brooches, and plaids are worn; and the woollen garments of these Asiatics are checked and striped in brilliant colours after the manner of clan tartans. Zanskar is simply Sanquhar.

ENLARGEMENT.

This parish was enlarged to its present size by the partition of the ancient parish of Kirkbride, between Sanquhar and Durisdeer, on the 19th of July 1727. In James IV.'s charter in 1507 that parish was called *Pan*-bride, or *Saint*-bride or Bridget, a name famous in the sanctology of Ireland and Scotland, the Pan being equivalent to the British Llan and the Gaelic Kil or Cil (Church). It retained the name Kilbride from the twelfth to the sixteenth century, when it was changed to Kirkbride, probably because one of the Reformation churches was erected there. Still, there must have been a church in that parish prior to the Reformation, as five merklands of old extent were attached to it, and were taken away at that period. (See Chalmers' Caledonia, 1824, iii. 171–73.)

That portion of the parish of Kirkbride which was added to Sanquhar lay between the heights of Stake-Moss, East Lowther, Auchenlone, Cairn, and Dalpeddar, and south of the Nith by the lands of Craigdarroch, and round by the Mennock stream and road over into the Wanlock, and up to the march with the Lanark county.

A portion of the parish of Sanquhar was in some respects taken away after the lapse of 130 years. In 1857 Wanlockhead was erected into a separate district for registration purposes, by order of the sheriff, and the same district was erected into a parish *quoad sacra*, or, in regard to ecclesiastical purposes, some years later.

COMMUNICATION.

(1.) *Roads.*—The great road from Dumfries to Ayr runs through the town of Sanquhar. Twenty-two miles of this road were cut by the Duke of Queensberry at an expense of £1500; also an additional road to the lime rock at Corson-Con, which cost £300. Statute labour by Act of Parliament was performed at 12s. per 100 merks in 1777. Toll-bars were thereafter erected, and by the revenue so obtained the road was much improved. A cross road from that great road, upwards along the Mennock stream to the eastern boundary of the parish, was also cut by the Duke of Queensberry at an outlay of £600; and another was projected to cross the Nith and go over into Galloway, which, although important, was not executed; but there is one from Sanquhar up the Euchan burn, one parallel with the Nith on the south-west, and another running above Sanquhar over towards Brandleys. These public roads, about 34 miles in length, with other branches, are maintained in good condition. Two handsome stone bridges span the Nith, and four smaller the Mennock. "The Dumfriesshire Roads Act, 1865," received the Royal Assent on 29th June 1865. The tolls of this district of the county were abolished at Whitsunday 1866, in virtue of the powers of that Act, and the whole roads, whether turnpike or statute labour, ceased to be so distinguished, and were all in-

cluded in one class termed " public roads." Prior to the passing
of the Act, the revenue derived from tolls maintained the turnpike
roads, and the conversion money the statute-labour roads. Since
the abolition of tolls an assessment has annually been imposed.
For 1874 the assessment was 3½d. per pound on the whole rental of
the parish and burgh of Sanquhar, payable equally by proprietor
and tenant. The expenditure in the parish and burgh for 1873 was
£280, 3s. Each parish in this district is separately assessed to
meet the expenditure therein. It would add greatly to the comfort
of the community were this plan generally adopted.

(2.) *Railway.*—The Glasgow and South-Western line of railway was
completed in 1850. The cost of making the line through the parish
was £75,000. Fifteen men are generally employed in the maintenance of way department. Their average time is 10 hours. A
large number employed on the line—" the flying squad "—paid at
the rate of 20s. per week, have been engaged in putting in rails,
fish-jointed and a half longer than those formerly used, which are
accounted safer and more durable.

The length of line through the parish is 4 m. 61 ch., and through
the burgh 55 ch.—in all, 5 m. 36 ch. The tunnel in the parish of
Durisdeer is about 1400 yards long, and cost about £45 per yard,
or £63,000. The first contractor failed, causing delay ; so that it
was about three years in execution. Some important bridges were
erected along the line—the Crawick Viaduct spanning the Crawick
Valley at the march of the parishes of Kirkconnel and Sanquhar.
Another magnificent bridge of five arches spans the viaduct of the
Mennock. In addition to the general railway station at Sanquhar
burgh, a " lie " or " siding " for goods at Mennock foot is chiefly
serviceable for despatch of lead bars and reception of coal for the
mines at Wanlockhead. Particulars for 1873 :—Number of passengers booked, 19,599 ; receipts, £1632. Goods—Tonnage, outwards,
1743 ; inwards, 2282. Minerals—Tonnage, outwards, 1588 ; inwards, 4694.

It would be a great benefit for Wanlockhead were the slow pas-
senger trains to take in passengers also at Mennock ; and a greater
still were a branch line constructed, as was at one time contem-
plated, up the Crawick and Wanlock. This, if carried over to the
Caledonian, would prove advantageous both to Dumfries and Galloway, as affording more direct communication to Edinburgh and
Leith. It seems surprising that the villages of Wanlockhead and
Leadhills, containing a population of nearly 2000, requiring almost
every necessary to be imported, and having such a large export
trade in lead, &c., should have been so long overlooked both by the
Caledonian and South-Western Companies. As, however, it is expected that coal will soon be obtained for the Duke of Buccleuch's
works at Whitecleuch on the Crawick, a branch railway may be
expected to accompany or follow that desirable acquisition.

HISTORY.

" O these are voices of the past,
Links of a broken chain ;
Wings that can bear me back to times
Which cannot come again.
Yet God forbid that I should lose
The echoes that remain."

THE INDICATIONS OF ANTIQUITY

POINT to two periods, that prior to, and that after the subjection of Scotland to the Roman Pontiff.

1. Moonlight glimpses are afforded of the earliest period by

(a) *The Celtic*, or, as it is popularly termed, the *Deil's Dyke.* This is manifestly the workmanship of former inhabitants. It begins at Lochryan, comes on through Galloway to the heights above the Afton ; then turns down the west side of the Nith, on through Annandale to Carlisle. It is constructed of stones and earth, is of considerable width, and passes over soft as well as hard land, running thus for a hundred miles. Its course through the parish runs from Drumbuie at Kelloside through Barmoor, and on through Cairnhill, Craigdarroch, and Glengenny below Jock's Ruck. It is known that twenty-one tribes occupied all that was known of Caledonia in the first century of the Christian era ; and that the tribe of the Selgovæ—supposed to be Picts, who dwelt in the south-west as well as north-east of the Forth—long resisted the legions of Agricola and raised military works. It is thought that this dyke of some strength was erected as a dividing-line or territorial division between the inhabitants and their foes. It is well known that the ancient Caledonians swept down from their fastnesses and killed thousands of the Romans ; and that whilst Roman roads and camps were formed along the Nith by Durisdeer and the vale of Clyde, they did not appear to have occupied Galloway. The Picts and the South Britons were thereafter at war, as well as amongst themselves. In Roxburgh and Selkirk a similar dyke is called the *Catrail* or divid-

130

ing line, and this too was probably the boundary which the Southern Picts had resolved to maintain. Dr Jameson held that the Picts were of Gothic extraction—a view favoured by monosyllabic and other names, as well as by remaining customs and terms. Thus the power of pit and gallows of former days, and the terms still used as *Yule* and *Rood* and of many mountains and headlands refer to that early origin. Five of these Caledonian tribes, including the Selgovæ, occupied what came to be termed the province of Valentia, lying between the walls of Antoninus and that of Adrian. These were partially subdued and civilised and became citizens of the Roman Empire.

(*b*) *Kemp's*—or "*the Warrior's*"—*Castle* is beautifully situated on a neck of land, having a steep side, from 50 to 60 feet above the Barr Burn, and more gently sloping on the side of the Euchan, near the junction of these streams. There is a tableland of about 120 yards long by 20 broad in the middle, with three trenches, one well marked at the upper and narrowest point. All trace of building has been removed for fencing purposes. Some fragments of fused pieces have led to the conclusion that this was a vitrified fort, but they seem merely to indicate that the walls had been constructed by hot lime. They can be seen in the hut at the neighbouring quarry. The site of the castle being surrounded by trees, it now forms an agreeable summer retreat.

(*c*) *Druddle* or "*Druid's Hill*" and *Dalpeddar*, or Dal-pow-dar— "Field of the Stream-of-the-Oaks," if these terms are to be accepted as evidence. Oaks have been dug up in a moss above a retired dell, where possibly Druid worship may have been engaged in. But that is yet a matter which has not been conclusively settled as to the British Isles.

(*d*) *Sepulchral Remains at Cogshead.*—What are thought to be round graves, filled over by stones and earth, of various sizes, close upon the dwelling-house of that secluded glen ; and

(*e*) *Tumuli*, also supposed to be graves on the Town Common, a mile and a half from the burgh. These are filled in the same manner as those at Cogshead. Dr Simpson says they are the length of a man, and are scattered over the field, in many cases single, in others double, or of the breadth of four, with what he imagined as the chieftain's grave on an eminence at the head. And all lying north and south, he considered proof of an age prior to the introduction of Christianity.

(*f*) *The Stockaded Island*, on the Black or Sanquhar Loch. A person having been drowned by falling through the ice, this loch was drained to get the body, and then an ancient canoe, fashioned out of the trunk of an oak, was found on the north side, measuring 15 feet by 3, and having 5 plugged holes in the bottom. It was in the possession of Mr Walter Scott, Sanquhar. The islet is 50 feet by 39, with a mole or causeway a few feet broad, and sunk 4 feet below the water, which was 20 feet deep, the place exactly corresponding to descriptions given of Irish crannoges or little wooden islands—that is, islands of moss held together by a strong pallisading of oak sticks, driven down by their sides. These were common in the ninth century. The Roman army left at the end of the fourth century. Then, and onwards, the Selgovæ were assaulted by the Scots, who came from what we term Ireland, but which then was the home of these Celtic rovers. Though unable to resist these and other northern foes, the Selgovæ were not wholly driven out.

OTHER HANDWRITINGS ON THE EARTH

point us back to "the people of the woods," who were stirred to patriotic exertions, and who, by the labours of the Culdees, were brought to embrace and practise the religion of Christ in its simplicity and power. And similar hints are given as to the time when, through the Saxons in South Britain, and eventually by Malcolm Canmore and his sons, the Popish system began to, and did prevail. Thus—

(a) *The Round Moat at Ryehill* is a memorial of the Saxon period, some 800 or 1000 years ago—the word signifying a place of assemblage. These were either "Folkmotes," for assemblages of people, or "Wittenagemotes," where judges might hear and decide causes. This round green moat, level on the top, belonged to the latter class.

(b) Then these *castles* or *forts*—(1) the circular remains at Chapelcleuch, 12 or 14 feet thick; (2) at Southmains, and those of (3) Glenrae—a double circle of some 90 yards, with trench, on the bank above the burn; (4) Clackleith; (5) Gilmour, at Auchengrouth; (6) Ryehill, (7) as also the Peel of Sanchar—refer to pre-Reformation times.

(c) The *Chapelyard* of Dalpeddar, with, Dr Simpson says, a golden toe found there, once possibly devoutly kissed, and (d) Auchentaggart, *the field of the Priest*, evidently speak of subjection to and worship in connection with Rome.

(e) What may be termed *Pangrains Kirk* is a cross tumulus on the green table-ground rising up from the side of Mennock, lying under the White Dod Hill, and the Beer or Bir (short) Burn purling some 20 feet below. On ascending this eminence close to the round "stell" or shelter for sheep, almost in the centre of the table, lies a cross composed of closely-packed stones and turf, similar to the tumuli at Cogshead and on the Common. The transverse sections measure about 60 feet each way, and intersecting not at the centre, but so as to make one of the lengths next to the hill 42 feet long. The breadth throughout is about 6 feet. The impression that this may have been an old "stell" for sheep cannot well be retained, as, first of all, there seems no reason, if so, why two of the lengths— the foot of upright and the top of the cross—should be so much out of proportion, as about 42 and 12, instead of some 26 or 27 feet each. Then it seems improbable, unless regarded with reverence, that the stones of which it is composed should not have been again used when the circular form of the "stell" was adopted, rather than to have brought others from the streams below. The name of the sharp projection round which the traveller turns e'er he comes in sight of this table-ground appears also to refer to a place of worship in the neighbourhood. "The Starn Capel Nuik" may be read "The corner of the chapel on the height." Then the designation of the stream "Mennock," or "Monk's Water," speaks for itself. Such romantic and secluded places, it is well known, were chosen by the persecuted Culdees, and it is highly probable that in such hiding-places pure religion was retained long after the term "Monk" was applied to all who were devoted to a religious life, whether or not they had taken vows of subjection to the Pontiff. Finally, the term *Pan*-grains as fully indicates as does the term Pan-bride that a church stood here, that early prefix, as plain as by the original "llan" or the "kil" or "cil," being applied to a spot devoted to religious worship.

(*f*) The ancient church and hospital at Sanchar, with the well of St Bride or Bridget, now covered by the railway embankment, where till recently girls on May-day paid tribute of nine smooth pebbles, tell of pre-Reformation times. The account of 1792 says—"There is a figure as large as life near the entrance to the church, cut out of stone, which vulgar tradition calls 'the saint of the choir.'" This may be the figure called the "Bishop of Sanquhar" at Friars Carse. The walls of the old church were nearly 5 feet thick, and so compact as to require to be blasted with powder. The foundation of an ancient structure, deep in the soil, 4 feet thick, and running to the south of the church, was then discovered, in which were some carved stones. An enormous quantity of bones were dug out of the floor of the old church. These things testify that the place was at once esteemed sacred as a sanctuary for worship and refuge, and also as a place of interment, centuries prior to the Reformation.

The Saxons, who had obtained "a very thin settlement" in Dumfriesshire at the close of the seventh century, gained possession by marriage and otherwise. Gregory, King of Scots, and his people migrated to Wales. Returning, they were defeated at Lochmaben in 890, after which the early inhabitants were unknown as a separate people. Consequently, the Selgovæ, Scots, and Saxons were the progenitors of the following generations. Up to the eighth century the Selgovian or old British tongue would prevail, and Gaelic during and long after the ninth. Some strongly hold that Gaelic preceded the old British—if it was not spoken in Eden itself (!). Then Saxon came, and by the Norman Conquest and intermarriage, a new speech, the Scoto-Saxon, a kind of modern Doric, was introduced before the end of the twelfth century. Thereafter Gaelic was banished north of the Firths of Forth and Clyde. But up till that period "Stra-nid" or Strath of the Nith was Celtic both in people and institutions.

Sir James Balfour, in his MSS., wrote thus regarding the people who dwelt in the district in old times :—"This Nidisdale, together with Annandale, breeds a warlike sort of people called Selgovæ, but infamous for their depredations. For they dwell upon Solway, a formidable arm of the sea, through which they often make excursions into England for booty, and in which the inhabitants on both sides, a pleasant sight and sport, *hunt salmons* (whereof there is great plenty) with spears on horseback, or, if you had rather call it so, *fish* for them." Sibbald's Description (p. 907–10) also says— "What manner of *cattle-stealers* they are that inhabit these valleys in the Marches of both kingdoms, John Lesley, a Scotchman himself, and Bishop of Ross, will inform you. They sally out of their own borders in the night in troops, through unfrequented byways and many intricate windings. All the daytime they refresh themselves and their horses in lurking-holes they had pitched upon before, till they arrive in the dark at those places they have a design upon. As soon as they have seized upon the booty, they in like manner return home in the night through blind ways, and fetch many a compass. The more skilful any captain is to pass through those wild deserts, crooked turnings, and deep precipices, in the thickest mists and darkness, his reputation is the greater, and he is looked upon as a man of an excellent head. And they are so cunning that they seldom have their booty taken from them; unless, sometimes, when by the help of bloodhounds, following them exactly upon the track, they may chance to fall into the hands of their adversaries. When being taken, they have so much persuasive eloquence, and so many smooth insinuating words at command, that if they do not move their judges, nay, and even their adversaries (notwithstanding the severity of their natures) to have mercy, yet they incite them to admiration and compassion."

In former times the monks in some instances rented their lands to freemen, who, enjoying long leases, applied greater skill and labour and began a better system of husbandry; but the great body of cultivators were bondmen attached to the castle or glebe. In charters of Robert I. and David II. we read of poundlands, merklands, shillinglands, pennylands, halfpenny and farthing lands. Some farms still retain the names of these old valuations. Artificial draining was unknown. Horses were then of more value than cows.

Chalmers says that the barons, monks, and the tenants had enclosed fields—hay, mills of every sort, brew-houses, fish-ponds, the usual appendage of orchards from the Britons, saltworks on the Solway, wheel carriages and artificial roads, all during the early part of the thirteenth century. Animal food, in addition to the oaten diet, was more plentiful than at present. Sir W. Scott says that—

> " The rafters of the sooty roof
>   Bore wealth of winter cheer—
> Of sea-fowls dried, and solands store,
>   And gamonds of the dusky boar,
>   And savoury haunch of deer."

ANTIQUARIAN CURIOSITIES

connected with the parish may be seen in Dr Grierson's Museum in Thornhill:—(1) Two coins called bodles of the reign of James VI., with the thistle; (2) a large amber or lamar bead found in 1825; (3) a stone celt found in the loch; and (4) whirlstanes used anciently in the spindle; copy of the last number of the "Sanquhar Times" newspaper. Other two articles may be said to be connected with the district—namely (5) the sword and (6) the Bible of a Covenanter, who carried them into banishment, and brought both back with him after the Revolution. It is also understood that (7) a valuable chain of heavy links of silver was found near Wanlockhead not many years back; and that (8) a large cannon-ball, 27½ lb. weight, was got in the same neighbourhood; (9) a quantity of broad gold pieces was found near the site of the Castle at Southmains. A silver coin, James VI. and the national arms quartered, was found on the top of Coom Law, and is possessed by the writer.

OTHER ANTIQUITIES.

(*a*) The old bridge at the braehead, Sanquhar.

(*b*) The small bridge near the gateway of the Castle ruins, where the avenue terminated, is supposed to be one of the oldest arches known.

(*c*) As it is understood that the Marquis of Bute has obtained the consent of the Duke of Buccleuch to search the tumuli at the Castle, it is expected that some antiquities may be discovered.

(*d*) Two pieces of the old cross of Sanquhar remain, one on the porch of the Free Church, and the other, till lately, used for tying up cattle in a butcher's shop.

(*e*) Black-letter stone, built into one of the farm offices at Blackaddie.

(*f*) A fort and trench at Broomfield, the removal of which by the Railway Company was arrested.

(*g*) Stone implements—one pointed—in possession of Mr A. Sloan, found on the farm of South Mains. Another found at Broomfield, 10 lb. weight, supposed to have been used for slitting wood—in possession of J. G. Clark, Esq.

(*h*) Two plates of old Castle, of date 1790, in possession of J. R. Wilson, Esq., solicitor, Sanquhar.

(*i*) In Sanquhar Churchyard, the top of a throughstone, with a beautiful border of ivy leaves, was exhumed by Mr Wilson, solicitor, It bears this inscription:—"Here lyes Christopher Pearson, overseer of the Lead Works in Wanlockhead. He was born at Bishopfield, in the paroch of Allenindale, in the county of Northumberland, and dyed July the 27th 1710, aged 41."

There are some others of Wilsons and Dalziels, &c., in the Wanlockhead corner. One bears—"This is William Wilson in Wanlockhead, erecht his burial place," &c., 1752.

(*k*) A portion of a sculpture of a sword and handle, with scissors at the side, probably broken from a tombstone, is built into the churchyard wall.

THE "PEEL" AND ITS BARONS.

" The Borderer—bred to war,
He knew the battle's din afar,
And joyed to hear it swell:
His peaceful day was slothful ease;
Nor harp nor pipe his ear could please
Like the loud slogan yell.

" On active steed with lance and blade,
The light-armed pricker plied his trade,
Let nobles fight for fame;
Let vassals follow where they lead,
Burghers, to guard their townships, bleed;
But war's the Borderers' game.
Their gain, their glory, their delight
To sleep the day, maraud the night,
O'er mountain, moss, and moor."   MARMION.

THE CIVIL HISTORY

OF the "old town" parish may be said to arise from the feudal period. The baron who owned the king as his liege lord received in return a grant of the land. On that land sprang up his castle, and the general attendants, a kirk, a mill, a brew-house, with huts of wattle-and-turf in the neighbourhood for his retainers.

The date of the original fort or castle of Sanquhar is involved in obscurity. The baronial castle was erected on the same site at the end of the twelfth or beginning of the thirteenth century. The ruins manifest that it was built for strength in barbarous times. The walls, of great thickness, have by time and spoliation become much dilapidated. The strongholds of Dumfriesshire are of three classes :—(1) The massive fortresses of Caerlaverock and Lochmaben; (2) smaller fortresses; and (3) keeps or fortalices, having thick walls made of burnt shells of lime mixed with sand poured hot among loose gravel between the outer blocks. Morton and Sanquhar occupied the second position. It is considered that if not built, the castle was occupied, in the time of David I. (1124–52), by Dunegal, one of the Dougalls or M'Dougalls of Galloway, who ruled as patriarch or legal superior. He was at the head of the Scot clan M'Gowan that inhabited the upper part of Nithsdale after the original Selgovæ. This chieftain of Stra-Nith, however, held the tower of Morton as his principal residence. The people were allowed to occupy the soil according to real or supposed relationship to him as head of the clan. This Dunegall was a witness to a grant made by David I. in 1124 to Robèrt Brus of Strathannand, or Annandale. The estate bestowed is described as " Extrahannet or Strathannand, and all the land lying from the division of Dunegal de Stranid, &c." This was, of course, a grant under the usual conditions of feudal service. David I., having spent his boyhood at the English Court, became familiar with many Annan barons, who, when he succeeded to the Scottish crown, followed him and received grants of land. Rodolph, the eldest, having inherited the largest share of the property, lived at Morton; Dovenald received Sanquhar, Eliock, Dunscore, and other lands. He was slain in the Battle of the Standard. His son Edgar succeeded, and Edgar's children adopted that title as the family name—one of the earliest instances of the use of surnames. Richard Edgar owned, with the castle, only half of the barony of Sanquhar; and his son Donald held the appointment of captain of the clan M'Gowan from David II. It was thereafter possessed by his son Dunevald. Land began to be partially divided into " royalty" and "regality " in the middle of the twelfth century. Regalities held their own courts for the trial of offenders; royalties were subject to the king and his judges; and Nithsdale, being a sheriffdom, was superintended by the king's bailies or judges.

SIR WILLIAM WALLACE AND THE DOUGLAS.

In the time of Sir William Wallace (1296–1305), Captain Beaufort and a party of English held the " old town " peel— every stronghold from Carlisle to Ayr having been seized by the Southerners. Sir William Douglas having been urged, came to its rescue. His patrimony of Douglasdale being confiscated, he determined to dispute the supremacy of the English. He first subdued the small castle of Durisdeer, and then took the Peel of Sanquhar by stratagem. Concealing his men by the "Witches Linn," on the Crawick, during the night, a plan devised by Dickson of Hazelside, on Douglas Water, was successfully executed in the morning. Exchanging clothes with the carter who took in the firewood—who was equally desirous at once of the gold bribe and the defeat of the English—Dickson, in the dusk of the morning, demanded admittance for his load. So soon as the portcullis was raised, and the strong gate unbarred, he drove the loaded cart till firmly jammed in the entrance. Douglas and his men were instantly within, and slaughtered the garrison. Sirs Henry de Percy and Robert de Clifford, with other English leaders and followers, were soon at the castle, and endeavoured to starve out the successful party; but Wallace, a fortnight after, came to their assistance, Dickson having escaped and carried the tidings. Upon this the besiegers fled, were overtaken, and some 500 slain on Dalswinton Plain. Thereafter, joined by a body of Dumfresians, many more of the English were drowned in the Solway or slain at Cockpool. Wallace rested at Caerlaverock, and on the following day was gratefully received by Douglas at Sanquhar Peel. In reward for his services, Douglas was constituted the Governor of the entire district from Drumlanrig to Ayr. A wing of the old castle is called Wallace's Tower, where tradition ascribes unequalled deeds of valour to our great Scottish patriot.

THE ROSSES OF RYEHILL.

Another castle is thought to have stood at Ryehill, but all knowledge of it—if, indeed, it ever existed—is lost, except that the place belonged to a family of the name of Ross. About the end of last century a stone was found bearing the following inscription :—

Hir lys
The gude Sir John Ross
of Ryehill.
Hir lys
The gude, gude Sir John Ross
of Ryehill.
Hir lys
The gude, gude, gude Sir John Ross
of Ryehill.

Each successor was better than his predecessor. That stone is now *non est*. An ancient ballad also says—

> " Sir Rab the Ross of laits,
>   Thane of hie Sanquhar's peel ;
> On his caprousie,* heezed the cross,
>   He stalwart was and leel."

This would rather indicate that the " Peel," and not Ryehill, was his residence, and that he was baron of the district, although tradition points to the bank at Ryehill, now covered with trees, as the site of the castle. Probably he may have been an Anglo-Norman vassal to whom David or his successors made a grant of Sanchar for distinguished services, thereby removing the heirs of Dunegal.

John Crichton of Ryhill, second son of Robert, second Lord Crichton, had a charter to himself and Christian Dalzell, his wife, of the lands of Ryhill, 1611, wherein he is described as brother-german of William, Lord Crichton.

THE CRICHTONS OF SANQUHAR.

The opinion that the Rosses had received possession of the castle and lands is strengthened when it is found that in the reign of Robert the Bruce (1305–29) only the half of the barony was held by Richard Edgar, while the other by William de Crichton, was held in the right of Isabel de Ross. He died in 1360. The Crichton family thus obtained their position at first by marriage. The family was of Celtic origin. In the reign of Malcolm Canmore a Celtic chief, possessing the lands of Crichton, in Mid-Lothian, took this title as his surname. Two centuries later his descendants are found in Upper Nithsdale. Thomas, supposed son of Thurstanus de Crichton, swore fealty to Edward I. It was his second son, William, who married Isabel, daughter of Robert de Ross, a relative of the Lord of the Isles. The other half of the barony having been purchased by Crichton, it became the chief title of his family.

In 1433 Sir Robert de Crichton held charters of the entire barony, and was Sheriff of the county of Dumfries. He married Isabel, daughter of Sir William Kinnoull in Perthshire. His son, with the same title, signalised himself in

---

* Frontal of helmet.

repelling the incursions of the Duke of Albany—second son of James II.—and the Earl of Douglas at Lochmaben in 1484, and in 1487. As a reward for this service he was created a Peer of Parliament, with the title of Lord Crichton, by James III. His wife was Lady Marion Stewart, daughter of the first Earl of Lennox. That first Lord of Sanquhar died in 1502, and in 1507 a piece of needlework was executed which is in the possession of Miss Bramwell, Gullaberry—a sampler on canvas, done in the usual manner by Lady Isabel Penelopé Crichton. On the one side is sewed the words—"*Giv God the first and last of the deys thoght;*" on the other: "*Mathov VII., 10. Whatsoever I would that men should do to yov, do I even so to them; for this is the la and the profets*"—sentiments that with profit might well be engraven on every heart.

Robert, the second Lord of Sanquhar, married Elizabeth Murray, daughter of Cuthbert of Cockpool. In 1508, four years after James IV. had held a "justice ayre," or criminal court, at Dumfries, a deadly struggle took place between the Lords of Maxwell and Sanquhar, who had both grown in power since the fall of the Douglasses. The Lord of Sanquhar having been appointed sheriff and gaining power in Nithsdale, an old feud was intensified. Lord Maxwell exclaimed, "We must teach this aspiring chief a lesson. Let him see who is the real master of Dumfries." On the 30th of July, instead of being able to hold his court as Sheriff of Dumfries, Lord Sanquhar was attacked by Lord Maxwell and Sir William Douglas of Drumlanrig in a "grate feight," in which "Laird Crichton was chasset with his company frae Dumfries, and the Laird of Dalyell and the young Laird of Cranchlay slain, with divers uthers, quhareof there appeared great deedly feud and bludshed," but "partley be justice and partley be agreement, the whole cause was suddenly quyted and stanched." When a steward of one portion of Nithsdale could make a murderous onslaught upon the sheriff of another with impunity, little protection from outrage and oppression could be expected.

Sir William Douglas of Drumlanrig, one of the parties in that strife, was a very powerful baron. He was ancestor of the noble house of Queensberry, married Elizabeth, daughter of Sir John Gordon of Lochinvar, and fell at Flodden, September 9, 1513.

The strife led to an action before the Lords of Council, and an "Act anent the Resset of Rebellis," and caused a great sensation.

Robert, third Lord Maxwell, fell at the fatal field of Flodden.

On the other hand, his antagonist, Robert, second Lord Crichton of Sanquhar, ancestor to the Earls of Dumfries, survived many years. His son William, the third Lord Crichton of Sanquhar, was stabbed to death in the house of the Governor of Scotland, the Duke of Chatelherault, by the Lord Sempill.

Bishop Lesly gives the following statement under the year 1553: "At same time the Lord Semphill stabs to death the Lord Creychtoun of Sanchar, in the Governor's own house, upon a sudden within the town of Edinburgh, and had been execute therefor, were not the great labours made by the Lord Sanchar's friends for safety of his life, through an agreement that was 'laboured' betwixt them by the aid of the Bishop of St Andrews and other friends at the time." Pitscottie, however, animadverts sharply on the scandal of compounding for so heinous a crime, and states that "no correction was made therefor, because he (Lord Sempill) was the Bishop's good-father. But the plague of God never left the Bishop's house thereafter, because they left the public fault unpunished, conformable to justice" (C. Trials, I. pp. 353–54).

This Robert, third Lord Sempill, married first Issobel, daughter of Sir Wm. Hamilton of Sanquhar; and secondly Elizabeth Carlyle, a daughter of the family of Torthorwald. There seems to be no doubt that he owed his life to his daughter's corrupt influence over the Archbishop, who swayed his brother the Regent. The injured relations of the murdered lord, finding themselves compelled to yield to the force of circumstances, were induced to give the use of their names, as concurring in the application for pardon.

This third Lord Crichton, who was slain almost in the presence of the Governor—the Duke of Chatelherault—married Elizabeth, daughter of Malcolm, third Lord Fleming.

On the 6th September 1550, "Robert Master of Sempill became in her Majesty's will for art and part in this cruel slaughter on the 11th June last."

The Raid of Lochmaben-Stane shows the distracted condition of the country. Under date May 12, 1557, "Johnne Crechtoune, Tutour of Sanchare, alleges that the house of Sanchare was never in use to keip ane Wardane Raid sene [since the time] thai war Wardanis thameselffis. Item, secondly, allegis that he is nocht hakin [liable?] be vertew of the Proclamationne, to haif past to the said Raid, becaus he is nocht ane landit manne." This was in justification of his abiding from a warden raid, or "Day of Frew."

Same date, May 12, 1577, Robert Johnstone of Cottes, Robert Moffet of Grantonne, &c., alleges that they upon the 15th day of February last by past, which is the night before the day of meeting contained in the Proclamation, they being in readiness, and having their horses saddled, to come to the said day of Frew, "Jok Johnstoun, callit the Gallzeart; Jok J. bruther Willie of Kirkhill; Willie Grahame, callit fingand Willie; Ade Armstrang of Hairlaw, and Cristie Armstrang, callit the Bull, and thair complices, come to the Winter-cleuch about mydnycht, and thair tuke away the hale gudis" [stock of sheep], being thereupon pertaining to James Johnstone, father of the said Robert of Cottis, extending to the number of twelvescore sheep and the keepers thereof; and the hue and cry coming to the ears of the said persons, they, for rescuing and recovering of the said stock, with their servants and friends followed the drove until the said 16th day of February, at eight hours before noon, and recovered one part thereof, and in default of sufficient power to follow for recovering of the rest of their flock were constrained to leave off the pursuit. Then they made to come forward from the fray to the "Day of *Frew*," until they came to the water of Annan, which was so great that they might not ride it; and there they remained until they got sure word that the "Wardane" was returned, and the "Day of Frew" past.

May 14, 1557. "Johnne Creychtoune, Tutour of Sanchare," amongst others, found caution to underly the law at the next aire of Dumfries, for Abiding from the Queen's Army ordained to convene at Lochmabene-Stane."

So also are named Robert Johnstone, &c., above.

In the stirring times of the Reformation the Lord of Sanquhar took a part. First, along with others, he entered into an agreement for the defence of Queen Mary, when her marriage with Darnley raised disturbances against her. Again, in 1567, along with Douglas of Drumlanrig, he is found drawing sword in opposition to the Queen, Douglas being appointed Warden of the Western Marches by Regent Murray. Lord Crichton again changed sides, joining the Queen at Hamilton and fighting for her at the battle of Langside. For this offence the Peel was besieged by the Regent in person, and forced to surrender in 1568.

On the 22d December 1593, a Commission was granted to Lord Herries, Sir John Gordon of Lochinvar, Alex. Stewart of Garlies, James Douglas of Drumlanrig, &c., in order to the "establishing and making of quietness and good rule within the bounds of the next marches," which amongst other causes mentions the treasonable rebellion of Sir James Johnstone of Dunskellie, and that he most cruelly and barbarously murdered the true men "induellaris in the Sanquhair, in the defens and faulftie of thair awne guides."

December 29, 1598. James Crichton, son of William Crichton, tutor, in Townhead of Sanquhar, and John Edgar of Ingliston, were "dilatit" for art and part of the slaughter of Patrick Maxwell of Dalquharno. Mr Robert Crichton of Carco, and Mr William Crichton, Townhead, were heavily fined for the non-appearance of the former to answer to the charge. "Crechtoune and Edzer" were adjudged to be denounced rebels, and all their movable goods forfeited.

The story, one of those dreadful clan struggles for which the Borders were noted, is graphically told in one of our Border ballads. The Johnstones of Annandale came to revenge some insult, real or imaginary, upon the inhabitants of Nithsdale :—

THE "PEEL" AND ITS BARONS.

"O heard ye o' that dire affray
   Befell at Crichton Peel, man?
How the reeving bands o' Annandale,
Of a' the Border thieves the wale,
   In heaps fell on the field, man?

     •   •   •

"The warder blaws his bugle loud,
   It sounds far o'er the wild, man,
'Tell Clenrie's clan and Carco's men,
Their flocks within their folds to pen,
   And arm and tak' the field, man.'

"The lady in the peel sits wae,
   Her heart shakes like the leaf, man;
To think her lord is far away,
With hounds he keeps the stag at bay,
   But brings her no relief, man.

"Rouse up the men o' Yochan fair,
   The dwellers on the Scar, man;
The bravest sons o' Menick's rills,
Frae a' the woods the songster fills,
   The bowmen frae the Snar, man.

"Ye doughty sons o' Crawick's vale,
   Frae where Powcraigy roars, man;
In a' ye'r glens and fairy neuks,
In a' ye'r dells and winding cruicks,
   Come forth in warlike corps, man.

     •   •   •   •

"Let all the clans frae Corsancone
   To Kello's bosky streams, man,
All from Kirkconnel's sunny braes,
Wha in the sweetest woodland straes,
   For war resign the team, man.

     •   •   •   •

"The page like arrow from the bow,
   Out by the postern fled, man;
And, hasting o'er the moorland wastes,
Charged with his lady's high behests,
   To noble Douglas sped, man.

     •   •   •   •

"Ere dawn of day old Sanquhar heard
   The Douglas slogan shrill, man;
Which soon bade every fear depart,
And quick made every drooping heart
   With martial ardour thrill, man.

143

" The clans on every side pour in,
 Like ravens to the wood, man ;
And all the gallant band wi' speed,
In that dool hour of Crichton's need,
 The reevers fierce withstood, man.

  . . . .

" The reevers fierce frae Annandale
 Were worsted in the frae, man ;
And few returned to that sweet vale
To tell their friends the waeful tale,
Who deeply did their fate bewail,
And never sought they to assail
Old Crichton Peel for their avail,
 E'en from that dismal day, man."

         —*Simpson's Hist.*

Such scenes are only matter of history, but Nithsdale has made reprisals on Annandale in a different mood by conferring on a descendant of the "reeving" Johnstones the highest honour in her power to bestow, viz.,—to legislate for and represent her in the British House of Commons.

The sixth Lord Robert Crichton, at whose instance the barony burgh of Sanquhar became Royal, in 1598, and who though styled by King James "our beloved cousin," was executed at Great Palace Yard, Westminster, June 29, 1612, for being accessory to the far-famed murder of John Turner, a fencing-master, who had thrust out one of his eyes, while they were practising together, with his foil. It is asserted that his lordship bore his misfortune patiently, until, happening to be at the Court of Henry the Great of France, the King inquired "How he had lost his eye ?" "By the thrust of a sword," replied his lordship. "Does the man yet live ?" rejoined the King ? From that hour he is reported to have determined on putting Turner to death ; who not being his equal, he resorted to the horrible expedient of assassination, which was effected by a fellow of the name of Robert Carlyle, who, with the assistance of an accomplice, pistoled the unfortunate fencing-master.*

Calderwood said—" This lybell was affixed in open places "—

" The Scots doe whippe our noblemen with rods ;
 They kill our fencers traitrously under trust."

This was when James VI. having ascended the English throne, numbers of needy adventurers went south, the Scotch being exceedingly unpopular in England ; which feeling seemed to be the only excuse offered for the cruel and despotic death of a Thomas Ross by order of the king. They had killed the English fencing-master at Innes, while he was putting the cup to his head.

* Crim. Trials, i. p. 77.

THE "PEEL" AND ITS BARONS.

KING JAMES I. OF ENGLAND AT THE "PEEL."

William, the seventh Lord, was served heir to the preceding Lord Crichton in 1619. Living in the castle prior to this formality, King James spent the last night of July 1617 with him there. Spottiswood says that the King and Crichton, the lord of the manor, had been intimate companions, and that James on a tour through Scotland fourteen years after he had ascended the English throne, came through Ayrshire, and down Nithsdale to Sanquhar, to visit Crichton in his "Peel." The occasion was one of popular excitement and hilarity. The stately avenue of lofty trees, which arched overhead, cut down within the last generation, one or two excepted, was lined with the people, and the hoofs of the horses of the royal cavalcade were "bathed in the bluid red wine." It is said that Crichton, in the excess of his delight, burnt, in the presence of the King, an account of a debt due by his Majesty for borrowed money; and that this excess of loyalty was one cause of bringing the estate into the market shortly thereafter. Some appear to confound this last Lord Crichton with the successor to the barony in this reception. Thus it is said that Sir William Douglas, in a grand Latin poem not only welcomed his "Sovereign" Grace, but proclaimed the honours of his own family—

> " Why ranks this mansion high in storied fame ?
> 'Tis gilded by the glorious Douglas' name ;
> And now new lustre o'er its turret falls
> Since Sovereign Majesty has graced its halls,
> This kingly visit leaves a brilliant trace
> Which Time's destroying hand shall ne'er efface."

Though that visit is remembered, the remains of that mansion are fast passing away. The object of the visit of King James —viz., the establishment of the ecclesiastical system of England on the ruins of "haughty Presbytery"—eventually prevented the accomplishment of the wish towards the house of Stuart with which that welcome concluded—

> " May Britons aye be bound by love and trust,
> And have the fortune on their throne to see
> A noble branch spring from the good old tree."

History of Dumfries.

EARLS OF DUMFRIES.

William, seventh Lord Crichton of Sanquhar, was advanced to the dignity of Earl of Dumfries, Viscount of Air, Lord Crichton of Sanquhar and Cumnock, 1633. William, second Earl of Dumfries, was a Privy Councillor to King Charles II. William, third Earl of Dumfries, succeeded his grandfather 1691, died 1694. Penelopé, Countess of Dumfries, inherited the title in virtue of the patent 1690, married her cousin, the Hon. William Dalrymple of Glenmure, and died 1742. William, the fourth Earl, their eldest son, succeeded his mother 1742, was promoted in the army, and died at Dumfries House, Ayrshire, 1768, without issue. He was succeeded in the title by his nephew, Patrick Macdowall of Freuch, county Wigton, as the fifth Earl. He was the son of Lady Elizabeth Crichton Dalrymple, eldest daughter of the Countess, and of her husband John Macdowall of Freuch. John, sixth Earl of Dumfries (the eldest son of Lady Elizabeth Penelopé Crichton and John Viscount Mount-Stewart, the eldest son of the Marquis of Bute), was born 1793, and succeeded his grandfather, Patrick, 1803. He obtained licence to assume the surname Crichton, in addition to, and before that of Stuart, and to bear the arms of Crichton quarterly with the arms of Stuart, in accordance with a deed of his great-uncle William, sometime Earl of Dumfries and Stair.

THE OLD PEEL AND THE NEW CASTLE.

In the beginning of the reign of Charles I., Lord Crichton sold the Barony and Castle of Sanquhar to Sir William Douglas, Viscount of Drumlanrig, who was created Earl of Queensberry in 1639. The sale was confirmed by charter in 1630. This duke resided in the Peel whilst building the Castle of Drumlanrig.

At length, removing thither, he only slept one night in the new castle, for, taking unwell in the night, and unable to make the servants hear him, he returned in disgust to the Peel for the rest of his days. He was also so disgusted with the immense cost of the new castle, that he wrote on his bundle of accounts, "The deil pyke oot his een that looks herein." On his death, the Peel was so far dismantled, and by a shameful Vandalism not only allowed to fall into ruin, but portions of it have been demolished to build the Town Hall and other edifices. On the death of William, Duke of Queensberry in 1810, the estate was inherited by Henry, third Duke of Buccleuch and Queensberry.

Major Thomas Crichton of Auchensheoch was appointed chamberlain to Duke Henry of Buccleuch on his accession in 1811, and continued till 1843. He was succeeded by William Maxwell, Esq. of Carruchan, and in 1863 by John Gilchrist Clark, Esq. of Speddoch.

Queen Anne, who succeeded to the throne on the death of William in 1702, appointed James, second Duke of Queensberry, the leading nobleman in Dumfriesshire, to be her High Commissioner in Scotland for promoting the Union. He was born in 1662 at Sanquhar Castle.

For his services in carrying the Union movement to a successful issue he received a pension of £3000 a year, the entire patronage of Scotland was conferred on him, and he was created a British peer, with the title of Duke of Dover, Marquis Beverley, and Baron of Ripon. He died 1711, four years after he had attained the object of his ambition. His wife died in 1709. A magnificent mausoleum, containing marble figures of the deceased, was erected over their remains in Durisdeer Church. (See Illustration.)

In 1706 the " Union Duke " resigned into the hands of the Queen his titles of Duke of Queensberry, Marquis of Dumfriesshire, Earl of Drumlanrig and Sanquhar, Viscount of Nith, Torthorwald, and Ross, and Lord Douglas of Kinmont, &c., for a new patent, granting those titles to him and his heirs of entail, male and female, *succeeding to the estate of Queensberry*, with this proviso, *that such heirs of entail should be descended from William the first Earl.* In this resignation the titles of Marquis and Earl of Queensberry, Viscount of Drumlanrig, Lord Douglas of Hawick and Tibbers, not being included, their descent to his heirs-male was not affected by the change.

Charles, his third son, succeeded him in 1711. He possessed 150,000 acres, chiefly in Upper Nithsdale. As he did much to promote the interests of Dumfries, his portrait was put into the Town Hall in 1769, and a Doric pillar was erected to his memory in Queensberry Square.

On the death of Charles in 1778, the Dukedom of Queensberry devolved on his cousin, William, Earl of March, and on his death in 1810, the male line of William, the first Duke of Queensberry, terminated. The titles and property then, by virtue of the first patent and of a second, executed by the second Duke, devolved on Henry, third Duke of Buccleuch, the heir of line in right of his grandmother, who was thenceforward designated Duke of Buccleuch and Queensberry. Thus the famous old Border family of the Scots became the leading one in Dumfriesshire; but property valued at £30,000 went with the Marquisate of Queensberry. See Dr Ramage's " Drumlanrig," p. 58.

His son, Charles William Henry, succeeded in 1812 as fourth Duke of Buccleuch and sixth of Queensberry.

Walter Francis Montague Douglas Scott, the nobleman who now worthily wears the united Dukedoms of Buccleuch and Queensberry, with numerous other titles, was born on the 25th November 1806; succeeded whilst a minor in 1819 to the estates; married, 13th August 1839, Lady Charlotte Thynne, youngest daughter of the second Marquis of Bath, and has issue :—

1. William Henry Walter, Earl of Dalkeith, Lord-Lieutenant of Dumfriesshire.

2. Lord Henry John.

3. Lord Walter Charles.

4. Lord Charles Thomas.

5. Lady Victoria Alexandrina, married to Lord Schomberg Kerr in 1865.

6. Lady Margaret Elizabeth, married to Donald Cameron, Esq. of Lochiel, M.P., December 1875.

7. Lady Mary Charlotte.

The Buccleuch and Queensberry rental approximates to upwards of £113,000 per annum. The original Queensberry family are represented by the descendants of Sir Charles Douglas of Kelhead.

THE CRICHTONS OF ELIOCK.

The estate of Eliock ("a little rock") was at that time in the possession of Sir Robert Crichton, probably a brother of the Lord of Sanquhar. Sir Robert was a distinguished lawyer—first Lord Advocate, and then a Lord of Session in the reigns of Queen Mary and James VI. He married three times. His first wife was Elizabeth Stewart, who was directly descended from Robert, Duke of Albany, son of Robert II., King of Scotland, and closely connected with the Tudors. They had two sons, James and Robert, the latter being afterwards known as Sir Robert Crichton of Cluny. James was born on the 19th August 1560, when the Free Parliament and nation of Scotland were renouncing Popery and embracing anew the Protestant religion. This James Crichton, or, as he wrote it, Chrichtone, became at a very early age one of the most remarkable students, so that he has been generally distinguished by the title of

THE ADMIRABLE CRICHTON.

Considerable dubiety has prevailed as to the place of his birth; but the matter may be regarded as settled in favour of Eliock House, not merely from the tradition which points to the little chamber where the event occurred, but from the fact that the estate of Cluny was not conveyed to Sir Robert till 1562, two years after the birth of James, and Eliock was not sold till 1592. The first documentary evidence as to his education is furnished by a MS. in St Andrews, showing that he became a Bachelor of Arts in the College of St Salvator on the 20th March 1573-74, when he was between thirteen and fourteen years of age. He is said to have confined himself to no single study, but that he ranged alike through all the sciences; and as he was a youth of universal erudition and superior talents of memory, he at one time excelled in polemical, at another in rhetorical studies; then again, he would devote himself to philosophical, and after that to theological subjects, and this too with a success that he was accounted most versed in every kind of science; and all this though he was only seventeen years old. He had the happiness also of having been selected as one of the fellow-students and companion of King James VI., under the direction of the celebrated George Buchanan, at Stirling. It is confidently affirmed that he was versed in twelve different languages, viz., Hebrew, Syriac, Arabic, Greek, Latin, Spanish, French, Italian, English, Dutch, Flemish, and Slavonian. Though some of the accounts handed down are not sufficiently reliable, there appears to be no doubt that from 1578 Crichton spent two years in France in the study and profession of arms, where not only his person but his feats of grace and strength were greatly admired, and that he took part in the wars against the Huguenots of Henry III. of France. Further, that after a visit to Genoa, he arrived at Venice in 1580, whither his literary fame had preceded him. Having been introduced to the Doge and Senate, he sustained his literary reputation by a brilliant discourse. Thereafter he disputed upon theology, philosophy, and mathematics before a great assembly of the learned. A similar disputation was sustained at Padua, which he commenced by an extemporaneous poem in praise of the city; and once more at Venice for three days, the programme or challenge of the discussion having been preserved by Aldus. It was from these disputations, which drew forth unbounded admiration of his talent and erudition, that he obtained the title of the "Admirable Crichton." He perished at the age of twenty-two, having been run through in a dastardly manner by a young and dissolute prince to whom he had been engaged as tutor. His marvellous gifts place him at the head of the eminent men born in the parish. Whether more lasting results might not have been produced by a more limited selection of subjects is another question.

THE VEITCHES.

The estate of Eliock was sold by his father in 1592 to a gentleman of the name of Dalzell (afterwards Earl of Carnwath). It thereafter became the property of the Hon. James Veitch, one of the Senators of the College of Justice. Four farms of that estate were some time ago sold to the Duke of Buccleuch. On the death of James Veitch, Esq., at the end of 1873, his brother, the Rev. William Douglas Veitch, a clergyman in the Church of England, became the proprietor. The fine old mansion is in good condition. It contains some fine portraits of the family, but most of them, and the library, have been recently removed. The small room in which the Admirable Crichton was born has a window facing the river Nith. It is certainly to be regretted that this beautifully-situated mansion—the only one of any consequence in the parish—should remain untenanted.

AGRICULTURE.

" How lovely Nith, thy fruitful vales,
Where spreading hawthorns gaily bloom !
How sweetly wind thy sloping dales
Where lambkins wanton through the broom !"

THE SOIL

AT the foot of the hills is partly moss and partly clay. In many places where oats are sown the want of a southern exposure and the spongy nature of the ground causes a late and precarious harvest. The south-west end of the parish is of a light gravelish soil, which in dry seasons produces only a moderate crop. If rain falls in April and May, it is more abundant and earlier ripe than in other parts of the parish.

About the centre of the parish the soil is deeper, particularly the holm-lands on the banks of the Nith. Though not a rich loam, with a plentiful supply of manure and lime, excellent crops are yielded. It is also well adapted for grazing.

CROPS.

A very inconsiderable part of the land is under tillage. Formerly not more than 600 or 700 acres were under the plough. Consequently the whole grain yield was not sufficient for the inhabitants for one-half of the year, and an annual supply of meal was imported from Dumfries and neighbourhood. The Inland Revenue returns show a considerable increase. The grain commonly sown is oats, barley, or rather bear, peas, turnips, and potatoes. Ryegrass seed and clover were not formerly sown.

AGRICULTURAL IMPROVEMENTS

have been carried on to a great extent. Agricultural implements, of the most approved description, have been introduced with decided advantage ; better draining and breaking up of the soil, as also deeper ploughing. A stimulus was given by the disannulling of the old Queensberry leases about a century ago, although at the

151

time regarded as a most ruinous and calamitous event. Activity and enterprise were thereby evoked, and a higher state of cultivation reached.

Liming.—Observation of the good effects of putting lime on the land led to its adoption about 1790, a plentiful supply being brought from the Corsonconehill, ten or twelve miles distant, at the boundary with Ayrshire. A cart-load contained 12 or 14 bushels, for which 3d. per Winchester bushel was paid; but there is less lime used than formerly.

Fencing.—The mania for thorn hedges has gone past; now wire fences or drystone dykes are more effective. The cost of this fence is some 10s. per rood—6s. 6d. for quarrying and building (which is generally defrayed by the proprietor), and 3s. 6d. for carting, borne by the farmer.

THE DURATION OF LEASES

on the Eliock estate in several cases is for nineteen or more years; on the Queensberry estate fifteen instead of nineteen, as formerly. Power to reserve or resume possession of cottages and cottage gardens is retained by the proprietor. Rents payable at Candlemas and Lammas, instead of Martinmas and Whitsunday, giving three months' time, which may have some reference to the law of hypothec. A five-years' rotation is stipulated, but most work in a six years' rotation, by which two years of pasturage are obtained, half of the ground being generally under pasture all the three years. The improvement of the land must take precedence of the improvement of the stock, as to bring on a new stock suddenly would be destructive. The tenant is required to do the whole of the carriages necessary for building or repairs; and the proprietor reserves right to replace stone dykes with thorn hedges, but provision is made for the settlement of all disputes by arbitration. The penalties stated in the leases have never been exacted. Farmers don't generally object to the shortening of the period of leasehold. If the land be improved, they get the benefit. On the other hand, if likely to be lost, it may not be too highly enriched. Not only are the farms on the Queensberry estate let at a very moderate rate, the comfort of the tenantry is so much attended to that his Grace is very highly esteemed both as a man and a landlord. The houses of the shepherds are superior to many farm-houses in other parts, whilst the farm-houses are superior to the dwellings of the proprietors of former days. Gardens and shrubbery adorn the front, whilst the steadings at the back are all that can be desired.*

---

* For rental and agricultural statistics, see Appendix.

WOODS.

" *The mountain ash*
No eye can overlook, when 'mid a grove
Of yet unfaded trees she lifts her head
Decked with autumnal berries, that outshine
Spring's richest blossoms . . . The pool
Flows at her feet, and all the gloomy rocks
Are brightened round her."   WORDSWORTH.

THE parish, excepting the estate of Eliock, is rather naked. On that estate a fine natural wood fringes and adorns the banks of the Nith for two miles in length. On the banks of the Yeochan, Crawick, and other streams, there are delightfully-wooded walks, which at length lead to spots where

"Round the sylvan fairy nooks
  Feathery breckans fringe the rocks ;
'Neath the brae the burnie jouks,
  And ilka thing is cheerie O."

The last Duke of Queensberry destroyed the woods on his estate till he died, being apparently in need of money. At that time one side of the Yeochan was cleared. The wood on the other still remains.

" Degenerate Douglas—oh, the unworthy lord !
 .   .   .   .   that he could send forth word
To level with the dust a noble horde,
A brotherhood of venerable trees,
Leaving an ancient dome and towers like these
Beggared and outraged."   WORDSWORTH.

A good deal of Scotch larch, silver fir, New England pine, balm of Gilead fir, old oak, elm, birch, beech, ash and mountain ash, Spanish maple, and hazel have been planted and enclosed. The annual value of the manor-house and grounds of Eliock is stated at £50, and the woodlands at £20 in the rent-roll, and the saw-mill is let at £18, on a nineteen years' lease. 450 acres were planted on the Eliock estate, but a considerable number of trees have recently been cut down. 282 acres of the Duke of Buccleuch's land are covered with natural wood by banks of streams. It was cut down about 1795. The trees are thus small, mostly shoots from roots of large trees. The chief kinds of wood grown on the Queensberry lands are oak, larch, spruce, Scotch fir, and sycamore. At present there are ten woodmen employed in the parish—wages 17s. per week. No rough timber is sold, as all the wood is used for cutting up for fences. Disease prevails in the larch and Scotch fir.

The wood employed by house and cart wrights is mostly American, procured on the Ayrshire coast, and home grown from Closeburn, as that sold on the Eliock estate is generally disposed of in lots too large for their purpose. Joiners' wages—formerly for lad at apprenticeship, 1s. per week and food; journeymen, now, 20s. and board.

LARGE TREES AND RATE OF GROWTH.

Dr Ramage, of Wallace Hall, has noted the size and growth of trees on the estate of Eliock from data furnished in 1872 by the late James Veitch, Esq. The measurements, which were taken three feet from the ground, were continuously kept from 1847. Many of the trees are computed to be two hundred years old. The silver firs were planted in a row of twenty. Of five larches, which were brought from Taymouth by the late Lord Eliock, three were blown down, and the two measured suffered from a prevailing disease in Dumfriesshire. The largest of the larches grew $35\frac{3}{4}$ inches in forty years, from 1807 to 1847; while from 1847 to 1872, twenty-five years, it grew only 18 inches. By the former rate it was growing 22 inches in twenty-five years; so that, as might be expected, it had ceased to grow as rapidly as it did in its younger days. The measurements were, in inches, in 1807—No. 5, $84\frac{1}{4}$: in 1847, No. 5, $120\frac{1}{2}$; No. 6, $82\frac{1}{4}$: in 1872, No. 5, $138\frac{1}{2}$; No. 6, $90\frac{1}{2}$.

The larch, which is 11 feet $6\frac{5}{8}$ inches in girth, is not equal to some larch-trees on the Duke of Buccleuch's estate near Langholm, No. 1, at the surface of the ground, being 14 feet in girth; at 8 feet up, 9 feet; and upwards of 100 feet in height. There are found specimens of growth rarely to be met with in this country. The silver fir in Eliock is the largest in Dumfriesshire. In 1847 it measured $132\frac{1}{2}$ inches; in 1872, 156 inches. The ash, in 1853, $122\frac{1}{2}$ inches; in 1872, 142 inches. The largest oak, in 1847, 119 inches; in 1872, 136 inches. Old Scotch fir, in 1872, 107 inches.

These details are interesting as is the leafing of trees, of which a popular rhyme says—

> " If the Oak's before the Ash,
> Then you'll only get a splash;
> If the Ash precedes the Oak,
> Then you may expect a soak."

FARM LABOURERS.

The average remuneration of farm-servants has greatly increased of late years, ploughmen ranging from £38 to £45 per annum, with free house, garden, firing driven, potato-land, and food during harvest. The time of labour (5 A.M. to 9 P.M.) at the plough, and then in the barn in the evening, during winter, is long ; but the employment is healthy, and there are sundry breathing-times. It is consistent with the necessities of existence and the preservation of civil society, as well as of higher considerations, that the period and remuneration of labour should keep pace with the progress and wealth of the country.

Their general character is that of a respectable, humane, active, decent, contented people, the pursuits of agriculture and pastoral life being favourable to integrity and simplicity of manners. The education of farm-servants still is generally defective. There is an improvement in reading, little in writing, and many are unable to do a sum in arithmetic. In general deportment, employers complain that servants are "less biddable and more independent" than formerly ; and that whilst poaching is almost unknown, and there are few cases of petty theft, and not more drunkenness, that profane swearing amongst males and females, and licentiousness, are more prevalent, and that these evils are to be traced to a large extent to the absence of parental instruction and supervision.

Many young men migrate from the district for various parts of the world, miners going out not only to the iron, coal, and lead districts of Scotland, England, and Ireland, but to the United States, Canada, and Australia. Most of those who leave the agricultural districts, with some others, go to England to "carry the pack," or become travelling drapers, one-half of whom, at least, are found to be well conducted and successful.

THE BARONY AND THE BURGH.

" Happy the man who sees a God employed
In all the good and ill that chequer life !
Resolving all events with their effects
And manifold results into the will
And arbitration wise of the Supreme."

THE sixth Lord Robert Crichton, as stated, secured that the "old town" was erected into a royal burgh in 1598. It had already been created a burgh of barony in 1484 by James III.—a kind of re-erection, as is supposed. Now James VI., by a charter under the Great Seal at Falkland, on the 29th day of August 1598, declared that "the said burgh of barony be now, and in all time to come, erected and created a free royal burgh, with all the other immunities and privileges which it shall please us to grant to the same," &c.

Royal burghs were established on the exclusive system. All merchants within them were by means of a burgess ticket authorised to "pack and pell." Without this they were liable to fine and imprisonment as rebelling interlopers. No one could carry on a mechanical occupation unless he had served an apprenticeship to it, and had acquired the freedom of the burgh by favour, marriage, or purchase. Every trade had its incorporations ruled over by its deacon, and the merchants were organised into guilds for the protection of their interests. Business was carried on in booths or covered stalls in the principal streets on Mondays and Fridays, and in addition to these *market-days* spring and autumn fairs were held. The houses were usually constructed with their gables to the street, having a sunk kitchen, a shop, dwelling, and dormitories, where apprentices lodged and journeymen had food with their masters. Outside the walls and liberties inferior huts sheltered "outland folk," "gangrel bodies," and "broken men," who were the continual annoyance of the privileged craftsmen. Everything had to be vended or made under specified conditions. The breach of these rules was punishable with fine, imprisonment, or forfeiture, and even banishment from the burgh. Whisky was unknown in the seventeenth century, ale being the national liquor. Burgesses alone were allowed to brew or sell it, by license from the magistrates, the "change houses" being placed under rigorous inspection. By an Act passed in 1689, innkeepers required to possess accommodation for quartering "four footmen and two horsemen in meat, drink, and bedding." The following declaration was required of all licensed persons :—"That no vitious or scandelous personnes shall be harboured or resett in our houses, and that we nor any of our families sall be found drunk, and that we sall resett no drunken personnes whatsoever, and that we sall not sell drink to any personne nor personnes within our houses on the Sabbath, and sell nor resett nor give drink to any personnes after nine o'clock at night ; and that we sall be at any time found contravenors of these presents, we sall pay for the first fault five merks, for the second ten merks, and for the third fault to be deprived of the libertie of brewing." French wine was the favourite beverage of the upper classes. See History of Dumfries.

THE BRIDGE BENEFIT.

The Sanquhar Bridge claims to a greater antiquity than any other in the Upper Nithsdale, although the ruins of the north end of it may still be seen between two thorn-bushes at the "Brigbrae" at Sanquhar, and nearly one hundred yards northward of the present channel of the Nith. Then the Burgh of Sanquhar was made a royal burgh by James VI. on 18th August 1598. The King granted to the Provost, Bailies, Councillors, community, and inhabitants of the Burgh of Sanquhar, and their successors for ever, "the bridge of the said burgh." The next notice of this bridge is an Act of Parliament of Scotland passed in 1661. That was the year in which the great Marquis of Argyle, and the Rev. James Guthrie of Stirling, were led to the block as the first victims of "the killing-time." A strong stone bridge of three arches was erected some distance above the charter-bridge in 1855. The Act shows that the charter-bridge was a source of revenue to the burgh, and the curious fact that its erection was by the aid of a public collection throughout the churches south of the Forth. It is copied from vol. iii. of the Acts of the Parliament of Scotland in the Advocates' Library, Edinburgh, edited by the late Thomas Thomson, the celebrated legal antiquarian, and printed by Royal Authority on 1st August, 1820. The Act, which is very interesting, is as follows :—

"A.D. 1661. Act in favours of the Burgh of Sanquhar—Our Sovereign Lord and Estates of Parliament takeing to their consideration a supplication presented to them by Johne Williamson, Commissioner for the Burgh of Sanquhar, in name and behalff of the said Burgh, Shewing that the said Burgh of Sanquhar, being situat and builded upon the said Water of Nyth, ane verie great considerable river which, in the Winter tyme is noways passable at the beist dureing the tyme of any raine or storme. The bridge which wes therupon being now totallie fallen down and ruined, which is very prejudiciall not only to the said burgh, bot also to the haill Cuntrie neir the saime, and all others who have occasion to passe that way, who sumtyme will be forced to staye three or four dayes er they can passe over the said water. And the said burgh, thro the calamaties of the tyme and great sufferings they have had, are now redacted to such povertie as they are noways able to build up the said bridge, which so much concernes the weill of the said burgh and the publict good of that Cuntrie. And, therefor, craveing ane recommendation to the severalle presbetries within this Kingdome upon this side of fforth for help and supplie for building up of said bridge, which so much concernes the weill of the said burgh and all that Cuntrie. And also seeing such a contribution will be inconsiderable for so great a work, therefor also craveing ane certaine small custome to be payed at the said bridge for such years and aff such persones and goods as should be thought fit. And having considered ane testificat of verie many Noblemen and Gentlemen in the Shire and circumjacent bounds, Testifieing the necessity and conveniencie of the said bridge, and haveing heard the said Johne Williamson thereanent, who, in name of the said burgh, had undertaken the building of the said bridge within the space of two years. And haveing also considered the report of the Commissioners of Parliament appointed for bills and tradeing (to whom the said mater was referred) thereanent, His Majestie, with advice and consent of the said Estates of Parliament, Have ordained and ordaines ane contribution and Voluntar collection to be made and ingathered within all paroches, both in burgh and landward, on the South side of the water of fforth, for building of the said bridge. And that either personally or parochially, as the Magistrats of the said burgh shall desire. And hereby Seriously Recomends to and require all Noblemen, Gentlemen, Magistrats, and Ministers of the law and gospell, within the said bounds, to be assisting to the said Magistrates of Sanquhar for so good a work, and for ane liberall Contribution for that effect. And seeing it is expected that the foresaid collection will not be so considerable as to defray the charges of so great a work, Therfor His Majestie, with advice and consent foresaid, hath given and granted, and hereby give and grant, to the said burgh, ane custome to be lifted by them, or any other they shall appoint for uplifting thairof, for the space of Twentie seven yeers after the building thairof, at the rates following—viz., for ilk footman or woman, two pennies Scots, for ilk nolt beast or single horse, four pennies, for ilk horse with his load or rydder, six pennies Scots, And for ilk sheip two pennies Scots money. And ordaines all passengers whatsomever to answer, obay, and make payment of the said custome, at the rates abovewrin, to the said burgh and their collectors thairof, dureing the space above mentioned, but any obstacle or objection whatsomever. With power to the said Magistrats to put this Act to dew execution, Conforme to the tenor thairof in all points."

In the charter above referred to we have reliable documentary evidence that Sanquhar Bridge existed in 1590; and if it was then in good repair, its origin cannot be ascribed to a later date than the beginning of the fifteenth century or at latest, to 1484, when Sanquhar was erected into a burgh of barony.

"In old times," says Symson, "the citizens were stout men, who, with assistance of their neighbours of the parish without the burgh, made usually an effective resistance to the Borderers, making inroads for prey in part of this parish, and oftentimes pursued them with loss, though their numbers were considerable.

"In the year 1653, when the loyal party did arise in arms against the English in the West and North Highlands, some noblemen and loyal gentlemen, with others, were forward to repair to them with such parties as they could make, which the English with marvellous diligence, night and day, did bestir themselves to impede, by making their troups of horse and dragons to pursue the loyal party in all places, that they might not come to such a considerable number as was designed. It happened one night that one Captain Mason, commander of a troup of dragoons that came from Carlisle, in England, marching through the town of Sanquhar in the night, was there encountered by one Captain Palmer, commander of a troup of horse that came from Air, marching eastward, and meeting at the town-house or tolbooth, one David Veitch, brother of the Laird of Dawick, in Tweddale, and one of the loyall party, being prisoner in irons by the English, did arise and came to the window at their meeting, and cryed out that they should fight valiantly for King Charles, wherethrough, they taking each other for the loyall party, did begin a brisk fight, which continued for a while, till the dragoons, having spent their shot, and finding the horsemen to be too strong for them, did give ground, but yet retired in some order toward the Castle of Sanquhar, being hotly pursued by the troup through the whole town, above a quarter of a mile, till they came to the castle, where both parties did, to their mutual grief, become sensible of their mistake. In this skirmish there were several killed on both sides, and Captain Palmer himself dangerously wounded, with many more wounded in each, in a pass betwixt two hills near to Crawford Moor."

The rebel army must have passed through Sanquhar in December 1746.

"The body of 4000 marched into Dumfries, where they lodged until Monday the 23d, and imposed a contribution on the town of £2000 sterling, to be paid directly. Although this was remonstrated against, as a thing not only hard, but impracticable, yet it was peremptorily insisted on; but at last £1100 was accepted in ready money. They took Mr Riddel and Mr Crosby as hostages for the payment of the remainder. The rebels also insisted on 1000 pairs of shoes, paid nothing for their quarters, and at their marching off ordered their baggage to be sent after them; and if any person durst presume to molest any of their stragglers, the hostages should suffer for the fault. They continued their march from Drumlaurig to Glasgow, at which city they arrived on the 25th."

MAGISTRACY.

The chief magistracy or provostship of the royal burgh has been held by—

1. *Small* George Ker, Chamberlain to the Duke	. .	1680
2. Provost Allison (see Woodrow) . . .	. .	1684
3. Abraham Crichton of Gairland . .	. .	1715
(He led Sanquhar volunteers against the rebels to Dumfries, and retained Lord Kilmarnock prisoner in Sanquhar for a night.)		
4. James Hunter	. .	1720
5. John Crichton of Carco, Chamberlain and Justice	.	1721
6. Abraham Crichton of Carco (of "ghostly" memory, and under whose magistracy the present Town House was erected)	. .	1733
7. Charles Crichton, merchant . . .	. .	1744
8. James Crichton	. .	1765
9. Robert Whigham of Hallidayhill . .	. .	1772
10. Provost Lorimer	. .	1789
11. Mr Johnstone of Blackeddie . .	. .	1791
12. Edward Whigham, a Leadhills boy, a friend of Burns		1793
13. Dr Otto (founder of the town library) . .	.	1800
14. Provost Hamilton . . .	. .	1812
15. Provost Crichton, Chamberlain to the Duke of Buccleuch		1815
16. William Broom of Panbreck (the first Dissenter who held the office)	. .	1832
17. Provost Braidwood . . .	. .	1836
18. „ Gibb (of Castlebrae) . .	. .	1840
19. „ Williamson, merchant . .	. .	1850
20. „ Whigham . . .	. .	1858
21. „ Williamson again . .	. .	1862
22. „ (Dr) Kay . . .	. .	1866
23. „ (Dr) Kennedy . . .	. .	1872

The government is maintained by a Provost, a Dean of Guild, two Bailies, a Treasurer, and four Councillors, who are elected. Of those who have held this honourable position, six were of the name of Crichton. The fifth (James Crichton, 1765) being the father of Dr Crichton who had been in the service of the East India Company, returned in 1808, and purchased the estate of Friars' Carse, where he died in 1822. He left £100,000 to found a University at Dumfries, or to be spent for benevolent purposes "in any way that his dear wife thought proper," along with the other trustees. The first idea being impracticable, at the instance of Sir Andrew Halliday, a model house for the treatment of the insane was established and partially endowed, on forty acres of ground, part of the estate of Mountainhall, near Dumfries. The building, which cost £50,000, was ready in 1839, and £40,000 additional was spent in its completion. This Crichton Royal Institution receives one hundred and twenty patients, whose minds are soothed, alleviated, and in many cases restored. In 1848 a supplementary structure, the Southern Counties Asylum, was erected for pauper patients. Dr W. A. F. Browne was the first medical superintendent, who having retired, was succeeded by Dr James Gilchrist. (See Appendix.)

REPRESENTATION.

County voters in the parish, 44 ; burgh voters, 243 ; total, 287. (a) Sanquhar burgh unites with (b) Dumfries and Maxwelltown, (c) Annan, (d) Lochmaben, (e) Kirkcudbright, in returning a representative to Parliament, and have in all 2553 voters.

Burns wrote thus of a former election struggle :—

> "There were five carlins in the south,
>   They fell upon a scheme,
> To send a lad to Lon'on town
>   To bring them tidings hame."

Then after describing four of these he adds :—

> "Auld black Joan frae Crichton Peel,
>   O' gipsy kith and kin—
> Five wighter carlins werena foun'
>   The south countrie within."

And again :—

> "Says black Joan frae Crichton Peel,
>   A carlin stoor and grim,
> The auld guidman and the young guidman
>   For me may sink or swim.
> For fool will freit o' right or wrang,
>   While knaves laugh them to scorn ;
> But the sodger's friend has blawn the best
>   So he shall bear the horn."

PRIVILEGES.

The gross revenue of the burgh in 1793 scarcely amounted to £50 per annum. For the year ending 9th October 1874 the revenue from all sources amounted to £277, 19s. 8d. Formerly a very small return was derived from land, but in 1830 the heritors of the burgh of Sanquhar raised and carried out an action of *souming* and *rouming* against the Provost, Magistrates, and Town Council of the burgh, decree in which action was pronounced on 8th July of that year. By this action one-half of the Common or Moor was allocated among the heritors found legally entitled to rights of pasturage thereon, while the other half was set apart to the burgh. The part which thus fell to the town now forms Lochside Farm, and by judicious improvement it yields with the shootings the sum of £203 yearly. A small portion of the Common still remains in a waste state, and was retained at the time of division for a resting place for sheep and cattle as they pass by the drove-road leading from Sanquhar into Lanarkshire, and in it is situated the Black Loch containing the lacustrine dwelling formerly mentioned. The remainder of the revenue is received from customs leviable by the burgh, rents under long leases, rents of small properties, and various other sources. Coal was formerly worked on the Common of Sanquhar, and the right to all minerals within the Common as divided is still possessed by the burgh. About two years ago the Town Council carried out boring operations with the view of again working the coal, but it was found that any coal which remained could not be profitably worked on account of the great depth, thinness, and derangement of the seams. Being on the verge of the eastern outcrop of the Upper Nithsdale coal measures, it seems very doubtful if the burgh revenue will ever be greatly augmented from mineral sources.

The valuation of the whole properties within the burgh of Sanquhar at different periods is shown by the following schedule :—

1855.	1861.	1867.	1872.	1874.		
£2163	£2381	£2706	£2845	Lands, &c.,	£2960	16 11
				Railway,	531	0 0
					£3491	16 11

In 1875 the lands were valued at £2977, 17s. 11d.

TRADE.

The knitting of stockings was at one period a considerable branch of industry in the burgh. The " patriotic Duke of Queensberry " and the trustees for the encouragement of manufactures gave annually a premium of £40 each, to be divided in part to those so employed in Sanquhar ; and in part to those employed in any other useful manufactures within the bounds of the Presbytery. As these were chiefly exported to Virginia, this branch was extinguished by the American War of 1776. Though mostly of coarse quality, some were so fine as to be drawn through a ring for the finger. These were so admired as to be worn by the then heir-apparent to the Throne. One manufacturer alone sent south 4800 pairs of stockings annually.

Possessing superior natural advantages for woollen manufacture, in the midst of a pastoral district with abundance of water-power in the several streams, and coal close at hand, two branches of carpet manufacture were carried on for some time on the banks of the Crawick. In the one department ten or a dozen hands were employed in weaving. In one year they threw off 12,000 yards. Stuffs, serges, plaids, and flannels were also produced. The other branch employed an equal number. In one of these a carpet was wrought in twenty-eight different parts. At present a few hands only are employed in woollen manufactory.

Brick and tile works were established twenty years ago. The clay, which is got on the ground, is more porous, and when manufactured is not so brittle as that got elsewhere. The fire-clay is found lying below freestone. Five miners and twenty other hands are employed at an average of 4s. per day of nine hours ; boys and girls earn 10s. per week. The process in crushing the clay by ponderous wheels, its conveyance by small railway cars to the machine where it is sent out in tiles, &c., the drying, cutting, and firing, is very interesting. Twenty tons per day of clay, making 14,000 tiles, can be manufactured, or 4,368,000 per year.

Some miners who work in Kirkconnel parish reside in Sanquhar town. A forge for making shovels has been erected.

The wages of working people generally are greatly improved— quarrymen receiving 24s. ; masons, 35s. or 36s. per week ; surfacemen on public roads, 18s.

PAUPERISM.

The administration for the relief of the poor is managed by a board of 53 members, composed of four classes—(1) Proprietors of £20 and upwards annual value ; (2) members of the Kirk Session of the Established Church ; (3) the Provost and Magistrates of the burgh ; and (4) four members elected by the ratepayers. A collector, inspector, clerk, and medical officer are appointed annually. The Board possesses a joint-proprietorship in the Upper Nithsdale Combination Poorhouse. Each parish is entitled to receive a certain number of billets. A levy is made per billet for general expenses. The parish is entitled to fill up these billets, and in addition have to pay 3s. or 3s. 6d. per week for the board of each pauper. The poor were formerly maintained by public collections in the church, the interest of a small sum saved, and an annual gratuity from the Duke of Queensberry, as well as by money arising from penalties, the use of mort-cloths, &c.

Being on the highway from the west of Scotland to England, the parish was and is infested by shoals of foreign beggars. The people are charitable, but are often imposed on. The assessment is now 9d. per £ ; it was formerly 10d. and 11d. per £. A General M'Adam, ten years ago, capitalised £350, yielding from £15 to £18 per annum, administered by Kirk Session and Parliamentary Board conjointly. A mortification of £200, left by Mrs Carmichael, and £100 from Dr Crichton of Friars Carse. For medical relief the parish receives a Parliamentary grant of £14 on condition of the expenditure amounting to £28. The lunatics are sent to the Southern Counties Asylum. The parish pays at the rate of £20 per annum for each inmate—that institution being partially endowed from the same fund as the Crichton Institution.

In 1793 there were 35 on the roll. There were 80 in 1873.

The income of the Parochial Board was £920, 3s. 0½d., with a balance at credit of £123, 1s. 4½d. ; but against this must be noted this item in the yearly abstract : " Interest of loan, £337 from the M'Adam Bequest Trustees ; one year at 4 per cent. per annum, £13, 9s. 7d."

Five licences are granted for the sale of excisable liquor in Sanquhar police district ; 45 persons were apprehended for crimes and offences in 1873, but 6 of these were non-resident, and 5 were unable to write or read.

EDUCATION.

The *Crichton School* was endowed in 1821 by £3000 by the Trustees of the late James Crichton, Esq. of Friars Carse, he being a native of Sanquhar. This was for the education of the poorer classes. The ground and buildings cost £1259 ; 140 are in attendance, of whom 15 are educated free, and 25 at a reduced rate.

A private school for young ladies is taught by the Misses Laurie.

Board Schools.—On the 14th April 1873, the first School Board of Sanquhar parish was elected under the Act to amend and extend the provisions of the law of Scotland on the subject of education. 209 out of 241 electors, including 31 ladies, recorded their votes. The parish school only was placed under the Board. Latin, Greek, and French are taught in addition to elementary education. The teacher's income is over £200. In 1793, it was £40. An assistant has been appointed at £70 per annum. The school also derives benefit from the interest of £100, mortified by the Rev. William Martin. This mortification, along with £20 for prizes and £100 for the poor, is held by the Kirk Session. 200 is the average attendance. The school maintains its character for education. One pupil teacher is allowed for every 40 after the first 20. The fees are, 10d. to 2s. 4d. per month. The Board are making some improvement in the school buildings.

Mennochfoot and Wanlockhead Schools are still retained under His Grace's management.

RETURN OF CHILDREN.

Name of School.	Accommodation. No. of Scholars.	No. of Scholars on the Roll.
Sanquhar (public late parochial)	270	220
Crichton School, Sanquhar	140	130
Mennock Bridge School	75	47
Wanlockhead School	135	135

The total number of scholars of school age in the parish was 572, and there is accommodation for 620 children. In December 1872, there were 121 children between 5 and 13 not attending school— 68 in Sanquhar and 53 in Wanlockhead district—but measles caused at Wanlockhead an unusually large number of absentees. During the year ending 23d March last, 81 scholars were in the male and 76 in the female department of Wanlockhead School, which are distinct—157 in all—rather in excess of the accommodation. The school has not hitherto been under official inspection, and the Sanquhar Board decline to inquire further than as to accommodation and attendance. The second Board was elected, Friday, 14th April 1876.

RECREATION.

Recreation is promoted in various ways, as by the bowling green and quoiting. Commodious bowling and croquet greens were constructed in 1871. There are sixty members who contribute 7s. 6d. per annum, under the presidency of Mr J. A. Wilson, solicitor. In no recreation is more interest taken than in the game of curling. The Sanquhar Curling Society dates as far back as 21st January 1774—the centenary of its institution having been celebrated on the first month of 1874. On that occasion a silver jug was presented for future competition by the president. It bears that it was "Presented to the Sanquhar Curling Club in commemoration of its hundredth anniversary, by James Kennedy, Brandleys, President for twenty-seven years." Wanlockhead had the honour to carry it off at the first competition at the close of 1874. The game had been long practised—from 1774 it was carried out by a systematic organisation. The Society appears originally not to have been exclusively a parish one, for in the first list of members there occur the names of persons living at a considerable distance.

At a very early stage of its history a dispute had arisen among the members as to what was the true curler word and grip ; and the Society found it necessary to issue an authoritative declaration on the subject, which is in these terms :—" In order to prevent all dispute concerning the Curling Word and Grip, the Master, who always is preses during his office, and the rest of the Society, agreed that the following shall be held and reputed the Curling Word and Grip of this Society for the future—

The Curler Word—
> 'If you'd be a Curler keen—stand right, look even,
> Sole well, shoot straight, and sweep clean.'

"*The Curler Grip, with the Explanation—*Gripping hands in the common manner of shaking hands is the gripping the band of the curling stone. The thumb of the person examined or instructed thrust betwixt the thumb and forefinger of the examinator or instructor signifies ' running a port.' The little finger of the person examined or instructed linked with the little finger of the examinator or instructor means an ' inring.' " A list of 171 original members is given, as also of office-bearers to the present date. The Wanlockhead curlers were originally part of that society ; but in 1777 they broke off in order to have greater liberty of action, and formed a club by themselves. It is questionable if in any district of Scotland more keen or firstclass curlers could be found. Their societies partake of a masonic and martial character, there being a " master " and " grandmaster," and the skips being commanders. Six rinks were named after their respective commanders, as a standing veteran army, and a seventh as a *corps de reserve* with a qualified commander. A committee of the best qualified persons tried and examined the rest as to the "word and grip." The terms of admission were obedience to the master, discretion, civility to the members, and secrecy, with a fourpenny fee for those in the parish, and sixpence for those outside. At the celebration referred to, Mr Brown, the Secretary, said :—"We can point to no stroke of policy by which anger and strife have been pacified and divisions healed amongst us, but we can point to something better, for during twenty-seven years anything like anger, strife, or division have been happily avoided. Distinctions of rank are lost sight of, and the greatest freedom of intercourse allowed."

SAVINGS.

In addition to the Branch Offices of the British Linen and Royal Banks, there is a District Savings Bank, instituted 1818, and the Sanquhar Post Office was opened for Savings Bank business on Feb. 17th 1863. Number of depositors' accounts, 39 ; of which 16 were open and 23 closed to the 31st December 1873.

Amount due to depositors, Jan. 1st 1873, .	£400 13	6
" of deposits in year 1873, . . .	80 10	0
" of interest, ...	6 16	2
	£487 19	8
" of withdrawals in 1873, . . .	172 15	3
Amount due to depositors Dec. 1st 1873, .	£315 4	5

Interest allowed in the Post Office Savings Bank at the rate of $2\frac{1}{2}$ per cent. per annum.

There is also a penny savings bank.

The inhabitants are generally an industrious, intelligent, and religious class of people, regular in attendance on Divine ordinances, and paying a proper regard to the duties of social life, though still capable of farther improvement. Neither very rich nor very poor, and possessing a competent share of the comforts of life, they were at one time, although not now, destitute of its luxuries. Political collisions were formerly said to have proved injurious to social, moral, and religious obligations ; as also the substitution of dram shops for alehouses ; but, as compared with that condition, drinking and other customs have changed for the better.*

When the Reform Bill agitation was at its height, the Radical reformers of Sanquhar were so incensed at a statement reported to have been made by a certain nobleman in Parliament to the effect that "Reform meant cheap whisky," as to burn his effigy; when a zealous burgher, rushing forward, emptied a half-mutchkin measure upon the figure in the fire, exclaiming, "Hae ! there's some cheap whusky for ye, Watty !"

---

* For Statistics of Population see Appendix.

SCENES ON THE CLYDE AND THE NITH.

ENGRAVED CHIEFLY FROM SKETCHES BY THE AUTHOR OF THE "TREASURE HOUSE."

Part IV.

ITS "GATES OF ZION."

" O Scotland, thou art full of holy ground—
From every glen I hear a prophet preach—
Thy sods are voiceful—no gray book can teach
Like the green grass that swathes a martyr's mound.
And here where Nith's clear mountain waters flow
With murmurous sweep round Sanquhar's hoary tower,
The place constrains me, and with sacred power.

" What Scotland is to Scottish men I know ;
Here first their youthful hero preacher raised
The public banner of a nation's creed ;
Far o'er the land the spoken virtue blazed,
But he who dared to voice the truth must bleed."

PRE-REFORMATION CHURCHES.

CRAWFORD CHURCH was dedicated in old times to a St Constantine, probably a chieftain who, in 606, became ruler of the ancient kingdom of Strathclyd. It is mentioned under this title in 1164, 1175, and 1178. In 1223 the monks of Newbottle held the teinds of the lands. Thereafter David Lindsay granted to the monks of Newbottle, between 1224 and 1232, his land "from the head of Glengonar to the land of the church of Crawford, and by the top of the hill, between the said church lands and Glencaple, to the head of Hurl-burl, and so . . . to

169

Glengonarhead." By another charter, the lands between Glengonar and Elwyn were conveyed to the same abbey, and in 1327 exempted from the barony of Crawford, and erected into a separate barony by King Robert the Bruce in favour of that abbey, with the title of "Friar's-mure." At the Reformation this barony was valued at £111, 5s. a-year.

The church and lands were attached to the Abbey of Holyrood till the Reformation. In 1606 these were included, when the possessions of the abbey were given for a temporal lordship to John Bothwell, created Lord Holyroodhouse. To this grant was attached the condition that 400 merks, with the glebe, should be paid to the minister serving the curé of Crawford. This grant being surrendered to Charles I., that king bestowed it upon the bishopric of Edinburgh; and when Episcopacy was overthrown, the patronage reverted to the Crown, till its abolition by the Act of 1874. The valuation of the rectory in 1228 was 20 merks annually, the vicar receiving 100s. then at £40 a-year. In 1561 the canons of Holyrood let parsonage and vicarage for £86, 13s. 4d., the vicar-pensioner retaining his portion at £32, 10s.

Prior to the Reformation in 1426, William Clark was vicar. John Mason, 1435, exchanged with Duncan Zhaluloh in 1459. Patrick Donaldson, 1498. This vicar-pensioner had a stipend of 15 merks, with 12 merks for a curate, or 27 merks, free of burdens, if he served himself, with house, croft, and pasture for two cows.

The Crawford Church originally stood on the farm of Kirkton, where the churchyard occupies its original position. A charter of Bishop Walter conveys, along with the church, two ploughgates of land; but the church lands were absorbed after the Reformation into the barony of Crawford-Douglas—as indeed were church lands generally.

CRAWFORDJOHN.

In the reign of Malcolm Canmore, in the twelfth century, 1153–65, a charter was written, by which Wicius of Wiceston, in addition to the "church of my town of Wyceston," gave "its two chapels, namely, the town of Robert (hence Roberton) and the town of John, the stepson of Baldwin" (hence Crawfordjohn), to the monks of Kelso. In 1300 the curé was served by a vicar appointed by them, when it is recorded that £6, 13s. 4d. of dues were paid to the monks from Crawfordjohn—the earliest record of this singular name. The monks transferred their rights to the lord of the manor in the fifteenth century, when the living was rated at £10, 13s. 4d. In 1450 Robert de Glendonwyn was rector. There is not sufficient evidence to show that the church was dedicated to St Anne. The idea may have arisen from a fair, held on the 26th July, having been authorised in a charter in favour of Anne, Duchess of Hamilton.

SANQUHAR.

The earliest notice remaining of a Churchman connected with Sanquhar is found in "The History of King John and King Henry III., and the most illustrious King Edward I., wherein the ancient sovereign dominion of the Kings of England, Scotland, France, and Ireland, over all persons and all causes, is asserted and vindicated against all encroachments and innovations whatsoever: by William Prynne, Esq., keeper of His Majesty's Records in the Tower of London," published in 1670. In vol. III., page 659, the signature of "Barthelmeu de Egglesham, Chapeleyn, Gardein de novel leu de Seneware," occurs immediately before that of "William de Taillur, Patrick or Matheu de Parton, del Comte de Dumfres." These, along with many of the Scottish gentry and clergy, went to Berwick, and there swore fealty to Edward I. That document is thus not only proof of that "disgraceful year" 1296, but unfolds who ministered then at neighbouring altars.

In the fifteenth century the rectory of Sanchar was constituted a prebend (or stipendiary) of the Cathedral Church of Glasgow, with the consent of the patron, whose right of patronage and of the prebend was continued. The benefice was usually conferred on the younger son, or other relation of the family. Mr Ninian Crichton was parson of Sanquhar in 1494; Mr William Crichton, son of Wm. Crichton of Ardoch, was rector during the reign of James I. Among other altars in the Church of Sanquhar there was one which was called the "Altar of the Holy Blude." Sir John Logan, the vicar of Colvend, granted certain lands and rents within the Burgh of Dumfries for the support of a chaplain to celebrate Divine service at the Altar "Sacri cruons domini" in Sanchar Church. This was confirmed by the King in November 1529. (Privy Seal, Reg. VIII., 114.) In Bagimont's roll, as it stood in the reign of James V., the rectory of Sanquhar, thus a prebend of the chapter of Glasgow, was taxed at £10.

Two orders of religious knights had settled in the county—the Templars or Red Friars, and the Knights Hospitallers, who, it is said, had their largest hospital under the shadow of Sanquhar Castle. "Barthelmeu" was pastor of that Hospital Church. The masters of both orders having submitted to Edward I. in 1296, were confirmed in their possessions by precepts addressed to the Sheriff by the King. "Many ages after all traces of it had disappeared, the plough turned up numerous relics of its inmates, the mouldering memorials of a brotherhood now forgotten throughout the district. At the Reformation, the property being secularised, Ross of Ryehill is said to have obtained a considerable portion of it."— *M'Dowall's "History of Dumfries."*

Lord Sanquhar and Douglas of Drumlanrig both signed the First Book of Discipline, a test of their approbation of the change. Readers, men of simple faith and purpose, were much employed at that time, ministers being scarce, and it is probable that this parish benefited by their services. John Semple, one of these, came to assist at a Sacrament, from Carsphairn. He had walked twenty miles over the hills, but the ministers were only rising. He took the opportunity to administer a rebuke to them, remarking that he had found all the shepherds out on the heights looking after their flocks while they had been asleep.

PARISHES AND PATRONAGE.

In the 8th and 9th centuries the word Parochia was applied to the territory cared for by the bishop or presbyter, which in that Culdee period were the equivalent terms for ministers of religion. When the power of Popery became consolidated in the middle of the 12th century, the proper division of each parish was settled by charters and other formal writings. Parochial clergy, with fixed districts or parishes, were recognised in Canons of the Scottish clergy passed at two of their General Councils, held in 1242 and 1269—the bishops holding the power of uniting or disjoining the parishes. That power after the Reformation was intrusted to a Royal Commission, and every district recognised by it was accounted a civil parish. That power, along with the fixing of stipends and regulation of teinds, was thereafter intrusted to the Court of Session, under consent of the principal heritors, and some additional powers were added in 1844. The civil parish possessed the greater power over the ecclesiastical—or the *quoad omnia* over the *quoad sacra*—in registration, proclamation, burial, provision, and assessment for the poor and education of the young.

The patronage of the Sanchar Church continued with Lord Sanchar till 1630, when it was sold, with the barony of Sanchar, to Sir William Douglas, Drumlanrig; and the barony and patronage have since belonged to this opulent family. On the death of William, Duke of Queensberry, in 1810, the patronage of the Sanchar Church went along with the Queensberry estates to the Duke of Buccleuch and Queensberry, to whom it belonged, and who has generously yielded that right without compensation on the abolition of patronage, January, 1875, an example unfortunately not followed by many landed proprietors. The church was undoubtedly the parish church before the Reformation.

"Near to the water of Crawick stands the Church of Sanquhar, a considerable and large fabrick, consisting of a spacious church, and a stately quire, where are the tombs of severall of the Lord Crichtons of Sanquhar, wrought in free-stone, and before them some Lords of the name of Ross." The manse was built in 1755.

REFORMATION TIMES.

For perspicuity, instead of continuous and separate lists, contemporary ministers may be grouped together in periods, and taking first the

MINISTERS.

From the Reformation to the Revolution, three periods may be regarded,—1. From 1560 to 1610; 2. 1610 to 1661; and 3. 1661 to 1689. A glance at the Chronological Diagram (on page 180) along with these notes, will more readily call up the condition of men and parties in these parishes of Crawford, Crawfordjohn, and Sanquhar, during these periods.

FIRST PERIOD—1560 to 1610.

In 1581 there were 924 Kirks in Scotland, but the Assembly finding that many of the congregations were small and the buildings ruinous, the charges were reduced to 600, which were apportioned in companies of 12 to 50 Presbyteries.

I. CRAWFORD.

Richard Weir was Reader November 1570. He "left the office." In 1574, William Levingstoun was translated from Liberton, being presented by James VI. Stipend, £52, 10s. The Reader had the Kirkland and 20 merks. Then Crawfordjohn was within the charge stipend, also said to be £4, 7s. 6d. In 1588, Robert Landellis; he was translated to Carmichael in that or the following year. In 1593, James Fotheringhame was promoted from Crawfordjohn, and was continued in 1601. William Wilson, in 1607. He died September 1623, and left money to be distributed to the "puir of the Kirk be the elders betwixt and Yuill."

II. CRAWFORDJOHN.

Charles Forrest is named as exhorter. He had 40 merks of salary as assistant to WILLIAM LEVINGSTOUN, 1567, "pait by Sir James Hamiltoun," who held Liberton also.

In 1583, JOHN HAMILTOUN, parson, was included in the general Act of Restitution. He and his servant were, in 1605, indicted "for the hurting and wounding and mutilation of Alexander Lockhart, tutor of Mickelshaw, of his left hand, and dismembering of him of his mid finger nearest his little finger of his said hand, and bearing and wearing of pistolettis."

In 1589, JAMES FOTHERINGHAME, formerly of Roberton; he is named as Reader, 1590–91, and John Hamilton of Bagra, elder, in 1583.

In 1603, ROBERT LINDSAY, A.M. (Degree from Glasgow). He contributed 20 merks towards erecting the Library in the College of Glasgow in 1623. Died 7th June 1651, aged 70.

III. SANQUHAR.

The earliest introduction of the Scriptures in the South of Scotland was by means of a copy of Wickliffe's Testament, studied by Alexander Gordon of Airds, in Galloway, and Alexander Gordon, younger of Garlies. William Harlaw was the first Protestant missionary who, in Dumfries, on the 23d October, 1558, "nine houris afore noon, denounced the Mass as rank idolatry, and proclaimed the pure faith of salvation in Christ. He had begun his mission at Garlies, and then at three o'clock in the morning, preached in the free hall of Robert Cunninghame within the burgh of Dumfrese." The Dean sent a legal emissary requiring him "of quhais authoritie, and quha gaif him commission to preach, he beand ane laitman, and the Quenis rebel, and excommunicate, and was repelled furth of other partis for the said causis." To which Garlies boldly replied—"I will avow him, and will maintain and defend him against you and all other kirkmen that will put at him." And to the honour of the Magistrates, it is recorded that they refused to interfere, and so the work was allowed to go forward; and, by and by, when the Reformation was accomplished, the deaneries and religious houses in subjection to Rome were all suppressed.

On the visit of Knox in 1562, Robert Pont was elected as superintendent over Dumfries, Galloway, and Carrick, and soon after the Presbyteries of Dumfries, Penpont, Lochmaben, and Annan, and as parts of the Synod of Dumfries, were formed.

On the 19th May 1563, John, Archbishop of St Andrew's, and forty-seven others, were charged with celebrating Mass, and attempting to restore Popery at several places in the West, in which is mentioned, "the said Mr Robert Crychtone, parsone of Sanchar, in Will for the Cryme foirsaid, committit be him in the Parroche Kirk of Sanchar, the tyme foirsaid," and with others, warned " that they should neither complain to the Queen nor Council, but should execute the punishment that God hath appointed to idolaters in His law, by such means as they might, wherever they should be apprehended."

In 1574, JOHN FOULLARTON was translated from Kirkconnel, having also Kirkconnel and Kirkbride in charge, with jc. and fi. of stipend. He was a member of the Assemblies, August 1575, and April 1576 ; and was continued in 1579. He returned to Kirkconnel about 1580.

ROBERT HUNTER, A.M., in 1594. He was laureated at the University of Edinburgh, 12th August 1592, and on the exercise there 6th August 1594. He was presented by James VI., 16th December following, and to the vicarage pensionary of Kirkbride 1st February 1602 ; was a member of Assembly same year, and also in that of 1610.

JOHN BLAKET, in 1607.

SECOND PERIOD—1610–61.

I. CRAWFORD.

JOHN WILSON, A.M., attained his degree at the University of Glasgow, in 1613. He was presented by James VI., 8th September, and admitted, 13th November 1623. He was suspended, 1st October 1646, for admitting William, Marquis of Douglas, to the Lord's Table while under censure, and for associating with James, Marquis of Montrose. He was also ordained, 1st July 1647, "na to marie any quhen there is so great multituds and pypers at brydalls." He died December 1649, aged 57, in the 27th of his ministry. In 1624 a collection was made in the Upper Ward for Dunfermline. Crawford sent £17.

In 1649 and 50, the trial of eleven poor women, informed upon by "Janet Cowts, a confessing witch," is detailed. The charges are very curious ; as that Janet M'Birnie "at one time followed William Brown, sclater, to the house in Water-meetings, to crave somewhat, and fell in evil words. After which, within twenty-four hours, he fell off an house, and brak his neck." Again, that "after some outcast, she prayed that there might be bloodie beds and a light house. And after that, the said Bessie Acheson, her daughter, took sickness and the lass cryed 'There is fire in my bed,' and died. Also, the said Bessie Acheson, her goodman dwyned." Marion Laidlaw, too, had differed in words with Jean Blackwood, "about the said Marion's hay, and after that the said Jean's kye died. That she had her husband by unlawful means, and had a berd (beard) !" Fortunately, nothing was found proven against them, especially as Janet Coutts afterwards confessed that the accusations were false and malicious.

GILBERT HAMILTON, A.M., was laureated at the University of Glasgow, in 1643, called in 1650, and admitted 15th January 1651. He was cited before the Privy Council in 1669, but not called, indulged in West Kilbride in 1672, and again cited before the Privy Council, 11th August 1677.

The Presbytery recorded in 1656, that "the minister regrettis the incomodious situation of the Kirk, being in the outmost corner of the parish, and desires the Presbyterie to lay it to hart how it may be helped, and that it might be thought on how a bridge might be builded over the river, sieing the most part of all the people are separated from the Kirk by the Clyd being many times impassable."

II. CRAWFORDJOHN.

In 1624 this parish contributed £93, 13s. on behalf of the town of Dunfermline, the most liberal of any in the Presbytery.

In 1631, Hamilton of Gilcherscleuch was accused of burying his child in the Kirk, and ordered to attend the next meeting of Presbytery.

In 1632, James Hamilton of Gilcherscleuch, a descendant of the Hamiltons of Crawfordjohn, gave ten merks to the library of the College at Glasgow; and in 1633 and 1643, he was appointed one of the committee of war for the county. In 1645, the Presbytery of Lanark personally thanked him for his " commendable adherence to the Covenant, and resolute resistance to the enemy in this difficult time." And he served again on the committee in 1646 and 1648. In 1650 a discord having arisen between him and William Carmichael, the Presbytery ordained that he should not be admitted to the communion till they became agreed; but in 1656, his children were ordered to be baptized because " he subjected himself to tryall and censure." He was also subjected to severe fines, because his lady befriended the ousted ministers, and allowed conventicles to be held in their house. The property of that family is now possessed by Colonel Walter Hamilton, who distinguished himself in the Indian Campaign and relief of Lucknow.

In 1647, it was recorded (1) "that sundrie of this paroche appeared before the Presbytery, desyring that they might remove the through stones that lyes above their predecessors when they were buried; and seeing that they have not now libertie to bury in the Kirk, that they might transport them where they were at libertie to bury. The Presbytery, considering the same now inexpedient, appointed that these stones should remain still quher they were." (2) Considering that the Kirk of Crawfordjohn has long time been without a kirk-box, and how hurtful that might prove unto the poor, ordained the minister and elders to get ane box, and that the poor moneyes in safetie might be kept therein." (3) That a man and his mother who had used scandalous words "should stand at the kirk-doore, with a paper on his browe, in sackcloth, and afterward with her in the place of repentance." (4) A petition was presented from "sundrie gentlemen of the paroche, complaining that they were in the kirk without accommodation, for want of seats to sit in, and that diverse who had less interest in that part kept use of seates ; whereupon they appointed that seates should be set up in an orderly way in the kirk, and that this should be done according to the interest thereof."

ROBERT HUME, A.M., in 1652, Degree from Edinburgh. Called unanimously. Continued 1657. "Their cruelty," says Baillie, 11th April 1659, "against poor Mr R. Hume is strange."

WILLIAM SOMERVEL, A.M., 1660, Degree from Edinburgh. One of the protesting party, 24th Nov. 1660. Deprived by the Acts of Parliament 11th June, and of Privy Council 1st Oct. 1662. He was afterwards indulged at Carmichael.

III. SANQUHAR.

In 1617.—WILLIAM LEVINGSTOUN, A.M. He was laureated at the University of Edinburgh, 8th December 1618; continued 11th December 1622, when he entered burgess and guild-brother of that city in right of Barbara, a daughter of the Logane, burgess, whom he had married, 6th May 1617. A son, William, was served heir 7th May 1645. JOHN M'MILLANE, A.M., in 1632, acquired his degree at the University of Glasgow, and continued 2d August 1638. GEORGE JOHNSTOUN, translated from Linton, Peeblesshire, after 7th March 1639, translated to Kirkwall, 15th June 1642.

Mr JOHN CARMICHAEL of Kirkconnel and Sanquhar ; Mr ALEXANDER STRANG, Durisdeer ; and Mr THOMAS SHIELS, in Kirkbride, were ejected in 1661 for their adherence to the principles enunciated in 1638. This was effected by the decree of the packed Parliament, who conferred on Charles II. absolute power over the Church and nation, requiring every minister to renounce Presbytery and to embrace Prelacy. 400 ministers refused to allow the remaining vestiges of liberty to be swept away, and were in consequence subjected to incredible suffering. The successor of Carmichael, Mr James Kirkwood, though a prelatist, had kindly feelings towards, if he did not actually sympathise with, the sufferings of the Covenanters. "Off with your coats and join our game," he cried to two fugitives who had dashed through the river from their pursuers. It is believed that they were even permitted to hold secret night meetings within the church. If they would but come over the Kirk stile he would report favourably.

He is said to have been of a humorous turn, and capable of dealing out merited rebuke with keen satirical effect. Thus, when the Earl of Airlie in pursuit of the fugitives was at " The Peel," Kirkwood was not suffered to go till daylight of the Sabbath morning, Airlie pressing him, " Come, Mr Kirkwood, another glass and then." Airlie, anxious to see how he would acquit himself, sat in front of the preacher in the church. Taking for his text, " The Lord shall destroy the wicked, and that right early," he waxed warm in his extemporaneous delivery, laying particular emphasis upon the word early, pointing with his finger to the Earl, till the attention of the audience was fixed upon him ; and then calling down again and again to the clerk to turn the sand-glass by which the half-hours were measured, he cried, " One glass more—one glass more and then."—(Dr Simpson's Sanquhar, p. 73–77.) Trying to urge his horse where she had formerly sunk, without effect, he cried, as it was frosty, " You have a better memory than judgment"—the saying passed into a proverb : " Like Kirkwood's horse, mair sense than judgment."

ADAM SINCLAIR, A.M., translated from Morton ; admitted before 25th January 1650 (Woodrow makes him at Morton, and one of the deprived in 1662. There must be some mistake). He died 25th July 1673, aged about 71.

THIRD PERIOD—1661–1689.

I. CRAWFORD.

ROBERT SMITH, A.M., Teacher at Peebles, ten years a preacher, presented by George, Bishop of Edinburgh, 1666. Continued, 1681, and probably vacated the charge on not taking the test.

JOHN BROWNE, A.M., degree from St Andrews. Presented by John, Bishop of Edinburgh, 1682. Purchased lands in 1707. Ousted at the Revolution. Alive February 1696.

With other western counties, Lanark had its full share of the persecution caused by the resistance of Scottish Presbyterians to the " black prelacy," which was sought to be imposed upon them by the Stewarts. The punishment inflicted by the " Highland Host," the battles of Drumclog and Bothwell, with the sufferings unto death of the heroic people, are all well known. At the Revolution of 1688, the declaration of the Prince of Orange was published at Glasgow, before any other part of Scotland. Lanarkshire, that ardently favoured the Revolution, as bitterly opposed the Union with England, in 1707. Following the lead of the Duke of Hamilton and several of the barons, scarcely a town or village but demonstrated their antipathy to that measure.

II. CRAWFORDJOHN.

WILLIAM THOMSON, A.M., degree from Edinburgh. Licensed by George, Bishop of Edinburgh, 1665. Continued 1681, and probably deprived for not taking the test. His widow got a discharge from the Kirk Session, 1st June 1700.

In 1666, the miller and his wife were cited for Sabbath breaking, by grinding of meale on Sabbath, after the sunset. In 1667, the Session Book was not produced to the Presbytery.

The farm and hill of Shawhead are memorable from a pointed sermon delivered in its neighbourhood by Richard Cameron. The cothouse, which was the homestead of that farm, was occupied by a tenant who removed to Canada. He was a specimen of several in the district who reared a respectable and prosperous family. " Many," it is said, " are still alive, who remember the late tenant of Shaw-head, an elder in his parish church, living full eight miles west, the road rough, the weather often wild, but rare was it that the good man failed to find his way to his place of worship—staff in hand, plaid over shoulder, his daughter on a pony, his boys following after."—(Upper Ward.)

JOHN NESBIT, A.M., degree from Edinburgh. Presented by William, Duke of Hamilton, 1682. Translated to Houston, 1686.

SAMUEL HOWAT, A.M., formerly of Kirkconnel, 168–. Ousted by the people, 1688, and went to Ireland. Returning, was recommended by the Archbishop of Glasgow to the charity of all good Christians, because of his wife and family, which was responded to by the Kirk Session of Muthill and Scoonie. In April 1702, imprisoned by Magistrates of Edinburgh, for celebrating clandestine marriages, &c. Died in that city, 20th July 1717, aged 68.

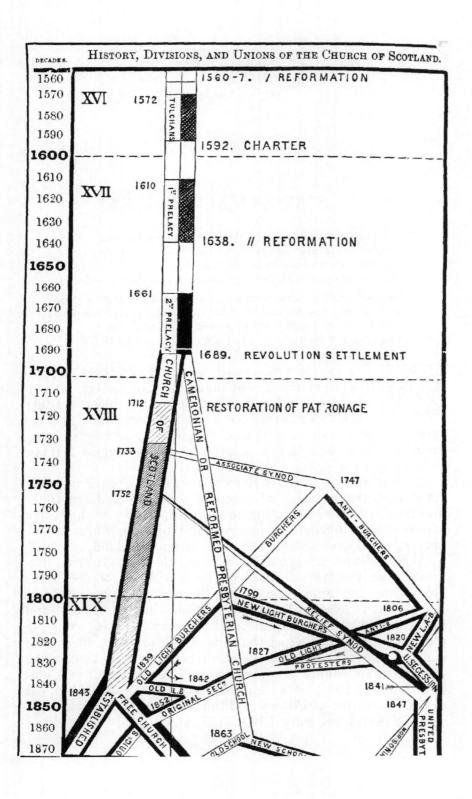

STRUGGLE AND VICTORY.

" O wild traditioned Scotland, thy briery burns and braes
Are full of pleasant memories and tales of other days.
Thy story-haunted waters in music gush along,
Thy mountain-glens are tragedies, thy heathy hills are song.

Land of the Bruce and Wallace, where patriot hearts have stood :
And for their country and their faith like water poured their blood :
Where wives and little children were steadfast to the death,
And graves of martyr'd warriors are in the desert heath."

THE struggle maintained by our forefathers, prior to the Revolution, was not, as some assert, a mere absence of toleration acting upon a bigoted adherence to an unreasonable form of worship. It was a struggle for freedom, civil and religious, as a constitutional right, by those who drank inspiration at the highest fountain of life and liberty.

Its first victory was the Reformation from Popery in 1560 ; its second, the national adoption of the Covenants in 1638 ; and its third, the Revolution settlement of 1688, with all that steady and well-grounded progress and blessing which as concurrent tides have elevated our people and our land.

Absolute and irresponsible power—the right to rule irrespective of the law of the land or the Word of the living God—was the grand aim of the Stewart dynasty ; and that not merely in relation to outward action—human thought and belief must also be subject to their sway. Prelacy was the tool employed, and which lent itself willingly, to effect this end. Presbytery was the agent of resolute resistance, along with national bonds or covenants. "The Godlie," or Common Bond of 1557, with that of 1559 (1581 and 1588), led to the overthrow of Popery and the recognition and establishment of Scriptural truth 1560, 1567, and 1592.

Previous efforts to dominate gathered force from the ascension of James VI. to the throne of Britain in 1603. Prelacy as his handmaid was elevated anew, with "consecrated" vessels from 1610 to 1638—while the "Court of High Commission" banished such godly ministers as Rutherford of Anworth and Dickson of Irvine.

THE "TABLES" AND THE COVENANT.

Roused to action by the imposition, of a religious service-book,

> " Then her stool seized Jenny Geddes,
>   Hearty hater of humbug ;
>   Would you not be sent to Hades,
>   Lay no masses at her lug."   —*Proudfoot.*

That was but the straw indicating the direction of the current. Some 60,000 persons flocked to Edinburgh to petition for redress of grievances. Four "Tables," or Committees, were their extemporised Interim Government, and, under its direction, the Covenants were sworn.

That renewal of ancient national covenants, with adaptation to the pressing emergency, in the church and churchyard of Old Greyfriars, and throughout the land, in 1638, is one of the noblest acts in Scottish story. Alexander Henderson's prayer, the Earl of Loudon's explanation and vindication, Johnstone's reading of the parchment, the answers given to objectors by the Earl of Rothes and David Dickson, the first signature of the aged Earl of Sutherland, the signing on the flat gravestones—some with their own warm hearts' blood, others with the affix "till death," the resolute activity and eagerness of the people which made it possible that at that period it could be signed over most parts of the country in the course of two months, the healing of old feuds, the solemn swearing by the great name of God to hold fast by the gospel, and to defend each other in the maintenance thereof—all this is not only deeply impressive, it proclaimed emphatically that the people were ONE AND FREE.

Then followed the overthrow of Prelacy and the restoration of Presbytery in the Assembly, which met in the venerable Cathedral Church in Glasgow, closed by the memorable words of Alexander Henderson : " We have now cast down the walls of Jericho ; let him that rebuildeth them beware of the curse of Hiel the Bethelite."

THE KILLING TIME.

Brief was the respite granted to the Covenanters. From 1640, twenty-eight years of as severe conflict as ever nation encountered, were intensified emphatically into the "killing time," until the shadows broke up and the darkness passed away.

The Scottish people had but two things to crave at the hands of the king. These were—A FREE PARLIAMENT, AND A FREE ASSEMBLY. Both were denied: "I give you leave to flatter them with what hopes you please," were the deceitful secret instructions of Charles I. to Hamilton. "Declare them not traitors till my fleet be ready to sail for Scotland." But they knew the man with whom they had to deal. "We know," said Loudon, "no other bonds between a king and his subjects but those of religion and laws. If these are violated, our lives are not dear to us. Overborne by threatenings we will not be. Such fears are past with us."

Animated by such a heroic resolution, the Covenanters went calmly and firmly onwards in defence. Their "information of the crisis" was published. The Castles of Edinburgh and Dunbar occupied, Leith fortified, beacons ready to be lighted on every mountain height, deputations sent to, if possible, avoid a conflict. Then, 30,000 strong, they marshalled on Dunse Law, with banners that told the reason why. If they must, they will, to maintain "CHRIST'S CROWN AND COVENANT." No wonder that despots trembled, and that no blow was struck. Hearing that morning and evening by sound of drum the Covenanters assembled to supplicate the aid of their Covenant God, they could not but feel and say, "These men will conquer or die."

How political scheming broke up that unity and power; and how the people of England became convinced that they must ultimately become the victims of a monarch whom no treaties could bind; or, that they must secure their own lives by his death, resulting in the tragedy at Whitehall in 1649, are subjects worthy of consideration.

THE SCONE PALACE WARNING.

Attached to monarchy, the Scottish people hesitated not to proclaim Charles II. king, but his coronation at the Old Palace of Scone was a solemn farce—because of his insincerity. Holding that the end sanctified the means, and no help appearing from any other quarter, Charles embraced the Covenants to gain the crown.

On the 1st January 1651, Robert Douglas preached. "Our king receiveth this day a power to govern, *limited by contract.* To these conditions he is bound by oath. There must be no tyranny upon the throne." The Covenants were read, and then the prince lifting up his right hand swore: I, Charles, King of Great Britain, France and Ireland, do assure and declare, by my solemn oath, in presence of Almighty God, the Searcher of hearts, my allowance and approval of the National Covenant, and of the Solemn League and Covenant, and faithfully oblige myself to prosecute the ends thereof." These documents he subscribed; and then took the Coronation oath; "To maintain the true religion of Jesus Christ, and to rule the people according to the Word and command of God, and loveable laws and constitution of the realm." The Crown having been set upon his head by the Marquis of Argyll, the people then with uplifted hands took oath:—"We become your liegemen, and truth and faith shall bear to you, and live and die with you against all manner of folk in your service, according to the National Covenant and the Solemn League and Covenant." "Sire!" Robert Douglas exclaimed in concluding the ceremony—"Sire! destroyers are prepared for the injustice of the throne. Execute righteous judgment. IF NOT, YOUR HOUSE WILL BE A DESOLATION."

This compound of falsehood, treachery, and vice, hardened and matured rather than improved by adversity, proved utterly false to all these solemn engagements, and the prophecy was fulfilled. His house did become a desolation. But not until he had been made a terrific scourge.

Defeated at Dunbar and at Worcester by Cromwell, for ten years Charles and royalty were banished the kingdom. Restored as by miracle on the 29th May 1660, Clarendon, Middleton, and Sharp, were the instruments by whom Charles sought "to tame, shape, and strike terror into the hearts of the Covenanters." His remaining years were employed in using the entire power at his command to destroy the Covenants and the Covenanters he had so solemnly sworn to uphold.

THE PRINCE VASSAL,

the mighty Marquis of Argyll, was his first selected victim. And this stroke of terror was repeated on prince and peasant, holy men, and tender women and children, till the nation, maddened and bleeding to death, arose, and, by one of her sons, pronounced that doom of the house of Stewart which shortly thereafter was carried into execution.

Lured by false promises to London, the Marquis was sent from the presence chamber to the Tower, and thence to Edinburgh, where, on a charge of treason, Scotland stood on her trial in the person of her representative. Death predetermined, Argyll received his sentence kneeling. "I had," he said, "the honour to set the crown upon the king's head, and now he hastens me to receive a better crown than his own." "The Lord will require it!" cried the Marchioness. "Forbear!" said Argyll. "They know not what they do. They cannot shut out God from me, and He lets not out too much of His communications here, for He knows I could not bear it." "My Lord," exclaimed the Rev. James Guthrie to him upon the scaffold, "such is my respect for your Lordship, that if I were not under sentence of death myself, I could cheerfully die for you." With steady step, calm pulse, and unmoved countenance, at peace with God and man, this true patriot fell by the axe of the Scottish "Maiden" on the 27th May 1661.

Argyll was pre-eminently a martyr on the altar of religion and liberty. His greatness consisted not merely in being able to bring forth some 20,000 men at his call from the forests of Badenoch to the Mull of Kintyre; it lay rather in that principle of wisdom, so necessary for every one to cultivate—he governed others by being able to govern *himself*. Then he acted upon three grand maxims, not less important in modern times :—*First*, CONSTITUTIONAL MONARCHY; but rather let the throne be vacant than that it should be occupied by a despot. *Second*, LET HIERARCHIES PERISH, for they can only live by eating into the flesh of free men. *Third*, CONFIDENCE IN COUNTRY. Never abandon truth and freedom although opposite principles for a time prevail. Happy would it be for our people and our land were these three principles fully understood and translated into practice.

A HISTORY WRITTEN IN BLOOD

is that of the following twenty-seven years in Scotland. It has not, it could not be, fully written. Mere gleanings have been gathered of that red vintage, as of "the Pentland Rising" in 1666, the battle of Drumclog, 1679, and the sad tale of Bothwell Brig, where

> " When the enemy had won the bridge,
>   The Westland men did flee ;
>   The English men and Clavers' both
>   Did kill them grievously.
>   And all along through Hamilton town
>   They did both kill and wound ;
>   Until the streets with bodies dead
>   Were covered in the town."

The mountains and glens in the South Highlands are everlasting memorials of the heroic sufferings of Covenanted sires, who secured our freedom with their blood.

PEDEN'S GLENS.

Thus, a stream and glen that run down from the Lowthers still bear the name of Peden, as that man of God often found shelter in a shepherd's cottage there, and by that burnside enjoyed precious seasons of communion with God.

Glendyne, a long winding deep glen running up from the Mennock to the Blackhill, dividing it from the Wanlock, was another of his favourite retreats.

Dr Simpson gives a tradition, that mosstroopers coming suddenly upon him, Peden fled, and that when about to pass a burn, he crept into a cavity, and that the hoof of one of the horses actually grazed his head and pressed his bonnet into the clay ; but that, left uninjured, he found in the deliverance matter of praise. Again, "In Auchengrouch Muirs, Captain John Mathison and others being with him, they were alarmed with a report that the enemy were coming fast upon him. But he not being able to run hard by reason of age, he desired them to forbear a little until he prayed, when he said, 'Lord, we are ever needing at Thy hand, and if we had not Thy command to call upon Thee in the day of trouble, and Thy promise of answering us in the day of our distress, we wot not what would become of us. If Thou have any more work for us in Thy world, allow us the lap of Thy cloak this day again.' When ended, he ran alone a little, and came back quickly, saying : 'Lads, the bitterest of this blast is over ; we will be troubled no more with them this day.' Foot and horse came the length of Andrew Clark's, in Auchengrouch, where they were covered with a dark mist, and roared out because they could not get the execrable Whigs pursued for it."

RESCUE AT COGSHEAD.

"Drumlanrig himself conducted the troopers over the north height of Glendyne, and descended on the Water of Cog to 'The Martyr's Knowe,' a romantic elevation at the lower end of an abrupt ravine called 'The Howken.' They seized a boy who was returning from Glenhilloch to Cogshead, carrying an empty wooden vessel, called a *kit*, in which were several horn spoons— a proof that he had been conveying food to some persons among the hills. They strictly interrogated the boy, but to no purpose. The firmness of the youth enraged Drumlanrig, who drew his sword with the intent to run him through the body, and would have slain him on the spot—but he caused him to be bound hand and foot, while he sent out the soldiers in the direction in which he had been seen returning. The soldiers found the men in their hiding places, and secured Dun, Paterson and Richard, while Brown, Morris and Welsh made their escape. But the soldiers were visited with one of those hasty thunderstorms which are frequent amongst the hills. When the dragoons who led the three prisoners were within a short distance of Drumlanrig's station on the Martyr's Knowe, the first burst of thunder rattled its startling peal over their heads. The rapid descent of the hail, the loud roaring of the thunder, and the flashing of the sheeted lightning in the faces of the animals, rendered them unmanageable, and they scampered off. In the confusion, Drumlanrig, himself panic-struck, fled reckless both of his men and his prisoners, provided he could find shelter, and the soldiers followed his example. The prisoners making use of their opportunity fled; but as they passed the Martyr's Knowe they saw the boy lying apparently lifeless. Untying and advising him to seek concealment, they went westward and found a retreat among the wilds of Galloway."

Dr Simpson hands down another tradition concerning Alexander Williamson, who lived at Cruffell, near the source of the Yeochan, who carrying his child over the hills to Carsphairn to be baptized, left his wife exposed to a rude assault from the soldiery in his absence; and relates the gratitude which in all probability would be felt when the family gathered in safety once more around the family altar. Glenglas is also mentioned, as a spot to which the persecuted fled for shelter.

Again, he tells of a servant favourable to them, who waited on Dalziel of Carnwath, who kept a small troop of dragoons at Elioch House. This man used to go out and address a huge tree that grew upon the side of the Carple Burn, in such terms as these : "O fair and stately tree, many a time have I stationed myself in meditative mood under your wide-spreading boughs and mantling foliage, to listen to the delicious murmuring of the gentle stream, and to hear the delicious music of the songsters—but mayhap to-morrow by this time I shall be elsewhere, as I shall be called to follow my master, with his band of troopers, to pursue some of those unhappy Covenanters, who are understood to be lurking in some place near this." Thus without speaking to the man who occupied a cavity beneath, important warning was conveyed. South Mains is particularly mentioned as a place of refuge, which shared the attention of these "troopers." Cleuchfoot is noticed in connection with Patrick Laing's wanderings and escapes—his sword having been handed down as an heirloom.

John Willison of Glengeith in Crawford, had a room so constructed as to form a secret place of shelter for the persecuted. Cargill and other godly men often found there a resting place. But Glengeith was exposed to visits from the dragoons who were stationed in Crawford; and a heroic defiance uttered by his wife to a rude soldier has been handed down, declaring that without the permission of God he could not touch a hair of her head.

The Clarks of Brandleys, Auchengrouch, and Glenim, are also placed amongst the worthies of those days of trial.

Of course Dr Simpson gives these and other stories merely as traditions handed down, which he clothes in interesting and instructive language. But in regard to the sufferers "the half has not been told," nor ever will be known until that day when all secret things shall be revealed.

The rescue of a minister during the Covenanting struggle was planned and carried out by some of the miners in Wanlockhead and Leadhills. Wanlockhead was long the haunt and refuge of the persecuted, and a meeting of Covenanters was held in Wanlockhead in 1680, when they resolved that duty and safety seemed to require them to rise in a posture of self-defence—not suddenly; not at all, if only for England, but when the whole country pressed to declare themselves.— (*Faithful Contendings*, p. 356.)

At the time of the Revolution the Cameronians were called to Edinburgh to protect the Scottish Parliament while deliberating on the transfer of the Crown to William of Orange against the plots which environed them. For this service they were publicly thanked by Parliament, whilst they refused to receive any pay. They served not as mercenaries, but as men devoted to the Covenant. The following account has been preserved, amongst others, of one

RESCUE IN ENTERKIN PASS.

"Enterkin is an exceeding large and lofty mountain, along whose side the road wynds with a moderate ascent for upwards of a mile, till about midway it becomes more steep, the aclivity on the other side being nearly perpendicular; while, on the other, a tremendous precipice, dark and horrid, descends into a narrow, deep bottom, only broad enough for the wintry torrent, whence again the mountain rises immediately, and almost equally abrupt, to a stupendous height. The road then was so narrow that two horsemen could with difficulty march abreast, and the least stumble endangered their being precipitated over the edge, in which case there was no possibility of recovery. Through this pass the soldiers were proceeding with the minister (supposed to be Mr Welsh of Irongray) and the other prisoners—the front reaching near to the top of the hill, and the rest stretching along the steep path—when they suddenly heard a voice calling to them from above. It was misty, and nobody was at first seen; but the commanding officer halted and asked who they were, and what they wanted? He had scarcely spoken, when a dozen countrymen made their appearance upon the side of the hill above him. When the officer repeated his inquiry and ordered them to stand, one, who appeared to be their leader, ordering his men to make ready, asked the officer—'Sir, will you deliver our minister?' 'No, sir,' with an oath, was the reply. On this the other fired immediately, and with so true an aim that he shot him through the head, and he instantly fell. His horse started and staggered over the precipice, and, rolling to the bottom, was dashed to pieces. The rest of the twelve men were preparing to fire, when the officer next in command demanded a truce for his party, which was in such a situation that not a man of them durst stir a foot or offer to fire a shot, as, had their opponents given a volley, in all probability they would have driven double their number down the side of the mountain into the dreadful gulph at the bottom.

"'We wish to hurt none of you,' said the countrymen, 'only restore our minister and other friends and prisoners.'

189

To this the soldiers were constrained to consent, and they were loosed and let go. When the minister had proceeded a few steps the officer said—'I let you go, and I expect you to promise to oblige your people to offer no hindrance to our march.' This the minister promised to do. 'Then go,' cried the officer, 'you owe your life to this cursed mountain.' 'Rather say,' answered he, 'to that God who made the mountain.'

Meanwhile, some travellers appeared in the pass, which being too narrow for both, they went a little up the hill to allow the soldiers to march on. The officer, observing them, and thinking they were a part of his armed opponents, called to the leader to be as good as his word, and order off the fellows he had posted at the end of the way. 'They belong not to us,' said the honest man, 'they are unarmed people, waiting till you pass by.' 'Say you so,' replied the officer; 'had I known that, you had not got your men so cheap, nor have come off so free.' 'An' ye are for battle, sir,' retorted the countryman; 'we are ready for you still. If you think you are able for us you may try your hand—we'll quit the truce.' 'No,' said the officer, 'I think ye be brave fellows: e'en gang your gait.' The prisoners (nine in all) were being brought from Dumfries Jail to Edinburgh, escorted by a guard of twenty-eight soldiers. This was in 1686. The rescue was followed by an ambulatory commission, who interrogated upon oath the population in the neighbourhood above the age of fifteen, and the justices were compelled to execute sentence passed within six hours after its being pronounced."—(See *Dodd's Covenanters*, p. 373.) Defoe gives another account, and it is supposed that Enterkin was the scene of several such successful rescues. (See Illustration, Enterkin.)

The deep impression produced upon a sensitive mind by the silent and solemn grandeur of this mountain pass is indescribable. A rock sofa on the side of the path, affords a rest to the pedestrian, who seems to be climbing up a ladder to the skies. In this "Deil's chair,"—probably so named as the resting-spot of the baffled dragoons when the rescue was made—time is afforded to meditate on the mysterious and yet gracious workings of God to men, churches, and nations, so as to the full accomplishment of His sovereign will. Or, again nearing the summit, and embracing the small crystalline spring denominated "Katie's well," the traveller cries—

"Wow, but the braes are dour tae spiel,
And what wi' loupin' hags and burns,

It's richt weel pleased I am to kneel
  Beside thee, till my breath returns.
And restin' here, tae feel the calm
  O' this lown glen come owre my min',
While memory lea's me in a dwaum,
  Wi' gowden glints frae auld lang syne.

Wha kens but Peden's haly lips,
  Or black M'Michael's bearded mou',
At times may hae been fain tae dip,
  Where mine but gethert strength enow?

O winsome well that rins sae clear
  In this far hid unheard-o' glen!
'Twas Heaven alane that prankt thee here,
  Sic gift nae ither han' could sen'."   —*Reid.*

Impressive at all times, when thick mist fills the pass, and you perceive no height, depth, length, or breadth but that on which you tread, the scene is overwhelming.

Noble and peasant have felt and acknowledged the majesty of the scene. Sir Thomas Kirkpatrick of Closeburn—probably the same whose mansion was burned down in 1748 — riding down this pass in company with the farmer of Newton, Mr John Ross, had here a narrow escape for his life. His horse stumbled, and Sir Thomas was all but thrown over the rocks into the chasm below. Regaining his feet without injury, he called to his companion to alight—" John, come down, and let us kneel and give thanks to God "—an impressive occurrence, which the farmer ever after was delighted to rehearse as a pleasing trait in the character of his laird.

" Fifteen years ago," said a young man in my hearing, " I passed down the pass of Enterkin, thoughtless, Christless. Suddenly eternity arose before my mind, and how unprepared I was to enter upon it. I resolved to go no further in that wretched condition. I stopped, threw myself on my knees, implored the Divine mercy through the merits of the Redeemer, and solemnly gave myself away in covenant to be now and for ever the Lord's. And since that time I have been much helped through grace."

· THE SANQUHAR DECLARATION.

Sanquhar was chosen by Richard Cameron, his brother Michael, and twenty armed horsemen, for the publication of the famous declaration denouncing " Charles Stewart " for his " perjury and usurpation in Church matters, and tyranny in matters civil," and " disowning him that has been reigning, or rather tyrannising, on the Throne of Britain." This was read and afterwards affixed to the Market Cross on the 23d June 1680. In 1675 the Earl of Queensberry, Lord Chancellor of Scotland, directed the work of putting down the insurrection which broke out in 1666, but no such severities could quench the spirit of freedom. The "Queensferry Paper," prepared early in 1680 by the Covenanters, rejected the King and his associates, because they had " altered and destroyed the Lord's established religion ; overturned the fundamental laws of the kingdom ; and changed the civil government of this land, which was by a King and Free Parliament, into tyranny." And now Cameron chose this anniversary of the defeat at Bothwell Brig and this centre of martyrland to proclaim openly what had already been privately subscribed. They deemed it a part of God's controversy with them that they had not long ago disowned the perjured King. A patriotic and consistent defiance was made by the inhabitants of this district to the doctrine of passive obedience to despotic authority. (2) A second declaration was published at Sanquhar by Mr Renwick on the accession of James, Duke of York, " witnessing against the usurpation by a Papist of the government of the nation," on the 28th May 1685. Other declarations were published by the " Cameronians " at the same place ; (3) on the 10th August 1692 ; (4) on the 6th November 1695 ; (5) the 21st May 1703 ; and again (6) in 1707, when the Cameronians regarded the union between England and Scotland as the consummation of national guilt, being a direct violation of the great Covenants by which both kingdoms were solemnly bound. The first of these declarations was by far the most important. (See Appendix and Illustration.)

Mr Cameron declared that the Sanquhar declaration would shake the Throne of Britain, and the prediction was verified in the Revolution. The nation acted upon the very same principles in 1688 which in 1680 were boldly declared by Richard Cameron at the Cross of Sanquhar.

It is a singular coincidence that Sanquhar was visited by James VI. (1617) shortly after he ascended the British Throne, he having come north purposely to plan out more fully the suppression of all opposition to his despotic authority ; and that in that same royal burgh the doom of his house was publicly pronounced by servants of Christ, who had been goaded to desperation by sixty-three years' carrying out of such plans ; and which desolation, as predicted by Douglas and pronounced by Cameron, was actually accomplished in 1688.

James Hislop, a poet of the district, has feelingly described the brief conflict on Airs' Moss, in which Cameron was killed, in a piece entitled

"CAMERONIAN'S DREAM.

" 'Twas morning, and Summer's young sun from the east
Lay in loving repose on the green mountain's breast;
On Wardlaw and Cairntable the clear shining dew
Glistened sheen 'mong the heath bells and mountain flowers blue.

" 'Twas the few faithful ones who with Cameron were lying
Concealed 'mong the mist where the heath fowl were crying,
For the horsemen of Earlshall around them were hovering,
And their bridle reins rang through the thin misty covering.

" Their faces grew pale, and their swords were unsheathed,
But the vengeance that darkened their brow was unbreathed;
With eyes turned to heaven, in calm resignation,
They sang their last song to the God of salvation.

" When the righteous had fallen, and combat was ended,
A chariot of fire through the dark cloud descended;
Its drivers were angels on horses of whiteness,
And its burning wheels turned on axles of brightness.

" On the arch of the rainbow the chariot is gliding,
Through the path of the thunder the horsemen are riding—
Glide swiftly, bright spirits, the prize is before ye,
A crown never failing, a kingdom of glory."

Two hundred years after Cameron's declaration was published, a commemoration was held at Sanquhar on the 22d June 1860, and a grey granite monument was erected at a cost of £80. It bears that it was erected "In commemoration of the two famous Sanquhar declarations, which were published on this spot, where stood the ancient cross of the burgh, the one by the Rev. Richard Cameron on the 22d June 1680, the other by the Rev. James Renwick on the 29th May 1685."

THE KILLING TIME.

" If you would know the nature of their crime,
Then read the story of that killing time."

At that demonstration Professor Blackie read a sonnet which he had composed in the Sanquhar Hotel after a journey of twenty miles over the hills from Carsphairn, which says, regarding Richard Cameron's declaration, that

" Men called it rash—perhaps it was a crime—
His deed flashed out God's will an hour before the time."

Don Carlos, who crossed over from Boulogne to Folkstone,

and arrived in London on March 4th 1876, who expresses confidence in the resuscitation of his cause, and who was received with groans and hisses by the representatives of various English societies who happened to be present, both at Folkstone and London, is said to be not only the representative of the Spanish branch of the Bourbons, but by his grandfather, the late Duke of Modena (who left him a fortune of eight millions), the surviving head of the Scottish Stewarts, and is thus held by some to be, by right of birth, *King of Great Britain* no less than King of Spain.

His Stewart pedigree is thus traced as distinct and unquestionable. Henrietta, the daughter of Charles I., educated in France as a Romanist by her mother, became the wife of Philip, Duke of Orleans, the ancestor of Louis Philippe. A princess of the House of Orleans, sprung from this union, married into the House of Savoy, and a princess of Savoy, their lineal descendant, was the mother of the late Duke of Modena, whose daughter in turn became the mother of this Don Carlos. The male line of the Stewarts being extinct, the representation of the family is thus held to rest with him.

As the representative also of Ultramontanism or Popery in its most virulent form, he doubtless understands, and desires to be avenged of the Revolution of 1688, as he has tried to emulate the romantic adventures of Charles Edward in Northern Spain.

It is thus evident how easily, at the beck of the Vatican, God might permit a scourge to arise and chastise Britain for her past and continued unfaithfulness as a nation to the truth of Christ, with which she has been intrusted, and to which she solemnly pledged herself. And it will be interesting for future historians to mark whether, as a reward of Britain's repentance and the performance of "the First Works," the doom pronounced by James Douglas at Scone in 1651, and by Richard Cameron in 1688 continues to rest upon the Royal House of the Stewarts. There would undoubtedly be greater confidence enjoyed by many, who consider the rapid advance of Popery to power and influence in Britain, were the people of God to enter into a solemn compact to plead that none but truly Christian princes might be permitted to sit upon the British Throne.

Is there no cause to mourn over our national rejection of God and His law? Assuredly if ever nation was by repeated and most solemn acts yielded up in covenant bonds to be for Christ and not for another—this is that land. It does not

194

follow, that to maintain this covenanting testimony men are bound to renew the Covenants in precisely the same way, or in the identical terms in which our fathers were called upon to pledge themselves to one another and to God. And yet the matter as conclusively presents itself to the mind, that if ever there was a time when the gathering forces of infidelity, irreligion, rationalism, ritualism, popery, ignorance, radicalism, rascality, and revolution, required that the people of God in the several Churches of Great Britain should nationally unite in binding themselves solemnly to each other and to God, in order to the firm resistance of these evils, and to advance those interests of truth and righteousness which can at once save our nation from every danger, and make her, as in times past, great, glorious, and free—the present is such a time.

Surely every true patriot ought to yield himself, and endeavour to influence others to (1) acknowledge the supreme authority of God's Word, (2) to do homage to the Lord Jesus Christ as King of nations in every proper and possible way, and (3) to uphold and strengthen the Protestantism of the National Constitution, while resisting and repelling whatever would subvert our religion and our liberty. It would be a hopeful and blessed event were multitudes of men and women found flocking as of old with eager, warm, and enlightened hearts to sign and maintain such a sacred bond.

A shepherd Covenanter—the author of "Truth frae 'mang the Heather," justly observes that—

"The father-in-law of the great Hebrew Lawgiver addressed this counsel to his friend—'Thou shalt provide out of all the people able men, such as fear God, men of truth, hating covetousness, and place such over them to be rulers.' The man according to God's own heart left this as his dying testimony—'The God of Israel said, the Rock of Israel spake to me, He that ruleth over men must be just, ruling in the fear of God.' And if it ought to be so with the rulers, so also with those who have the power of election, for those who hold that power are in a secondary and subordinate sense the rulers themselves. One end for which society is organised is to promote its peace and order, and that peace and order is enjoyed exactly in proportion as the precepts of the moral law are respected and obeyed; therefore to encourage obedience and restrain disobedience is the first duty of rulers. And if there is one lesson more than another to be learned from the history of nations, it is this : *That the rejection of God and His law is the most dangerous social foe against which a nation requires to be protected.*"

The Rev. Dr Wylie, Professor of the Protestant Institute,

Edinburgh, recently stated his belief *"that if the agencies which were at present in operation went on unchecked for several years, England would again be a Popish country,"* which meant the fall of liberty over half the globe."

On the other hand, many have been greatly encouraged to hope that by the tardy act of justice rendered by the Legislature in 1874, in the complete abolition of patronage in the Established Church, a way may yet be found for the re-union of the separated branches of our Scottish Zion.

A real revival and practical manifestation of godliness in all the land is much required. With the poet, have we not to confess that in many places there's little

"To mind ye o' the brave auld times—the Covenant times awa."

Does he not speak with much truth when he says

" The braid blue bannet still may cleed the pows in green Glencairn,
The laverock wake the mavis yet in howes o' auld Carsphairn;
But waes me for the Covenant psalm that echoed aince amang
The wastlin' hames o' Scotland, mair sweet than mavis sang.

" Aince gaed ye east, or gaed ye wast, on howm or heather braes,
In clachan, cot, an' shiel was heard the e'enin' lilt o' praise;
And i' the calm o' morn and even, the solemn sounds o' prayer
Frae Scotland's hames amang the hills, went floatin' up the air.

" Frae Solway to Dunottar, frae the Bass to Fenwick Moor,
The Covenant life was bonnie aince, the Covenant faith was pure;
The flowers o' heaven were rife on earth—Frae 'neath the auld blue bannet
Cam' croonin' up King David's psalm, or aiblins Erskine's sonnet.

" But noo nae mair amang the glens, nae mair amang the hills,
The simple strains o' Covenant times, the muirlan' shepherd trills;
Ye'll wander far afore ye hear the e'enin' psalm ava,
The bonnie flowers o' Scotland's faith are nearly wede awa."

—*George Paulin.*

196

CHURCHES SINCE THE REVOLUTION.

" I seek divine simplicity in him
Who handles things divine."
COWPER.

THE interval from the Revolution settlement to the present time may conveniently be divided into two periods—(1) from 1689 to 1800, about which time (1799 and 1806) two divisions in the Church arose out of the "New Light" of opposition to the connection between Church and State; (2) from 1800 to this date. The *quoad sacra* churches of Leadhills and Wanlockhead, non-established churches, and the old church and parish of Kirkbride will then come under the eye.

FIRST PERIOD—1689-1800.

I. CRAWFORD.

In 1693 the Presbytery recorded that the offering at Crawford included "two bad shillings, a thrie, and a babie."

James Hepburn, 1698; died 5th July 1738, in 71st year and 41st ministry. On the induction of Mr Hepburn in 1698, a report shows that £286, 13s. 4d. Scots was expended on the manse, £10 for thatching, £80 for offices, and that, in addition to other wants, a kitchen, a brew-house, a bell with glass windows and seats for the church, were required. There was £100 salary for the schoolmaster, but no schoolhouse. Then also gross scandals had fallen out, so that application was to be made to the sheriff that some public stigma should be put upon the guilty.

John Hepburn, son of former, presented by George II., 1738; died 27th April 1759, in 50th year and 20th ministry.

John Kingan, licensed by Presbytery of Kirkcudbright; called in consequence of the *jus devolutum*, 1760; died 9th February 1781, in 59th year and 21st ministry.

James M'Conochie, licensed by Presbytery of Strathbogie, 1781; died 29th June 1806, in 25th ministry. Published—Sermon on National Fast, 1794; Discourses concerning the Writer of the Fourth Gospel, 1803; and Thoughts on National Defence, 1813.

The Stipend (1792) was £1000 Scots, and the King patron; "but some say that the right was vested in the family of Douglas." The church manse and school old buildings. The schoolmaster's salary £100 Scots. 30 children in attendance. Only 15 or 16 paupers on the roll.

II. CRAWFORDJOHN.

The oldest register of births and marriages commenced in 1690.

John Bryce, 1693; died 1704, in 11th of ministry.

In 1696 several of the entries in the session-book were declared to be illegal, and in 1704 that book was written "ill-spelled and ill-worded," whereby it is unintelligible and nonsense in some places. That volume, beginning in 1693, and ending in 1709, is still in existence. On the 27th June 1704, the Presbytery found that the church furniture consisted of "two silver communion cups, table cloaths, a pewter basin and stoupe for baptisme, communion tables, and a sand-glass"—for measuring the time of service.

Robert Lang, licensed by Presbytery of Biggar; nominated by the Presbytery *jure devoluto* 18th November 1708. The Act 1690 was then in force. It vested the patronage in the heritors and kirk-session, and the appointment was the occasion of much angry contention and riot. Lord Selkirk and some of the elders wished to elect Mr Wilson, another heritor with supporters favoured Mr Wood, and a third was proposed by some others. The Presbytery, on the very day six months after the death of the late minister, resolved to exercise their right, and to appoint a fourth. The matter being carried before the Synod and General Assembly, its decision was adverse to the views of all the four parties. At length Mr Robert Lang was appointed to preach 26th December 1708. His reception was far from cordial. When he went to preach, he found the church doors locked and nailed up, so that he preached in the churchyard. The chamberlain having caused the locks of the manse to be removed and replaced by new ones, refused to give him possession five years after the vacancy had occurred, on which the Presbytery communicated with the Lord Advocate, who advised "that application be made to the Justices of the Peace to make open doors and repossess him." Translated to Newburgh 1711.

Robert Davidsone, licensed by Presbytery of Hamilton. Chaplain to Lady Blantyre. Ordained 1713; died 7th January 1749, in 68th year and 36th of ministry. "Amiable and faithful, always prepared for emergencies. Instantaneously penetrated the motives of human conduct, and by practical exposition of absurdities, with humorous representation of real occurrences, at once maintained the ascendancy of a superior mind, and contributed to the harmless amusement of his friends and associates." One son became minister of Old Kilpatrick, and another, Dr Archibald, Principal of the University of Glasgow.

William Millar, licensed by Presbytery of Paisley; presented by Commissioners for Dunbar, Earl of Selkirk, 1750; died February 3, 1801, in 82d year and 51st of ministry. "A Nathaniel indeed—contemned meanness, exposed artful designs, and denounced prevarication and hypocrisy." When offered an augmentation of his stipend by the heritors, he is said to have declined receiving it. Published New Statistical Account of Parish.

III. LEADHILLS.

The Presbytery of Lanark appear to have exerted themselves by communications with the Hopetoun family, in order to secure the services of a resident minister for the Leadhills Village. At length the sanction of the General Assembly was obtained, in 1736, for an ordained chaplain or preacher, *without providing a permanent endowment*, as required by the laws of the Church. Lord Hopetoun, however, retained power to employ a preacher or not, as he should think right. Immediately following this decision, a wing of "The Ha'" or mansion-house was converted into a chapel, as it stands at present, with a private entrance leading from "The Ha'" into "His Lordship's Loft," or gallery.

SUCCESSION OF MINISTERS AT LEADHILLS.

A preaching-station had been proposed on the 15th October 1699, and a preacher was provided by Charles, Earl of Hopetoun, 19th May 1738. It has since that time been supplied as follows:—1722, Mr Edward Buncle, afterwards of Kirkmahoe; 1722, Mr Alexander Duncan; 1728, Mr Alexander Henderson, afterwards of Portpatrick; 1732, Mr Robert Hunter, afterwards of Kirkconnel; 1746, Mr William Moncrieff, afterwards of Annan.

ORDAINED MINISTERS.

1785, Mr William Peterkin, afterwards of Ecclesmachen; 1788, Mr James Sanson, was a tall, awkward, bashful gentleman, generally termed "Dominie Sanson" by the inhabitants. Fond of playing at curling; when he made a good throw with his stone, he was in the habit of exclaiming "Prodigious!" This eccentricity observed by a boy (afterwards Mr John Irving, W.S.), being related to his friend (afterwards Sir Walter Scott), probably originated the story wrought out under the title of "Dominie Sampson."

Mr William Lang, 1796; died 8th April 1819, in 66th year and 23d ministry.

IV. SANQUHAR.

"The whole Churches of the Sheriffdom of Nidesdale and Stewartry of Annandale, being four presbyteries," says Symson, "did constitute one provincial synod, until the late restitution of Episcopacy; but since that time all the four presbyteries are within the Diocese of Glasgow."

Patrick Inglis, A.M., translated from Annan before 12th February 1686; was ousted by the people in 1689.

After the revolution of 1688, the first minister settled in Sanquhar was Thomas Shiels, who was one of the 400 ministers in Scotland and 2000 in England ejected in 1661 because they declined to own the King's supremacy in all causes ecclesiastical. He was translated from Kirkbride; called in September 1691; admitted 2d August 1693; died 8th February 1708, in his 78th year and 53d ministry. The tombstone of the Rev. Thomas Shields is the earliest in the churchyard, of a minister. One of the most peculiar stones near it is coffin-shaped, with a smaller one by its side. It bears a sword and the initials R. H., near the front door of the church.

Mungo Gibsone, translated from Abbotrule; called in November, and admitted in December 1713; died between 17th December 1735 and 4th February 1736, in 38th ministry. He had two sons, George and William, and a daughter, Janet. His official usefulness was terminated by a paralytic stroke in the pulpit. (See Kirkbride.)

John Sandilands, licensed by the Presbytery of Biggar 30th August 1733; called 29th December 1737; and ordained 27th April thereafter; died (in consequence of a fall from his horse) 29th August 1741, in 4th ministry.

John Irving, translated from Wamphray; called 17th February, and admitted 9th June 1743; died 14th September 1752, in 20th ministry. His books brought £43, 1s. 4½d. sterling. He married Helen Irving, who died 25th October 1739.

William Cunninghame, A.M., translated from Durisdeer, presented by Charles, Duke of Queensberry and Dover, in February, and admitted 29th May 1753; died 25th August 1768, in 32d ministry. He was clever and accomplished, and pleasing and elegant in his manners beyond most of his day, so that Catherine, Duchess of Queensberry, made him, when in his former charge, her daily companion, which led to his being termed "the Duchess' walking-staff." He married in 1645 Helen Sinclair, who died 15th January 1785.

John Thomson, licensed by the Presbytery 1st April 1767, presented by Charles, Duke of Queensberry and Dover, 9th October 1768, and ordained 7th September following; translated to Markinch 2d March 1785.

This Rev. John Thomson was the father of the Rev. Andrew Thomson, of St George's, Edinburgh, who was born in the old house on the margin of the River Nith. He was the first ordained minister of Sprouston, translated to East Church, Perth, in 1810 to New Greyfriars, Edinburgh, and in 1814 to St George's, Edinburgh, the second Presbyterian Church erected in the New Town, at a cost of upwards of £33,000, a pastorate of great success and power. As a preacher, a member of Church courts, a literary man, a controversialist, a patriot, a prilanthropist, Dr Andrew Thomson maintained his pre-eminence until his sudden death in 1831. His services in the Apocrypha controversy, in the cause of civil and religious liberty, and of negro emancipation, ought not to be forgotten. He was one of the most eminent of the men to whom the "old town" parish has given birth.

1785.—William Rankin, licensed by the Presbytery of Kirkcudbright 7th October 1778, presented by William, Duke of Queensberry, in August, and ordained 22d September 1785; died 7th October 1820, in his 70th year and 36th ministry. He married, 8th December 1788, Margaret Barker, who died 25th March 1837, and had Thomas, Solicitor Supreme Courts, Edinburgh ; and Margaret, who married Lieutenant David Adam of the Royal Marines. Publication— Account of the Parish (Sinclair's Statistical Account).

THE SECESSION CHURCH.

What is now termed the South United Presbyterian Church was first erected in 1742, and rebuilt in 1841, containing 450 sittings. The Rev. John Hepburn, inducted in 1680 as incumbent of the parish of Urr, is regarded as the originator of the Secession movement in the south of Scotland. His concern for the spread of evangelical truth led him to preach in other parishes without asking or obtaining the permission of the ministers. He was suspended in 1696, and eventually deposed in 1703, for "intruding himself and exercising his ministry without taking the oaths of allegiance and subscribing the assurance." These sentences he disregarded, exercising his ministry over Dumfriesshire and Galloway till his death in 1723. Thereafter, many of his adherents followed the "M'Millanites or Mountain Men." On the rise of the Secession, ten years later, they formally acceded to the Associate Presbytery under the designation of South and West." At that time Sanquhar, Kirkconnel, Wanlockhead, and Closeburn, were supplied with occasional preaching, and also Moniaive and Thornhill. Adherents in these two villages were formed into another congregation when the Sanquhar Church was built.

Another circumstance tending to foster dissent was the compulsory reading of the Act for bringing to justice those who had executed Captain John Porteous. One minister gave the people a hint to leave the church before the reading, declaring that whilst that was compulsory, the Act contained no clause to compel them to hear it. These and other proceedings probably afforded grounds for the accusation of the Duke of Argyle that "seceders were fanatical persons, instilling into the minds of the vulgar and ignorant such enthusiastical notions as are inconsistent with all government, by making sedition and rebellion a principle of their religion." In 1734 the reclaiming party in the parish of Troqueer, who seceded afterwards, helped to form the first Associate Synod.—*Annals and Sketches of the U. P. Church, by Rev. Dr M·Kelvie, pp.* 148-9.

The General Associate (Anti-Burgher) Synod formed a " Presbytery of Sanquhar" in 1755, and was changed to the "Presbytery of Dumfries" in 1788.

The first minister of this church was Mr Thomas Ballantyne, ordained 1742.

An inscription upon his tombstone in the parish churchyard says that "Here lies the Rev. Mr Thomas Ballantyne, ordained minister of ye Associate Congregation at Sanquhar, September 22d 1742, died 28th Feby. 1744, aged 30, the first of the Associate ministers who died after renewing our solemn Covenant.

> "This sacred herald, whose sweet mouth
> Spread gospel truth abroad,
> Like Timothy was but a youth,
> And yet a man of God.
>
> "So did the young yet ready scribe
> A friend for Christ appear,
> And was among the ancient tribe
> A covenanted seer.
>
> "He for ye Reformation cause
> Contending for renown,
> Among that noted number was,
> The first that gained the crown.
>
> "His dauntless soul with hasty pace
> Did mortal life despise,
> To feed ye lambs around ye place
> Where now his body lies."

The congregation adhered to the Anti-Burgher Synod during the vacancy. Mr John Goodlet, author of " Vindication of Associate Synod," was ordained in 1749. Mr Andrew Thomson, in 1776, died 1815.

V. WANLOCKHEAD.

THE MORTCLOTH DISPUTE.

An interesting document has been preserved as a memorial of the causes that led to the separation of Wanlockhead from Sanquhar ecclesiastically. The extracts refer to the period from 1735 to 1779. Up to that time the dead were carried all the way from Wanlockhead to Sanquhar for interment, either by Glendyne or Mennock, and the scenes on such occasions were frequently far other than edifying or solemnising. Surrounding parishes, from which the inhabitants were drafted, shared in the interments till a graveyard was obtained at Meadowfoot, on the Wanlock, more than a hundred years ago.

From "Extract Minutes of Penpont Presbytery anent Wanlockhead," dated Penpont, April 2d, 1735, it is found that there was "a representation and petition from the Kirk Session of Sanquhar presented to the Presbytery, bearing that the inhabitants of Wanlockhead had neglected and slighted the Session of Sanquhar in expending the poor's money collected among them, and when they had a preacher there, needlessly and superfluously in buying mort-cloths for themselves, when the Session of Sanquhar can answer them with all sorts, fine and coarse, large and little, and therefore requiring that the Presbytery interpose their authority, and cause the inhabitants of Wanlockhead deliver the collection now in their hands to the Session of Sanquhar, and to be accountable to them in all time coming. There was a representation and petition from the miners in Wanlockhead presented to the Presbytery, which was read, bearing that they being above five miles of very bad way from Sanquhar could not easily attend gospel ordinances there, had, with consent of Presbytery and Minister of Sanquhar, hired a chaplain of their own, and that they had collected the poor's money every Lord's Day as in planted congregations; there being neither elder nor deacon among them, they collected it by turns, and in regard they wanted a mortcloth to serve themselves, the mortcloths in Leadhills and Sanquhar being either very dear or lent out frequently when they wanted them, were often put to an inconvenience. They therefore stented themselves voluntarily in order to get a mortcloth for their own use, without any design to lend it to any other. And as to the poor's money, they allege the Session of Sanquhar can pretend no right to the distribution of it, seeing they neither send any of their number to collect it, nor yet supply any of the poor in Wanlockhead, except one, alleging also that the practice of the miners of Leadhills pleads for them, who had the same demand made on them by the Session of Crawford, and yet could never obtain it. They therefore humbly crave that the Presbytery may reprise the demand of the Session of Sanquhar, and allow them to keep their own cloth and distribute their own collection to their own poor."

Again, by appointment, the Presbytery met at Wanlockhead, on September the 24th, 1735. The Presbytery "resolved to desire the Commissioners in Sanquhar to give in a list of such persons in Wanlockhead as they judged fit for the office of elders. Accordingly they gave in the following list, viz.:—Mr Alexander Henderson, preacher of the gospel; William Telfer, Alexander Telfer, James Tait, John Campbell, James Alston, and Ninian Cunningham, which list the Presbytery approve, and appoint their edicts to be served the first Lord's day that a minister preaches at Sanquhar, and to attend to be ordained the next Lord's day that a minister preaches there, which elders, after they are ordained, the Presbytery appoint to collect for the poor in Wanlockhead, and to distribute the money so collected according to the necessities of the poor within their bounds; and in the meantime they are allowed to buy a mortcloth with the money already collected, and are appointed to keep their mortcloth within the precincts of Wanlockhead—that is, *they are not to lend it to any other within the parish of Sanquhar but miners;* and the said elders are to employ the emoluments of the mortcloth for the use of the poor in Wanlockhead only; and the preacher at

Wanlockhead is to keep a regular account of the collections and distributions, and give an extract of it to the Sanquhar Session to be registrate in their Session-Book yearly."

A preacher having been sent in 1733, and a chapel having been built, preachers or ministers were for a long period employed as chaplains.

SUCCESSION OF MINISTERS.

1735—Alexander Henderson, preacher ; 1750—Rev. Mr Laurie ; 1772—Mr John Williamson, afterwards of Tinwald ; 1777—Mr Bryce Little, afterwards of Covington ; 1789—Mr John Williamson, afterwards of Durisdeer ; 1794—Mr John Henderson, afterwards of Dryfesdale ; 1800—Mr James Ritchie.

SECOND PERIOD—1800-1876.

I. CRAWFORD.

John Ross, licensed by Presbytery of Forres. Tutor in family of Lord-Register (Colquhoun), and through his influence presented by George III. 1806. Died 2d October 1828, in 22d ministry.

Thomas Anderson, tutor in family of Lieut.-Col. Alexander Mac-Lean of Ardgour ; licensed by Presbytery of Haddington ; ordained by Presbytery as Catechist or Chaplain at Leadhills, 1829. Presented to this parish by George IV., 1829. Published New Statistical Account of the Parish.

Mr William Morrison, ordained assistant and successor, 1863. Died in street in Edinburgh, 1869.

Mr James Alexander Burdon, translated from Perth in 1870. Ordained there in 1863.

The old church had its seats (for some 320) repaired in 1835 ; but after a commodious manse had been erected in 1872, a beautiful new church to seat 280 was opened on the 17th October 1874. A harmonium was then introduced, but being petitioned against, was shortly thereafter silenced. These buildings are supposed to have cost about £4600. The communion cups bear date 1692, and the plates that of 1746. There are over 200 members, 98 males, 102 females on the roll ; a Sabbath-school with 5 teachers, and somewhere about £30 are raised for missions. The stipend, consisting of 19 chalders of oatmeal = 152 loads, along with barley—Given in Return to the House of Commons, 1874 :—Stipend, £304 ; Communion elements, £8, 6s. 8d. ; manse, £30 ; glebe, £37, 1s. 10d.—total annual value, £379, 8s. 6d.

Murray says in his "Upper Ward" that the schoolhouse of Crawford was erected by the Railway Company, as the line ran through the old one ; that "the teacher is an example of intelligence and of hospitality. Whether the latter virtue be in odour at the manse is doubtful, as the occupants of such superior dwellings

seem to have small affection for 'chiels amang them takin' notes ;'"
and he adds that the stipend has been improved by the interest of
£600 paid by the Railway Company for traversing the glebe.

The Rev. J. A. Burdon was elected minister of the church and
parish of Lasswade on the 11th March 1876.

II. CRAWFORDJOHN.

John Aird, presented by George Colebrooke of Crawford-Douglas,
1801 ; died 23d April 1815, in 70th year and 14th of ministry.

"When the salary of the parish schoolmasters was increased, and
the rate fixed at three grades of emolument, the heritors," says
Murray, "met and moved that the oldest and best-liked of the
teachers should be placed upon the lower rate. The minister
opposed, and when votes were offered, he demanded the production
of his mandate from one, popularly supposed to be the greatest man
present, who represented another. Not having anticipated this,
the mandate was not forthcoming, and the minister triumphed."
Murray also mentions that when the "New Statistical-Account"
appeared, the minister of Crawfordjohn affirmed that five articles
of the twenty on the Ward overlauded their heritors, and that
"*it was strange that the writers were all the sons of tailors.*"

William Goldie, licensed by Presbytery of Perth ; presented by
Trustees of George Colebrooke, Esq., 1816 ; died 9th March,
1862, in his 74th year and 46th of ministry. Published, Remarks
on the Striking of Fiars in the Country.

Mr John Allan Hunter Paton, 1862 ; translated to Duddingston
1866.

Mr James Cowan, 1866.

Crawfordjohn Parish Church was built in 1817. It is seated for
350. Return to House of Commons, 1874, of members, 315—131
males, and 184 females. Stipend—Teinds, £356, 13s. 9d. ; Communion elements, £8, 6s. 8d. ; manse, £24 ; glebe, £20—total annual
value, £409, 0s. 5d.

The Free Church was built in 1850, renovated internally in
1875, at a cost of £61. Seated for 120. It was supplied by
preachers until the settlement of Mr Logan, when it was annexed to
Abington.

ABINGTON.

The ministers of the United Presbyterian, formerly the Relief,
Church at Roberton for above seventy years, conducted religious
services at Abington. At one time that congregation reached to
Leadhills and Wanlockhead. It still has members in Crawfordjohn,
although no service is conducted there.

The Rev. Robert D. Scott was ordained in 1845, and there are
125 communicants, contributing above £143 per annum, of which
above £44 go for missions. The old church at Roberton was
erected in 1800, the new in 1873, and contains 250 sittings.

Free Church services were commenced about 1844, the church was erected in 1861. The beautiful manse was a gift from John Logan, Esq., Edinburgh, the father of the present minister, with the exception of a small sum from the congregation. The Rev. Robert Logan was ordained in 1866, and has preached at Crawfordjohn every Sabbath, Elvanfoot once a month. There are 116 communicants, who raised above £133 for all purposes, or at the rate of about 20s. per member for the Sustentation Fund. The congregation was put upon the platform of the equal dividend in 1875, and received grant from the Fergusson Bequest Fund.

The Established Church minister of Crawfordjohn also preaches every Sabbath at Abington in the schoolroom.

III. LEADHILLS, Q.S.

Mr Thomas Anderson, 1820 ; translated to Crawford, 1829.
Mr John Hope, 1834, translated to Dunscore.
Mr Stewart Smith, 1847.

The chapel, with a certain district, was erected into a *quoad sacra* parish by the Court of Teinds 17th July 1867. The income guaranteed being only £110, with manse and land, valued at £18, 10s., the congregation ought to provide an adequate income for the excellent minister, of whose accomplishments and library notice has been taken. The church is seated for 500, and there are 384 communicants, stated in Parliamentary return as 363—167 males and 196 females. Some £12 contributed for missions, and recently an addition for the Spanish Evangelistic Association.

The Sabbath-school, superintended by Mr George Wilson, has 157 scholars and 28 teachers. £2, 10s. raised for missions.

Free Church service was opened 9th January 1870, by Rev. J. Moir Porteous, and has been conducted fortnightly. The Sabbath-school, numbering 10 teachers and 50 scholars, superintended by Mr James Weir, elder.

In addition to soirées, Sabbath-school walks are given to the children, on two occasions to Abington House, where they were handsomely entertained by Lady Colebrooke, who also takes much interest in the welfare of the young women of Leadhills.

IV. SANQUHAR.

1821.—Thomas Montgomery, presented by the tutors of Walter Francis, Duke of Buccleuch and Queensberry, in February, and ordained 5th June. He got a new church built in 1827, and died 3d June 1861, in 40th ministry. He married 26th October 1826, Mary Brown, who died 21st April 1843, aged 50. Publication—Account of the Parish (New Statistical Account).

The Rev. John Inglis, the senior minister, was ordained in 1845 as assistant and successor, and attained to full status in 1861. On the 3d August last he applied for the appointment of an assistant and successor; and, after the various steps of procedure required by the laws of the Church, and the regulations of the General Assembly framed for carrying out the provisions of the recent Patronage Abolition Act, the congregation met on 27th December last, and by a very large majority elected the Rev. James M'Donald Inglis, M.A., assistant in South Leith Parish Church, to be assistant and successor. On this the first occasion of election under these regulations in the Presbytery, their suitability was fully attested. Mr Inglis was formally ordained and inducted on the 24th February last. The provision made by the incumbent for him is £100 per annum from the stipend, £10 annually for Communion elements, and the exclusive right of occupying the manse and glebe.

The parish church is situated at the west end of the town of Sanquhar, is of elegant architecture, on an elevation, and accommodates 1000 sitters, with 60 free sittings. The manse (value £40) was built with the church about the year 1826. The glebe, of about 20 acres in extent, was recently let at £107 per annum. The stipend was formerly 18 chalders, one half meal, and the other half barley—£390, 19s. 11d. The Old Statistical Account gives it at £105, 11s. 1½d. Now it is 21 chalders, supposed to be worth £18 per chalder, and £10 for Communion elements. The communicants number 340. The Sabbath-school is attended by about 100 children.

The collections and contributions last year for religious, educational, and charitable purposes amounted to £154, 15s. 10d.

PROCLAMATION OF BANNS

in this parish, according to the return obtained by Mr Ernest Noel, cost £9, 2s., of which £6, 6s. were appropriated to the session-clerk, and £2, 16s. to session or other purposes. There were 24 proclamations—2 on one day at £1, 1s., 21 on two days at 6s. 6d., and 1 on three days at 3s. 6d. Since the decision regarding *quoad sacra* churches, proclamation has begun to be made at Wanlockhead and Leadhills. If, however, the proposed Bill be enacted to entrust the matter to the Registrars, the triumph over *quoad civilia* will be shortlived. It ought to be noted that the suggestion of such an enactment first emanated from the Free Church minister and Session of Wanlockhead.

SOUTH UNITED PRESBYTERIAN CHURCH.

Mr James Reid, 1816 to 1849. Mr David M. Croom, 1838; called to Portsburgh, Edinburgh, 1852; author of "Harmony and State of Doctrine in Secession Synod." Mr Forbes Ross, 1854 to 1860. Mr Matthew Crawford, 1858; to Duke Street, Glasgow, 1869. When the previous reading or singing of the line of the psalm by the precentor, prior to its being sung by the congregation, was given up, an elder of the name of Harper arose and left the church.

Thenceforth the tune sung that day obtained the designation of "Harper's March." Rev. John Sellar, 1870. There are 285 communicants on the roll. The income for 1873 was £270, 8s. 4½d.; expenditure, £267, 19s. 4½d. Church accommodates 500.

THE NORTH UNITED PRESBYTERIAN CHURCH

was formed by adherents of the Associate (Burgher) Synod, receiving supply from the Presbytery of Annan and Carlisle, 1815. Church built in 1818; enlarged, 1830, with 500 sittings; brought down by mining operations; a new church built in 1849, with 550 sittings.

The Rev. Robert Simpson, D.D., was settled as pastor of the congregation in 1820; he died in 1867. Degree conferred by Princeton College, U.S., 1853. Author of "The Two Shepherds," "The Minister and his Hearer," "Traditions of the Covenanters," "Life of the Rev. James Renwick," "A Voice from the Desert," "Memorials of Worth," "History of Sanquhar," "Martyrland," "Cottars of the Glen."

He was succeeded by the Rev. James Hay Scott in 1868.

A very neat grey granite memorial column stands in front of the North United Presbyterian Church, bearing the following inscription :—

In Memoriam.
Rev. ROBERT SIMPSON, D.D.,
Minister of the North United Presbyterian Church for forty-eight years.
Died 7th July 1867, aged 75 years.
Author of "Traditions of the Covenanters," &c., &c.
Erected by Members of his Congregation and Friends.

The session consists of eight members, who have charge over as many districts. The board of management consists of fifteen members, one-third retiring annually. Quarterly contributions in support of ordinances are taken instead of seat-rents. The income and expenditure for 1874 was £263, 14s. 9½d.; of that sum £41, 9s. 7d. was applied to mission purposes.

SANQUHAR FREE CHURCH.

The Free Church was erected in 1845, worship having been conducted for a time in what is now the South United Presbyterian Church. The top of the old cross of Sanquhar is placed on the dome of the porch. The Rev. William Logan, from Lesmahagow, was settled as the first minister in 1844. His labours were highly appreciated, as a minute unanimously recorded by the Free Presbytery of Penpont declares. It states that he was for seven years Presbytery clerk, and that, ordained in 1820, he had been nearly 40 years a minister; that "he was a sound and judicious expounder of the Word of God, a faithful and laborious pastor, eminently successful in teaching the ignorant, warning the careless, reclaiming the backslider, and building up the Lord's people;" that "his singularly amiable and gentle disposition secured for him the attachment and commanded for him the respect of the community;" and that he was "most sincerely attached to the principles, while he was feelingly alive to the interests of the Free Church." He died after labouring there for twenty years, and was succeeded by the Rev. Stevenson Smith, who was ordained in 1863. There is an excellent manse on an elevation on the north-west of the town. The congregation has a Sabbath-school library. The church has 500 sittings, and there are 217 members on the roll. Contributions for the Sustentation Fund, year ending 15th May 1873, £123, 16s. 3d.; £59, 9s. 1d. for congregational objects; mission objects, £31, 15s.—in all £215, 0s. 4d. Minister's income, 1874-75, £198, 19s. 3d., of which £36 from Surplus Fund.

THE EVANGELICAL UNION

or "Morrisonian" Church, was commenced in March 1864. There are 300 sittings; 92 communicants were on the roll in 1873. The Rev. George Gladstone was ordained on 26th January 1865, removed to Govan on 1st August 1871, was succeeded by the Rev. George Bell, M.A., on the 1st December 1871, who was translated to Falkirk. The income for 1873 was £125, and the stipend £99.

The Anabaptists, or "Baptists," have still a place of worship. They are a small community, but are generally esteemed.

V. WANLOCKHEAD, Q.S.

Mr William Osburn, formerly of Tillycoultry, 1803, who died 25th June 1812, in the 68th year of his age and 39th of his ministry.

Mr John Henderson, formerly of Middleburgh, 1813, who died 14th September 1814, in the 62d year of his age and 29th of his ministry.

Mr Robert Swan, 1814, of Cockermouth.

1835—Mr Thomas Hastings, Holywood, and who joined the Free Church in 1843.

1843—Mr Patrick Ross, Birkenhead.

1847—Mr John Inches Dickson, Kirkbean, afterwards of Paisley and Kirkbean.

1848—Mr James Laidlaw, formerly of Bewcastle.

The chapel was built in 1755 by the Mining Company, and cost only £70 or £80. It was rebuilt and enlarged in 1848. The stipend was only from £60 to £65, with a house and an acre of land. Wanlockhead was erected by the Court of Teinds as a *quoad sacra* parish 27th January 1861, at the sole expense of the proprietor, Walter Francis, Duke of Buccleuch and Queensberry. The deed of his Grace conveying two farms in perpetuity for the endowment of this *quoad sacra* church, and accepted by the Court of Teinds, says—" The petitioner will give security over the lands of Carcoside and Orchard, both belonging to him, in fee-simple, and lying in the barony of Sanquhar and parish of Kirkconnel." The present value of these farms is £230 and £45 respectively. The sittings in Wanlockhead Established Church number 325 ; communicants, 140—as presented to the House of Commons in 1874 : 67 male, 75 female—total, 142. The collections for congregational purposes were, in 1874, £10, 12s. 10½d ; do. missions, £8, 7s. 9d.

The population, by Government census of 1831, was 675, and by ecclesiastical survey 1836 it was 716—of whom 678 belonged to the Church, 24 were Dissenters, and 14 nondescripts.

The Communion is observed twice in the year, on the last Sabbaths of April and of September. On the "Fast," or day of humiliation, the works are stopped, and there is a good attendance at all the diets of worship.

WANLOCKHEAD FREE CHURCH.

The Rev. Thomas Hastings received the appointment of Chapel-of-Ease minister at Wanlockhead 40 years ago, from his Grace the Duke of Buccleuch. Along with 200 communicants in Wanlockhead and 50 in Leadhills, he joined the Free Church in 1843, when he was elevated to the platform of the equal dividend of the Sustentation Fund. He was thus for eight years chaplain or minister in the Established Church. Then for nearly ten years he lived in one of the little cottages, entering the manse in 1852, and the church in the year 1859. He expended a great amount of labour, and had to withstand during these sixteen years great severities of winter. His attachment both to the place and people could not well be surpassed. In the beginning of 1862 he commenced a MS. history of Wanlockhead, along with suitable and profitable reflections. That history he re-wrote, and presented to the village library in 1869. In it he states that he had baptized above 1000 children, and had seen upwards of 1600 of the inhabitants laid in the silent grave. Further, that he had assisted some 42 individuals to obtain a classical education, some of whom became teachers, ministers, and missionaries. His desire was that, as the population had long enjoyed a good reputation, not only for industrious labour, but also for intelligence, they would not only maintain that high standing, but grow in grace and increase in knowledge as they advanced in life. He died on 30th April 1875, in his 80th year, and was buried beside his wife, in the churchyard of Monswald.

The Rev. Dr Chalmers preached in the tent on the hillside at Wanlockhead Hass in the summer of 1846. There never had been such a gathering of worshippers at that place. It was computed that there were, at least, 2500 persons present. When the venerable man of God looked around, and had given out his text, his first words were, "Now I can tell you nothing new." Although his MS. was before him, he spoke with his wonted fervid eloquence and power, and, to the delight of the villagers, "without reading." As it was long before a site was obtained for a church, many men of mark—Drs Pitcairn, Clason, Candlish, and Guthrie, &c.—gave similar countenance to the congregation. When Dr Candlish preached, the rain fell in torrents, and little that he said could be heard, owing to the pattering of the rain upon the umbrellas. Dr Guthrie wrote thus in 1870, "I well remember preaching, under a cold wintry sky, to the good and brave people of Wanlockhead— I honour them highly."

The Rev. James Moir Porteous, author of "The Government of the Kingdom of Christ," &c., was ordained as colleague and successor 19th November 1868, and became sole minister 1st May 1875. The church and manse, although not too commodiously for the people, are pleasantly situated, overlooking the village. The church is seated for 400. A cottage has been recently erected beside it, in terms of the lease. The membership in 1873 was 276, including 18 office-bearers, with 281 contributors to the Sustentation Fund, which amounted to £72, 8s. 3d. The total amount raised by the congregation for that year was £156, 4s. 4d.—of which £79, 5s. went to general funds and schemes, £17, 14s. 10d. for local building, and £59, 4s. 6d. for congregational purposes. Average of contributions per member to Sustentation Fund for 1875 was 5s. 4d., consequently no benefit is derived from the Surplus Fund.

Fortnightly service has been maintained in the Library Hall on the Sabbath evenings for seven years. There are 84 scholars and 17 teachers in the Sabbath-school, which, however, vacates for some winter months; but female Bible-classes are continued.

Wanlockhead is the first place in the south of Scotland where the "spelling bee" was introduced. It was in connection with the Free Church Sabbath-school annual excursion to the hills. Assembling at the church at eleven o'clock on the 18th September 1875, they marched by Mennock "Hass" and the Middle Moor, with their teachers and banners, first to the top of the Black Hill, and then to that of the Stood or Green Hill, above 1820 feet high. On each of these resting, beside refreshments, they partook of the enjoyment of "spelling bees," when it was found that seven girls and four boys could not be put out, were entitled to prizes, and each was afterwards presented with a book. In former times trenches were cut on the hills to receive the rainfall, and then the water was sent gushing down the hillside, thereby cutting up the ground and exposing the veins of lead, which were anxiously sought. In one of these "Hush Dams," clothed with a soft carpet of green, the school assembled, listening to addresses from the Rev. J. M. Porteous and the elders, Messrs Weir, Scott, Gracie, and Gemmel, and singing some sweet songs of Zion, which were distinctly heard in the village below. The views of Glendyne, the surrounding mountain-tops, and especially of the entire village, which is had above Glencrieff, together with their exercises, gave much pleasure to the children ; so that after descending the steep and rugged hillside, and ascending through the village to the manse, and partaking of a service of fruit, they were prepared to give three ringing cheers of acknowledgment to those that had during that lovely day ministered to their enjoyment.

THE GRAVEYARD AT MEADOWFOOT,

well fenced and encircled with a row of trees, lies in the sheltered and retired valley a mile below the village. The tombstones, which are numerous, are well lettered, and in good preservation, none being defaced or obliterated. The earliest interment recorded is that of a child in 1751, so that it has not been used for much more than a hundred years. The inscription runs : " Here lyes the corps of William Philip, son to William Philip Minder in Wanlockhead, who departed this life April the 2 day 1751, aged ten months." The next date reads thus : " Here ly the corps of William Adamson, son unto William Adamson Mason in Wanlockhead, who died March 23, 1753, aged 16 years." Another, in memory of Jean Watt, spouse to James Ramage in 1761, says—

> " Here now she rests who when in life
> Was a chaste maid and pious wife,
> A constant consort, faithful friend
> And still proved better to the end."

One stone, in recording that " Here lyes the corps of David Stewart son to James Stewart in Wanlockhead, who died January 19, 1773, aged near 5 years," says on the other side—

> " Bright as the gems the welthy orients boast,
> Sweet as the odours of the spicey coast,
> A pearly dew drop see some flower adorn,
> And grace with all its pride the rising morn.
> But soon the sun emits a fairer ray
> And the fair fabric rushes to decay.
> Low in the dust the beauteous ruin lyes
> While the pure vapour seeks its native skies.
> A fate like this to the sweet youth was given,
> Who sparkled, bloomed and was exhaled to heaven.
> Immortality and things below, I have no time and compliments to show,
> So farewell to you all in haste, I look for heaven to be my place."

FROM THE REVOLUTION.

Two flat stones, side by side, mark the spot where rest the remains of the Rev. William Osborne, who died in 1812, at the age of 68, and of the Rev. John Henderson, minister of the Gospel at Wanlockhead, who died 14th September 1814. This stone was erected by his only son, John Hally Henderson, Kingstone, Jamaica.

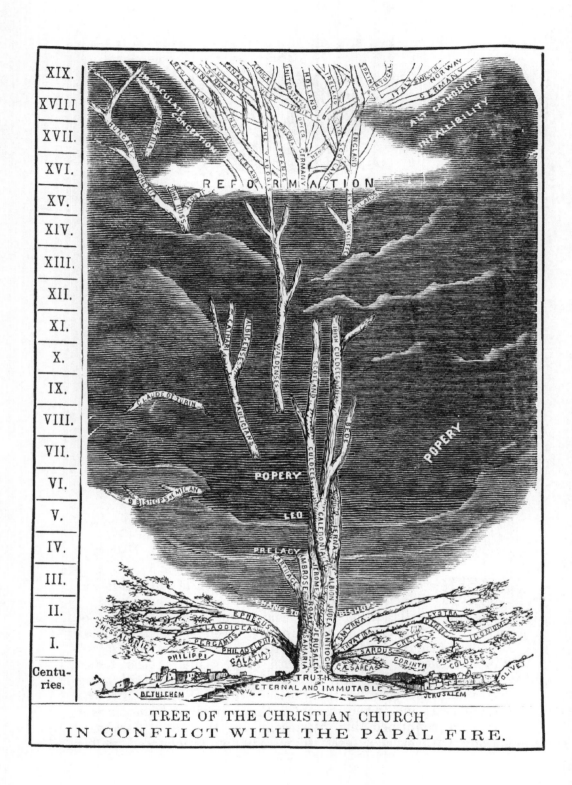

TREE OF THE CHRISTIAN CHURCH
IN CONFLICT WITH THE PAPAL FIRE.

KIRKBRIDE.

TO KIRKBRIDE IN RUINS.

" Hail Mountain-Pharos, like a star
Thy steady ray once shone afar.
Thou wast the lighthouse of the Nith,
From Corsincon to Solway Frith.
When midnight darkness reigned around,
And Truth no tabernacles found,
O'er south and west in circuit wide
Was reared this Shiloh of Kirkbride.

" Could they who saw thee long ago
Now view thee in thy weeds of woe ;
Could they who saw thee in thy pride
Visit again forlorn Kirkbride—
Even the most skilled could scarcely trace
A likeness in thy furrowed face."   DALZIEL.

PORTION of the ancient parish of Kirkbride was added to Sanquhar in 1727.

Tradition states that, prior to the building of the church, worship had been there maintained under a thorn ; and that it was one of the "Seven Sisters," or churches erected in the south of Scotland at the Reformation, which had the honour conferred upon it of being cursed every year by the Pope. And a Rev. Dr Browne some years ago, when present with his pupil at Rome, is said to have confirmed this, by recognising the name Kirkbride along with other subjects of malediction pronounced in his

hearing. Of this a worthy farmer in the neighbourhood of
Drumlanrig writes—

> "The foremost thou to join the strife
> And fight for freedom as for life,
> To spurn Rome's penalties and pains
> And burst her soul-debasing chains.
> Thence comes her deep and deathless hate
> Which your destruction cannot sate;
> For yearly still at Carnival
> On thee her maledictions fall;
> O'er church, and graves, and churchyard mound,
> Her dread anathemas resound."

"The origin of this *ecclesiola*, which is unique in appearance, is unknown, but being close to Coshogle, where many
different proprietors have resided, it is likely to have been
founded by one of these families. The name was *Kilbride*
from the twelfth to the sixteenth century. Curiously enough,
in James IV.'s charter, in 1507, it is called *Pan*-bride, as synonymous with *Kil*-bride. . . . In the sixteenth century the
name of Kilbride was changed to Kirkbride. . . . The Church
was sacred to St Bridget, an Irish saint, to whose memory we
find many churches dedicated, not only in Ireland, but in
every part of Great Britain, though how she acquired this
honour is a mystery. . . . She was the daughter of Cadwrthai,
being born in Ulster soon after the establishment of Christianity, and receiving the religious veil in early youth from St
Mal, the nephew and disciple of St Patrick. St Bride formed
for herself a cell under an oak, called Kildara, the cell of the
oak. She was regarded as the patroness of that country, and
is supposed to have lived in the early part of the sixth century,
being first mentioned in the martyrology of Bede. . . . Such
was the saint to whom this parish was consecrated.

"The Church is first mentioned in a charter of William,
Bishop of Glasgow, in 1240, where it is called 'The Church
of St Brigid de Stranith.' (Macfarlane's Coll. MSS.) It belonged in the reign of Alexander II. (1214–49) to the monks
of Holyrood House, and it was confirmed to them by William,
Bishop of Glasgow, in 1240, but seems afterwards to have been
relinquished for some other acquisition. It continued a rectory
or parsonage till the Reformation. We find Walter de Lilles-
cliff, the parson of Kilbride, swearing fealty to Edward I., and
obtaining from him a precept to the Sheriff of Dumfries, in
September 1296, for restoring his possessions (Rymer II. 723).

Its value, according to Bagimont's Roll, about 1275, was taxed at £6, 13s. 4d."

"The Church lands of Kirkbryde passed into lay lands. In 1541, the Rector, with consent of the Archbishop of Glasgow, and of the Provost and Chapter of Lincluden, granted a charter and seisin in favour of John Menzies, brother of Edward Menzies of Castlehill, giving to him and his heirs general the whole Church lands of Kirkbryde, making 5 marks A.E., and lying by annexation in the Barony of Drumlanrig, for the payment of 10 marks yearly. They were then passed to Sir William Douglas of Coshogle for life, and to his son James in fee. In the year 1543 we find James Douglas of Drumlanrig obliged to find surety to appear to 'underly the law for art and part in the slaughter of Mr Hector Sinclare, Rector of Kirkbryde.'" Pitcairn's Crim. Trials, I. 1, 329.

In Kirkbride "dwelt formerly the Lairds of Corshorogell of the name of Douglass, and the Lairds of Mackmath of Achenson. But these lineages being now extinct, the whole parish pertains to the Duke of Queensberry."

Pitcairn, in his "Criminal Trials," relates that one of the Coshogle family of the Douglases was accused of witchcraft, and condemned to be burned on the Castle Hill of Edinburgh. Under date 8th May 1591, he relates that Barbara Napier, spouse of Archibald Douglas, an Edinburgh burgess, and brother of the Laird of Coshogle, was accused of sundry points of witchcraft in a charge given in against her by Mr David M'Gill of Cranstoun, and that the verdict was that the said Barbara Napier, be "fylit' and convicted of "consultation from Anne Sampsonne ane wich, for the help of Dame Jeane Lyonne, Lady Angus, to keip hir from vomiting. Item, for the consulting with the said Annie Sampsonne, for causing of the said Dame Jeane Lyonne, Lady Angus, to love her, and to gif hir the gier awin hir agayne, and geiving of ane ring for this purpois to the said Anne, quhill sche had send hir ain courchie (kerchief) of linning and swa for contravening of the Act of Parliament," &c. Accordingly "dome was prononceit against Barbara Napier" (Drumlanrig, pp. 78, 112–16).

The list of ministers of Kirkbride transmitted gives, from 1560 to 1610, that of Thomas Weir, reader, 1567; Thomas Macgunzeon, 1568; Alexander Myll, 1571–74; William Runcyman, 1574–78; William Douglas, 1579; and Simon Purdie, 1585–91.

Those of the second period (1610 to 1661) were John Forke,

1615; Robert Blackwood, 1634; and Thomas Shields, 1655. Because of his adherence to the Covenants, he was deprived by the Acts of Parliament 11th June, and of Privy Council 1st October, 1662.

The third period (1661 to 1689) presents the name of Robert Lockhart, 1677. In 1691-93 he is said to have "molested the parish, though legally cast out, and prevented them getting another minister." Dr Simpson relates a tradition of "Rabbling," which is generally ascribed to Lockhart. Six stalwart men, fully armed, appeared at the manse demanding admission. Finding that they were determined to be in, and guessing their errand, he ran off, and never returned. But when the Revolution had been effected, Thomas Shields returned (1689), and was restored by Act of Parliament 25th April 1690.

In 1703 Peter Rae was appointed, who became clerk to the Presbytery of Penpont, and Synod of Dumfries. But Kirkbride was suppressed, and ceased to be a distinct parish, and Mr Rae was translated to Kirkconnel in 1732. The divisions of Kirkbride were annexed to Durisdeer and Sanquhar by the Lords Commissioners of Teinds on the 19th July 1727. The name of Peter Rae is usually associated with the rebellion of 1715, as he was the author of a "History of the Late Rebellion raised against his Majesty King George by the Friends of the Popish Pretender. Dumfries: Printed by Robert Rae, 1718." He published several treatises of divinity, was held to be a good scholar and philosopher, as well as an able divine. His brother, who printed the volume, was at that time the only typographer in the south of Scotland. His father was a clockmaker in Dumfries. An ancient clock made by him was lately presented to Dr Grierson's Museum; it goes twenty-four hours, and has an ornamental brass face. But Peter himself was no mean mechanic, as he constructed a musical clock, still in the castle of Drumlanrig. He was attacked in a pamphlet of bald poetry and prose because of his authorship. Kirkconnel having been destitute of a minister for fifty years, his first sermon there was upon the Ark abiding in Kir-jath-jearim twenty years, and all the people lamenting after the Lord. He died in 1748. (See Drumlanrig, p. 164.)

Mr J. R. Wilson writes me—"I recently found among the Sanquhar Communion tokens a Kirkbride token of 1725, circular, and about the size of a sixpence, and of lead. It had K B on one side, and the monogram ℞, 1725, on

218

the other. This indicates "Peter Rae, Minister." I gave Dr Grierson the token for his museum. The Rev. Mr M'Kenzie, of Durisdeer, tells me he has several of these tokens."

This ancient church still stands in a ruinous condition. Many attempts were made to abolish it, which met with the most determined opposition on the part of the population generally. So great was the aversion of the people to the change, that several joined the Cameronian party, refusing to be longer connected with a Church guilty of the sacrilege of dismemberment; and many stories are yet current which, although they have gathered somewhat of the imaginative around them, are yet truthful in the main.

Thus, it is said that the Rev. Mr Gibson, the first day he preached in the united parishes of Sanquhar and Kirkbride, was struck dumb when attempting to give out the Psalm, he having been attacked by paralysis. His offence was that he had declared it was of no use to keep up Kirkbride as a separate parish. The event has been thus described—

> " The day of trial comes—the day
> Of rest when Christians meet to pray.
> Yeomen, with grudges ill-suppressed,
> Slunk in the union to attest;
> And shepherds came with visage stern
> From lone Glenim and bleak Glenwhairn.
> With vigorous tread and haughty air
> The parson mounts the pulpit stair
> And forward steps, 'mid breathless calm,
> To read the wonted morning psalm.
> But lo ! the offended Lord hath come
> To strike the braggart hireling dumb ,
> The tongue, that erst could vaunt at will,
> Forgot at once its former skill.
> Sounds indistinct and strangely blent,
> Proclaim to all his punishment."

It is farther asserted that Abraham Crichton, Provost of Sanquhar, had gathered a number of workmen to the spot, declaring, " I'll sune ding doon the Whigs' sanctuary ;" and, though failing of his purpose, he some time after fell from his horse in Dalpeddar, and broke his neck. Being buried in the churchyard of Sanquhar, the Provost would not lie, and servant-maids could not milk their cows because Abraham's ghost kept grinning over the kirk dyke, till Mr Hunter of Penpont had laid the ghost. Drawing a circle, and muttering a magical incantation, the shade of Abraham made a revelation which no other than the hearer might know, "and then sunk doon." But Abraham was not alone. Every one who had any hand in the spoliation of the "Auld Kirk" met with some disaster. An old wife who carried off an iron "stenchel," or iron bar of a window, fell, along with her cuddy, down Enterkin, and broke her thigh-bone. A man who took away a stone for a corner of a steading never wrought more. Taking ill immediately, he soon after died. Then Crichton, the factor, afraid of some such ill-luck befalling him, said to a farmer, "You may tak' some o't if ye like, but I'll no touch't." The farmer, on hearing this, replied, "Weel, we'd better let it alane!" Visiting the ruins recently, the writer found the belfry and the font there, and the iron support of the basin for baptisms, with other movables, lying untouched in the grated window. No wonder that the interesting ruins still remain.· But that is not all. Bands of angels, they say, have been heard, high up in the air, singing the seventy-fourth Psalm—

> " To these long desolations
>   Thy feet lift, do not tarry;
> For all the ills thy foes have done
>   Within thy sanctuary."

" Major Crichton gave orders to an official at Drumlanrig, long since dead, to have the bell removed for safe custody, but he entreated that he should not be employed in such a dangerous business." The bell remained for a time, till it was carried off by a company of tramps, but parts of it were got long afterwards on the farm of Ardoch, and a quarry hammer lying alongside of the fragments. A portion is preserved in Dr Grierson's Museum. A piece of freestone, with black letter characters on it, is also preserved. This took place about ten years ago. But prior to that event several masons had, at their own free will and expense, repaired the damage that had befallen the "auld wa's." Some years ago a good fence was put around the graveyard by the Duke of Buccleuch.

The old church stands on a height, near to Enterkin-foot, looking down the valley of the Nith. And in addition to the romantic and well-wooded ravine of the Enterkin, it has another glen, "the Lime-cleuch," upon its right side. It could not have contained many worshippers, being only 46 feet by 20. (See Illustration.)

Most impressive must have been their assembling, as thus described—

> " Our fathers worshipped in this place,
> And still their steps I seem to trace ;
> With plaided form and bonnet blue,
> With reverent face and heart so true.
> I see them slowly wend their way—
> On rainy or on snowy day—
> Down deep ravine or steep hillside,
> Or up the brae to loved Kirkbride.
> But seldom now the measured tread
> Of those who bear their kindred dead,
> Or earth thrown on the sounding bier,
> Disturbs the echoes slumbering here."

The graveyard—where sometimes an open-air service has been conducted on a summer Sabbath-day—is not less full of interest.

There is a monument in the church, of one John of Rockell, with this inscription, "Hic situs est, Joannes de Rockell, Jurisconsultus Ecclesiæ."

A "thrauch stane" in the old churchyard marks the resting-place of the grandfather of Allan Ramsay, the poet, who was born in Leadhills in 1686—when the persecution of the Covenanters was at its height. It bears to have been erected to the memory of "Robert Ramsay, servitor, to Lord Hopetoun, who died December 1674." The poet's father acted as "grieve" or "oversman" for the Earl of Hopetoun ; and as there was no graveyard then in Leadhills, the dead were carried for sepulture either to Crawford, Durisdeer, or Kirkbride.

Another fact speaks volumes as to the attachment of the people to the place. A native who, though only half a year at school, spent the most of his spare money and time in books, and who left pieces of poetry which would have done no discredit to one more highly favoured, when dying, at the age of sixty-five, made this one request to those about him—" Bury me in Kirkbride, for there's much of God's redeemed dust lies there."

> " Among the last who here was laid
> Was one who long had plied his trade
> Beside the hill; who, ere he died,
> Said, 'Bury me in old Kirkbride.
> That spot I love, though chill and bare,
> For much redeemèd dust lies there.'"   *Dalziel.*

Another poet of the district, quoting this fact, says—"Taking advantage of the licence which all rhymers are apt to arrogate to themselves, I have in the following poem put the above beautiful words into the mouth of an old Covenanter who is supposed to have survived the persecution.—*Rob. Wanlock.*

' Bury me in Kirkbride,
　　Where the Lord's redeemed anes lie !
The auld kirkyaird on the grey hillside,
　　Under the open sky ;
　　Under the open sky,
On the breist o' the braes sae steep,
　　And side-by-side wi' the banes that lie
Streiked there in their hinmaist sleep.
This puir dune body maun sune be dust,
　　But it thrills wi' a stound o' pride
Tae ken it may mix wi' the great and just
　　That slumber in thee, Kirkbride !

. . . .

' Wheesht ! did the saft win' speak ?
　　Or a yaumerin' nicht-bird cry ?
Did I dream that a warm haun' toucht my cheek,
　　And a winsome face gaed by ?
　　And a winsome face gaed by,
Wi' a far-aff licht in its een—
　　A licht that bude come frae the dazzlin' sky,
For it spak' o' the starnies' sheen.
Age may be donart, and dazed, and blin',
　　But I'se warrant whate'er betide,
A true heart there made tryst wi' my ain,
　　And the tryst-word seemed—" Kirkbride."

' Hark ! frae the far hill-taps,
　　And laich frae the lanesome glen,
Some sweet psalm-tune, like a late dew, draps
　　Its wild notes doon the win' ;
　　Its wild notes doon the win',
Wi' a kent soun' owre my min',
　　For we sang't on the muir—a wheen huntit men—
Wi' oor lives in oor haun' langsyne ;
But never a voice can disturb this sang,
　　Were it Claver'se in a' his pride,
For it's raised by the Lord's ain ransomed thrang
　　Foregather'd abune Kirkbride.

222

KIRKBRIDE.

' I hear May Moril's tongue,
  That I wistna tae hear again,
And there—'twas the black Macmichael's rang
  Clear in the closin' strain ;
  Clear in the closin' strain,
Frae his big heart bauld and true ;
  It stirs my saul as in days bygane,
When his guid braidsword he drew :
I needs maun be aff tae the muirs ance mair,
  For he'll miss me by his side ;
In the thrang o' the battle I aye was there,
  And sae maun it be in Kirkbride.

' Rax me a staff and plaid,
  That iu readiness I may be,
And dinna forget that *The Book* be laid
  Open across my knee ;
  Open across my knee,
And a text close by my thumb,
  And tell me true, for I scarce can see,
That the words are, ' Lo ! I come.'
Then carry me through at the Cample ford,
  And up by the lang hillside,
And I'll wait for the comin' o' God the Lord
  In a neuk o' the auld Kirkbride.' "

January 1876.

KING WINTER'S REIGN IN THE SOUTHERN HIGHLANDS.

· " God's Treasure-House in Scotland."

APPENDIX.

APPENDIX.

A.—NATURAL GRASSES AND METEOROLOGICAL OBSERVATIONS.

1. STOOLBENT OR ROSEBENT (*Juncus squarrosus*).—Always green and eatable, springing as early as January.

2. DRAW-MOSS.—Bushy on moorland, and without seed. Growing at all seasons, it is green summer and winter. Long and wiry. Sheep fond of it in snow-storms. They pull it up by the length of the stalk, when it comes out in slips at the root.

3. MOSS-CROPS.—Cotton Grass or Wild Cotton (*Eriophorum augustifolium, et E. Polystachion*).—The latter found only in wet ditches or bogs. Marked feature where boggy ground whitened with cotton-like seed-tufts. Flowers in April, but tufts remain later.

4. DEER'S HAIR (*Scirpus cæspitosus*).—Abounding on deep mossy moors in the end of April and May. The heather is burnt to allow of its growth.

5. FLYING-BENT OR BENT GRASS (*Agrostis vulgaris*).—Common on dry heaths. An elegant grass, which in "saft weather" has its graceful and branched funicle beaded prettily with dewdrops.

6. "AE POINTED GRASS" (*Carex paniculata*).—Early in February on Lowthers. Tufts in moss-hassocks.

7. AE SPRET, SPRAT, OR SPROT (*Juncus acutiflorus*).—Rush common in watery places. "Not much danger of lairing where sprats grow." Coarse. Grows below the snow in December, at its height in August.

8. WILD LEEKS OR RAMPS (*Allium ursinum*).—May and June. Green all the year. The beauty of its white flowers dimmed by strong smell of garlic. Reckoned poisonous. Cows that eat it have their milk and butter tainted.

9. PRYGRASS (*Hordeum pratense*).—Generally rare, but here abundant. Green all the year. Good for sheep.

10. WINNEL-STRAE OR BULL'S-FACES (*Aira cæspitosa*).—June, July. Flowered stems ornaments for fireplaces. The stalks a pipe by which to slake thirst, or thirst appeased by chewing its sapid culms, when the peat-bog water is "pushonable." Fergusson speaks of

"A set o' men,
Wha, if they get their private pouches lined,
Gae na a windle-strae for a' mankind."

227

11. THRESHES, RUSHES, OR RASHERS.—The three species, *Juncus effusus, conglomeratus,* and *glaucus.* Eaten during storms by sheep. Children

"Pulled the rushes from their watery bed
To plait the belt, and helmet for our head."

"Step on a rasher bush, and it will no deceive you."

12. TATH GRASS.—Luxuriant grass from dropped manure. Grows tender at "stell-dykes." Eagerly eaten by cattle and horses.

13. DOG GRASS (*Triticum canina*).—Long, broad, raspy. Green all the year. Scarce, uncommon. A quick vomit for, and eagerly eaten at times by, dogs; sheep fond of it in a snow-storm, and it has not the same effect upon them.

14. LIVER GRASS (*Potentilla anserina, Merchantia polymorpha,* or *conica*).—Not eaten by sheep. Made into pills, and given by shepherds to dogs. Was formerly thought to be "the sovereign'st thing on earth to cure a cold"—the decoction sweetened with liquorice.

15. BESOM FOG.—Silver or sponge heather (*Polytrichum vulgare*). Long moss, not eaten by sheep.

16. BLAEBERRY BUSHES (*Vaccinium myrtillus*).—Crop supposed to come only in alternate years.

17. HEATHERS.—Eaten at all times by sheep. By Act of Parliament no burning from March till the corn be cut down. Blooms about the middle of August. The bee-hives are carried to the moors, or bees come from a long distance.

(1.) LING (*Calluna vulgaris*).—Burnt every three or four years.
(2.) PURPLE BELL.—Flowers twenty-fold more numerous, and yield more honey.
(3.) WHITE VARIETY.—Rare.

18. NETTLES (*Urtica dioica*).—Eaten by cattle and swine. Companion of man, but lives in deserted places. Herbs in spring.

19. BRECKEN.—Long and sharp, eaten; and FERN, broad from the roots, eaten (*Ptenis aquilina*); bracken or brakes. Mown and dried for litter.

20. BROOM (*Spartium scoparium*).—Lambs fond of. Grows to perfection in seven or eight years, then dies. Some years elapse before the seed vegetates.

21. THISTLES (*Onopirdum acanthium,* &c.)—Lambs fond of. Maintains itself unsown. Bog thrissel (*O. palustris*), with white flowers.

22. HEMLOCK (*Conium maculatum*).—Roots eaten by cattle when unwell. Valuable medicine. The name given by peasants to several large umbelliferæ. A valuable poultice for sores.

23. CRACKERS, FOX OR FOLKS GLOVE (*Digitalis purpura*).—Not eaten. Medicine of energy and value. Administered by country quacks, not always with impunity.

24. COLT's-FOOT OR HORSEHOOF (*Tussilago Farfara*).—Also used for colds.

25. DOCKEN (*Rumex obtusifolius*).—Grows on waste ground. A healing salve made from its roots. Leaves, with oatmeal, given to poultry.

26. CRAWBERRY OR CRANBERRY (*Vaccinium onycoccus*)—

"He pu'd me the crawberry ripe frae the boggy fen."—*Tannahill.*

27. TORMENTIL (*Tormentilla officinalis*).—The root called *Shepherd's Knot*, boiled in milk for diarrhœa. The plant dried—flesh and blood—astringent medicine for children.

28. BLUEBELLS, BLUEBOTTLES, OR BLA'WORT (*Centaurea cyanus*).—

"Of colour like a bla'wort blue."—*Ramsay.*

29. HORSE TAIL (*Equisetum fluviatile*).—Gregarious in boggy places.

30. YELLOW RATTLE, GOWKS' SIXPENCES OR SILLER (*Rhinanthus Crista galli*).—From shape of leaf and rattle of seed.

31. RAGGED ROBIN (*Lychnis flos cuculis*).—White variety rare.

32. SHEPHERD'S OR LADIES' PURSE (*Thlaspi bursa pastoris*).—Great variety. Birds fond of seed. Children cry, "Tak' a haud o' that." It cracks, and then a shout, "You've broken your mother's back."

33. VIOLETS (*Viola odorata, canina*, and *lutea*).

34. WILD STRAWBERRY (*Fragaria vexa*).

35. TWA-BLADE (*Listera ovata*).—Sports into monstrosities.

36. SORREL (*Oxalis acetosella*).—Gowk's meat. Its acidity more agreeable and delicate than the lemon.

37. BURDOCKEN (*Arctium bardanna*).—The burr. In ditches, &c.

38. QUEEN OF MEADOW OR MEADOW SWEET (*Spiræa ulmaria*).—Wholesome for cattle amongst meadow hay. In olden time valued when

"With rose and swete flores
Were strawed halles and bouris."

39. RIB GRASS OR KEMPS (*Plantago lanceolata*).—Eaten with avidity. Used by children at play. One is held, and if decapitated, is thrown aside. He who at last has the parcel or "Kemp" entire is victor. Kemp is thus synonymous with hero or champion.

40. BLUE BONNET OR DEVIL'S-BIT (*Scabiosa succisa*).—Common on moors.

41. LADIES' MANTLE, DUCK-FOOT, AND BEAR'S-FOOT (*Alchemilla vulgaris*).—The most elegant plant of all our natives. At sides of burns.

42. CRAW-TAES OR CAT'S CLOVER (*Lotus corniculatus*).

43. MILLFOIL, YARROW, HUNDRED LEAF, OR WILD PEPPER (*Achilla millefolium*).—White and pink flowers.

"The yarrow wherewithal he stops the wound-made gore."

44. DANDELION (*Leontodon taraxacum*).—Jagged edges of the leaf resembling rows of teeth of the heraldic lion. Medicinal for chest disease, &c.

· 45. CLOVERS (*Tipolium repens, pratense,* and *medium*).—Red, white, and yellow.

46. SCOTCH TIMOTHY OR SOLDIER'S FEATHERS (*Phleum pratense*).—Seeds carried from Virginia to North Carolina by Timothy Hanson—hence the name.

47. MEADOW VETCHLING OR WILD PEA (*Vicia sylvatica*).

48. FAIRY LINT OR MOUNTAIN FLAX (*Linum catharticum*).—On the pastures. For linen of the " good people " supernaturally.

&c. &c.

METEOROLOGICAL OBSERVATIONS AT DRUMLANRIG AND WANLOCKHEAD.

Station and Observers' Names	Height of Station above the sea at point of observation (Feet)	1873 Months	BAROM. Monthly Range	THERMOM. Monthly Range	THERMOM. Mean Temperature	HYGROM. Dry Bulb	HYGROM. Wet Bulb	DEDUCTIONS. Glaisher's Tables, 2d Edition — Dew Point	Elastic force of vapours	Humidity (sat. 100)	WINDS. Number of Days it blew in certain directions — N.	N.E.	E.	S.E.	S.	S.W.	W.	S.W.	Calm or Variable	Mean Pressure on Square Foot	RAIN. No. of Days it fell	RAIN. Amount in inches
			Degs.	Degs.	Degs.	Degs.	Degs.	Degs.												Lbs.		
DRUMLANRIG— Mr David Thompson, gardener to the Duke of Buccleuch.	191	Jan.	1·972	35·0	38·4	38·4	37·6	36·5	·116	94	2	1	...	4	16	4	2	8	...	...	15	10·10
		Feb.	1·886	37·0	34·0	32·5	31·8	30·4	·170	92	15	1	...	1	4	3	...	4	...	...	5	1·20
		March	1·236	44·0	39·8	39·2	38·8	38·3	·232	97	6	1	2	5	6	3	...	8	...	...	13	3·70
		April	1·002	45·0	45·0	45·0	44·5	43·9	·287	96	7	5	...	2	3	4	6	8	...	...	...	...
		May	1·094	40·0	46·9	47·6	47·3	47·0	·322	98	5	...	1	3	7	2	2	6	...	...	12	2·39
		June	0·856	39·6	56·0	56·2	55·0	53·9	·416	92	8	2	1	2	10	3	...	2	...	...	11	1·63
		July	...	...	...	...	...	...	...	...	...	...	...	...	...	...	...	...	...	...	25	7·70
		Aug.	...	...	...	...	...	...	...	...	...	...	...	...	...	...	...	...	...	...	25	5·90
		Sept.	1·232	41·0	49·6	49·0	47·9	46·7	·320	92	10	...	...	1	4	3	...	8	...	...	13	4·30
		Oct.	1·558	40·0	43·5	41·4	41·0	38·2	·231	89	8	4	2	...	8	6	4	6	2	...	15	8·10
		Nov.	1·816	38·0	39·9	39·6	38·3	36·6	·217	90	6	...	...	...	5	4	3	2	1	...	12	3·60
		Dec.	1·384	35·0	41·0	41·2	40·2	38·9	·237	92	4	...	...	2	7	12	3	4	...	...	14	3·50
Sum of Ten Months, Means			1·401	39·4	43·4	43·0	42·2	41·0	·264	93	71	14	6	20	70	44	24	51	3	...	160	52·00
WANLOCKHEAD— Mr Gilbert Dawson, schoolmaster.	1334	Jan.	1·850	31·0	34·9	35·2	34·8	34·2	·195	96	1	...	3	2	2	14	8	1	...	2·56	24	12·52
		Feb.	1·760	30·4	30·2	29·2	28·8	28·2	·155	96	8	2	5	2	...	2	6	3	...	0·61	4	1·85
		March	1·220	34·2	36·4	35·2	34·5	33·4	·192	93	10	2	12	1	4	4	4	2	...	1·28	14	5·38
		April	0·820	34·6	42·0	40·7	39·3	37·6	·225	89	10	2	4	1	2	2	8	1	...	0·67	7	0·23
		May	1·070	32·4	43·4	42·6	41·5	40·2	·249	91	1	...	6	2	2	3	14	3	...	1·10	15	3·73
		June	0·890	23·0	52·4	51·6	50·4	49·2	·351	92	1	1	4	1	2	6	12	3	...	0·98	13	3·64
		July	...	...	...	...	...	...	...	...	...	...	...	...	...	...	...	...	...	...	18	12·95
		Aug.	...	...	...	...	...	...	...	...	...	...	...	...	...	...	...	...	...	...	15	6·74
		Sept.	1·140	28·2	47·4	46·4	45·4	44·3	·292	93	4	1	2	2	...	7	14	2	...	1·49	22	6·39
		Oct.	1·560	30·6	40·8	40·3	39·9	39·4	·242	97	1	...	2	1	2	10	15	1	...	1·28	17	7·83
		Nov.	1·790	27·1	36·8	36·8	36·3	35·6	·203	95	1	...	6	...	2	8	10	1	...	2·19	16	4·80
		Dec.	1·380	24·5	38·4	39·1	35·8	38·4	·233	98	...	...	...	...	...	12	18	1	...	2·10	...	5·86
Sum of Ten Months, Means			1·339	30·3	40·3	39·7	37·9	38·0	·234	94	29	8	44	11	16	68	109	18	...	1·43	190	71·94

NOTE.—As the observations for July and August were not taken at one station it is thought better to omit them in calculating, so as to give a more accurate comparison.

B.—SHEEP AND SHEPHERDS.

The short blackfaced sheep, which fattened from 10 to 14 lbs. per quarter, are the old residenters found to be best suited to the district. Attempts were made without success to introduce white-faced, long-bodied sheep of the Bakewell breed. The climate and coarseness of the pasture, high winds and heavy rains, were thought to be insuperable difficulties. Now both Cheviot and blackfaced short-woolled sheep are fed ; the Leicester also, but not upon the hills.

The shepherd is considered " puist," " bien," or well-to-do, having in general a good table. His conditions of servitude are totally dissimilar from those of the farm servant. Four loads of meal and two cows' grass is a common allowance. Then he may have fifty sheep of his own stock, worth say 20s. each, which, with lambs, share in the fortune of the general sales. It has, however, become customary to give money instead of sheep pasture. But inadequate provision tends to the benefit of neither party. The shepherds' houses are now much improved. He is also allowed a dog. Generally shepherds are found to be more intelligent, respectable, and respected than some others, and to take a deeper interest in their master's property. Lectures have been delivered on these hills by a shepherd which would have done no discredit to an LL.D. or D.D. And yet a rougher party can rarely be met with than that of some young shepherds when " whuskied " at a village fair. Then " the drink madness shows the dark beginning of the darker end."

The lambing season is perhaps the most anxious and laborious period of shepherd life. In hilly districts it usually begins from the 17th or 18th of April, and lasts for six weeks. During that period the shepherd has a hired assistant or assistants, and the traversing of the hills goes on incessantly from early dawn till late at night. And often he may be seen with a little lamb in the bag slung across his shoulders, which he is carrying either to suckle on cow's milk at home, or to get attached to a ewe in a little fold, when it has lost its own lamb.

The clipping of the sheep is another busy time to the shepherds. (1) That of those termed " eill " or " yell ewes " or " hoggs " begins from the 20th to the 24th June ; (2) Cheviots from the 1st July ; (3) blackfaced from the 10th or 12th ; and (4) milk ewes from the 1st to the 15th of July.

The smearing is another important operation. It begins from the 7th or 8th of October. Pouring from the 20th. Dipping is practised at all times. Although dipping is much in use, shepherds in upland districts value the smearing or pouring before it. Without this, in snowstorms the sheep are liable to become " batted up " with drift and frozen snow, which becomes so heavy on their heads and sides as to fix them to a spot. But this does not usually happen, and the sheep are kept warmer when some oil or grease is used. The practice of salving or smearing was thought to improve the quality, to increase the quantity of wool, to preserve and to defend against attacks of vermin. This last is now regarded as the chief evil to be guarded against, and so dipping in a solution of arsenic, sulphur, juice of broom, tobacco, or other mixture is generally substituted for the tar and butter of former times. Where oil is used, five gallons are counted sufficient for 100 sheep. Shepherds dislike the arsenic, as many have been killed thereby.

THE DISEASES OF SHEEP chiefly arise on marshy ground.

1. Rot—a bag growing in their necks below the chin, which is found to be full of water. As a preventative, marshy, low-lying land would require the drains to be cleaned out every six or seven years.

2. Sturdo, or water in the head, for which the brain is sometimes pierced. Hard winters are supposed to be the chief cause.

3. Braxy, or inflammation, frequently in the bowels, for which the sheep are bled, and the mutton considered a rarity.

4. Trembling, or "the loupin' ill," from the sheep jumping up when attacked, is frequent on the west side of the Nith, and more sudden. Death in violent cases is immediate. Sheep recover from less virulent attacks by careful treatment.

Mossy land, where, as at the edge of lochs, the grass has not a firm hold of the soil, but which springs up quickly and is eagerly sought after by the sheep, is found to be injurious, much soil being swallowed. So also is the smoke of the lead furnaces, which is seen in the morning lying as dew upon the heather or grass; but the recent smoke-extracting apparatus employed on the Wanlock tends to counteract this evil there.

The average price of sheep in 1793 was £8 to £12 per score of three-year-old wedders—and when kept to Michaelmas, from £6 to £7; lamb, £4, 10s. to £5. At present, *Lambs*—(1) Half-bred (from Cheviot ewe and Yorkshire tup), 26s.—a few kept for feeding; (2) cross (from blackfaced ewe and Yorkshire tup), 22s.—for fatting and killing, not breeding; (3) (from Cheviot ewe and tup), ewes, 30s.—lambs, 18s.; (4) blackfaced ewes and tups, 24s.—lambs, 17s. —turned off in sixth year. *Wethers* (stopped breeding)—(5) Tups (*a*) Yorkshire, £7; (*b*) Cheviot, £5; (*c*) blackfaced, £5.

C.—GEOLOGICAL GROUPS.

"By taking a section from near Crawfordjohn, across the Snar Water, Leadhills, and the Green Lowther, to the valley of the Potrail Water, the Lower Silurian rocks traversed may be regarded as forming *one great synical trough.* . . . . Two divisions of that system are here represented—the Llandeilo and the Caradoc beds. . . . . In ascending order they consist of—

"(*a*) Queensberry Grit group.

"(*b*) Hartfell Shale group.

"(*c*) Daer group—a mass of strata drained by the Daer Water and its tributaries, north-westwards to a line drawn from Durisdeer, by Well Hell, Coom Rig, to Tomont Hill. It consists of hard blue and purplish gritty greywacke, accompanied by and interbedded with grey shales and shaly greywacke. . . . . The latter often contains much diffused iron, which oxydises, and causes it to assume a dull-red colour. . . . . The prevailing strike is north-easterly.

"(*d*) Dalveen group—well exposed in Dalveen Pass. Their bedding is sometimes much jointed, contorted, slickensided, and veined with quartz. . . . . This group of beds in the Dinabid Linn passes under a bed of coarse pebbly conglomerate.

"(*e*) Haggis Rock group, along north-west margin of the Silurian area from the Clyde at Mote, by Crawfordjohn, Fingland, and Kirkland Hill to the edge of the Sanquhar coalfield. . . . . Its general dip is south-easterly. It consists of thin-bedded, shaly greywackes, hard red mudstones, and fine conglomerates, ... locally known as 'Haggis Rock.' The pebbles are chiefly of quartz, jasper, and Lydian stone, varying in size from a pea to a walnut. . . . . The same strata are found on the north-west slope of Lonsie Wood Law . . . . prolonged beyond the other side of the Clyde across the Cakelaw and Glespin Burn. The south-east dip, with which the Haggis Rock group plunges under the Lowther Hills, is succeeded by a dip to the north-west, so that the ridge of the Lowthers lies in a synical trough, and the Haggis Rock group is brought up again along its south-east flank.

"(*f*) Lowther group, overlying the former—a great thickness of finely-laminated and flaggy blue felspathic greywackes and thin-bedded shales—seen in all the streams descending from the crest of the Lowther ridge. . . . . To the north-west the whole thickness of the group is met with along the ridge which, between Leadhills and Crawford, separates the valley of the Elvan and Glengonnar Waters. The best section of these strata occurs in the cutting of the Caledonian Railway at Crawford. It is in this group of strata, as developed along the Leadhills line of outcrop, that the mineral veins of Leadhills and Wanlockhead chiefly occur.

"(*g*) Black Shale group, distinguishable from the former by the occurrence of bands of red and green flinty sandstone, and of black anthracitic, pyritous, occasionally gnarled shales, containing grapto-lites. . . . . It has its centre occupied by the Caradoc group of Duntercleuch and Glendowran. The black shale bands are nume-rous, and the group containing them may be traced by their means along the southern side of the basin in a zone of over a mile in breadth, from Cogshead, by the smelting-mills at Waulockhead and Leadhills, to Laggen Gill, near Abington. Good sections of the graptolitic shales may be seen in Cog Burn, Wanlock Water, near Raecleuch Hill, Sowen Burn, behind the Wanlockhead smelting-mill and Glengonnar Burn (east of Black Hill). The lowest beds of this series may be seen resting on the Lowther beds in the burn south of the Wool Law, Leadhills, while the uppermost beds dip under the Caradoc group at a high angle in Blackburn, Wanlockhead, and Glenkip Burn, Leadhills. . . . . The flinty mudstones consist of indu-rated green, red, or chocolate-coloured mudstones or shales, with thin courses of dark flinty shale or Lydian stone. The latter are shat-tery, and much-veined with quartz. . . . . The fossils of this group prove that it belongs to the upper portion of the Llandeilo series. The fossils show that the rocks of the district belong to the Caradoc or Bald series." (See list given p. 13 and 14 of Memoirs.)

"In the Sanquhar district, or that portion of the Silurian area which lies to the south-west of the Nith, the geological structure is less easily traceable. . . . . It occupies a broad synclinal fold, inter-rupted at the head of the Afton. . . . . There is reason to believe that these folds are actually inverted. . . . . The group which is most easily followed, and from the convolutions of which the complicated geological structure of the district can best be seen, is that of the black shales. . . . . Each of the metamorphic areas consists of a central nucleus of granite, with a varying band of altered rocks around it. The largest area is that which is traversed by the Spango Water; it lies on the outcrop of the Haggis group and the lower part of the Lowther beds, having a breadth of about two miles and a length of about four. . . . . The granite occupies the area once filled by an equivalent mass of Silurian strata. . . . . It is a fine-grained mixture of pink orthoclase, with a little oligoclase, quartz, black mica, and hornblende. . . . . It weathers with com-parative rapidity into a rusty-coloured sand. . . . . A white, coarser variety of granite occurs at the Knipes, the Afton Water, &c. . . . . In it a vein of antimony glance has been worked, at a place called Hare Hill, south-east of New Cumnock, and though discontinued, many tons of the ore are to be found near the mouth of the mines."

"THE SANQUHAR COALFIELD is entirely made up of strata belong-ing to the true coal-measures. With the exception of the small faulted outlier at Whitecleuch, all the Carboniferous districts lie to the north of the great boundary fault, and outside of the Silurian region. This field is a prolongation of the Ayrshire coal-measures. . . . . On the north-east side of the field lies a portion of the upper barren red sandstones, which, as in Ayrshire, overlap the older portions of the Carboniferous system. Near Bankend they spread over a fault of 90 fathoms, without being themselves disturbed. Yet that these red sandstones are of Carboniferous and not of later age is indicated by the occurrence in them of at least two coal-seams (one of which is two feet thick) and one of blackband ironstone, seen in the stream near Kirkland. . . . . One distinguishing feature is the fact that along the south-west half of the field the strata are traversed in a north-west direction by at least three narrow doleritic dykes, which send out intrusive sheets along the whole coal-seams. . . . .

"Between the villages of Leadhills and Crawfordjohn there occurs a singular detached area of breccia, about a mile broad and two miles long. It fills a depression in the Silurian rocks, and may once have stretched into and along the Duneaton Valley, which is filled at Whitecleuch with Carboniferous deposits. . . . . It is inferred to be of Permian age."

"LIMESTONES are confined to the Carboniferous districts. The cornstones belonging to the calciferous sandstone series are extensively worked at Craigdullyeart, north-west of Corsoncone, for agricultural purposes. . . . . They are also worked at Wildshaw and Whitecleuch.

"BRICK CLAYS and red marls, lying in the upper part of the coal-measures, are used at Sanquhar for the coarser kind of pottery and terra-cotta, as also bricks and stiles.

"MINERALS.

"MINERAL VEINS are found traversing the Lower Silurian rocks round the villages of Wanlockhead and Leadhills, the one running north-west and south-east, the other west-north-west and east-south-east. These veins contain—

"(1.) Lead or Galena. Further westwards a true vein of galena was tried at in the Silurian rocks to the south of New Cumnock, but was abandoned. The general character of the veins is seen in a description of a part of the New Glencrieff vein laid open in December 1868. The vein here hades to the east at 70° to 75°. Beginning at the east or 'hanger' side, the order of metals is as under:—(a) Greywacke; part of the general Silurian rock or 'country.' (b) 'Black Jack' (zincblende), decomposing into clay. ½ inch. (c) 'Vein stuff;' greywacke ground up and mixed with quartz. 1½ inch. (d) Calcspar. ½ inch to 1 inch. (e) Galena. ½ inch. (f) Vein stuff, similar to (c) quartzose, and graduating into pure quartz near the floor of the level. 2 to 3 inches. (g) Blue greywacke; joints veined with calcareous matter. 3½ feet. (h) Hard, fine, compact quartz, with iron pyrites in 'flowers,' i.e., the crystals are scattered through the mass, and are not connected. 7 inches. (k) Alternating irregular layers of barytes and galena.

8 inches. (*l*) Vein stuff, similar to (*c*). 4 inches. (*m*) Greywacke (the ledger side of the vein), marked with vertical slickensides.

"The section is about six feet high. A 'string' of 'Black Jack' commences at the roof of the level in (*g*), and cuts through all the layers on to (*m*), which it enters near the floor. (*a*), (*g*), and (*m*), are 'country.' The other layers and the string are properly the vein. The veins vary at every step, and are sometimes remarkably rich in lead ores ; while on the other hand, the levels are sometimes driven for many fathoms without meeting with any.

"(2.) Iron.—Hæmatite, but not in workable quantity, found on the Ponnel Burn (north-east), also on the slope of Lewsgill, east of Abington. It occurs also in the veins of the lead tract.

"(3.) Small quantities of antimony are met with in the mineral veins.

"(4.) Manganese.—On the old Sanquhar road, about a mile north-east from Wardlaw Hill, a vein of barytes occurs, containing small quantities of finely-mammillated pyrolusite. The same ore is also met with in the lead veins.

"(5.) Zinc.—'Black Jack,' or sulphuret of zinc, is a common constituent of the galena veins, and occurs sometimes in considerable quantities.

"(6.) Copper.—Copper-pyrites is an occasional constituent of the Leadhills and Wanlockhead mineral veins.

"(7.) Silver.—The galena of Wanlockhead is sufficiently argentiferous to allow of the extraction of the silver with profit.

"(8.) Gold has been collected for three centuries from the alluvia of the streams of the district.

"(9.) Barytes.—A vein may be traced from near the head of Gass Water for two miles north-west to Knockbreck. Another, three feet thick, sometimes containing hæmatite, on the flank of Auchensaugh Hill, east of Douglas coalfield.

"(10.) Teal.—Carboniferous tracts furnish the coals of Muirkirk, Cumnock, Glespin, and Sanquhar. In some of these fields the shales are sufficiently bituminous to be capable of being used for the manufacture of paraffin oil."—(See Memoirs of Geological Survey, No. 15.)

VARIETIES OF LEAD.

There are not less than ten varieties of lead in the Susanna vein, Leadhills ; as (1) carbonate of lead, (2) phosphate of lead, (3) sulphate of lead, (4) sulphide of lead, (5) lanarkite, sulphato-carbonate of lead, (6) lead-hillite, sulphato tri-carbonate, (7) Susannite (different chiefly in specific gravity), (8) cromophosphate of lead, (9) Linarite, cupreous-sulphate, (10) vanadiate of lead.

Crumbling of silver-lead bars.—Specimens of bars containing the richest proportion of silver, which being exposed to air for five or six years, have crumbled down, are to be seen in the Museum of Science and Art in Edinburgh. This remarkable fact has been pointed out to me by Mr Gellatley, the curator there.

THE REGALIA OF SCOTLAND.

Fanny Kemble states that Sir Walter Scott informed her that when the Scottish Regalia was discovered in its obscure place of security in Edinburgh Castle, pending the decision of Government as to its ultimate destination, a committee of gentlemen were appointed its guardians, amongst whom he was one; and that he received a most urgent entreaty from an old lady of the Maxwell family, to be permitted to see it. She was nearly ninety years of age, and feared she might not live till the crown jewels of Scotland were permitted to become the object of public exhibition, and pressed Sir Walter with importunate prayers to allow her to see them before she died. Sir Walter's good sense and good nature alike induced him to take upon himself to grant the poor old lady's petition, and he himself conducted her into the presence of these relics of her country's independent sovereignty; when, he said, tottering hastily forward from his support, she fell on her knees before the crown, and clasping and wringing her wrinkled hands, wailing over it as a mother over her dead child. Sir Walter's description of the scene was infinitely pathetic, and it must have appealed to all his own poetical and imaginative sympathy with the former glories of his native land.

Some grains of gold, two small nuggets, and quartz with gold spread upon it, in addition to the Martin nugget from Leadhills, are exhibited in the Edinburgh Museum of Science and Art.

GOLD IN MYSORE.

The Madras newspapers have lately given some account of the Colar gold-fields in Mysore, and of the operations which have just been commenced there by the Oorogum Gold-Mining Company. The auriferous quartz reefs are said to extend for a length of nearly twenty miles, and are about twelve miles distant from a station on the Madras Railway.

These facts are interesting, and may be advantageous to man; but another fact should ever be present to the mind. It is that—

> " Gold healeth none,
> It hath no balm for wounds,
> It binds no broken hearts,
> It smooths no ruffled brow,
> It calms no inner storm.
> It cannot buy from heaven
> One drop of rain or dew,
> One beam of sun or star,
> Far less the heavenly shower,
> Or light, that hath the healing in its wing."

D.—EARLS OF CRAWFORD AND LINDSAY.

" Grey Crawford Castle's ruined wa's,
Sweet Clutha glides in reverence by.
Nae mair sae lichtly thro' the ha'
Treads Scotia's royalty the dance:
Nae mair at morn the hunters ca'
Or cavalier wi' haughty glance.
All weirdlike as the daylight wanes,
Dim spectre o' some ghaistly tale."

LORDS CRAWFORD (MENTIONED IN CHARTERS, &C.).

1. Galfridus and Gaulterus de Crawford, 1189-1202.
2. Reginald de Crawford, 1128.
3. Sir John de Crawford, 1248.

DE LINDSAYS, EARLS OF CRAWFORD.

Family of Lindsay in eleventh and twelfth centuries in England, name derived from manor in Essex.

William and Walter obtained lands in Clydesdale, &c., from David I., 1145, 1160.

Robert, 1199.

William (hostage for release of William the Lion), 1174

David, 1200, 1227.

Sir David, 1244; Regent, 1255; Great Chamberlain, 1255; died in crusade.

Sir Alexander, 1290, 1296, 1297, 1304.

Sir David, signed letter to Pope John 6th April 1320, asserting independence of Scotland, 1323, 1328, 1364. Keeper of Castle of Edinburgh, 1366.

Sir James, 1357.

Sir James, 1370. At coronation of Robert II., 1371. Baron of Crawford Lindsay, 1381-82, 1397.

Sir James de Lyndesay of Crawford was taken at Otterburn. Richard II. issued an order to Henry de Percy, Earl of Northumberland, 25th September 1388, regarding him.

Sir Alexander, 1366. Died in Candia on pilgrimage to Jerusalem, 1382.

Sir David, 1397. At tournament at London Bridge, 1390. Treating of peace with England, 1404. Created first earl, 1406. Died 1412.

Alexander, second earl, 1416, 1421. Hostage for James I., 1424, when his annual revenue was estimated at 1000 marks. Slain 1445-46 at Aberbrothwick.

Alexander, third earl, 1446. Rose in arms to avenge death of

239

Douglas, to whom the king had granted a safe-conduct. Defeated and forfeited, 1452, but pardoned. Died of fever, 1454.

David, fourth earl, 1458. Duke of Montrose, 1488, which was lost on accession of James IV., and restored by charter. Died 1494.

John, fifth earl, styled Master of Crawford, 1494.

Alexander, sixth earl, 1476–1517.

David, seventh earl, 1526.

Alexander, Master, 1527.

David of Edzell, eighth earl, 1550. Father of Sir David Lindsay of Edzell.

David, ninth earl, 1559. Joined association for Queen Mary, 1568. Married daughter of Cardinal Beatton of St Andrews, with dowry of 4000 marks, a month before the murder of the Cardinal.

David, tenth earl, 1581–1607.

David, eleventh earl, 1608–1621.

Henry, twelfth earl, 1623. Order of Bath, 1603.

George, thirteenth earl, 1623.

Ludovick, fourteenth earl, 1641. Joined Marquis of Montrose on behalf of Charles I. at Dumfries, 1644, for which excommunicated by the Commission of the General Assembly. Forfeited 1644, but restored as Earl of Lindsay. Excepted from pardon 1646, but allowed to be transported. Died in Spain.

Lord Spynier died 1672, when John Lindsay of Edzell became male heir, and entitled to the earldom. The title was taken up by the Earl of Lindsay 1650, 1661.

LINDSAY, EARL OF CRAWFORD AND LINDSAY.

Sir William Lindsay of Byres, and family, descended from Sir David Lindsay of Crawford.

John, fifteenth earl, Lord Lindsay of Byres, 1596, on the forfeiture of Ludovick, 1644, received title and estate, and thenceforth designated Earl of Crawford-Lindsay. Entered into engagement, 1648. Confined in Tower, and excepted out of Cromwell's Act of pardon, 1654. Released by Monk, 1660. Opposed " Act recissory." Against restoration of Episcopacy. Greatly esteemed. Died 1676, aged eighty.

William, sixteenth earl, and second Earl of Lindsay, concurred in Revolution. President of Privy Council, 1689.

John, seventeenth earl, third Lord Lindsay, Privy Councillor, 1702–13.

John, eighteenth earl, fourth Lord Lindsay, engaged in military exercises abroad. Charging French infantry, he cried, " Hark, my dear lads ! trust to your swords, handle them well, and never mind your pistols." They were victorious. Died at London, 1749. On account of the great debts of the family, William, fourteenth earl, was, in 1678, obliged to dispone his estate to trustees, and the debt had increased. Dying without issue, the titles of Crawford and Lindsay devolved on George, Viscount of Garnock, descended from the Hon. Patrick Lindsay, second son of John, fourteenth earl.

George, fourth Viscount of Garnock, in 1749 became nineteenth Earl of Crawford and fifth of Lindsay.

George Lindsay Crawford, twentieth earl, 1781.

The Earl of Balcarres submitted to the House of Peers his claim to the earldom of Crawford.

SIR ALEXANDER HOME had a charter of the king's land of Roberton, 1450. Mariot, his daughter, was married to John, fifth earl of Crawford, but had no issue.

Of an offshoot of the family, the last Lord Lindsay of Covington, the ruins of whose tower may be seen not far from Thankerton Station, a singular story is told. He had a remarkable beard. He sickened, was laid out as dead, friends invited to his funeral, and due preparation made, " when the great-grandchild of the dead nobleman whispered in her mother's ear, ' The beard is wagging, the beard is wagging.' When approached, Sir William awoke from his trance; but with the humour characteristic of the man, he forbade that the preparations made should be interfered with. When the funeral party arrived, the door was opened, and, leaning on the arm of the minister of the parish, the pale nobleman appeared, and explained to the wondering guests that he was alive, glad to see them, made thanks be returned for his rescue from the grave, caused dinner to be served, and spent, as was the wont of those days, a jovial evening." He died about 1688, the era of the Revolution; but having squandered his estate, his family were reduced, but thriving farmers of the name of Lindsay are still to be found in the parish of Covington. (See Upper Ward, vol. i. p. 488.)

CRAWFORD AND LINDSAY ARMS.—Quarterly, 1st and 4th, gules, a fess cheque, argent and azure, for Lindsay; 2d and 3d, or, a lion rampant, gules, debruised with a ribbon, sable, for Abernethy. Crest—An ostrich proper, holding in its beak a key, or. Supporters—Two lions sejant, gules, armed, or. Motto—*Endure Fort,* or *Endure Furth.* (See Illustration.)

E.—PROPRIETORS AND RENTAL OF CRAWFORD AND CRAWFORDJOHN PARISHES.

I. CRAWFORD VALUATION, 1875–76.

Subject.	Proprietor.	Occupier.	Rent.
Farm, Up. How-cleuch	Wm. Bertram of Kerswell, Carnwath	John Paterson	£314 18 0
Sheep-f., Cramp	Ditto	Robt. Paterson	320 0 0
Shootings	Ditto	Allan Home	15 0 0
Tollhouse, Glen-geith	Big. and P. Road T.	Ten. under £4	6 10 0
Farm, Kirkhope	Duke of Buccleuch	J. T. Milligan, Hayfield, Thornhill	608 15 0
„ Whitecamp	„	Richd. Vassey, Far., Morningside	530 0 0
Ho. and garden	Robt. Baird, shepherd	...	4 0 0
Manse	Minister	...	30 0 0
Land	„	...	16 0 0
Ho. Crawford	Thos. Cranstoun, labourer	...	2 10 0
Ho. Crawford inn	Hrs. of A. Cranstoun, innkeeper	...	14 0 0
Ho. and gar., C.	Wm. Carmichael, labourer	3 ten. under £4	4 15 0
„	„	Empty	1 15 0
Man. Ho. land, and shootings, Newton	Mrs Louisa Catterson	J. A. Callender, Braemain Villa, Morningside, Edinburgh	145 0 0
Woods	Ditto	Mrs L. Catterson	5 0 0
F., Over Fingland	Ditto	Wm. Rae, Gateslick, Thornhill	300 0 0
F., Shortcleuch	Ditto	Alex. Paterson, Carmacoup, Douglas	300 0 0
F., Boghead	Ditto	John and Robt. Paton	100 0 0
F., Newton	Ditto	John A. Callender	200 0 0
F., pt. of Inches	Ditto	Robt. Boreland, Andinicairn	15 10 0
Waterpower, Leadhills	Ditto	Leadhills Mining Co., W. Muir, 7 Wellington Street, Leith	20 0 0
Land, Inches	Ditto	Gideon Pott, Gengeith	1 10 0

CRAWFORD VALUATION, 1875-76—*continued.*

Subject.	Proprietor.	Occupier.	Rent.
Game on Fingland	Mrs Louisa Catterson	Robert Leach, Thos. Harridge Rochdale, and Thos. Cradwick	£50 0 0
F., Castlemains	Sir F. E. Colebrooke, Bart., M.P.	David Tweedie	571 8 0
F., Southwood and Murdoch Holme Park	Ditto	,,	150 0 0
F., Kirkton	Ditto	Hope Hunter	264 14 0
F., Normangill	Ditto	Richd. Vassie	883 16 0
F., Netherhouse-cleuch and Bid-house	Ditto	John Paterson	520 0 0
F., Elvanfoot and Stoneyburn	Ditto	D. Tweedie	541 6 0
F., Midloch	Ditto	John A. and W. Johnstone	499 7 0
F., Crookedstone	Ditto	Robt. Boreland	1,112 11 0
Ho., yard, &c., C.	Ditto	Ten. under £4	25 19 0
Game, Normangill	Ditto	R. Vassie	10 0 0
Ho. and land, C.	Ditto	R. Ramsay	14 0 0
Land, C.	Ditto	Alex. Cranston	52 0 0
,, C.	Ditto	Eliz. Russell	10 0 0
,, C.	Ditto	Matt. Henderson	5 0 0
,, C.	Ditto	,,	4 10 0
,, C.	Ditto	Wm. Kerr, farmer	13 10 0
Land and wool-carding mill, Glengowan	Ditto	Hunter & Co.	10 0 0
Shootings, Elvanfoot, &c.	Ditto	Allan Home	85 0 0
Land, C.	Ditto	Thos. Henderson	2 0 0
Ho., C.	Ann Cranstoun	...	4 0 0
Tollhouse, Elvanfoot	G. & C. R. T.	Alex. Dempster	4 0 0
House	,,	Jas. Crawford, grocer	5 0 0
Police station, Leadhills	Commrs. of Supply	...	14 0 0
Ho. and land, C.	George Dickson	...	4 0 0
Ho., C.	,,	2 ten. under £4	3 5 0
Tollhouse, Newton, and bedhouse	Elvan Water Road Trustees	Ten. under £4	4 10 0
F., Nunnerie, Wintercleuch, Sergeant Land, and Craikburn	Robt. Wm. Ewart, of Allershaw	J. Wilson	1,360 0 0
Shooting Lodge, N.	Ditto	Robt. Maddison, R. Warwick, Ch. J. Ebden, Esq.	75 0 0
Shootings	Ditto	Ditto	160 0 0

Subject.	Proprietor.	Occupier.	Rent.		
Ho., C.	Eliz. Gilchrist	...	£2	0	0
Ar. and pas. F. C.	Alex. Goodfellow, portioner	Alex. Murray	45	0	0
,, land and ho., C.	Ditto	Alex. Goodfellow	37	10	0
Houses	Ditto	...	4	0	0
F., pt. of N. Shortcleuch	Earl of Hopetoun	Thos. Gibson	175	0	0
Game grounds, Leadhills	,,	,,	8	0	0
Cowgang and pt. of N. Shortcleuch	,,	Ten. under £4	56	0	0
Sheep pas., F., ¼ of S. Shortcleuch and N. ditto	,,	Alex. Paterson, Carmacoup	118	0	0
F. Smithswood and Watermeetings	,,	Wm. Wilson, Watermeetings	• 725	0	0
F., Glenocher and Glengeith	,,	G. Pott, Mrs Pott, Mr S. Tait, Mrs Tait	1,350	0	0
F., Glencaple	,,	John French, far.	400	0	0
Ground, Leadhills	,,	Jas. Glasgow	12	0	0
Ho., land, hotel, Leadhills	,,	Wm. Noble	60	0	0
Ho., land, do., with bakehouse	,,	John Wright	10	0	0
Lead-mines	,,	Leadhills Mg. Co.	1,618	7	0
Houses, Leadhills	,,	Ten. under £4	13	0	0
Game ground, do.	,,	E. of Hopetoun	50	0	0
Holms of Glengeith	,,	Robt. Boreland, Auchincairn, Closeburn	50	0	0
Cottage, Leadhills	,,	John Gill, overseer of mines	15	0	0
Gamekeeper's ho. and land	,,	Jas. Glasgow, gamekeeper	10	0	0
Ho., Elvanfoot	Hrs. of R. Hunter, farmer	Robt. Brown	4	0	0
F., Whelphill	Countess of Home	Robert Fletcher	455	2	0
F., Little Clyde	,,	Archd. Thomson	160	0	0
Ho. and gar., Crawford	John Hair, platelayer, 86 Kippoch Hill Rd., Glasgow	2 Ten. under £4	3	5	0
Ho., Elvanfoot	Wm. Kirkpatrick, 41 Main Street, Motherwell	3 ten. under £4	7	10	0
Ho. and gar., C.	Wm. Kerr, farmer	...	5	10	0
Ho., C.	,,	4 ten. under £4	9	0	0
Ho. and smelt-mill, Leadhills	,,	Workmen	16	0	0
Ho. and land, Bellfield	Mrs Barb. Menzies	John Paterson, Howcleugh	£120	0	0
Ho., C.	,,	4 ten. under £4	9	0	0
Ho. and land, Bellfield	,,	Mrs B. Menzies	15	0	0

CRAWFORD VALUATION, 1875-76—*continued.*

Subject.	Proprietor.	Occupier.	Rent.		
Grass parks	Mrs Barb. Menzies	J. Paterson, H.	£3	0	0
Shootings	,,	Sir F. E. Cole-brooke	7	0	0
Ho. and land, C.	Mrs D. Murray	...	50	0	0
Plantations, C.	,,	...	0	5	0
Ho. and gar., C.	,,	Ten. under £4	4	0	0
,,	T. Murray, mason	Robt. Murray	5	0	0
,,	T. Martin	Ten. under £4	1	10	0
,,	N. Murray	...	7	0	0
Ho. and land, C.	Rev. J. G. M'Vicar, D.D., Moffat, Tr. of Morrison's school.	Jas. Gilchrist	45	0	0
Ho. and gar., C.	William M'Lean, labourer	...	2	0	0
,,	G. Robertson, slater	...	6	0	0
,,	T. Robertson, slater	...	8	0	0
Ho. and land, Lead-hills	Rev. S. Smith	...	15	0	0
Land	,,	...	3	10	0
Sheep-f., Troloss	John Wilson & Co.	...	550	0	0
Game	,,	...	50	0	0
Ho. and gar., Elvan-foot	Jas. Wight, sheep-drover, Elvan Villa, Moffat	...	4	0	0
Ho. and gar., Lead-hills	John Weir, senior, miner	...	3	0	0
Land, L.	...	...	5	0	0
		Total,	£15,817	8	0
Caledonian Railway Co.	. . . . .		7,657	0	0
			£23,474	8	0

2. CRAWFORDJOHN, LANDS AND RENTS, 1876.

Subject.	Proprietor.	Occupier.	Rent.		
Limeworks, White-cleuch	D. of B.	Jas. Murdoch	£10	0	0
Farm, Upper White-cleuch	,,	D. and W. Camp-bell	325	0	0
Farm, Shieldholm	,,	,,	75	0	0
Ho. and gar., White-cleuch	,,	Ten. under £4	5	0	0
Ho. and shop, C.J.	A. French or Black-ley	E. Watson	8	0	0
Ho. and gar., C.J.	J. Boe or Forrest	Mrs Forrest	315	0	0
House, C.J.	,,	Ten. under £4	25	0	0
Farm, Netherbal-gray	Sir T. E. Colebke.	Jas. Black	119	11	0
Ho. and gar., Ab-ington	,,	Mrs Capie	5	0	0

CRAWFORDJOHN, LANDS AND RENTS, 1876—*continued.*

Subject.	Proprietor.	Occupier.	Rent.		
Farm, Newscastle	Sir T. E. Colebke.	Wm. Coke	£204	7	0
„ Mosscastle	„	Ebenezer Law	190	0	0
Ho., Duneattonford	„	J. Hallidaw	7	0	0
Farm, Eastertown	„	D. French	260	10	0
„ Mountherrick	„	J. French	285	10	0
„ Boghouse	„	A. Dalgleish	358	8	0
Mill and land, C.J.	„	W. C. & W. Gibb	170	0	0
Ho. and land, Min. Park	„	Rev. J. Cowan	12	12	0
Farm, CrossKnowes	„	H. Haddow	60	3	0
„ Craighead	„	W. Hunter	249	18	0
„ Goal and Liscleuch	„	J. Williamson	373	12	0
„ Parkend	„	J. Hunter	11	9	0
„ Over Abington	„	J. Paterson, sen. and jun.	338	19	0
„ Gilkerscleuch Mains	„	T. Jack	354	13	0
„ E. Glentewing and Cleuch	„	J. & W. Coke	151	9	0
Land and schoolmaster's park	„	Wm. Stewart	6	10	0
Farm, Greenfield	„	J. Dalgleish	198	12	0
„ N. Abington	„	Rps. of T. Morton	610	0	0
„ C.J.	„	E. Watson	276	19	0
Man.-Ho., Abington	„	Sir T. E. Colebke.	100	0	0
Ho. „	„	A. Hunter	4	0	0
„ „	„	W. Corrie	4	0	0
Woodlands on estate	„	Sir T. E. C.	88	8	0
Ho. and gar., Meadowbank	„	Ten. under £4	65	16	0
Ho., Abington	„	W. M'Multree	4	0	0
Police Stn., A.	„	Comrs. of Supply	8	0	0
Grass parks, A.	„	Sir T. E. C.	120	0	0
Sawmill, Abington	„	Hope Macqueen	12	0	0
Ho., Burnpark	„	S. Forrest	6	6	0
Land, pt. of Eastertown	„	A. Renton	10	9	0
Ho. and steading, Gilkencleuch	„	G. Hunter	43	0	0
Grass park, Abington	„	D. Tweedie	19	16	0
Ditto	„	„	19	4	0
Ho., C.J.	J. Coke	Ten. under £4	9	15	0
Ho. and shop, A.	R. Coltart, 194 Main St., Glas.	Mrs Coltart	6	0	0
„ „	R. Coltart	Wm. Brown	13	0	0
Ho., Abington	„	Ten. under £4	5	0	0
Land, „	„	Mrs Coltart	3	10	0
Ho. and offices, A.	Commercial Bank	A. Paterson	40	0	0
Manse, C.J.	...	Rev. Jas. Cowan	24	0	0
Glebe, „	...	„	20	0	0

CRAWFORDJOHN, LANDS AND RENTS, 1876—*continued.*

Subject.	Proprietor.	Occupier.	Rent.
Game, Whitecleuch Birkcleuch, and Myres	Mrs Catterson	A. Renton	£15 0 0
Farm, Nether W.C. &c.	,,	,,	195 0 0
Farm, Birkcleuch	,,	T. Lammie	250 0 0
Ho. and smithy, Burnside	...	R. Forrest	7 0 0
Ho., C.J.	James French	Ten. under £4	8 10 0
,, ,,	A. Watson or Forrest	W. Thomson	2 12 0
,, ,,	Ditto	Ten. under £4	2 0 0
,, ,,	Ditto	Empty	2 8 0
,, ,,	Hrs. of J. Simpson	Ten. under £4	9 5 0
,, ,,	,,	A. Renton	6 0 0
Tollhouse, A.	G. and Car. Road Trust	J. Allan	3 0 0
,, Duneatton, Braehead	Ditto	,,	4 0 0
Ho., C.J., Overtown	Hrs. of J. and W. Gall	Misses Thomson	10 0 0
Ho., C.J.	W. S. Gall, 135 Moore St., Glasg.	Ten. under £4	2 10 0
Ho. and stable, Redwors	Css. of Home	J. Lindsay	4 0 0
Farm, Stonehill	,,	T.A.Greenshields	641 0 0
Ho. and gar., Stanemuir	,,	J. Watson	5 0 0
Farm, Blackburn	,,	E. Watson	33 5 0
,, Greenburn	,,	J. Willison, s. & junr.	250 0 0
Ho. and Lands, Glespin	,,	J. Bell	9 0 0
Farm, Netherton, Blackhall	,,	T. French	826 0 0
Farm, Shawhead	,,	J. & D. French	315 0 0
,, Netherton and Glespin	,,	T. Haddow	237 12 0
Ho. and Lands, Wr. Netherton	,,	Mrs Gillespie, Parkhall	1 0 0
Farm, Sheriffcleuch	,,	G. Paterson, Glentaggart, Douglas	150 0 0
,, Glendorch	Earl of Hopetoun	P. Stewart, Middlegill, Moffat	220 0 0
Ho. and shop, A.	Hrs. of G. Hunter	G. Hastie	12 0 0
,,	,,	Mrs Galloway	7 0 0
Ho., Abington ,,	,,	Ten. under £4	4 0 0
,, ,,	Wm. Hunter, Craighead	,,	3 10 0
Inn, ,,	Mrs Hunter	(Mr Pollock)	16 0 0
Ho., ,,	Hrs. D. Hunter	Ten. under £4	3 0 0
Ho. and gar., A.	E. Hunter, Craighead	,,	2 10 0

CRAWFORDJOHN, LANDS AND RENTS, 1876—*continued.*

Subject.	Proprietor.	Occupier.	Rent.
Ho. and gar., Dun-eatton Bge.	W. Hunter	Ten. under £4	£2 0 0
Land, Lettershaw	J. E. Hunter, 14 Walmer St., Gl.	R. Watson	80 0 0
,, Glentewing	Ditto	W. Watson	227 10 0
Farm, Snarshead and Glenbeith	J. A. Johnstone, Archbank M.	J. A. Johnstone	400 0 0
Game	Ditto	,,	60 0 0
Ho. and gar., C.J.	R. Lewis	R. Lewis	5 15 0
Ho., C.J.	...	Robert Lindsay	2 10 0
F.-C. Manse, A.	...	Rev. R. Logan	25 0 0
Ho. and shop, A.	J. M. Macqueen, Raemuir Cottage, Juniper Green	Hope Macqueen	14 10 0
,,	...	Robt. Macfarlane	8 0 0
,, C.J.	J. Pennan, dress-maker	...	2 15 0
Ho., store, and gar. C.J.	A. Renton	E. & M. Renton	9 0 0
Houses, C.J.	,,	Ten. under £4	19 0 0
Grass Parks, Town-head	,,	A. Renton	3 0 0
Ho., Abington	...	Thomas Ramage	3 5 0
Ho. and gar., C.J.	...	Wm. Slimmon	3 15 0
,,	...	Hugh Steel	6 0 0
Farm and Wood-land, Holmhead	Michael J. Stewart	R. Watson	110 0 0
Ho. and gar., C.J.	School Board	W. Stewart, jr.	10 0 0
Ho., Abington	Wm. Thomson	Ten. under £4	3 0 0
Farm and game, Glendowan	Trs. James Thomson	J. Williamson	197 0 0
Ho. and shop, Abington	E. B. Oswald and L. Alexander	J. Hunter	20 0 0
Farm, Strangcleuch	G. Williamson, builder, Well Road, Moffat	Alex. Williamson	250 0 0
Shootings	Ditto	J. A. Johnstone	20 0 0
Ho. and gar., C.J.	W. Williamson	W. Williamson	8 0 0
Inn and stable	,,	S. Marchbank	9 0 0
Ho. and gar., C.J.	Robert Williamson	Ten. under £4	4 0 0
Ho. and stable, C.J.	Jas. Watson	J. Watson	5 10 0
Cot. and gar., C.J.	Hrs. of J. Watson	J. & M. Stevenson	8 0 0
Houses, C.J.	Robert Young	Ten. under £4	2 10 0
			£10,076 19 0

F.—CRAWFORD AND CRAWFORDJOHN—CONDITION AND ELEVATION.

The best authorities give as the extent of

(1) Crawford—118¼ square miles, or 60,183 Scots statute acres—23 Scots being equal to 29 imperial acres.

(2) Crawfordjohn—26,251 land, 106 roads, 103 water—in all, 26,460 acres statute.

In CRAWFORD parish hills are called "watches," where in troublous times the watcher gave notice of the approach of the foe, the notices being telegraphed from hill to hill, in smoke by day, in fire by night. Tinto signifies "the hill of fire" on this account.

The population in this parish has been reduced one-half by the engrossing of farms, an evil which still goes on. In some instances where five families resided, one farmer holds the land. The practice termed "bowing" being prevalent here and in Nithsdale, a number of cows are put under the care of a man and his wife, who take the entire risk, and if they can, make a little profit, after paying rent to the farmer at the rate of £10 per cow.

The rearing of horses was formerly much practised, as the roads were too bad to admit of wheel-carriages, and numbers of horses were employed.

The valley of the Elvan was farmed at one time by seventeen tenants ; now there are only four.

The population of Crawford in 1792 was 520 ; Leadhills, 970 ; total, 1490 ; of whom only six were Seceders, and twenty Cameronians.

About the year 1780 a road was made from Douglas Mill to Moffat, which opened up the country.

The Crawford Inn, in coaching days, enjoyed the patronage of honeymoon parties, who now pass on by rail to Beattock, or northward to Edinburgh and Glasgow.

The Board of Supervision for Relief of the Poor states that £555, 8s. 4d. had been expended in Crawford parish for 75 paupers or dependants, 8 of whom were casual, and 2 were lunatics in the asylum.

The sum paid by the Caledonian Railway for poor-rates is nearly five times the amount in which the heritors formerly assessed themselves.

A valuable mineral spring still flows at Trolass. Formerly many woods must have existed, as indicated by the designation "shaw" applied to several places ; now, with the exception of some wood at Newton House, opposite to Elvanfoot station, and at Abington House, there are few trees in Crawford. Peat is little used since coal was obtained by the Caledonian line.

CRAWFORD.

"The Paradise of Scotland" is a title which was "justly" claimed for the beginning of Clydesdale, from "Arick-stone," sixteen miles above Lanark, by William Lithgow, who, born in that town 1583, published a remarkable book of his travels and voyages (mostly performed on foot) over various portions of the world. He thus addressed that paradise, after he had been arrested and "reduced to a martyred anatomy in the Inquisition"—

> "Where, whence (O natal place) my soul did coil
> Blood, spirit, flesh, birth, life, love, and soil."

"The Beauties of Scotland" says that "the village of Crawford had a peculiar constitution. Till about the year 1785 twenty freedoms were held run-rig—that is, in feu under the families of Crawford or Douglas. The masters of these freedoms were called *Lairds*, and their wives *Ladies*. A subordinate rank feued ground for a house and yard. The freedom consisted of four or five acres of croft land, with a privilege of feeding some cattle on the hill. A *birly* court, remarkable for its noisy meetings, governed this small republic, in which every freedom laird had a vote, or his tenant in his absence, the business being the allocation of cows, sheep, or horses on the pasture. These old times, when the court adjourned to the alehouse, and little work was required or performed, are still regarded as a sort of golden age.

The ancient practice of *riding the stang* was sometimes employed when a husband was known to beat his wife whose character was good. The women, uniting in conspiracy, seized the offender, and having placed him astride a strong beam of wood, tied his legs beneath; then raising him aloft, he was carried in derision round the village, exposed to the jeers and hisses, and having his legs pulled by the indignant community. In extreme cases a ducking brought the punishment to a termination, the grown-up men remaining all the while at a respectful distance from the scene.

Crawford was often the scene of more direful scenes in former days. Thus, William Johnstone of Wamphray, surnamed the Galliard, came and ravaged the lands of Lord Sanquhar. Taken by the Crichtons, he was converted into a "tassel" for the gallows-tree. He pleaded hard, offering bribes to Simon of the Side, his chief captor—

> "O Simmy, Simmy, now let me gang,
> And I'll ne'er mair a Crichton wrang;
> O Simmy, Simmy, now let me be,
> And a peck o' gowd I'll gie to thee!"

His successor, another William Johnstone of Kirkhill, mustered afresh for booty and revenge—

> "Back tae Nithsdale they hae gane,
> And awa the Crichton's nowt hae ta'en;

And when they came to the Wellpath head,
The Crichtons bade them light and lead.

" Then out spoke Willie of the Kirkhill,
Of fighting, lads, ye'se hae your fill,
And from his horse Willie he lap,
And a burnished brand in his hand he gat.

" Out through the Crichtons Willie he ran,
And dang them doun baith horse and man.
Oh but the Johnstones were wondrous rude
When the Biddes burn ran three days blude.

" As they cam in at Evan head,
At Ricklaw Holm they spread abroad ;
Drive on, my lads, it will be late ;
We'll hae a pint at Wamphray gate.

" Where'er I gang, or where'er I ride,
The lads of Wamphray are on my side,
And of a' the lads that I do ken,
The Wamphray lad's the king of men."

VERE IRVING OF NEWTON.

The history of the Veres, or Weirs, of Newton, whose mansion-house lies opposite to the foot of the Elvan, is not without interest. The " Upper Ward " says that it " originated in a cadet of the Veres of Blackwood, in Lesmahagow, who acquired lands in Crawford, in which parish we find them established early in the sixteenth century. William Vere of Newton served upon an assize in 1512. In 1528 his widow, and John Weir his son, entered a protest in the High Court of Parliament that they should not be prejudiced by the forfeiture of the Earl of Angus. The representative of this family, in the latter part of the seventeenth century, appears to have taken an active part on the patriotic side during the troubles which marked the reigns of the later Stuarts. In 1662 an Act of Parliament was passed declaring that His Majesty Charles II. has thought fit to burden his pardon to some (whose guiltiness hath rendered them obnoxious to the law, their lives and fortunes at his Majesty's disposal) with some small sums. Among this list of these appears John Weir of Newton for £360 (most probably Scots money). In 1682, the Duke of York having left Scotland, and intrusted its affairs to the Earl of Aberdeen, Chancellor, and the Earl of Queensberry, Treasurer, " a very arbitrary spirit appeared in' this administration, a gentleman of the name of Weir was tried because he had kept company with one who had been in the Rebellion, though that person had never been marked out by process or proclamation. The inferences upon which Weir was condemned (for a prosecution by the Government and a condemnation were in Scotland the same thing) hung upon each other after the following manner : No man, it was supposed, could have been in a rebellion without being exposed to suspicion in the neighbourhood. If the neighbourhood suspected, it was to be presumed that each individual had likewise heard of the grounds of suspicion. Every man was bound to declare to the Government his suspicion against every man, and to avoid the company of traitors. To fail in this duty was to participate in the treason. The conclusion on the whole was, You have conversed with a rebel, therefore you are yourself a rebel. A reprieve was with some difficulty obtained for Weir." The person referred to by the historian is the same John Weir of Newton, and the family tradition as to the manner in which the reprieve was obtained is, that he had a sister who was married to a cadet of the Irvings of Saphock, and that the latter was usher to the Privy Council. By his connivance his wife obtained access to the council-chamber, and implored the Lords to grant a pardon to her brother—at first in vain. Being, however, near her confinement, her agitation brought on the pains of labour. She nevertheless refused to be removed, and continued her frantic entreaties for mercy until the Chancellor exclaimed, "Take away the woman, and make out the pardon;" upon which Weir swore, that be the bairn lad or lass, it should inherit his lands, as its coming had saved his life. The tradition appears confirmed by a deed executed by him about this date, by which he conveys his property to his sister and her husband, on condition that they should take the name and arms of Vere. No sooner, however, was John Vere out of one scrape than he was into another; for we find him, in 1685, forfeited by Parliament for the crime of treason, the accusation being that he, along with others, "went to London, pretending to negociat the settlement of ane Scots collonie in Carolina, but trewlie and realie to treat anent and carie on a rebellion and conspiracy with the Earls of Shaftesbury and Essex, and Lord Russell and others, in England." He remained under this ban until the Revolution, when it was removed by the General Act repealing previous forfeitures, passed in 1690. The farms of Harthope and Raecleuch were held by branches of the Johnstone family, while the lands of Ellershaw, Trolass, and part of those of South Shortcleuch, were possessed by other sub-vassals.

The late George Vere Irving, Esq., wrote the valuable archæological and historical papers which form a choice portion of Murray's "Upper Ward of Lanarkshire" which appeared in 1864. He died in London in 1869. It is said that the property was left to his widow during her lifetime, and thereafter to Mr Barker, an artist. His widow has married again. Whether it may return to the family of the Irvings may be a disputed point.

CRAWFORDJOHN,

in its improved condition, was thus concisely described by Mr Macqueen, Abington, at an annual festive reunion of its natives in Glasgow—

"Who knows better than the natives of Crawfordjohn what a great place it is and has been? It was once the seat of royalty. That was the time when the Castle of Boghouse, with its stately towers and battlements, bade defiance to every invader. Many important documents, still in existence, relating to Scotland, were signed there; but, like every other thing in this world, it was doomed to decay, and at the present time not one stone is left standing upon another. The farm-steading of Boghouse is built on the ruins of the castle. Then on the Abington side of the hill we have the ruins of the abbey that gave Abington its name. Some of the walls remain, and form part of the farm-offices of Upper Abington. It must have been a grand place in its day, judging from the way the land around it has been laid out and nicely studded with fine old trees. But the age of progress in Crawfordjohn dates from the time Sir E. Colebrooke became principal proprietor in the parish. Good roads are the first thing to improve a country side. Well, previous to that time they were so fearfully bad that it was a rule in the parish that, when farmers were carting peats, never fewer than two carts and two horses were to go in company, so that when one cart and horse got into a hole, the other was always at hand to help to pull them out again; but great improvements have been made since then. There are about thirty miles of as good statute-labour roads as you will find in any moorland parish in Scotland. Then the next thing that improves a place is shelter. Sir E. Colebrooke and his able factor, Mr M'Kenzie, within the last thirty years, have laid out upwards of a thousand acres of healthy, thriving plantation. These have changed the whole landscape. They have also spent thousands of pounds in fencing and draining the estate, so that now may be seen the deer feeding on rich, green pasture, by the side of pretty plantations, where, forty years ago, it was not safe for a hare to wade through. 'These were the places where the stirkies drowned.' The next thing that adds comfort to the population of a place is good houses. I am glad to say the proprietors of Crawfordjohn have not been backward in this respect; none of your mud-cabins nowadays, but good houses done up in modern fashion, with all the modern improvements. They can stand favourable comparison with the buildings of any estate in Scotland; and the cottages, particularly in Abington, are returned by the Government Inspector as first-class. And what is the result of all this? A thriving, intelligent, improving tenantry, that need not be ashamed to show their faces in their line of life in any part of the world. And when you find the land well managed, you generally find the stock equally well improved; and I am glad to say Crawfordjohn is no exception to the rule, for there are herds, not a few of both sheep and cattle, in the parish that stand very high in the best show-yards in the land. In regard to the two chief towns in the parish, Abington and Crawfordjohn, it was long a disputed point which was to outstrip the other. It was resolved to decide on the icy board whether Abington was to get over the kirk and the bell. At that time Crawfordjohn was scarcely ever beaten there; but as luck would have it, on this particular occasion Abington was victor. Then the next thing was how to get over the kirk, and, to settle all disputes, a Crawfordjohn worthy said we might take the kirk, but that they were determined to keep the bell and the stipend. Neither changed hands at that time; but as years rolled on Abington got a church and bell of its own, so I suppose all parties will be pleased. But the finishing touch to Abington was Sir Edward's taking up his abode amongst us, building his house in the middle of the village, and laying out the grounds with pretty clumps of plantation, intersected with beautiful walks, which are kept open all days of the year; and at the present time, I believe, if it were possible to bring old Hope Hunter, the founder of the village, again on the scene, were it not for Tinto and the neighbouring hills, he would not believe it was near the place of his birth. Then we are a reading population in Crawfordjohn parish. We have two circulating libraries, containing about 5000 well-read volumes—the one in Crawfordjohn village being the oldest and largest, so that, everything considered, the natives of Crawfordjohn have no occasion to think shame of the place of their birth.

CRAWFORDJOHN.

Schools.—Public (late Parish) School, Female School, and Abington School. The Public School has accommodation for 70 scholars, the average attendance for past year, 45. The attendance at Female School will be between 20 and 30.

The first School Board was elected March 19, 1873.

After many attempts had been made, a parish library was established in Crawfordjohn in 1840. It numbers upwards of 3000 well-selected volumes, and has 94 subscribers—Dr Proudfoot of Kendal, a native of the parish, having bequeathed 1352 works to it.

In 1836 there were eight, now three public-houses are found in the parish.

ABINGTON CATTLE-SHOW.

In September the annual exhibition of stock belonging to the members of the Abington Agricultural Society and the Highland Society's District Show of Cheviot Sheep was held on a fine level haugh, skirted by the river Clyde, and contiguous to the pleasure-grounds and gardens which surround Abington House, the Lanarkshire residence of Sir T. E. Colebrooke, Bart., M.P. for the Northern Division, and Lord-Lieutenant of the county. The show-yard was visited by a large number interested in the proceedings, and nearly all the leading agriculturists in the district. The entries of cattle and horses were a full average; sheep were considerably in excess of past seasons. Ayrshire cattle always excellent. This being the centre of an extensive sheep country, the show was a good one. The blackfaced were decidedly superior. The exhibition of dairy produce was the best held for years, the specimens being all highly creditable to the dairies from which they were sent. Collie-dogs were a nice lot. Numerous prizes were awarded, and at the termination of the show a large number of gentlemen, including the judges, dined in the Abington Inn, the chair being occupied by Sir T. E. Colebrooke, Bart. The toasts usual on such occasions were duly proposed and honoured, and the meeting broke up shortly before four o'clock, to allow visitors from a distance to get home by the early afternoon train.

An annual cattle-show is also held in July at Crawfordjohn. An ornithological exhibition takes place each year on January 12th at Crawfordjohn.

At Abington there is a subscription library of 600 volumes and forty members, with occasional lectures.

Murray, amongst other interesting descriptions, gives this amusing account of the good old times in Crawfordjohn Parish :—"The Captain (at Glespin) subscribed for the 'Dumfries and Galloway Courier,' which was duly sent to the Douglas post-office, and the papers usually reached Glespin when a week, it might be two weeks, out of date. The newsmonger of the district was 'bowl Tammie,' who carried crockery about to barter for hare-skins, &c.; and the gossip was Bauldy Gaw the tailor,—a little man, but a wondrous talker; and shrewd, as his counsel to his apprentices when employed with him at the farm-houses was, 'Tak the kail, lads; if its guid, it's worth the supping, and if no, there's sma' chance o' ocht better coming after.' The clothing of the youngsters was of the stoutest, not home made, but probably from the loom of the 'customer weaver' of the district. When friends came to visit—it might be once or twice a year—some of the young ones were sent to Douglas on the east, or Sanquhar on the west, for 'loaf bread,' and what was left from the feast was put past and kept moist for the next stranger. Porridge, barley-meal scones, oatmeal cakes, ham, the salted meat, trout or game, was the feeding of the family, and it certainly produced hale and hearty lads.

"The barn at the Glespin being longer, better floored, more frequently empty than any other for miles round, was most convenient for the dancing-master to hold his balls in; and sometimes the rustics made an effort to get up the play of the 'Gentle Shepherd' —the Captain's eldest son doing the part of Peggy well. In the shooting season, quarters were needful for the servants, and at other times the outhouse apartments, above and below, were given rent free —the upper to Mary, a widow, and a reputed descendant of the old laird's. She was apparently of a gentler breed than those about her, had a smooth tongue, and an eye that, not over-young as she was, yet made half the shepherd's wives look well to their men when 'she cam about the toun.' She smoked and learned the men to smoke. Will, who was in possession of the lower room, was a hulking lout, jobbing about, working easily for his employer, but when on piece-work, hard for himself. When middle-aged, he wedded Jean, who was as tall and ungainly as himself, but pushed her man about, and made him to show more energy than was believed to be in him.

"The minister of the parish in his annual visitation used to muster the neighbours in the Glespin barn to 'say their questions,' and the after-part of the day was pleasantly spent at the 'house,' where some of the more respectable of the neighbours were asked to meet him. There was a spinnet, an antiquated sort of piano, rarely tuned, at Glespin; and afterwards, when a lady was brought home to the manse, a piano came with her; now there may be a score of pianos in the parish, and twice that number of smart girls who have been sent to finishing schools, in Edinburgh usually, before settling down at home; and some of the bachelors in Crawford-moor allege that wives nowadays are more burdensome to keep than they used to be in their mothers' time."—*Upper Ward*, vol. i. pp. 132-4.

A person termed "the King of Crawfordjohn," in his ninety-fifth year was living, who had seen four ministers who were within 122 years in the parish. He was strong-willed, but his wife is said to have known how to rule him. "John," she would say, "the morn's Douglas Fair, and the lauds 'll be wantin' to gang, but ye maunna let them." "What for shu'd nae I let them?" he would say. "Weel," was her rejoinder, "hae yere ain way, but ye maunna gie

CRAWFORDJOHN.

them ony siller to clod awa." "What for shu'd nae I gie them some siller?" "Weel, weel," she would add, "I'm sure, saxpence or a shillin' apiece is plenty." "Na, na!" he then shouted in triumph, "they sall hae a croon apiece." On another occasion, it is recorded that he seemed anxious that a friend should remain and partake of supper, while the person protested that it was impossible. "John," cried his wife, "why did ye press the man sae sair to bide, when ye kent he couldna?" "Whan else," said John, revealing his frugality, "whan else wad ye hae me to press him?" He always cut down some corn, ripe or not, prior to a particular fair or "preachings," that he might be able to boast to the passers-by that he had begun the harvest. A brother of this eccentric old man was for fifty years a respected teacher in Leadhills. Afterwards a manufacturer in Glasgow, his son is a wealthy calico-printer.

ABINGTON SCHOOL

has accommodation for 80, with 60 on the roll and 56 in attendance. Average fees, 3d. per week.

PAUPERISM.

Registered poor and dependants, 35; lunatics, 3; casual, 9. Although the gross rental is £9724, 17s., in the Assessment Roll it is only £9624, 18s., yielding £302, 14s. 10½d. Expenditure—£287, 3s. 6½d., being £14, 16s. 4½d. less than in 1865; but the population has decreased by 127, it being in 1865, 980, while in 1875 it is only 853. These facts have been kindly furnished by Mr A. Renton, Inspector, Crawfordjohn.

HEIGHTS, LAWS, HILLS, CAIRNS OR DODS.

1. CRAWFORD.—Green Lowther 2403, Dungrain 2186, Dun 2216, White 1941, Lousiewood 2028, Watchman 1487, Coupland Gair 1686, Faugh 1906, Riccartrig 1750, Laght 1662, Coom 2107, Rodger 2257, Ballencleuch 2267, Wedder 2185, Earncraig 2000, Hitterhill 1608, Midheight 1362, Tomont 1652, Ladycairn 1716, Coupland 1289, Rome 1852, Lewsgill 1867.

2. CRAWFORDJOHN.—Snar 1346, Windy 1391, White 1279, Ewe 1301, Shawhead (Cairn Kinny) 1616, Wedder 1507, Fingland 1511, Knees 1189, Mosscastle 1250, Mountherrick 1400, Black 1260, Drake 1584, Glendouran 1543, Brown 1603, Rake 1620.

CALEDONIAN RAILWAY TRAFFIC FOR 1875.

ABINGTON.—Passengers booked, 7231; arriving, 7720. Goods forwarded, 1322; received, 1376: minerals forwarded, 27; received, 2228. ELVANFOOT.—Passengers booked, 3563; arriving, 3947. Goods forwarded, 198; received, 846: minerals forwarded, 18; received, 1537.

The length of line through Crawford parish is 11 miles 2 chains, but the cost of construction is not stated in the Railway Assessor's Valuation Roll.

CRAWFORD SCHOOL.

Information has not been furnished. A new school was recently erected near the source of the Clyde, and other two are in contemplation by the Board.

G.—EARLS OF HOPETOUN.

.The surname of Hope is very ancient. John de Hope swore fealty to King Edward I., 1296. Another John de Hope, the ancestor of the family, came from France in the retinue of Magdalen, queen of James V., in 1537. Edward was a commissioner for Edinburgh in the Parliament in 1560, and promoted the Reformation. Thomas, the eldest son of Henry (a merchant), defended six ministers tried for treason, for denying that the king had authority in matters ecclesiastical, before the Scottish bar, with such success that he was always thereafter consulted by Presbyterians, and attained to the first practice in the kingdom. Having made a fortune, he purchased several estates. He was appointed King's Advocate, and created a baronet 11th February 1628; and as Sir Thomas was Lord High Commissioner to the General Assembly 1643, two of his sons being seated on the bench, Sir Thomas, while seated there, had the privilege of wearing his hat accorded to him, it being judged unbecoming that a father should appear uncovered before his children. He had fourteen of a family.

Sir James, his sixth son, was born on the 12th July 1614. Having, while practising at the bar, as stated, acquired by marriage the property of the valuable mines at Leadhills, he applied himself to mineralogy, and brought the art of mining to a high standard, so that in 1641 he was appointed Governor of the Mint, with power to hold courts in the Mint-house. He was also appointed a Lord of Session and one of the Committee of Estates, 1649. He died at his brother's house of Grantown, 1661, two days after he returned from Holland, whither he had gone on his lead business. He was buried at Cramond, where there is a marble bust of him. He also had fourteen children by Anne, the heiress of Robert Foulis of Leadhills. John Hope of Hopetoun, the seventh child of Sir James, was lost in the shipwreck of the "Gloucester" frigate, 1682.

Charles, his son, born 1681, was M.P. for Linlithgow, a Privy Councillor, created a peer 1703, and zealously supported the treaty for union with England. He was Lord-Lieutenant of Linlithgow, 1715, and Lord High Commissioner to the General Assembly, 1723, was invested with the Order of the Thistle, 1738, for four years represented the Scottish peerage, and died 1742. Hopetoun House, which he erected under the direction of Sir William Bruce, is a monument of the magnificence of his taste. He had seven children.

John, second Earl of Hopetoun, the third child of Sir Charles, was born 1704, was also Lord High Commissioner in 1754, died 1781. He was married twice, and had ten children.

James, third Earl of Hopetoun, born 1741, was the fourth child of the second earl. He served in the army in Germany, succeeded his father 1781, was for two years representative of the Scottish peerage. On the death of his grand-uncle George, third Marquis of Annandale, in 1792, his great estates in Scotland devolved on the Earl of Hopetoun, with the titles of Earl of Annandale and Hartfell, which, however, he did not assume, but added the name of Johnstone to his own. He was made colonel 1793, and a baron of the United Kingdom 1809, by the title of Baron Hopetoun of Hopetoun. He was also heritable Keeper of the Castle of Lochmaben, and Lord-Lieutenant of the county of Linlithgow. He had six children. His titles were James Hope Johnstone, Earl of Hopetoun, Viscount Aithrie, Lord Hope, and Hopetoun of Hopetoun. His seats were Hopetoun House, county Linlithgow ; Ormistoun Hall, and Keith House, county Haddington ; and Raehills, county Dumfries.

John, the fourth earl, born 17th August, 1765, who succeeded to the estates of his half-brother James, the third earl, 29th May 1816, was the General who successfully conducted the embarkation of the British troops after the battle of Corunna in Spain in January 1809. The narrative of the dispiriting retreat before the overwhelming forces of Napoleon in the midst of snowstorms, mountain passes, and disorganisation caused by the wine vaults of Bembibre, and then of the preparations for embarkation and of the battle and victorious repulse of the French troops, is one of the most stirring that can be read. Sir John Moore received his death-wound while animating the 42d to the charge. His remains were wrapped in his military cloak, and laid in a grave hastily formed on the ramparts of Corunna.

> " Not a drum was heard, not a funeral note,
> As his corse to the rampart we hurried ;
> Not a soldier discharged his farewell shot
> O'er the grave where our hero we buried.
>
>   .   .   .   .
>
> " No useless coffin enclosed his breast,
> Nor in sheet nor in shroud we wound him ;
> But he lay like a warrior taking his rest,
> With his martial cloak around him.
>
>   .   .   .   .
>
> " Slowly and sadly we laid him down,
> From the field of his fame fresh and gory ;
> We carved not a line and we raised not a stone,
> But left him alone with his glory."

Sir David Baird having also been wounded, " the command devolved upon General Hope, who conducted the remaining arrangements with that decision and judgment which afterwards became so conspicuous in the Peninsular War, and whose eloquent despatch announcing the battle of Corunna and the death of Sir John Moore agitated so profoundly the heart of his country. 'His fall' wrote General Hope, 'has deprived me of a valuable friend

,to whom long experience of his worth had sincerely attached me. But it is chiefly on public grounds that I must lament the blow. It will be the conversation of every one who loved or respected his manly character, that after conducting the army through an arduous retreat with consummate firmness, he has terminated a career of distinguished honour by a death that has given the enemy additional reason to respect the name of a British soldier.' The embarkation commenced at ten at night ; the troops were silently filed down to the beach ; put on board with admirable order. The French gave them no annoyance, so strongly had the bloody repulse of the preceding day inspired them with respect for British valour. With a courage and generosity worthy of the highest admiration, the Spaniards manned the ramparts when the last of the English forces were withdrawn, and prolonged the defence for several days, so as to allow the whole sick, wounded, artillery, stores, and even prisoners, to be brought away " (Alison's Hist. Eur. viii. ch. 55).

This earl, who bore the titles of Viscount Aithrie, Lord Hope, Baron Hopetoun of Hopetoun, Baron Niddry of Niddry, was a great favourite with the inhabitants of Leadhills. Frequently they unyoked the horses and drew his carriage into the village. On his arrival at the Ha', the first thing he handed out was " the Big Bible " he carried with him ; and on stepping out himself, he warmly shook hands with the miners who had assembled, asking after their welfare. When remonstrated with by some of his friends for this familiarity, he replied that he might well think highly of the inhabitants of Leadhills, as he had profited largely by them. He contributed handsomely towards their library, and they, to this day, point with pride to his portrait which they hung in the Library hall. He died 27th August 1823.

John, the fifth earl, born 15th November 1803, was not less deeply interested in the welfare of these people. During the times of depression in Leadhills, he found on one occasion that several of the old men had been dismissed, and being observed walking hastily and thoughtfully up to the office, it was found that he had given easier terms to the Company that employed them, on condition that they should all be re-engaged. And this favourable interest has manifested itself in succeeding members of the Hopetoun family, who deservedly stand high in public estimation. This earl died 8th April 1843.

John Alexander, the sixth earl, born 22d March 1831, was early cut off by death, 1st April 1873.

John Adrian Louis, the present and seventh earl, is a minor, being born on the 25th September 1860.

HOPETOUN ARMS.—Azure, on a chevron, betwixt three besants, or, a laurel leaf, proper (to denote his maternal descent from Foulis of Leadhills, who carried three laurel leaves). Crest—A broken globe, surmounted by a rainbow, proper. Supporters—Two women, their hair hanging down, with loose garments, holding anchors in their hands. Motto—*At spes non fracta.*

THE HOPETOUN FAMILY.

THE LAST PARLIAMENT OF SCOTLAND was held 3d October 1706 to 25th March 1707. The Duke of Queensberry could not vote, as representing the sovereign; but amongst the 47 peers who voted, and supported the Treaty of Union, were the Earls of Crawford and Hopetoun, there being 22 who opposed it.

H.—EXTRACT REPORT BY MESSRS HEADLEY & SCAIFE,

In illustration of method and varied success in the Leadhills Mines.

"The two foreheads—that is, the one at the nine and the other at the twenty fathom random below level—were both standing in a 'check,' three or four fathoms south of the Rushy-grain knot in June 1826; but the lowest forehead was begun to be driven towards the latter end of that month, and had not been proceeded upon more than three fathoms until another knot of lead formed in a rib from four to seven inches wide between roof and sole was cut, and was driven about two fathoms when the engine was stopped, and consequently the forehead, with little alteration in the appearance of the lead. This last knot of lead is quite a distinct one from the Rushy-grain knot, is of much finer quality, and dips to a greater depth, inasmuch as the Rushy-grain knot was never bound in the sole or bottom of the twenty fathom random, whereas the other is equally strong in the sole as it is in the roof or top of the drift. The low forehead is now nearly seventy fathoms from the surface. The lead in this vein, when under the designation of Brown's vein, has varied in thickness or width of the rib from one to three feet, and it was sometimes found in what is called 'knockings,' or large lumps not formed into a rib amongst the mineral soil. . . . . The lead was sometimes found at the astonishing width of 12 feet or more. . . . . Altogether this vein has been the richest vein of any in Leadhills, or even in Scotland. . . . . Some of the veins are most productive in the brow of the hill." It *lades*, or lies, with its foot to the east.

Reports on Leadhills mines were also given by Captain Vivian, July 1860, and by Mr Henry Thomas, August 3, 1860, to Messrs Currie, Hope, & Williams, recommending a liberal treatment of the Company, and that a sufficient quantity of water be kept for the use of the villagers; that the truck system be abolished, and all wages paid in money, and that the custom of allowing the miners lands and houses rent free be undisturbed, together with such practical methods of working the mines as have since been carried into operation.

Mr Vere Irving mentions as a striking instance of poetic justice, the fact that a rich vein of pure galena eighteen feet wide was discovered at the close of last century under Glendorch, by the descendants of the orphan-girl whom David Foulis had attempted to defraud, it having been missed by only a few inches when sought for by that David Foulis to his utter ruin.

I.—MOUNTAIN MEN.

Many have been amazed that any persons could possibly be induced to make these mountain glens their home. Almost every necessary has to be imported into the villages, and some creatures cannot live there. Thus hens cannot go at large, the particles of lead killing them. Dogs and cats are also shortlived. They take the "lead brash," wheel round, and die. Birds, too, are as great a rarity as flowers, sparrows are seldom seen; but that arises more from climatic than metallic influences. And the "Black Jocks"—blackcocks—oft come with their "bir-whir" nigh to the cottages, and so give warning of approaching storms.

And yet, not only is love of these hills and glens intensely engraven on their hearts, when compelled by circumstances to go forth to England, America, or Australasia, but no class of men are generally more prosperous, respected, or useful.

This has been traced to their libraries, and to an education which at one time was ahead of surrounding districts. And still, as of Sanquhar, it may perhaps be reported that "religious instruction of the most thorough and satisfactory description is given."

These, with other advantages, have been influential in producing an approximation to the eight characteristics of Scottish people which Professor Blackie enunciated in his lecture at Dumfries in December 1875. And we are convinced that in proportion as these advantages are thoroughly possessed, and dissipating practices are renounced, will these characteristics be more fully manifested by the Southern mountaineers.

The Professor thus quaintly describes a true Scot—

First—An animal of immense working capacity—The most laborious people are the German and the Scottish. And this is our great glory, for this is a working world. Whatever else we do, if not work, it is nothing.

Second— With power of enterprise and adventure—Thus the vast continent of Africa remained a mystery to the world till travelled over and discovered by a Livingstone and a Cameron.

Third—Combined with power of abstract thought and speculation —THINKING distinguishing the man of business from the man of bustle. As a metaphysician he seeks out the ultimate grounds of things, or as a theologian, the one self-existent Cause.

Fourth—Reined in by a predominant practical tendency—No mere speculatist, but inductively handling facts. Thus the Taylors and others laid the foundation of successful mining operations, or applied steam to the propelling of vessels.

Fifth—A cautious, shrewd, astute, and even cunning animal—Inheriting the sturdy independence of Knox and the Covenanters, but along therewith, as a besetting sin, putting too high a value upon money.

Sixth—Thoughtful, earnest, serious, religious—This tendency, the cause of all the good he has accomplished, has been recognised by such men as Froude, Kingsley, and Dean Stanley.

Seventh—In the realm of emotion capable of fervour and lyrical intenseness—Hence such effusions as this—

> " It cam in the faulds o' a love-note true—
>   This sprig o' heather,
> Straucht doon frae the mountains whaur it grew
>   In the warm spring weather ;
> Fresh, wi' the fresh wild air o' the glens,
> Dear, frae the dear young thing that kens
> Hoo fain my wearifu' heart wud be
> Tae bide wi' her ain on the muirland lea,
>   Amang the heather."—*Reid.*

Eighth—And his thoughtfulness tempered by a deep sense of the humorous—While the sparkling vivacity of the French and the ready wit of the Irish have little or no place, the true Scottish mind is alive to the delight of a humorous turn of events related or occurring under his eye, which relieve the deeper shades of his generally prosaic history.

It may not be out of keeping with these reflections to put together a statement gathered from the statistics of shops and stores in these two villages. It is not the amount of spirituous liquors imported and consumed—although that may form no inconsiderable item—part of which might *possibly* be well spared. It is simply to ask such thoughtful, practical, earnest, humorous men to conceive how much of their means they actually with their own mouths blow into thin air. Not less than the sum of SEVEN HUNDRED AND TWENTY POUNDS sterling was spent upon tobacco in the villages of Wanlockhead and Leadhills in the year 1875, whilst in the three churches not much above THIRTY POUNDS were contributed to promote the evangelisation of the world. And this summation does not include the entire quantity consumed.

And then, these villages are but specimens of what is going on in the three *quoad civilia* parishes, and in all the parishes in our land. When will thoughtful, shrewd, religious, and earnest Scottish men ask the practical question, " If so much is yearly spent on luxuries, and so little on the establishment of Christ's kingdom —when, humanly speaking, may an answer be expected to our daily petition—' Thy kingdom come ?'"

MOUNTAIN ·MEN.

The children of these hills can truly sing :—

"O Caledonia, stern and wild,
  Meet nurse for a poetic child !
Land of brown heath and shaggy wood,
Land of the mountain and the flood,
Land of my sires ! what mortal hand
Can e'er untie the filial band
That knits me to thy rugged strand !
Still as I view each well-known scene,
Think what is now, and what hath been,
Seems as to me, of all bereft,
Sole friends thy hills and streams were left ;
And thus I love them better still,
Even in extremity of ill."—*Sir W. Scott.*

K.—SANQUHAR: AGRICULTURAL STATISTICS.

In the beginning of the fourteenth century the cost of an ox was 6s. 6d. ; a fat hog, 2s. 2d. to 3s. 9d. ; a pig, 10d. A quarter of wheat, 7s. ; of barley, 4s. 4d. ; of rye, 4s. ; of oats, 2s. to 3s. 6d. ; of beans, 7s. 6d. A labourer could earn a quarter of oats in a week. Ale sold from 12s. to 18s. a butt of 108 gallons ; wine 30s. per hogshead of 54 gallons.

PRODUCE IN 1793.

Meal, 1s. 6d. to 2s. per stone ; barley, 2s. 4d. to 3s. per Winchester bushel ; oats, 2s. to 2s. 6d. do. do. Beef or cow, £6 to £7 ; beef and mutton, 3d. to 4d. per lb. ; hens, 6d. to 8d. ; eggs, 2½d. to 3½d. per doz. Butter 1s. per lb. of 16 ounces, equal to 8d. per lb. Black-faced wool, per stone of 24 lbs., at 5s.—now 16s. Wool, £3, 5s. per pack (6 to 8 fleeces to the stone)—if washed, 8 or 9. After teasing and carding, would have 22 lbs. out of 2 stones of tarred wool.

AVERAGE REMUNERATION OF FARM-SERVANTS.

Formerly (1760)—Men servants, £2, 10s. to £3 per annum ; 1793, £7 to £9. Women, £1, 10s. to £1, 15s. in 1760 ; and £3 to £4 in 1793. Present Rate of Wages—Ploughmen, £38 to £45 per annum, with free house, garden, firing driven, potato land, and food during harvest. Or it may be stated thus :—*Rate at Dumfries Hiring Fair in* 1874—Single ploughmen of experience, £13, 10s. to £15 ; less do., £10 to 12 ; lads and boys, £4 to £7, 10s. Byrewomen, £7, 5s. to £9, 5s. ; outworkers, £5, 5s. to £6, 15s. ; girls, £2 to £4, 10s.— for the half-year from Whitsunday, with board.

AVERAGE PRICE OF COWS AND HORSES.

Ayrshire, £14 ; Galloways, £16. The black Galloways give the thickest milk, though the Ayrshire gives more, and suits dairy purposes better. Bull stirks—Ayrshire, £14 ; Galloways, £16. Plough horses, £50.

At the cattle-show of the Farmers' Society, held at Sanquhar on the 14th May 1875, the entries were 120, as against 136 last year, and 129 in 1873. The show is confined wholly to the Ayrshire breed, in which the district excels, and the display showed that there is no deterioration in this respect, the quality of some of the animals from the ducal herd of Drumlanrig being scarcely surpassable. As usual, his Grace was an extensive exhibitor, and showed some of his stock which had taken a number of prizes elsewhere. Indeed this fact, as hinted by one of the judges, may have had the effect of deterring some of the less pretentious breeders in the district from entering the arena against such a powerful antagonist, and may explain the absence from the show-yard of some of the animals entered. The duke certainly proved no mean adversary, for in no class in which he competed was he beaten, except for aged bulls; but it should be remembered that besides contributing handsomely towards the support of the show, the rearing of good stock in the district has in a measure been due to the care with which his Grace's stock is selected. There was a capital display of horses.

THE SANQUHAR WOOL FAIR,

held in July, immediately after that of Inverness, regulates the price of wool for the south of Scotland. It is largely attended by flockmasters, dealers, &c. Sheep and lambs there also change hands. At the fair in 1875 prices ranged about last year's rates, buyers declaring it was then purchased too dear. The recent heavy failures in the tweed trade had also an adverse influence on the wool market. Wool-brokers, commission agents, and dealers in dipping materials were present in great force, and there was a fair demand for blackfaced wool, with the result above referred to. Cheviot was not so much inquired for, and few sales in white were effected. Prices for blackfaced ranged from 19s. to 20s. Cheviot brought from 31s. to 35s. 6d., averaging about 33s.—Highland wool sold at 20s.

BLACKFACED WOOL.—The Tinwald Shaws clip sold at 21s. 6d. Mochrum wool at 20s. A clip from the Isle of Arran at 18s. Lochenkit wool at 20s., which was 2s. up from last year. Glenlee and Monybuie white wool at 20s., being 1s. more than last year; and laid at 15s. Glenkiln clip at 20s., being 1s. 6d. of an increase. Coghead clip at 19s. Inverness white at 21s. 6d., being 1s. 6d. of a rise. Carsphairn clip at 20s. Burrance clip sold at 1s. above last year. Arkindale white at 20s. Brickhouse and Nethercray white at 21s. Barscobe white at 20s. Glaisters white sold at 19s. 6d. North white at 18s. 6d.—Rigg, Kirkconnell, bought at 19s.; Changue, Barr, at 18s. 6d.; Dalveen, at 19s.; and Dinmurchie, Barr, at 19s.

CHEVIOT WOOL.—Drumlanrig clip sold at 38s. Holm of Dalquhairn clip at 33s., being 1s. up on last year's price. Crawfordton clip at 33s. 6d. Cruden ewe wool sold at 31s. Glaisters clip sold at 35s. 6d. Annanlee clip made 34s. Shancastle brought 32s. Skeldon Mill purchased at 31s. to 34s. Merkland sold at 33s. Dunable brought 1s. more than last year.

HALF-BRED WOOL.—The only sales reported was the Glaisters clip, which brought 40s.

PRIZES TO SERVANTS AND WORKING MEN.

The Nithsdale Agricultural Society offer for award at their annual meeting at Thornhill on the third Tuesday of September the following prizes :—

Six guineas to the agricultural servant, male or female, who has been longest in the same service. Six guineas to the oldest working man who is still following his usual employment.

Candidates must be resident within the district, consisting of the Presbytery of Penpont, with the addition of any of the adjoining parishes in which shall reside at the time not less than five members of the society.

Candidates must also be persons of unexceptionable moral character, members of some Christian church, and regular attendants on public worship.

The term *agricultural servant* shall be understood to comprehend the domestic servants of agriculturists, as well as those more specially employed in farm labour, and such shepherds as are engaged at fixed money wages.

The term *working man* shall be understood to comprehend every man who earns his bread by manual labour, whether without or within doors.

Candidates must never have been on the roll of paupers, and must always have supported themselves by their own labour.

All information may be obtained from

JAMES RUSSELL, Secretary, Thornhill.

OF THE PAST WINTER

Mr William M'Caw, an observant shepherd, to whose literary productions reference has been made, wrote at the close of January :—"Old Winter has passed over us without presenting any peculiar features of character to keep its transit long in remembrance. In early November he threw his white mantle over the hills, just as if to remind us that the time had come when he had a right to rule ; but it was soon withdrawn, and the general character of his reign has been peaceful mildness. In December he overspread the ponds with a glassy covering, and afforded the curlers a few days of very pleasant amusement ; but the enjoyment, if sweet, was short, for he speedily changed his plan, and bestowed his favours on the flocks of sheep. Fine mild weather continued for a fortnight, while the green earth, the balmy air, and the genial sky presented a most remarkable contrast to the ermine coat and biting breath of his predecessor at the end of '74. He closed the old year with a deluge of rain, and opened the new with a bright sunshine, and then in his freaks overspread the earth for a few days with mist and darkness. On the 8th of January there was an interesting contest between the clouds and the barometer. The clouds would have a storm, and the barometer said no. In the evening the east wind howled and the snow fell, and the barometer was forced to yield a little ; but it was only a little, for next morning the clouds were beaten from the field, and the barometer went up in triumph, remaining for some time much higher than usual at that season of the year. From the middle of the month the weather was variable —frosts, winds, and calms, dark fogs, and drizzling rains prevailing, but neither snow nor sunshine in the south of Scotland. Peace to thy memory, thou Monarch of December! Very kind thou hast been to us. Thou art leaving us with green fields open to the plough, and hills fresh and unencumbered. And unless thou act the part of an usurper, and assert thy sovereignty in the months of spring, we shall not utter respecting thee an unfavourable word."

The Monarch addressed so asserted his sovereignty that many declare that they have no remembrance of such a month of March. On the hills the roads were for weeks together snowed-up, and in one glen the snowdrift was understood to be forty feet in depth. April seemed to pluck a few days from July and then suddenly returned to the biting blasts of winter.

Our ancestors always hoped for a dry and cold January, considering mild weather at this season to do more harm than good. This idea has been embodied in the following, among other proverbs—

> "If the grass grows in Janiveer,
> It grows the worse for't all the year."

> "A January spring
> Is worth naething."

> "March in Janiveer,
> January in March, I fear."

> "If January calends be summerly gay
> 'Twill be winterly weather till the calends of May."

L.—SANQUHAR: PROPRIETORS AND OCCUPIERS.

In the tax-roll of Nithsdale in 1554—that is, shortly before the Reformation—the gross annual value of the whole land was only £116 sterling, or £1400, 3s. 4d. Scots.

THE OLD VALUED RENTAL of the united parishes of Sanquhar and Kirkbride in 1671 was 7919 merks Scots, that is, £440 sterling—a pound Scots money being equal to about 20 pence of our currency; a merk, 13½ pence; and 1s. Scots, 1d.

Then the property now owned by the Duke of Buccleuch was valued at 6623 merks, 8s. 4d. (Scots), that is, £368 sterling. At that time the Eliock property was valued at 120 merks Scots, that is, fully £66 sterling. A John Crichton of Skeoch is entered in the old roll at 96 merks 3s. 4d. Scots, as proprietor of Goosehill, that is, fully £5 sterling.

In 1792 "the total rental of the parish, exclusive of the burgh, some spots of land about it, and Wanlockhead mines, was about £2500 per annum."

These valuations are, however, supposed not to be the actual value, but the low rate at which they were estimated by their owners.

THE ACREAGE OF THE DUKEDOM OF QUEENSBERRY in the parish of Sanquhar, according to the survey in 1856-57, is, including thirty-three farms, 34,814 imperial acres; public roads, 65 acres; railway, 39 acres; in all, 34,918 acres; while the acreage of the whole parish is 40,846 acres. The average rental of arable and pasture land is from 25s. to 30s. per acre.

SANQUHAR VALUATION ROLL, 1874-75.

Subject.	Proprietor.	Occupier.	Yearly Value.		
F., Matthew's Folly Land	Miss M. Broom	J. Colvin, Mains	£30	0	0
	,,	George Taylor	12	0	0
,,	,,	R. Grierson and J. Tweedle	10	0	0
,,	,,	Adam Brown	18	0	0
,,	,,	John Howat	8	10	0
,,	,,	Walter Scott	8	0	0
Ho. under £4 C.M.	,,	Sundries	14	4	0
F., Euchanhead	Duke of Buccleuch	T. & W. Milligan, Durisdeer	360	0	0
F., Auchengruith	,,	George Dalziell	565	0	0
F., Auchentaggart	,,	T. B. Stewart	330	0	0
F., Blackaddie, Glenmaddie, &c.	,,	A. C. Bramwell	335	0	0
F., Boggs, Brandleys, &c.	,,	Jas. Kennedy	500	0	0
Car. Manufac. C.M.	,,	J. Kerr	10	0	0
F., Clenries, &c.	,,	W. Hyslop, sen. and jun.	1900	0	0
Colliery	,,	M. K. Whigham	100	0	0
F., Conrick	,,	J Ingram	140	0	0

SANQUHAR VALUATION ROLL, 1874-75—*continued.*

Subject.	Proprietor.	Occupier.	Yearly Value.		
F., Corse	Duke of Buccleuch	J. Hair	£16	0	0
Cra. M. Land, &c.	,,	J. Kerr	85	0	0
F., Dalpeddar	,,	D. C. Willison	500	0	0
F., do. (part)	,,	J. Thorburn	4	10	0
F., do., Bridgend, &c.	,,	Geo. Corson	85	0	0
F., do., Over	,,	Mrs Thorburn	17	0	0
F., Glengape, Burn-foot	,,	M. K. Whigham	250	0	0
F., do. do., Glen-glass	,,	Dan. Craig	1060	0	0
F., Glengape, 2d div.	,,	Thos. Moffat	680	0	
F., Glenglass, Ban-park, &c.	,,	Wm. Blair	21	0	0
F., Glenim, Thir-stane	,,	A. Brown, Benan	400	0	0
F., Knockenhair	,,	J. Young	425	0	0
F., Newark	,,	Mrs S. Otto	60	0	0
F., Newark (pt. of)	,,	And. Williamson	9	0	0
F., Castlebrae (part of)	,,	J. & J. Murdoch	53	0	0
F., Greenhead, &c.	,,	J. Hair, sen. & jr.	120	0	0
F., Ryehill	,,	Wm. Stitt	290	0	0
F., South Mains	,,	J. Wightman	300	0	0
F., Ulzieside	,,	Sam. M'Call	540	0	0
F., Knockonny, &c.	,,	W. Hyslop, sen. and jun., Cosh-ogle, D.	53	0	0
F., Carcarse, &c.	,,	Jas. Henderson	230	0	0
Woodlands	,,	Proprietor	360	0	0
Pyetscleuch House, lands	,,	J. M'Call, joiner	12	0	0
Ho. un. £4, Sanq.	,,	Sundries	110	0	0
F. Heukeland, &c.	,,	J. Laidlaw	58	0	0
Lead Mines, Wanld.	,,	Proprietor	1500	0	0
Ho. and gar., ,,	,,	,,	20	0	0
F., Auchensow	,,	D. Fergusson	230	0	0
F., Mains of Castle-farm	,,	J. Colvin	190	0	0
F., Townhead	,,	J. Murdoch	16	0	0
Lands under £4, Glenim and Wnld.	,,	Sundries	30	0	0
Ho. Cra. Mill	,,	J. Hamilton	20	0	0
Land ,,	,,	Gav. Lindsay	4	0	0
Ho., gar., Wanld.	,,	Rob. Slimmon	14	0	0
,, ,,	,,	Mrs J. Hastie	14	0	0
,, ,,	,,	Gil. Dawson	5	0	0
Quarry, Euchan	,,	J. Murdoch	20	0	0
House, gar., field, Wanld.	,,	J. Wilson, M.D.	16	0	0
Do., Wanld.	,,	J. Reid	15	0	0
Do., Mennock Bge.	,,	R. Lees	8	0	0
Do., Barrbank	,,	Hugh Baird	35	0	0
Do., Cra. Mill	,,	J. Kerr	4	5	0
F., Lochside, B. of Sanquhar	,,	R. S. Laing	190	0	0

SANQUHAR VALUATION ROLL, 1864-75—*continued.*

Subject.	Proprietor.	Occupier.	Yearly Value.
Shootings	Duke of Buccleuch	D. of Buccleuch	£13 0 0
F., Muirlands	Mrs Croom	J. Laidlaw	22 0 0
Ho. und. £4, Windyedge and C.M.	,,	Sundries	23 10 0
Do., C.M.	Margaret Dickson	,,	5 10 0
Land, Townfoot	W. Dobson	John Kerr	17 10 0
Field, Muirpark	T. Fergusson	Thomas Scott	6 10 0
M., gar., land, Wanlockhead	Rev. J. Laidlaw	Proprietor	10 0 0
Field nr. Sanq.	G. M'Michael	,,	4 0 0
F., Muirlands	Mrs S. Otto and Mrs D. Barker	John Laidlaw	73 0 0
Brick and tile wks.	Ditto	Geo. Clennell	63 0 0
Land nr. Sanq.	Ditto	,,	11 0 0
	Ditto	Wal. Scott, sen.	24 0 0
F., Goosehill	Ditto	J. and D. Fergusson	125 0 0
Lands, Welltrees	Ditto	Jas. Murdoch	11 0 0
Ho. at Knowehead	Ditto	John Howat	4 0 0
High Corsepark	Ditto	J. and D. Fergusson	33 0 0
F.-C. M. and gar., Wanlockhead	Rev. Jas. Moir Porteous	Proprietor	10 0 0
F., Raefield	Robert Rae	,,	13 0 0
Ho. and gar., Raefield	,,	Empty	5 0 0
Ho. und. £4, Raefield	,,	Sundries	6 15 0
Do., C.M.	Mrs W. D. Russell	,,	2 10 0
F.-C. M., Sanquhar	Rev. Stev. Smith	Proprietor	20 0 0
F., Pennyland	T. B. Stewart	Geo. Clennell	25 0 0
Eliock Grange	Rev. W. D. Veitch	A. Lewis	253 0 0
Man.-Ho. and gar., Eliock Grange	,,	Proprietor	50 0 0
Woodlands, ,,	,,	,,	24 0 0
F., Craigdarroch	,,	J. Paterson	773 0 0
F., Haughcleuchside	,,	R. and J. Fergusson	310 17 0
F., Little Mark	,,	John Kirk	20 0 0
Sawmill, Eliock	,,	J. & Js. Penman	18 0 0
F., North Glengenny, &c.	,,	Hugh Baird	140 0 0
Laught at Sanq.	,,	Robt. Wallace, jr.	15 0 0
Ho. und. £4, C.M.	Mrs J. Crichton or Williamson	Sundries	6 0 0
		Total, . .	£14,524 14 10

Glasgow and South-Western Railway (lineal measure, 4 miles 6 chains; cost of stations, &c., £600, at 5 per cent., £30), value in parish 2,676 0 0

£17,200 14 10

Glasgow and South-Western Railway—Total cost in county of Dumfries, £18,100; total value in county, £37,229.

M.—POPULATION.

The census returns show that the population of Sanquhar burgh reached it highest point in 1851, and that in the next twenty years it decreased by 1057 inhabitants. Looking back ten years farther, it only contained 1700. The contrast of thirty years shows that it has decreased by 374, while Wanlockhead, in the same period, has increased by 104. Or again, taking the burgh, landward, and Wanlockhead portions together, there has been a loss of 539 inhabitants in comparison with the condition of the parish thirty years ago.

PARTICULARS OF CENSUS, 1871, from the Eighth Decennial Parliamentary Report, Vol. I.—

Sanquhar civil county and parish, 40,846 acres.

	HOUSES.		PERSONS.			Children from 5 to 13 receiving Education.	Rooms with one or more Windows.
	Inha-bited.	Unin-habited	M.	F.	Total.		
Total in Burgh . . .	297	30	698	878	1576	262	1025
Landward	283	7	723	739	1462	233	837
Total . . .	580	37	1421	1617	3038	495	1862

Census of Civil County with its Ecclesiastical Subdivision—

Sanquhar	406	35	999	1202	2201	352	1486
Wanlockhead	174	2	422	415	837	143	376
Total . . .	580	37	1421	1617	3038	495	1862

Comparison.

Burgh, 1861	328	6	950	1123	2073	...	976
„ 1871	297	30	698	878	1576	...	1025
	31 Dec.	24 Inc.	252 Dec.	245 Dec.	497 Dec.	...	49 Inc.
Landward, 1861 . . .	275	2	712	784	1496	...	823
„ 1871 . . .	283	7	723	739	1462	...	837
	8 Inc.	5 Inc.	11 Inc.	45 Dec.	34 Dec.	...	14 Inc.

In villages (reckoned to contain from 300 to 2000 inhabitants), 1871.

Sanquhar (as Par. Burgh)	243	15	583	741	1324	214	903
Wanlockhead	160	2	392	380	772	136	349
Total . . .	403	17	975	1121	2096	350	1252
Sanquhar Royal Burgh	248	23	546	706	1252	205	873

REGISTRATION.—The Rev. William Ranken states in the old "Statistical Account" that he desired the schoolmaster to begin a register for births, and proposed, for his encouragement, to collect sixpence from every parent who came to obtain baptism for a child. This payment being unpopular, many refused to register their children; but that people belonging to the Established Church came into the practice, from which Dissenters abstained, the average number of births registered exclusive of Wanlockhead being 50 per annum. The total number of births was then estimated at 70, equivalent to the present rate.

LONGEVITY AND DISEASE.—The causes of death must be thus stated:—Diseases: Chest and respiratory organs, 23; acute or inflammatory, 7; heart disease, 5; infantile diseases, 6; other causes, 25; unknown, 2; number of deaths, 68.

The longevity of the population is an important detail. Formerly it was said that stomach complaints, slow fevers, rheumatism, and nervous disorders prevailed, and that prior to inoculation the small-pox carried off large numbers, especially children; but that the general health improved with better modes of living and a greater attention to cleanliness. Ten years ago the late Dr Simpson stated that there were then living nearly forty persons above the age of 80, some above 90, and that one died shortly before that at the age of 101. Now, the registrars say, "We seldom record any above 90, owing doubtless to the severity of the climate, particularly in winter."

The following shows the ages at death in 1873:—Age: Under 1 year, 8; 1 year and under 2, 5; 2 years and under 5, 3; 5 to 20, 9; 20 to 50, 11; 50 to 70, 13; 70 to 80, 10; 80 to 90, 9; above, 0; total, 68.

SANQUHAR RETURNS.

The following are the returns of births, deaths, and marriages for Sanquhar (population, 2201), with Wanlockhead (837), for 1873:—

	BIRTHS.					DEATHS.			Mar.
	M.	F.	Tot.	Legit.	Illegit.	M.	F.	Tot.	
Sanquhar	21	23	44	41	3	19	25	44	11
Wanlockhead	10	17	27	23	4	10	14	24	7
Total . . .	31	40	71	64	7	29	39	68	18

It thus appears that whilst they are equal in the burgh, the births exceed the deaths by 3 in the entire parish, that the females born exceed the males by 9, the females who died exceed the males by 10, and that only 7 illegitimate births out of 71 are reported. Five of the mothers of the 7 were servants (one in another parish), and one no occupation.

The death-rate of Wanlockhead was high for 1873. In 1857, with a population of 842, it stood at 13. In 1873, during which year it is estimated that 100 had left the place, it stood at 24. But during the last winter, 1874-75, the death-rate in Sanquhar burgh has been higher than within the memory of the inhabitants, while in Wanlockhead it has been comparatively low.

The Wanlockhead registrar, in writing of the excess in March 1873, says—"Of the 10 registered, 7 occurred in January, and were mostly of persons advanced in life, who had been suffering from chronic diseases, such as heart, liver, phthisis, and paralysis." Again, "scarlatina has been prevalent," but no deaths. "Measles prevailed in the beginning of the (last) quarter, causing 1 death. There have been 2 cases of typhoid fever (both imported), one of which terminated fatally." Defective house accommodation, and consequent overcrowding, must also be regarded as an attendant circumstance; but several cottages have been rebuilt since then.

1875.—Births below average. Decrease of illegitimacy for some years, below 7 per cent. in 1875, higher wages stimulating to marriage. Deaths for the year, 69 ; 31 per 1000, unprecedentedly high, the average being 20 per 1000. Inflammatory diseases of the chest the chief cause, with scarlet fever and gastric fever prevailing in Wanlockhead.

CENSUS OF CRICHTON AND SOUTHERN COUNTIES ASYLUMS, DUMFRIES, 1871.

NAME.	PERSONS.			LUNATICS.			OFFICIALS.			FAMILIES OF OFFICIALS.		
	M.	F.	Tot.	M.	F.	Tot.	M.	F.	Tot.	M.	F.	Tot.
Crichton Royal .	102	92	194	79	46	125	16	30	46	7	16	23
Southern Counties	193	163	356	181	142	323	12	21	33	...	...	...
Total . .	295	255	550	260	188	448	28	51	79	7	16	23

BOWLING TOURNAMENT was held at Dumfries in July 1875, open to the world, on St Mary's Bowling-green. There were upwards of 150 entries, including several competitors from a great distance. Prizes to the amount of £100 were offered as follows :—First prize, £30 ; second, £20 ; third, £12. 10s. ; fourth, £8 ; four prizes, £5 each ; eight prizes, £1 each ; and a pair of prize bowls (value, £1, 10s.) to a player, not a prize-taker.

The Sanquhar Bowling Club have agreed that £56 in prizes should be given at the tournament to be held on the 25th of July next.

SANQUHAR RETURNS.

EDINBURGH DUMFRIESSHIRE SOCIETY.—The General Committee of this Society offer another bursary of £20 for students of the first year. The examination of competitors will take place in Edinburgh on the last Saturday of October, in the Library Hall of the University, where candidates must attend at nine o'clock A.M. The competition is open to all Dumfriesshire boys who have attended three years any of the public schools in the county, and subject to the approval of the General Committee and the other regulations of the Society. The bursary may be held for a period not exceeding four years. The subjects for examination are Latin, Greek, Mathematics, and English Grammar and Composition.— 2 Queen Street, Edinburgh.

THE SANQUHAR PUBLIC LIBRARY

contains about 2600 volumes. The regular readers number about 50, who pay 1s. quarterly.

N.—SANQUHAR : HEIGHTS AND BURNS.

HEIGHTS IN SANQUHAR PARISH (from Ordnance Survey).—
Rising from the Nith on the east border, E. and N.E.—Dalpeddar
Hill, 1291 feet ; Cairn Hill, 1471 ; Knockconey Dod, 1342 ; Three-
hope Height, 1802 ; Auchenlone Hill, 2068 ; Lowther Hill, or Five
Cairns, 2377 * (Green Lowther, in parish of Crawford, 2403) ; Stake
Moss, 1780 ; Wanlock Dod, 1808 ; Sowen Dod, 1784 ; Snarhead
Hill, 1663 ; Redcleuch Hill, 1419 ; Whiteside Hill, 1285. *Running
N. W.*—Clackleith Hill, 1256 ; Craignorth, 1386 ; Wedder, 1459 ;
The Dod, 1339 ; Conrig Hill, 1591 (*Nith*) ; Barr Moor, 1283 ; Black
Hill, 1642 ; Midd Hill, 1685 ; Poltallan Burn Height, 1796 ; Mag-
heuchan Rig, 1829 ; Blacklorg Hill, 2231.* *South*—Polvaddoch
Burn Height, 1965 ; Corse Hill, 1902 ; Rough Shoulder, 1831 ;
Cloud Hill, 1478 ; Corrodow Hill, 1521 ; Shiel Hill, 1566 ; Wether
Hill, 1568 ; Heathery Hill, 1657 ; Minny E. Hill, 1266 ; Jock's
Ruck, 955 (*Nith*). *In the interior, N.E.*—Glenrae Dod, 1322 ; Dun-
tercleuch, 1232 ; Lowmill Knowe, 1462 ; Glengaber Hill, 1689 ;
Stood Hill, 1925 ; Black Dod, 1801 ; Bail Hill, 1768 ; Willowgrain
Hill, 1686 ; White Dod, 1744 ; Brown Hill, 1544 ; Meikle Snout,
1337 ; Auchensow, 1378. *On S. W.*—Black Shoulder, 1821 ; Cruffell,
1695 ; Midrig, 1406 ; Cairn, 1097.

BURNS FLOWING INTO THE NITH.—*From the east side* the Nith
receives—1. *The Crawick*, rising in Crawick Moor, in Crawfordjohn,
which receives three streams—*The Corse Burn, Cog and Glensalloch,
The Wanlock*—into which fall the following *burns*—Clackleith, Back
and Glenbuie, Reave, Glenminsheuch, Shilling, Limpin, Lowen,
Glendorch, Seekly, Stakely, and Nicol Knees. 2. *The Mennock*, re-
ceiving these *burns ; on the north side*—The Bog, Fingland, and
Loch, the Shiel and Glendyne, Howat's, Glendauchan, Beer and
Glenclach Burns ; and *on the south side*—Auchinsow, Glenim, or the
Big Shaw, the Wee Shaw, Greig's Gutter, Whitsincleuch, and Moss
Burns. 3. *Knockengalle Burn* below Dalpeddar, at the junction with
Durisdeer. *From the west side*—4. *The Kello*, rising on the sides of
Blackcraig and Greenlorg Hills in Cumnock, receiving the Birk,
March, Glengap, and Big Burns. 5. *The Euchan*, receiving these
nine burns — The Barr, Poltallan, Midgrain, Polvaird, Glenglass,
Fenshaw, Glen, Glenmaddie, and Whing Burns. 6. *Eliock or Garple
Burn*, receiving the Back, Kirk, and Twentyshilling Burns. A few
smaller fall into the Nith, as the Brewster's Burn at Dalpeddar ; and
in the south-west the Glenwhern, Black, and Glengenny Burns flow
through the parishes of Penpont and Durisdeer.

---

* These heights formerly supposed to be—*East Lowther*, 3130 ft., 753 ft.
above Ordnance measurement ; *Blacklorg*, 2890 ft., 659 ft. above Ordnance
measurement.

O.—ORIGIN OF THE TITLE BUCCLEUCH.

" Such day of mirth ne'er cheered their clan,
Since old Buccleuch the name did gain,
When in the cleuch the buck was ta'en."
LAY OF THE LAST MINSTREL, VL

"A tradition preserved by Scott of Satchells, who published in 1688 'A True History of the Right Honourable Name of Scott,' gives the following romantic origin of that name. Two brethren, natives of Galloway, having been banished from that country for a riot, or insurrection, came to Rankelburn, in Ettrick Forest, where the keeper, whose name was Brydone, received them joyfully, on account of their skill in winding the horn, and in the other mysteries of the chase. Kenneth MacAlpin, then King of Scotland, came soon after to hunt in the royal forest, and pursued a buck from Ettrick-heuch to the glen now called Buckcleuch, about two miles above the junction of Rankelburn with the river Ettrick. Here the stag stood at bay; and the king and his attendants, who followed on horseback, were thrown out by the steepness of the hill and the morass. John, one of the brethren from Galloway, had followed the chase on foot, and now coming in, seized the buck by the horns, and, being a man of great strength and activity, threw him on his back, and ran with his burthen about a mile up the steep hill to a place called Cracracross, where Kenneth had halted, and laid the buck at the sovereign's feet.

' The deer being cureed in that place,
  At his Majesty's demand,
Then John of Galloway ran apace,
  And fetched water to his hand.
The King did wash into a dish,
  And Galloway John he wot;
He said, That name now after this
  Shall ever be called John Scott.

' The forest and the deer therein
  We commit to thy hand,
For thou shalt sure the ranger be
  If thou obey command :
And for the buck thou stoutly brought
  To us up that steep heuch,
Thy designation ever shall
  Be John Scott of Buckscleuch.

   .   .   .   .

' In Scotland no Buccleuch was then
  Before the buck in the cleuch was slain ;
Night's men at first they did appear,
  Because moon and stars to their arms they bear.

THE BUCCLEUCH TITLE.

Their crest, supporters, and hunting-horn,
    Shows their beginning from hunting come.
Their name and stile the book doth say,
    John gained them both into one day.
                   Watt's Ballanden.

The Buccleuch arms have been altered, and now allude less point-edly to this hunting, whether real or fabulous. The family now bear—*Or* upon a bend, azure, a mullet between two crescents of the field ; in addition to which they formerly bore in the field a hunting-horn. The supporters, now two ladies, were formerly a hound and a buck, or, according to the old terms, *a hart of leash,* and *a hart of grace.* The family of Scott of Howpasley and Thirlestane long retained the bugle-horn : they also carried a bent bow and arrow in the sinister cantle, perhaps as a difference. It is said the motto was, *Best riding by moonlight,* in allusion to the crescents on the shield, and perhaps to the habits of those who bore it. The motto now given is *Amo,* applying to the female supporters."

The only remains of any building at Buccleuch is the site of a chapel, where, according to tradition, many of the ancient Barons of Buccleuch lie buried. A mill is also said to have been there used to grind corn for their hounds.

THE BARONS OF BUCCLEUCH.

" In the reign of James I., Sir William Scott of Buccleuch ex-changed with Sir Thomas Inglis of Manor the estate of Murdiestone in Lanarkshire for one-half of the Barony of Branksome on the Teviot, that being in the vicinity of his domain in Ettrick, &c. Tradition imputes the exchange betwixt Scott and Inglis to a con-versation, in which the latter, a man, it would appear, of a mild and forbearing nature, complained much of the injuries which he was exposed to from the English Borderers, who frequently plundered his lands of Branksome. Sir William Scott instantly offered him the estate of Murdiestone in exchange. When the bargain was com-pleted, he drily remarked that the cattle in Cumberland were as good as those of Teviotdale, and proceeded to commence a system of reprisals upon the English which was regularly pursued by his successors. In the next reign James II. granted to Sir Walter Scott of Branksome, and to Sir David, his son, the remaining half of the barony of Branksome, to be held in blanche for the payment of a red rose. The cause assigned for the grant is their brave and faithful exertions in favour of the king against the house of Douglas, with whom James had been recently tugging for the throne of Scotland. This charter is dated 1443, and in the same month part of the barony of Langholm, and many lands in Lanarkshire, were conferred upon Sir Walter Scott and his son by the same monarch.

" The ancient Barons of Buccleuch, both from feudal splendour and from their frontier position, retained in their household at Branksome a number of gentlemen of their own name, who held
278

lands from their chief for the military service of watching and warding his castle.

> ' Nine and twenty knights of fame
>   Hang their shields in Branksome Hall.

> ' No baron was better served into Britain ;
>   The Barons of Buccleuch they kept their call,
>   Four and twenty gentlemen in their hall,
>   All being of his name and kin ;
>   Each two had a servant to wait upon them ;
>   Before supper and dinner most renowned,
>   The bells rang and the trumpet sowned.

> .   .   .   .   .

>   Every pensioner a room did gain
>   For service done and to be done ;
>   This I'll let the reader understand,
>   The name both of the men and land
>   Which they possessed, it is of truth
>   Both from the lairds and lords of Buccleuch.' "—*Satchells.*

Sir Walter Scott of Buccleuch, who succeeded to his grandfather, Sir David, in 1492, was a brave and powerful baron. His death was in consequence of a feud between the Scotts and Kerrs.

In the year 1526 the Douglasses held almost supreme sway, which displeased James V., then a minor, exceedingly. He wrote to the Laird of Buccleuch, asking him to meet him with his entire force at Melrose, "at his home-passing, and there to take him out of the Douglasses' hands." Buccleuch was delighted with this mark of confidence on the part of the king, "and so he brought with him six hundred speares, of Liddesdale and Annandale, and countrymen and clans thereabout, and held themselves quiet while that the King returned out of Jedburgh and came to Melrose, to remain there all that night."

But when the chiefs of the clan of Kerr took their leave of the king, then appeared the Lord of Buccleuch in sight on the back side of Halidon Hill, and Angus said to the king, "Sir, yon is Buccleuch, and thieves of Annandale with him, to unbeset your Grace from the gate (interrupt your passage). I vow to God they shall either fight or flee ; and ye shall tarry here on this knowe, and my brother George with you." "The laird of Cessford, and many other gentlemen and yeomen, were slain by the laird of Buccleuch," and then ensued a deadly feud betwixt the names of Scott and Kerr, which raged many years upon the Borders.

Buccleuch was imprisoned, and his estates forfeited, in the year 1535, for levying war against the Kerrs, and restored by Act of Parliament 1542. But the most signal act of violence to which this quarrel gave rise was the murder of Sir Walter himself, who was slain by the Kerrs in the streets of Edinburgh 1552. Of the Bethunes or Beatons, a French family, "was descended Dame Janet Beaton, Lady Buccleuch, widow of Sir Walter Scott of Branksome. She was a woman of a masculine spirit, as appears from her riding at the head of her son's clan after her husband's murder. She also possessed the hereditary abilities of her family in such a degree, that the superstition of the vulgar imputed them to supernatural knowledge. With this was mingled, by faction, the foul accusation of her having influenced Queen Mary to the murder of her husband. One of the placards of the time accuses of Darnley's murder 'the Erle of Bothwell, . . . the Quene assenting thereto throw the persuasion of the Erle of Bothwell, and *the witchcraft of Lady Buccleuch.*'"

Upon the 25th June 1557, this Lady Buccleuch and a number of the Scotts were accused "for coming to the kirk of St Mary of the Lowes to the number of two hundred persons bodin in feire of weire (arrayed in armour), and breaking open the doors of the said kirk, in order to apprehend the laird of Cranstoune for his destruction," for

> " The Lady of Branksome gathered a band
> Of the best that would ride at her command."

The Kirk of St Mary is said to have been burned by the Scotts at this rising.

> " The Minstrel gazed with wishful eye—
> No humble resting-place was nigh.
> The Duchess* marked his weary pace,
> His timid mien, and reverend face.
>
> . . . . .
>
> And he began to talk, anon
> Of good Earl Francis, dead and gone,
> And of Earl Walter,† rest him God,
> A braver ne'er to battle rode :
> And how full many a tale he knew,
> Of the old warriors of Buccleuch ;
> And would the noble Duchess deign
> To listen to the old man's strain.
>
> " Many a valiant knight is here ;
> But he the chieftain of them all,
> His sword hangs rusting on the wall,
>   Beside his broken spear.
>
> " Bards long shall tell
>   How Lord Walter fell
> When startled burghers fled afar
> The furies of the Border war ;
> When the streets of high Dunedin
> Saw lances gleam and falchions redden
> And heard the slogan's deadly yell—
> Then the chief of Branksome fell.
>
> . . . . .
>
> " In pity half, and half sincere,
> Marvelled the Duchess how so well

---

* "Anne, Duchess of Buccleuch and Monmouth, representative of the ancient Lords of Buccleuch, and widow of the unfortunate James, Duke of Monmouth, who was beheaded in 1685."

† Francis Scott, Earl of Buccleuch, and father of the Duchess. Walter, Earl of Buccleuch, her grandfather, and a celebrated warrior.

THE BUCCLEUCH TITLE.

His legendary song could tell—
Of ancient deeds so long forgot;
Of feuds whose memory was not;
Of chiefs who under their grey stone
So long had slept, that fickle Fame
Had blotted from her rolls their name,
And twined round some new minion's head
The fading wreath for which they bled."

See Lay of Last Minstrel, and Notes.

BUCCLEUCH ARMS.

In consequence of alliance with the heiress of the house of Montagu — Quarterly, 1. The arms of England, as borne by King Charles II., with a baton sinister, argent. 2. Montagu, argent, three fusils in fess, gules. 3. Monthermer, or, an eagle displayed, vert, beaked and membered, gules. 4. Scott, or, a bend, azure, charged with a star of six points, between two crescents of the field. Over all, on an escutcheon, the arms of Montague quartered with Monthermer, 1st and 4th Montague, 2d and 3d Monthermer. Crest—Upon a chapeau, gules, turned up, ermine, a dragon passant, or, chained and gorged with a crown of the same. Supporters—Dexter, an unicorn, argent, maned, and unguled, or, gorged with a crown, and chained, gules, for Scott. Sinister, a griffin, or, beaked and winged, sable, for Montague. Motto, *Amo.—Douglas's Peerage.*

At the Wanlockhead Smelting-Works the crest displayed is a flying heart surmounted by a coronet.

P.—RICHARD CAMERON AND HIS WORK.

"Cameron gave his name to the Strict Covenanters. It was the name they bore down to the Revolution, and after it, and it is even perpetuated until this day. The party themselves, indeed, did not assume the name, and with all their reverence for Cameron, repudiated such an application of it. But the world takes its own way in these things. They were known as CAMERONIANS so long as Covenanters existed, and those who claim to be their nearest ·modern representatives are still known by the selfsame title. Whenever a man gives his name to a sect, or to any considerable and enduring party, we may be sure that there has been something singular about him, something deserving the study of all who are interested in the aspects of human character.

"Although Cameron was a remarkable and 'representative man,' I do not claim for him any of the higher attributes of intellect. I do not mean that he was an original or profound thinker, a skilful director of affairs, or a man of literary attainment. On the contrary, his scholarship, considering his opportunities, must have been of as humble an order as a public teacher could well have. His management, in the eyes of the world, was utter foolishness—the blind frenzy of fanaticism. And his whole modes of thought were drawn from two very old sources—the Bible and the Standards of the Scottish Kirk. But he had an honest mind, that insisted on carrying out its convictions to their full legitimate consequences. He could not halt between two opinions. What to his mind was falsehood was a thing to be cast out, though it were a right eye. What to his mind was truth, was a thing to be owned, proclaimed, and acted upon, whatever the hazard, and though all men should be offended in him.

"To this zeal and directness of purpose he added an amazing courage, physical, mental, and moral. He had the firm front of the confessor, the strong nerve of the soldier, the unflinching spirit of the polemic, and—rarest, grandest, most heavenly gift !—he had the calm willingness to die for the cause which his conscience taught him to be of God. The people always love and follow the man who goes straight like an arrow to his mark, and is not eaten up of doubts and difficulties. Such a leader the Strict Covenanters obtained in Richard Cameron. In common with all men who bear sway over their fellows, the cause which he undertook was not a mere piece of business to be taken up and laid aside according to occasion. It was his *life*, that which alone bound him to earth, and gave his existence its meaning and interest. Hence the intense and lifelike power of that eloquence (rustic and primitive, no doubt, so far as regards artistic form) which he thundered forth in the moors and mountain recesses of Scotland.

RICHARD CAMERON.

It was not talk; it was not the perfume of the breath, the honey of the lip. In the few poor memorials we have of his discourses, snatched from oblivion by some fond disciples in the imperfect shorthand of the period, and under all disadvantages of outward circumstances, we see a brave, truthful, elevated soul, living and communicating kindred life to others. The function of the preacher is not to dig down in search of obscure and hidden dogmas; not to weave fine and intricate webs of argument; not to play off the legerdemain of style and unmeaning rhetoric; but seizing the great and necessary truths where all spiritual and eternal reality lies, so to flash them upon the hearts and consciences of men, that they shall be forced to exclaim, like the multitudes on the day of Pentecost, 'What shall we *do?*' what shall we do?' In this sense Richard Cameron was a MIGHTY PREACHER.

"Picture to yourselves this noble and majestic youth, with blooming countenance and eagle eye, standing on some huge rock uplifted in the wilderness. Ten thousand people are grouped around him: the aged, with the women and children, seated near this pulpit of Nature's handiwork; the men of middle age and the stalwart youths of the surrounding hamlets composing the outer circle, many of them with their hands on their swords, or their trusty guns slung by their side; and on each neighbouring height may be seen the solitary figure of the watchman, intently gazing in all directions for the approach of the troopers, who are now kept garrisoned in every district, and who night and day are on the prowl to catch some poor outlawed Covenanter, or surprise some Conventicle in the depth of the hills.

"It is a Sabbath in May. The great wild moor stretches out to a kind of infinity, blending at last with the serene blue sky. How sublime and peaceful the moment! even in this age of violence and oppression—of the dungeon, the rack, the scaffold, and murder in cold blood in the fields. Heaven smiles on the 'remnant.' All is hushed and reverent attention. The Word is precious. There are but three men now in Scotland who will venture their all to preach to the people, free from the chains of despotism, and asserting the independence of man's spirit and man's creed from all state control. These are faithful old Cargil, weary-footed, prophetic old Peden, and the youthful Cameron, who now stands before us. The Psalm has been sung, and the echoes of the myriad voices have died on the muirland breeze. The prayer has been offered, the earnest wrestling with Heaven of men who before sunset may themselves be an offering for their religion. The preacher rises. He eyes for a moment in silence that vast multitude gathered from all parts of the west. Always serious, always inspired with elevated feeling, there is in his manner more than the usual solemnity. There is a mysterious look, full of mingled emotion, of tenderness, sorrow, weariness, longing for rest, and the presentiment of Paul, 'I am now ready to be offered, and the time of my departure is at hand.' Yes! he knows that his days are numbered ; and that but a few more suns, the heather sod shall be his bed of death. A strange, almost unearthly, sympathy is visible, stirring these assembled thousands to the very depth of their being. Rousing himself from the reverie which had passed over him, the preacher announces his text, '*Ye will not come to me, that ye might have life.*' He commences by expounding the words ; he enters into a plain and forcible illustration of the various doctrines which lie imbedded in the text. Yet there is manifestly something weighing upon his mind, a vehement desire to throw aside mere general discourse, and to come into close interior contact—soul to soul—with the consciences and affections of the people. He may never see them more ; never again address them on the concerns of their eternal wellbeing. He bursts away from the trammels of common didactic speech. Hearken ! as that mighty thrilling voice startles the solitudes around.

" 'Are there any of you here saying, This doctrine is true that you are telling us ; you have told me the thoughts of my heart, for there is a great unwillingness in me to come to Christ. Alas ! ye come too easily by your religion in the West of Scotland, and so betides. You have taken it up at your feet. You have been born with it. O sad to think upon the West of Scotland ! The wild Highlands have not neglected so many calls as thou hast done. O ye in the West ! ye all have religion. Truly ye are like the Church of Laodicea, that lacked nothing, but knew not that she was lukewarm, poor, wretched, blind, and naked. It may be ye think ye have enough, and stand in no need of persecuted gospel ordinances. Yet ye are the people in all Scotland that are in the worst condition. My Master hath been crying unto you in the parishes of Muirkirk, and Crawfordjohn, and Douglas, "Ye will not come to me, that ye might have life." What say ye ? Shall I go away and tell my Master that ye will not come unto Him ? Ye that have been plagued with deadness, hardness of heart, and unbelief, He now requires you to give in your answer,—yes, or no. I take instruments before these hills and mountains around us, that I have offered Him unto you this day. Angels are wondering at the offer. They stand beholding with admiration that our Lord is giving you such an offer this day. What shall I say to Him that sent me ? Shall I say, Lord, there are some yonder saying, I am content to give Christ my heart and hand, house, land, and all I have for His cause ? Look over to Shawhead and all these hills,—look at them ! They are all witnesses now, and when 'you are dying, they shall come before your face.'

"The preacher trembles as he speaks, and the thousands around him, from the aged patriarch to the tender stripling, are touched with indescribable emotion. Language fails to paint the scene. Fancy cannot realise it. The old chronicler, with Hebraic beauty and simplicity, records—'Here both minister and people fell into a state of calm weeping.' *Calm weeping !* What a depth of meaning in that one phrase ! The Shawhead seemed to look down into their very souls. 'All those hills' became animated into living creatures with eyes of flame. Surrounding nature was bound over to appear as a witness against them at the day of dread decision ; and already they felt themselves amid all the fears and anxieties, the shadows and gleams of hope that wait upon a dying bed. 'The Shawhead and all those hills ! When you are dying, they shall come before your face.' After a long and affecting pause—after an interval where so many thousands were subdued into 'calm weeping' —Cameron, before again proceeding, offered up a prayer for the composing and tranquillising influences of the Holy Spirit.

"If you comprehend in the faintest measure the scene which I have endeavoured to depict, you have the key which at once explains the whole problem. How it was that Scotland could bear up for so many years, and grow in strength and fortitude, and ultimately triumph over the fiercest and most desolating persecution which perhaps ever descended upon any age or nation. The mother of sons like Richard Cameron could not be crushed.

"But Cameron was not merely the preacher of the persecuted remnant. He was the champion that was first to proclaim that the House of Stuart had forfeited the British throne. It was now necessary, in the evolution of circumstances, that the tie which had so long attached the Scottish people to their native dynasty should be gradually loosening ; and Cameron commenced this dissolving process amongst the strict Covenanters. In one of his earliest sermons, after his return from Holland, he thus expounds his views : 'The most part of the land cry out, We will have no other king but Cæsar, no other king but King Charles. We must cry, We will have no other King but Christ. *What say ye, Are ye against monarchical government ? We are not much taken up with that, if God let pure government be established, that is most for the advantage of civil and ecclesiastical society.* . . . . If you would have God be for you, you must cut off this king, and those magistrates, and make able men be rulers, men endued with suitable qualifications, both of body and mind. . . . . If ever ye see good days in Scotland without disowning the present king, then believe me no more. Indeed, that is not much ; but look to the Word of God. . . . . I know not if this generation will be honoured to cast off these rulers, but those that the Lord makes instruments to bring back Christ, and to recover our liberties, civil and ecclesiastical, shall be such as shall disown this king and the magistrates under him. . . . . Let them take heed unto themselves, for though they should take us to scaffolds, or kill us in the fields, the Lord will yet raise up a party who will be avenged upon them. . . . . We had rather die than live in the same country with them, and outlive the glory of God departing altogether from these lands.'

"In 1680 this was *treason:* in 1688 it became the *Revolution Settlement.*"—*Dodds's Covenanters*, pp. 276-85.

Q.—THE CHURCH OF THE REVOLUTION.

Happy as was the deliverance effected, two roots of bitterness were left to the Church by the Revolution settlement. First—The re-establishment of Presbytery was placed on no higher ground than the popular will. The Act simply gave as a reason for the change, that this was agreeable to the majority of the people, while the Acts that had cut off Presbytery were not cancelled. Secondly—A great number of men who held prelatic views were allowed to retain their position as Presbyterian ministers. If they had, on reasonable grounds, changed their views, this would have been a right course ; but it was questionable, when the outer change was only to secure the emoluments of office. One hundred and eighty of these men were, in 1692, assumed into ministerial communion and participation in Church government on subscribing the formula. Four-fifths of the prelatic ministers thus remained in possession of their endowments ; and, as to others, instead of having treated them with rigour, both ministers and magistrates contributed to their relief. This conduct towards their persecutors ought to be remembered to the honour of the Presbyterians of those days. But this act of kindness, as the result showed, was carried too far in admitting them to an equal share in a government to which they had proved themselves to be thoroughly opposed.

The Reformed Presbyterian Church arose out of these defects, a party of covenanters refused to receive the benefits of the Establishment on the grounds offered. They held, as was declared by Richard Cameron at Sanquhar in 1680, that Charles II., having broken the conditions on which he had received the crown—viz., adherence to the covenants—could no longer be regarded as a constitutional sovereign, and had forfeited all right to their obedience. Declining to take the oath of subjection to any sovereign who had not sworn to maintain the covenants, these parties have been popularly termed Covenanters or Cameronians. Various societies for spiritual improvement had been organised by Renwick. When their petitions to the General Assembly for relief to their conscientious convictions were utterly disregarded, and when Mr M'Millan was deposed in 1707 for holding the principles of these societies, that sentence was repudiated, and at length a Presbytery was formed in 1743, and a Synod in 1811. This first rending of the Church of the Revolution was thus the fruit of unjust domination. This was a fruit of that prelatic root. The " Vindication " prepared by Renwick, and their actions, show that at the beginning this Reformed Church did not stand so austerely aloof from all Churches, and from their duty as citizens, as some of their descendants. While repudiating the assertion that the dominion of Christ is founded in grace (see Goold in Enc. Brit.), their cardinal doctrine as a Church was the headship of Christ over the nations. Their position all along has therefore been in order to bring about a thorough harmony of our civil constitution and institutions with that doctrine. On this account, until 1863, they would neither take the oath of allegiance, nor employ others as their representatives who did so.

They said, even in that time of suffering, "Not that we would martially oppose and rise up against all such, but by our profession, practice, and testimony, we would contradict and oppose them ; we positively disown, as horrid murder, the killing of any because of a different persuasion and opinion from us." Declaring that there are men who have complied with the demands of the Government, whom we "love in the Lord, and acknowledge to be ministers of His Church," and "with whom we would not refuse accidental or occasional communion as brethren and Christians." They were willing to associate in common religious enterprises "with some as Christians, holding the same fundamentals." "As these people, however reproached by their enemies as the cold, anti-monarchical, enthusiastic, lunatic Cameronians, were amongst the first in Scotland who took up arms for the Prince of Orange, so they were the first men in Scotland that petitioned the Convention of Estates to place the crown of Scotland on the head of their deliverer, King William" (Crookshanks). In a single day they raised a regiment of 800 men, who, marching under Cleland to Dunkeld, defeated General Cannon at the head of 5000 soldiers.

The Reformed Presbyterians justify their refusal to embrace the Revolution Church on several grounds ; as that—(1.) The Church courts were composed of men against whom they had weighty objections ; (2.) The Assembly submitted tamely to the dictation of civil rulers ; (3.) The Reformation, in its most advanced state, was abandoned in the Revolution settlement ; and (4.) The principles on which that settlement was conducted were of a *political* rather than of a religious character. Still they do not maintain that even the second Reformation was free from blemishes, and they specify some actions that are justly censurable. (See " Test. of R. P. Church," pp. 65–105.) On the other hand, it has been felt that this most advanced state being confessedly imperfect, and the Revolution bringing about a normal condition, in which it was impossible to bring the nation back to that advanced state, it might be the best possible and most hopeful position to " let bygones be bygones," and to begin anew upon the Reformation basis. It became also a serious *civil* question, whether it is a right thing either for any who enjoy all civil benefits, to refuse allegiance to the supreme civil power as lawful magistracy, or for any to denude themselves of their privileges and responsibilities as citizens. If these positions were to be universally acted upon by Christian men, then necessarily the entire power and influence of the nation must pass into the hands of the irreligious portion of the community, and all hope of bringing about national subjection to Christ is gone.

Nevertheless, posterity have more effectually rescinded the act recissory than could have been done by the Revolution settlement, and there has confessedly been a gradual approach *practically* to the principles embodied in the documents of the second Reformation, and most Presbyterians would rejoice could they be fully acted upon.

New light dawned upon the majority, and in 1863 their restriction was removed. It was declared, " That members of the Church, who may be led by the resolution to exercise the elective franchise, or take the oath of allegiance, shall not be visited with the infliction of ecclesiastical penalties to the effect of suspension and expulsion from the privileges of the Church."

Some thought the old spirit of domination was manifested, when the protest presented by the faithful minority was shuffled out of the church in Glasgow where the Synod sat. That protest, signed by the Rev. William Anderson, and seven others, was "against the decision now adopted as the law of the Church by the majority of this court, as opposed to the Word of God and to the testimony of this Church, and unconstitutionally adopted ; and seeing that they have thereby abandoned the principles, we do hereby protest and claim for those adhering to us to be constitutionally the Synod of the Reformed Presbyterian Church in Scotland," &c. (See " Test. of R. P. Church." Glasgow, 1866.)

The new School of the Reformed Presbyterian Church has 6 presbyteries, 46 congregations, and 40 ministers, a divinity hall with 2 professors, and 3 missionaries, 300 elders, and 6736 communicants. In 1870 it raised £9445 for all religious purposes—£1, 8s. per member. Stipend of ministers, £120 to £125, with manse. The number of deacons or managers has not been taken.

The old School of the Reformed Presbyterian Church has 2 presbyteries, 11 congregations, and 8 ministers. It receives a supply of preachers chiefly from the Synod in Ireland. It had 1200 communicants, 2800 adherents, and raised £1500 in 1870. Average contributions, £1, 5s. per member. Stipend, £120 to £140. With the Irish Synod a missionary is supported in Syria.

True Presbyterians within the Church of Scotland were not fully satisfied with the measure of security granted at the Revolution. But it was felt to be a blessed relief after the death-struggle in which the Church and country had been engaged. They chose the least of two evils, and hoped for the best, and for a time stood upon their watch-tower.

Thus, at the era of the Union (1707) the Scottish Parliament passed an Act vesting the powers of the crown, in the event of a vacancy, in their own Parliament, directing to choose as sovereign only one adhering to the Protestant religion, and only on the condition of maintaining the complete independency of the nation, and the integrity of her institutions. The commissioners were thereafter forbidden to treat at all regarding union, unless certain fundamental principles were guaranteed. They were not to treat of "any alteration of worship, discipline, and government of the Church of this kingdom." Consequently the Scottish Act of Parliament ratifying the articles of union in 1707 confirmed these privileges. "And sicklike her Majesty, with advice, &c., resolving to establish the Protestant religion and Presbyterian Church government within this kingdom, has passed in this present session of Parliament an Act entitled "Act for securing the Protestant religion and Presbyterian Church government," &c., therefore her Majesty, &c., doth hereby establish and confirm the said true Protestant religion, and the worship and discipline and government of this Church, to continue without any alteration to the people of this land in all succeeding generations," &c. By Act of the English Parliament, ratifying the union, these Acts are declared : "Forever be held and adjudged to be observed as fundamental and essential conditions of the said union ; and shall, in all times coming, be taken to be, and are hereby declared to be, essential and fundamental parts of the said articles of union."

These solemn treaties were soon broken. Efforts were made to have the crown restored to the Popish brother of Queen Anne, an elder branch of the house of Stewart.

Then, in 1712, patronage was restored by a bill hurried through Parliament *in one month!* "The British Legislature violated the articles of union, and made a change in the constitution of the Church of Scotland. From that change has flowed almost all the dissent now existing in Scotland. . . . Year after year the General Assembly protested against the violation, but in vain ; and from the Act of 1712 undoubtedly flowed every secession and schism that has taken place in the Church of Scotland" (Lord Macaulay, Speeches ii. 180). Yet the patrons did not exercise their rights for several years, and enforced settlements of ministers, contrary to the wishes of the people, were not insisted on for half a century.

At length strenuous resistance to forced settlements arose. Ebenezer Erskine denounced the corruptions of the Church in a Synod sermon at Stirling, which led to his secession in 1733 (and deposition in 1749). This he did, however, not from opposition to the constitution of the Church as the National Church. He severed from "the prevailing party," or defective majority, appealing to the first free, faithful, and reforming Assembly. Others, who with him left the Church, refused to return, and formed themselves into the Associate Presbytery. Still, besides the so-called Moderate party adhering to patronage, another remained in the Church who upheld Calvinistic doctrines, and the liberties of the people. The constitution being unchanged, they had hope. (As the subsequent history of the branches of the Scottish Church is somewhat complicated, the chronological diagram prefixed to this chapter should be kept before the eye.)

The history of this secession is remarkable for the number of its divisions. This Associate Presbytery was in 1747 divided into two by the oath required of every person clothed with civil authority, in consequence of Jesuit intrigues, and dread of French invasion. That burgess oath declared that "the individual taking it would defend the religion of his country as by law established." One party in the Associate Synod held this oath unlawful, as approving of all the abuses of the civil establishment of the Church. Another party held that it simply bound them to defend the Protestant faith against secret and open enemies. Being free to take the oath, this party was popularly termed "Burghers ;" and those who refuse to be sworn, the "Antiburghers."

The Antiburghers went so far as to excommunicate and depose the Erskines and others of the Burgher party.

Both of these portions were again split up by controversies regarding the obligations of public covenants, and what was popularly known as *New Light* views, or plainly, the Voluntary principle. "A great majority in both Synods denied the right of the civil magistrate to interfere with the Church, and of the Church to accept support from the State " ("Hist. of Secession Church," p. 579). The abuse made them imagine that the thing itself was evil, and that continually. This change of sentiment was first publicly announced in a pamphlet published in 1780 by a member of the Burgher Synod. In 1799 the formula was, by a majority, altered to suit this change of sentiment ; a minority reforming and retaining the views of the *Old Light* Burghers. In 1806 a similar split into New and Old Lights took place amongst the Antiburghers. Dr Thomas M'Crie, the accomplished author of the "Life of Knox," adhering to the Old Light views and organisation, was deposed. The New Light Antiburghers departed furthest from the principles of the first seceders.

A union of the two parties that had embraced the New Light views took place in 1820, forming the United Secession Church, which had thus Voluntaryism for a cardinal position. A minority of ten New Light Burghers protested against that union and withdrew, and found a more congenial union in amalgamating with the Old Light Antiburghers in 1827 as the Original Secession Church.

Meanwhile, the Old Light Burghers were approximating towards and finally united with the Establishment in 1839, recognising the Assembly as now the free, faithful, and reformed, to which their fathers had appealed. A few, however, declined to do so, and preferred to enter the Original Secession Church in 1842. That Original Secession, ten years later, by a majority of one, entered the Free Church. Again the minority declining, remain distinct to testify of Original Secession principles.

The Synod of the United Original Seceders have 4 presbyteries, and 27 congregations ; communicants under 3000 ; 1 professor and 12 students, 1 foreign and 4 home missionaries. The majority of congregations are managed by committees. There are 3 congregations not connected with the Synod, 2 in Edinburgh, and 1 in Perth.

In 1752 another secession had occurred at Dunfermline. This was at the beginning of the " Robertsonian " era, so named from a Moderate leader. The Presbytery were by the prevailing party commanded to proceed with a forced settlement of a minister contrary to the expressed wish of the people. Six declined to comply. In consequence, one venerable man, the Rev. Thomas Gillespie of Carnock, was deposed from the office of the ministry for contumacy. To this sentence he meekly answered, " I rejoice that to me it is given, in the behalf of Christ, not only to believe on Him, but also to suffer for His sake." This second secession formed themselves eventually into the Relief Synod, which also, after the French Revolution, became very Radical in their views. They disapproved of public covenants and creeds or confessions, as tests of orthodoxy or terms of communion. The chief object of their separate religious fellowship was to afford relief to those suffering from patronage. At ordination, church officers owned the doctrine of the Westminster Standards, " except where said Confession recognises the power of the civil magistrate in religious concerns."

" The contest which ensued between the two branches of the Secession and the Relief is one of the most heart-rending pages in the ecclesiastical history of Scotland. It took place between parties professing in the main the very same religious principles " (" Hist. of Relief Church," p. 14). Nothwithstanding, drawing nearer each other daily, the Relief and United Secession formed in 1847 the United Presbyterian Synod.—*Government of the Kingdom of Christ*, pp. 484-491.

R.—THE UNION OF CHURCHES

has occupied the attention of four branches of the Presbyterian Church very specially for the past eight years, viz., the Free Church, United Presbyterian, Reformed Presbyterian (new school), and the English Presbyterian. Whilst all parties maintain that union is desirable, and ought to be promoted, if essential principles be conserved, it is contended by a considerable minority of Free Church ministers and elders, that the present proposal would subvert national subjection to Christ, and be in effect an alteration of the constitutional principles of the Church. The last Free Assembly adopted, by a majority, a resolution to continue the committee, and " to encourage and facilitate the cordial co-operation " of these Churches. The English Presbyterian has made a further advance towards incorporation with the five presbyteries of United Presbyterians that are in England.

The Established Church and others are meanwhile pointing towards a more comprehensive union, on the basis of the principles of the Reformation. Thus, in 1870, a motion was carried for the abolition of patronage, and another to this effect :—" The General Assembly having heard the overtures, desire to record their deep sense of the manifold evils arising from the ecclesiastical divisions of Scotland, and considering the great impiety and abounding wickedness in the land which the divided Churches have not succeeded in removing, the Assembly record their hearty willingness and desire to take all steps, consistent with the principles on which this Church is founded, to promote the union of Churches having a common origin, adhering to the same Confession of Faith, and the same system of government and worship."

In a recent lecture on " Ecclesiastical and Social Evils," the Rev. Dr Begg said :—" So far as Scotland is concerned, the far more desirable object would be not only to arrange, if possible, a union of all Presbyterians on the old basis of the Reformation, but to secure the appropriation for this purpose of all existing ecclesiastical means and revenues, whether held directly under the authority of the State or otherwise, including also the appropriation of all the unexhausted teinds, amounting to about £150,000 a year, and also embracing all the free-will offerings of the people. This would be a restoration of the grand system for which Knox, Melville, Henderson, and Chalmers pleaded. Every shilling of this should be devoted to the service of a united and extended Church. This would be a union worth speaking of and contending for. This would make it possible to redivide all the parishes of Scotland which require division, to support ministers and teachers as they ought to be supported, and to make an effectual inroad upon the heathenism of our large cities and mining districts."

All the six branches of the Church of Scotland remain, professedly and practically, Presbyterial and Calvinistic—if public professions are to be the test (see Diagram). When visited by " The Day-spring from on high," these branches will one day become one stick in the hand of the Great Shepherd of Israel (Ezek. xxxvii. 16-19).—*Government of the Kingdom of Christ*, pp. 502, 503.

INDEX.

INDEX.

Second Edition.—Crown 8vo, 600 pp., with an additional index,
price 7s. 6d.   London: J. Nisbet & Co.

THE

GOVERNMENT OF THE KINGDOM OF CHRIST:

AN INQUIRY AS TO THE SCRIPTURAL, INVINCIBLE, AND HISTORICAL POSITION OF PRESBYTERY.

BY THE REV. JAMES MOIR PORTEOUS,
WANLOCKHEAD.

IN THREE PARTS.

WITH OUTLINE, QUESTIONS, CHRONOLOGICAL TABLES,
STATISTICS, AND ILLUSTRATIONS.

PREFACE BY THE REV. HORATIUS BONAR, D.D.

————

PART I.—SCRIPTURAL PRINCIPLES.

THE KINGDOM.—The Monarch—Universal Sway—The Community—Invisible—Visible.

THE LAWS OF THE KINGDOM.—Reason Insufficient—The Statute Book—Use of Subordinate Standards.

THE GOVERNMENT.—

Temporary Officers. Apostles—Prophets—Evangelists—Apostolic Guidance.

Permanent Officers. Elders—Gospel Ministry—Titles Interchangeable—Number and Function—Position and Power—Deacons.

Call to Office. Inner and Outer Calls—Ordination.

Administration. In "the Churches"—Churches of a Locality—Deliberative Assembly—*Essential Scriptural Principles Combined.*

PART II.—PRESBYTERY—UNTENABLE OR INVINCIBLE?

CHURCH DIVISIONS—Unity of Apostolic Church—Evils of Division—Distinctions—Which, or Whether any Polity, essentially divine?

GOVERNMENT DEVISED.—

§ 1. *Separatism.* 1. *"The Holy."*—2. *Society of Friends.*—3. *Plymouthism,* Sphere, Origin, Views—Is every Christian entitled to assume the Office of the Ministry?—Are Public Ministrations by Women Legitimate?—Is a Settled Ministerial Income Unlawful?—Who is the Outward Guide of Assemblies?

§ 2. *Erastianism.* § 3. *Libertinism.*

GOVERNMENT LOCALISED.—*Independency.* The Church One Body, although Churches are widely scattered. *Congregationalism.* Have the People Authority to Rule?—Who are to Bear Office?—Ruling Elders Rejected, and Deacons Substituted—Elders have Official Authority—Rule by all Incompatible.

GOVERNMENT CENTRALISED.—

1. PRELATIC EPISCOPACY.—

§ 1. *Support in Scripture.* Bishops—Priests—Deacons.—Did Christ appoint Prelates? — Were the Apostles, Timothy, and Titus, Prelates? — Angelic and other Theories — "Apostolical Succession"—Is it Fact or Fiction?

§ 2. *What saith Antiquity?* The Church of the First Three Centuries—Testimonies—Can the Introduction of Prelacy be accounted for?

§ 3. *Expediency.* Three Views. *Conclusion.* No Support for Prelacy.

II. THE PAPACY.—

Supremacy—The Church—The Ministry—The Standard—Worship—The System Doomed.

GOVERNMENT HARMONISED.—THREE ESSENTIALS.—

§ 1. *Liberty,* by — Election — Representation — Assent or Consent—Appeal and Protest.

§ 2. *Authority,* from Christ—Not to Dominate—Manifestations—Argument from Monarchy—Tendency to Prelatic Episcopacy.

§ 3. *Unity* manifested (1) Locally, (2) Nationally, (3) Universally—Pan-Presbyterial Council—Desired by Reformers —When fully exercised.

PART III.—THE PAST AND PRESENT CONDITION OF THE PRESBYTERIAN CHURCH.

AN HISTORICAL CONFIRMATION.

STARS IN THE NIGHT.—From the Fourth to the Sixteenth Century.

THE CULDEES.—Introduction of Christianity—The Green Isle —Missionary Institutes—The Struggle.

THE WALDENSES. — The Valleys — Origin — Persecutions— Government—Condition.

THE REFORMATION—GERMANY. — The Presbyter—Protest— Confession—Positions—Present State.

SWITZERLAND.—Polity of Reformers—Practices of Prelatic Controversialists.

FRANCE.—Reformation—Persecution—Extensive Organisation— The Massacre and Medal.

CONTINENTAL CHURCHES.—*Italy.* Liberty and Infallibility— *Spain and Portugal—Austria—Bohemia—Hungary—Poland— Russia and Greece*—Denmark, Sweden, and Norway—Holland —Belgium.

ENGLAND. — Exceptional Adoption of Prelacy — Presbyterian Church—Westminster Assembly—Other Churches.

SCOTLAND.—Reformation—The Two Prelacies—Revolution and Dissenting Churches—Conflict and the Free Church—Established Church—Union of Churches—Episcopacy.

IRELAND.—Early Stages—Organisation—Derry and Liberty— Union—Reconstruction.

AMERICA.—Origin of Presbyterian Church—Branches and Unions —Re-united Church.

BRITISH COLONIES. — *North America — West Indies — South Africa—Australasia—New Zealand—China—India, &c.*

PRESBYTERIAL POSITION AND ANTICIPATIONS.—One Result — Adoption — Approximations — Obstructions, from without, from within—Rectifications—The Coming Glory.

LONDON: JAMES NISBET & CO., 21 BERNERS STREET.

"The means in these critical times of leading students into extensive and useful research."—*Rev. J. Collingwood Bruce, LL.D.*, Newcastle.

"This defence of Presbytery is most admirable, and much needed in these days."—*Rev. James Macgregor, D.D.*, Tron Church, Edinburgh.

"I am delighted with it, and with the amount of research and learning it exhibits. I consider it a book of great value."—*Rev. F. Thain Davidson*, Islington, Moderator of the Presbyterian Church in England.

"Methodical and readable, and so broken down as to be easily apprehended. It is gratifying to find that it has been presented to the students of the English Presbyterian College. And we trust that means will be devised to bring it within the reach not only of the ministers and office-bearers, but the young men of the churches, in whose intelligent and cordial appreciation of her principles—humanly speaking—lies the future advancement of Presbytery."—*Weekly Review* (London).

"We commend the work before us as a useful and clear treatise on the subject of Church Government, bringing out a great amount of important truth, which in Churches overshadowed by the Church of England, or its branches, it is of very great importance that the members should be made to know."—*British and Foreign Evangelical Review.*

"Carefully selected and arranged materials, which will furnish many a Presbyterian's Armoury. Most complete and thorough, without being unduly bulky. Two things will recommend it in many quarters:—the one is the logical precision with which it is arranged, so that anything desired can readily be found—the other is the vast amount of statistical information concerning the different branches of the Presbyterian Church. The controversial tone is firm, yet conciliatory. The principles of Presbyterian Church Government are fully stated and earnestly maintained, without any want of charity towards any branch of the Church, or any disregard of its excellencies. The chapters have questions appended, which should make the work useful to a solitary thoughtful reader, as well as to those who study it for an examination."—*Presbyterian.*

"This complete and masterly work . . . fairly exhausts the subject. Not a single point at issue between Presbyterians, Prelatists, and Independents is omitted. . . . Presbyterian readers must experience great satisfaction in finding the principles they hold to be capable of such clear and convincing and overwhelming demonstration. Part III. is a novelty in the discussion of the subject, but it is entitled to attentive consideration ; it will be found to be not only very interesting but pregnant with instruction."—*Daily Review.*

"In these days of instability, arising from imperfect knowledge and feeble principle, it is of much importance that Presbyterians should be clearly taught the Scriptural grounds of their own system. . . The subject is here discussed in all its bearings with much ability and learning, and, at the same time, in a thoroughly Christian spirit. A wide diffusion of such an able and comprehensive work among ministers, preachers, students of theology, as well as the elders, deacons, and members of the Church, might be expected to accomplish very important results." — *Rev. Dr Begg*, Newington, Edinburgh.

"Presbyterianism has made Scotland what she is—a great country. . . Queen Victoria has proved herself the best of all the Stuart race. And in the grandest days of her reign, we see a reaction taking place against the Anglomaniac weakness of the sons of true Scotchmen. The book before us awakened these trains of thought. It is a vigorous and manly defence of the Ecclesiastical policy of Scotland. . . Another service rendered by the Free Church to the best interests of Scottish patriotism."—*Edinburgh Courant.*

Kelso Courier.

' This is an extraordinarily clever little satire, well repaying perusal. We most certainly wish the book speed, characterising it as the work of a scholarly and comprehensive mind.'

Galloway Gazette.

' The *brochure* is cleverly written, and we predict for " Kirkcumdoon " a large sale.'

Brechin Advertiser.

'. The picture is strikingly vivid; while the scholastic qualifications of the divines are cleverly and warmly dissected.'

Northern Ensign.

' This is a well got up *brochure* written to show that the Auld Kirk would have been all the better had the Patronage Act of last year not been passed.'

Ardrossan and Saltcoats Herald.

' The chapters entitled " The Village Smithy," " The Kirkyard after Service," and " The Village Inn," are inimitable.'

Shetland Times.

' We recommend its perusal to all who can appreciate Scottish scenes in the Scottish vernacular.'

Shortly by same Author, price 3s. 6d., 12mo, cloth,

INNOVATIONS IN THE PARISH OF COLDSOULS.

Third Thousand—Price one Shilling.

SNOWED UP AT BALLINTARN;

OR, CONVERSATIONS ON RITUALISM & VATICANISM.

' Relates actual incidents of the past winter. The production betrays on every page the hand of a master.'—*Greenock Telegraph.*

' Worth its weight in gold.'—*Brechin Advertiser.*

' The argument is both logical and scriptural.'—*Edinburgh Courant.*

Second Edition, Crown 8vo, 600 pp., price 7s. 6d.

ENTERED IN LIST OF WORKS ON PRESBYTERY FOR PRESBYTERIAL COUNCIL.

THE

GOVERNMENT OF THE KINGDOM OF CHRIST:

AN INQUIRY AS TO THE

Scriptural, Invincible, and Historical Position of Presbytery.

By the Rev. J. MOIR PORTEOUS.

WITH STATISTICS OF THE PRESBYTERIAN CHURCH THROUGHOUT THE WORLD.

Preface by the Rev. HORATIUS BONAR, D.D., Edinburgh.

PART I.—SCRIPTURAL PRINCIPLES.

PART II.—PRESBYTERY—UNTENABLE OR INVINCIBLE?

PART III.—THE PAST AND PRESENT CONDITION OF THE PRESBYTERIAN CHURCH—AN HISTORICAL CONFIRMATION.

Sixth and English Edition.

Now Ready—Revised and Enlarged.   Crown 8vo, 224 pp., cloth, 2s 6d.

BRETHREN IN THE KEELHOWES;

BRETHRENISM TESTED BY THE WORD OF GOD.

BY THE REV. J. MOIR PORTEOUS,

AUTHOR OF 'THE GOVERNMENT OF THE KINGDOM OF CHRIST,' ETC.

'Capital! Cogent arguments.'—*Rev. C. H. Spurgeon.* 'Comes like the gentle dew from heaven.'—*Daily Review.* 'A keen eye to the beauties of nature.' 'Some made alive to the evil through your facinating exposure.'

With Coloured Geological and Mineralogical Map and Illustrations.

'GOD'S TREASURE HOUSE IN SCOTLAND;'

The Times, Mines, and Lands in the Southern Highlands,

WHERE SUPPLIES HAVE BEEN OBTAINED OF

GOLD, SILVER, AND LEAD.

BY THE REV. J. MOIR PORTEOUS,

AUTHOR OF 'THE GOVERNMENT OF THE KINGDOM OF CHRIST,' ETC.

'God's Treasure House in Scotland' is the title formerly given to that district where 'much fine gold' was obtained. The history, ancient and modern, includes Crawford, Crawfordjohn, Leadhills, Wanlockhead, and Sanquhar; and not only embraces its geology and mineralogy, with all accessible information as to the gold, silver, and lead workings, but gives interesting details as to properties and people, together with Church history from the Reformation to this date.

Crown 8vo, cloth, 7s. 6d.

THE SHADOW OF CALVARY:

GETHSEMANE—THE ARREST—THE TRIAL.

By HUGH MARTIN, D.D.,

AUTHOR OF 'THE ATONEMENT,' 'CHRIST'S PRESENCE IN GOSPEL HISTORY,' 'THE PROPHET JONAH,' ETC., ETC.

Scotsman.

'It will be seen that Dr Martin holds very definite theological views, and that he is neither ashamed nor afraid to proclaim them.

'These lectures abound in powerful appeals and stern warnings.'

Courant.

'Those who have read Dr Martin's previous works, or who know his ability as a preacher, will expect to find a more than ordinary book of sermons in his "Shadow of Calvary," just published, and they will not be disappointed. Dr Martin's Lectures are full of the theology of the Westminster Confession of Faith, presented not in cold, dry statement, but in its bearing on the hearts and lives of men.

'Whilst preaching according to the doctrine of Boston and the Erskines, his mode of treating his subject is suited to the present day, and his illustrations, are often both fresh and apposite.'

Glasgow Herald.

'The book has many merits . . . . Several sterling excellences come out prominently in the second part of the book, which, dealing with the objective, is much superior to the first part. . . Dr Martin has a remarkable knowledge of Scripture, not merely in its best known portions, but in many of its less turned pages. He has a full, rich, and varied power of evangelical language; he has no little spiritual insight, and he is a clearly intelligent defender of the old forms of faith. On the whole, this is not a book for the literary man; even the quiet Christian reader may be fatigued by some of its pages; but few men can read it without learning something, and being the better of it.'

Daily Review.

'The author writes with much vigour, occasionally throwing in an unexpected remark, which commends itself so soon as it is made. He states his facts clearly, gives the needed explanation and illustration, deduces, doctrines, and appends practical inferences. . . . He has produced an instructive and useful book, which we cordially commend to the attention of our readers.'

Glasgow News.

'Dr Hugh Martin is well known as a representative of the orthodox evangelistic Scottish minister, and the lectures of which this book is made up are written entirely from that stand-point. To those who desire a good specimen of such reasoning and interpretation of the cardinal doctrine of Christianity, they may be heartily recommended. But it would be unfair to allow the book to go out without some notice of the force and fire of its eloquence, the vigour of its style, and the earnestness of its spirit. More even than the distinctly doctrinal parts of the lectures, the convincing and powerful practical exhortation is noticeable. The book will, therefore, not only keep up Dr Martin's reputation as an orthodox theologian, but also raise him in public estimation for the worth of his pulpit rhetoric.'

Original Secession Magazine.

'We recommend the "Shadow of Calvary" to our readers as an excellent book for Sabbath reading, and we trust it will have a large circulation.'

'It abounds in close heart-searching appeals to the unbelieving and impenitent, and with rich consolations for the humble child of God.

Crown 8vo, cloth, 5s.

SERMONS BY MARTIN LUTHER,

WITH PREFACE BY ALESSANDRO GAVAZZI.

Edited, with LIFE OF LUTHER, by

Rev. JAMES KERR, Greenock.

' We hail with cordial satisfaction this re-issue of the Sermons of Martin Luther.

' The preface to these sermons is written by Gavazzi; and in the burning words in which he writes, the Italian preacher and orator speaks with no bated breath of the evils of Ultramontanism and Rationalism against which Luther preached, and in highest terms commends the sermons of the great Reformer. Prefixed to the sermons is a life of Luther, written by the editor, in which we have a brief, but graphic and most interesting, survey of the leading events in the great Reformer's life.'—*The Advocate.*

' The Preface by Gavazzi is characteristically pithy.'

' The Editor has enhanced the value of the volume by a short but comprehensive life of the Reformer.'

' We are grateful to the present Publishers for this modern edition.'— *Original Secession Magazine.*

12mo, cloth, Second Edition, 2s. 6d.

Happy Homes for Working Men, & how to get them.

By JAMES BEGG, DD.,

' A volume already well known to those who are interested in building societies.'—*Edinburgh Courant.*

' A handy little book, which every working man should buy and study carefully.'—*Glasgow North British Daily Mail.*

' This volume first appeared about seven years ago, when it met deservedly with a warm welcome from the social reformers of Scotland.'—*Edinburgh Daily Mail.*

12mo cloth 9d., or sewed, 6d.

OUR CHILDREN FOR CHRIST:

A Plea for Infant Church Membership; with Brief Notes on the Mode of Baptism.

By SAMUEL MACNAUGHTON, M.A. of Nova Scotia,

AUTHOR OF THE 'DUTY OF THE CHRISTIAN CHURCH IN RELATION TO THE TEMPERANCE REFORM' (a Prize Essay).

' The author has stated very concisely the arguments from Analogy and the Scriptures, for infant baptism.'—*Edinburgh Courant.*

' Our Children for Christ is a statement free from all controversial bitterness of the arguments for infant baptism.'—*Daily Review.*

' These arguments will, no doubt, be regarded as convincing by the numerous sections of the Christian Church who accept the doctrine.'—*Daily Scotsman.*

DEFENCE OF CHURCH ESTABLISHMENTS.

In Crown 8vo, Cloth, 5s., by Post, 5s. 4d.

STATEMENT

BY THE LATE

THOMAS M'CRIE, D.D.,

AUTHOR OF 'LIFE OF JOHN KNOX,' ETC. ETC.,

WITH PREFACE,

BY

GEORGE SMEATON, D.D.,

PROFESSOR OF EXEGETICAL THEOLOGY, NEW COLLEGE, EDINBURGH.

It is a masterly defence of the Principle of Establishments as a Scripture Truth; and the most complete vindication ever given to the world of the position occupied by the Reformed Church of Scotland on the whole subject of National Religion, and of the magistrates' legitimate power in promoting it.—*Preface by Professor Smeaton.*

A very important service has been rendered to the 'present truth,' by the republication of the very able work of the historian of John Knox, on the vital Principle of Church Establishments. . . . We would strongly advise all to study the subject; and for this purpose, to procure the masterly and exhaustive treatise of Dr M'Crie.—*Watchword.*

We do not know any treatise in which the entire argument is presented so lucidly and conclusively within so small a compass. All the leading objections of Voluntaryism, moreover, are swept away, with a logic always calm, but trenchant and decisive.—*Original Secession Magazine.*

We heartily and earnestly recommend all who are in doubt and difficulty, or who may wish instruction on the Voluntary Controversy, and the principles that underlie it, to this reprint of Dr M'Crie's Statement. Professor Smeaton has done good service in bringing it to light again at this special time.—*The Edinburgh Evening Courant.*

Apart from the Editor's commendation, anything from the pen of so masculine a reasoner, and so well practised a writer as Dr M'Crie must be worth reading; and whoever wishes to study the important subject here treated of, will do well to have the little book beside him.—*Scotsman.*

Lightning Source UK Ltd.
Milton Keynes UK
UKHW031505090223
416681UK00013B/2990